NOVEL
HISTORIES

Past, Present, and Future in South African Fiction

MICHAEL GREEN

WITWATERSRAND UNIVERSITY PRESS

Witwatersrand University Press
1 Jan Smuts Avenue
2001 Johannesburg
South Africa

ISBN 1-86814-000-0

Cover design by Sue Sandrock

Typeset by Sue Sandrock Design
Printed and bound by Creda Press

To Charles Albert King
whose early belief and great generosity
made the hope of anything like this possible

In memorium
Allan Murray Charles Green
and
Donnée Phelps Cawood

CONTENTS

———■———

ACKNOWLEDGEMENTS

■

In its long making, this book has gathered more debts than I could ever hope adequately to acknowledge. This only underlines the generosity of all those who have helped me in its process. While most of my scholarly debts should be evident in the pages that follow, my gratitude for the special combination of academic and personal support which I received from Jacques and Astrid Berthoud, Landeg White, Stephen Gray, and Michael Chapman goes far beyond footnotes and a bibliography. A largely unstated presence but one without which this book would probably not have appeared is that of Nick Visser. He exemplifies what we owe to our best friends and colleagues – our thanks for their rich disagreements.

The main title of this book I owe to my dear friend and partner Carole Anne Lynch, along with so very, very much more.

My thanks to Esthie and her family in any case, and to Donnée Hannah Green in every case.

I would like to thank the Institute for Research Development, the British Council, Rand Afrikaans University, and the University of Natal, Durban, for the funding and assistance which helped make this study possible; none of it conclusions, of course, should be attributed to them.

Material treated more fully here has appeared in *English in Africa*, the *Journal of Literary Studies*, the *English Academy Review*, *Wasafiri*, *Les Cahiers FORELL*, *Current Writing*, *Research in African Literatures*, as well as in *New Nation New History* (*New Nation* and the History Workshop, 1989); *African Studies Forum*, edited by Romaine Hill, Marie Muller and Martin Trump (HSRC, 1993); *Rethinking South African Literary History*, edited by Johannes A. Smit, Johan van Wyk and Jean-Phillipe Wade (Y Press, 1966); *Writing and Africa*, edited by Mpalive-Hangson Masiska and Paul Hyland (Longmans, 1977).

INTRODUCTION

——■——

The question which initiates a history
is neither simple or given.
– *Pierre Macherey (1978:9)*

This book was begun in one world and ended in another (South Africa 1986-1996). Its production is thus not surprisingly marked by a sense of process, one which has tended to reinforce what could be seen as a – once again – potentially suspect valorization of history. This is apparent in not just my choice of subject matter (uses of history in fiction), but also in one of the primary methods by which that subject matter is approached (reading works back into the history of their production and reception); it is a key criterion, too, in the 'evaluation' of my material (the degree to which fiction presents historical material as resistant to its formal production is central to the way in which works are placed in relation to my argument).

History, moreover, in its broadest sense of 'change over time', has occurred as an 'irruption' as much as a theme in this book; this is because its actions upon itself – the events that have affected the very way in which they are understood as 'events' – challenged both the many and often conflicting ways in which history appears in the fiction that is my subject and my own attempts to accommodate this variety in my versions of what constitutes the 'history' of that fiction. Acknowledging that history has a history or, more properly, many histories, only deferred the problems generated by the term and the vast range of discursive constructs (informed by and informing the power relations that give them their materiality) to which it is attached. In treating uses of the term 'history' historically, one is, after all, operating within a practice thoroughly implicated in its own reflexivity, a practice in which an awareness of contingency is constructed as a mode within other levels of contingency by the very practice which is in question.

Appeals to the particular and specific – history's time-honoured advantage and limitation – in an attempt to make manageable the problems proliferating from the consideration of history in abstract and general formulations is difficult to sustain once these problems are carried into the realm of the literary, a realm that has been identified in the most venerable distinctions between the two modes making up my topic as the quintessential expression of the extra- or transhistorical.

For some time now, of course, this distinction has been challenged by the increasingly influential practice within literary studies of reading the fictional back into the historical, but more recently practices of this sort have been forced to recognise their own limitations. These limitations have largely been defined by a thoroughgoing questioning of the nature and status of history. A major factor in this was the increasingly popular strategy of extending historiographical inquiries into discursive areas commonly associated with the fictional, and techniques of analysis developed within the study of the fictional into history writing and historiography. One of the clearest signals that the practice of fiction engaged in these strategies no less than the practice of criticism was Norman Mailer's division of his *The Armies of the Night* into two books successively entitled 'History as a Novel' and 'The Novel as History'. My own title is in part derived from the impulse behind Mailer's subtitles.

Novel Histories needed to go further, however, and take into account the ways in which discussions regarding the essentially narrative nature of history writing were soon overtaken by a full-scale assault upon the seductive closures of narrative in general, with history represented as perhaps the most insidious of the master narratives needing to be interrogated. Mailer's 'Novel of History' (1971:228 [1968]) exemplifies fiction's ability to open itself to history, and history to itself, but it is also an example of how the opening up of formal narrative elements can still carry the most blatant of narrative closures in anything approximating a political or historical sense.

It is not surprising, then, that current questions raised around issues such as the positionality and authority of those practising within the institutions of literature and history have begun to supersede those regarding the relative merits of a rhetorical or material emphasis in either area of practice. In both literary and historical studies, central contested issues have settled, for some time now, into areas of broad agreement – acknowledgements as to the plurality, constructedness, positionality, and contingency of literature and history, for example, have become tropes of late – but these now more or less established general insights have begun to take on the air of, at best, truisms, and at worst, banalities. One of the results of this has been the beginnings of a shift of interest away from history in literary studies. As concepts of historicity have become refined to the point of virtual non-existence, other concerns have begun to take precedence in critical practice. The reforegrounding of ethics would be one illustration of this: even in its contemporary recognition of the non-self-evidency of the moral, the implicit transcendental imperative of this mode serves to hold at bay the conventionally historical. Renewed interest in such perspectives has promoted much of the new suspicion of the once oppositional, but now in some quarters dominant, even orthodox, historical methods of literary analysis.

None of the analytical modes filling the vacuum created by the apparent vanquishment of the historical is unmarked by their having to work through the significance of history, however; the best examples of the ethical interest just mentioned tend to situate themselves within the specificities of particular conflicting contingencies, and it is my hope that the geographic and temporal location of the texts and issues considered in this book will help recreate for the reader what remains for me the continuing vitality of precisely located questions to do with the uses of history in fiction.

Yet it is exactly the particular conjuncture of time and place with which I am concerned that has disrupted the cohesiveness I had hoped to bring to my treatment of this topic. To situate the production of this book within the shifts sketched above, I began in the certainty of the once commonly acknowledged – even celebrated – intense historicity of South African literature of the period this study covers, that is, roughly the late 1930s to the mid-1980s. Such a certainty suited the materialist mood pervasive among 'progressive' elements within the academy, but – in the light of some of the later historiographical insights I have touched upon – it is now necessary to investigate the nature of that 'historicity'. This will make up the bulk of the chapters to come, but in brief, the 'history' with which South African fiction is so insistently associated is not usually evoked in the most prevalent sense I called upon earlier – that is, the traditional idea of process attendant upon concepts of 'change over time' – but rather by its being locked into what appeared to be the particularly intransigent set of circumstances signified by the word apartheid.

I use 'apartheid' in this introduction as Derrida does in 'Racism's Last Word' (1986) – and not, as McClintock and Nixon require in their critical response to that article, in relation to the word's 'own history' (although much of the analysis that follows is engaged with precisely this) – because it is in its coming into being out of the subjunctive mode invoked by Derrida in 1983 that the word apartheid is most appropriate here. The temporal looseness with which I use the word is indicative of this – anachronism gives way to the fact that it is pretty well impossible to approach any moment of modern South African fiction without having to read through a plethora of attempts to politically systematise difference.

'APARTHEID – may that remain the name from now on, the unique appellation for the ultimate racism in the world, the last of many,' writes Derrida in his contribution to the catalogue of the exhibition *Art contre/against Apartheid* (1985:291). 'Last' in this context is used to indicate not only 'the worst', but also 'the last of a series, ... that which comes along at the end of a history' and punctual transitions since 1990 in South Africa, which cumulatively fulfil the standard narratological requirements necessary for the status of an *event* ('the transition from one state to another state') in a rather literal political sense, have equally been forceful and public enough to qualify as a rupture, a break, an end to history itself as South African history has been so long conceived.

Of course end-of-history theses usually emerge (as in the case of Fukuyama's global suggestion that in 1989 'what we may be witnessing is not the end of the Cold War, or the passing of a period of postwar history, but the end of history as such: that is, the end point of mankind's ideological evolution and the universalization of Western liberal democracy as the final form of government' [Fukuyama 1989, 1992]) as conservative strategies aimed at exalting the present order of things; in South Africa's case, the almost immediate and drastic lowering of the country's international media profile following the ushering in of democratic structures suggests in very real material terms the stasis attendant upon her enshrinement as the model for the successful resolution of a traumatic *historical* – in the sense of developing through conflict – progression. The story of South Africa's struggle for democracy has taken on now in many quarters the most colloquial sense of being 'history' – that is, finished, done with – and the country's present transitional political mediations are treated with a certain tiredness by an international perspective that seems to consider the adoption in principle of democratic procedures as enough to signal the end of South African history as a spectacular phenomenon worthy of high-profile notice.

For those more intimately implicated in what 'apartheid' must now be made to stand for, the problem is that its apparent relegation to history has not automatically granted a coherent base – national, cultural, historical – from which to simply position it within the past. This effects every level of the reconstruction – better still, the reinvention – of what 'South Africa' will mean. Not least in such a project is cultural reinvention, which includes what this book inevitably will be seen in relation to, that is, the imagining anew of 'South African literary history'.

Each of the singulars here – national, literary, historical – reminds us that the first moves in such an enterprise are driven by a very immediate awareness of plurality, fracture, contingency, and contestation. The enormous failure of apartheid, in any of its guises, worked all too well at some levels of its economy of division, and recognising difference in the wake of its enforced institution-alisation haunts the liberatory effects conventionally associated with such recognition. At the conference on Literature and Society in Southern Africa held at the Centre for Southern African Studies in the University of York in 1981, Stephen Clingman answered Kole Omotoso's challenge as to why he read Gordimer rather than Mphahlele or La Guma with the comment 'that he was white and young and South African and that Gordimer writes of his situation'; it is unlikely that Omotoso would call this, as he did then, 'in every sense an honest reply' (White and Couzens 1984:9), if it were made now. Equally, the pressures which made me competent to focus only on South African historical fiction in English – with all the evident limitations of language, genre, gender, class, region, and race that this implies – make this book, like Clingman's reply, no less a document of apartheid than the works with which it is concerned. Apartheid (again, in the less than literal sense that Derrida correctly identifies as its dominant mode) is so implicit to the representation of the southern African region and its periodisation, governing these in the way even its most vehement opponents are constructed in relation to itself, that attempts to nullify it need to go beyond not just the anti-apartheid manoeuvres that characterise many of the works I deal with in this book, but even a post-apartheid vision that still defines itself (in the logic of its strategies as much as its grammatical formulation) in relation to the very things it wishes to leave behind.

What then could this book contribute towards the construction of new South African literary histories? I have already admitted that for the most part it does not go beyond the restrictions ingrained in the material it considers, or those of the times in which it was mostly conceived and written. My hope is that in extending its focus of attention – uses of history in fiction – to its methods (making, in other words, its content its form), it does present its limitations usefully, and make something significant of its failures. For my real topic remains important to the negotiation of the many other contested areas in the construction of a national literary history – from which more general historical concerns are clearly not absent – that have clearly defeated me; this topic is the modes by which we relate the various temporal allegiances of a culture more noticeably in process than many others.

My basic method is to turn back what particular works of fiction do with the history they make their subject upon larger literary-historical issues to do with the past, present, and future. My intention is to demonstrate that certain literary works can be instructive, as much in the failure of some as the success of others, with regard to the fundamental problem of historicism: how does one represent the past (or the future, or, indeed, even the present) without simply appropriating it to one's own position. The essential concern of the book is perhaps caught by the term 'resistant form', developed in Chapter One. 'Resistant form' refers to the search for a critical model as much as an aesthetic mode that can, at one and the same time, recognise the inevitable constructedness of its subject within its own productive processes, yet create that subject in such a way that that subject challenges the terms within which it is constructed – thus resisting the very forms within which it is produced. The all too obvious paradoxical element in this project is the overall theme of this book. My first chapter is an attempt to spell out its theoretical parameters, although finally the ground upon which I have attempted to work through its complex and necessary inconsistencies is the detailed readings of the works I have selected. It is in this way that the history of my project is implicated in the history of the texts it focuses upon no less than those texts are implicated in the history they make their subject; out of this comes the logic of the trajectory I follow, always in the belief that the tropes involved in both the modes and methods that interest me not only intersect with, but are not divorced from, a great range of social practices.

The South African location of my concerns poses certain quite specific literary/ historical questions in relation to those practices, as do the temporal limits I have employed. This study's earliest concerns (chronologically speaking) are with a work produced within the formative period of the modern 'South African' nation;

it then jumps to what I have rather self-consciously called the period of the 'classical historical novel' and traces various significant manifestations of the historical within the literary from there to the mid-1980s. I have deliberately stopped at what is for us now so clearly the beginning of an end of a certain sort – the early 1990s – but equally deliberately remained within that end, so that the future we now inhabit remains a matter of hypothesis and projection as far as the works considered are concerned. This particular definition of a 'period', when considered in relation to the time in which I brought my study to completion, provoked implicit over-arching questions like, for example: what is the current status of a literature that has been thrust, if not at a stroke, then somewhat more precipitously than many would have predicted, into something identifiable as 'the past'? How can a body of texts generated within, and in terms of dissemination and reception still held within, the episteme of *anti-apartheid* (in the only partially allegoric sense given to this term by Derrida) be meaningfully related to one beyond apartheid? How do we locate the products of a world which we are so energetically trying to put behind us, to lose in the past as it were, in relation to, if not a confident sense of the present, then at least a material hint of a future in which they may truly enter the past tense? Above all, perhaps, how do we register in the shift towards a more relevant discourse that this shift is all the more painful and difficult for its material conditions not yet being firmly in place?

What these questions imply is that, if this book is truly an attempt to treat the texts of an anti-apartheid period as the pre-history of post-apartheid, it must have, like all similar attempts, something of the utopian about it. For the utopian mode to be effective, however (as I shall argue at greater length later), it must not be used to cheat history, as it were; if my project is aimed at a future, its trajectory includes opening itself up to its own history.

This book, then, must join a growing number which present themselves as something other than the cohesive and coherent arguments traditionally expected of academic work. Central to the nature of scholarly endeavour is the time involved in researching and constructing an argument, but it is questionable whether the achieved argument should always suppress the tensions of its process or its history be lost in its finalised form. Certainly a text presenting itself as a book-length study should be more than an excuse for a bundle of loosely related essays, yet there are schemes in which the parts may mean more than their sum. This seems to me to be the correct attitude to take to a project like this, caught short not only in terms of my working towards any sort of finality on its arguments but more importantly by the history surrounding its production. Current events as much as personal repositionings have led at times to a feeling during the rewriting of this material that the 'I' that produced it should be addressed by my present self in the third person. As I put it to a friend and long-time cultural associate of mine, at times I found myself asking, 'Who is the arsehole who wrote this?' Steve's response has served as a useful and historically apposite corrective to this feeling: 'Remember,' he said, 'that arsehole has to have his chance too.' In respecting this, and the readers who recommended the publication of this work after seeing much of it in its original state, I have added, cut, changed a little here and there, but attempted not so much to smooth out the project's awkward moments and occasional inconsistencies as to restore to it often erased hints of its own history. I have framed that history within what I believe to be not only current but enduring questions to do with the main terms of my argument, but a brief recapitulation of what became the opening moves in approaching my topic will probably serve as the most useful way of giving some substance to these very general introductory observations and provide some pointers to the body of this work.

This study arose out of a preoccupation with the place of the referent in fiction. My South African context, certainly in the period of the mid to late 1980s when this particular project was begun, cast that preoccupation primarily in the form of the historical, so historical fiction seemed a natural focus. My own positioning limited that focus mainly to fiction in English. Any desire to present a comprehensive survey of South African historical fiction in English soon gave way, however, to the more fundamental problems of defining just what is at issue when considering uses of history in fiction.

The literary genre one would assume to be most central to such a project – the historical novel – turned out from the first to be suspect, not least because of the contestation surrounding the extra-literary discourse implicit in its definition as a specific literary mode. 'History', in line with its problematic conceptual status, is invoked in a bewildering array of guises in South African fiction – itself a contested category in both national and aesthetic terms – and my first attempts to give some cohesion to even selected examples resulted in further fractures in what was at first assumed to be a unified field. A key fracture became one of the organising principles of this study: the fiction of the period covered displays varying temporal allegiances, allegiances which, related as they are to the problems of just what conceptions of history are used in the fiction, it was not possible to ignore. The past began to emerge as only one of a broadened definition of historical fiction's focuses, dominant only in a particular phase of the area of 'South African literature' I had demarcated for myself. The future, and perhaps more surprisingly, the present, were equally logical subjects for 'historical fiction' in the new sense in which it is used in this book. As my field began to break up and reform around these varying temporal emphases, a work of historical fiction became for me any work that was engaged in the production of a particular sense of the 'historical' – itself a contingent term.

A key element of most conceptions of history, then, made itself felt even as dispersal set in in other areas of the literary history I was assaying: a sense of change over time could be maintained, even if this meant that the movement from past to present and present to future that characterises standard conceptions of change over time had to be read back into the material to be covered. If, however, a case could be made for the organisation of this material around differing temporal emphases in different phases of the historical fiction of the region, other factors worked against simply marshalling all the likely material into such a chronology.

A major factor was simply the matter of reasonable limits; the various literatures of the Southern African region in the period with which I am concerned, because of the ways in which they were inevitably caught up in the effects of the policies necessary to enforce segregation, were particularly sensitive and open to 'history' in the sense of the significant public events that marked the progress of such policies. A vast amount of material claimed my interest then, despite my now pretty indefensible decision to confine myself largely to literature in English. My first methodological manoeuvre, that is, breaking with the temporal restriction to the past in my definition of 'historical fiction', had, of course, simply extended my range of study. It thus became more necessary than ever that I find other ways to make manageable my desire to indicate a general pattern of literary history while maintaining the kind of detailed study essential to its adequate support.

Here something of the broad history of this study makes itself felt. My early 'theoretical' commitments were to the then-prevalent (in oppositional circles) effects of social history as it impacted on literary studies in South Africa; the first part of this book, 'Uses of the Past', reflects this primarily in its 'case study' strategy. Five detailed studies each focus on a particular facet of 'uses of the past', with the general implications of what these 'uses' suggest being more or less left to hover within the very specific examination at hand. It is apparent, I think, that some of the case studies show a movement away from the more readily identifiable influence of social history in the others. I make no claim, of course, that the necessity of this shift was directly attributable to the limits of social history; its many successes speak to its historical advantages over some other historiographical forms, but I think it fair to say that the history of historiography this book has traversed does indicate why other approaches begin to take over as my work proceeded. Indeed, it became necessary to reorder the case studies when it became obvious that the first studies I engaged in could only take on their full significance within my overall argument once I had worked through with the reader certain issues tackled much later.

When I came to treat works engaged with the present and the future as 'historical fiction', I was drawn into more overtly, for want of a better word, 'thematic' strategies; by this I mean that my methodology centred upon the contested issues of treating the present and the future as history, rather than concentrating on particular writers and texts as specific 'case studies'. The study of the case, derived from law and medicine, began to suggest a degree of empirical validity and historical reductionism that I was increasingly uncomfortable in claiming. This, plus my growing conviction that the usually unstated and often hidden central premise of the case paradigm – that is, that sufficient knowledge of the individual subject yields sufficient knowledge of that subject's broader category – needed to give way to a greater degree of theorising, made me make the second part of this book, 'The Present as History', more (although imprecisely) 'structural' in conception. Starting with the common analogy of the detective for the historian, I made the formal structure of detective fiction (overwhelmingly present-tensed) a model for the manner in which the present is treated as history.

Without wishing to impose too progressive an interpretation back upon the history of this project – indeed, I have maintained some of the earlier sections in pretty much their original form in terms of both method and subject precisely because they seem to me still of intrinsic interest – it does appear to me now that the third part of this book, 'Future Histories', was an attempt to shake loose from some of the rigidity of the formal structuralism of Part Two. The future, conceptually the least established as an historical mode, encouraged this, so the emphasis on the utopian as an heuristic device in this section moved the study away from both case and structure and into a more explicitly speculative commitment – without, I hope, as I hoped in the shift from Part One to Part Two, entirely abandoning some of the more valuable elements of the previous strategies.

Each of these ways of dealing with my material resulted in a certain concentration which occasioned, of course, the marginalising of much other material of significance and interest. Having abandoned any attempt at a totalising perspective, I felt a certain freedom in constructing my course through a literary history self-consciously as much of my own devising as determined by the material I selected. Practically speaking, there was a real pressure to limit what is already clearly a potentially unfair demand upon the reader's span of attention. My apparently arbitrary decisions at times to include or elide certain works or interests may be the source of some surprise, even resentment, but I believe my choices to be significant in terms of investigating what constitutes 'historicising form' within at least one fracture of southern African literature.

Having presented this brief history of my project, I must repeat that, like all histories, it is no simple linear and progressive one. Apart from the reordering mentioned above, several sections were worked on at different stages in the production of this book, and no section is free of the effects of rewriting – even if later interventions were often carried out with the intention of clarifying earlier positions. Each step in the adjusted positions that each section of this book represents, then, remains of equal importance as far as the overall project is concerned.

One last point to do with the restrictions I have imposed upon myself needs to be addressed before my introductory comments are complete. The issue of exposure has been brought to bear in the selection of material. 'South African literature', a field formulated in opposition to dominant metropolitan canons, was initially structured into a canon of its own as a defensive method of promoting its national and aesthetic validity. This meant it was as much a construct of the thing it was resisting as it was an independent area of institutionalisation, for it contained within itself the same principles of selective appropriativeness it was attempting to avoid in establishing itself. As a contribution to a national literary history, this book represents an attempt to avoid falling into the essentialisms that recent critical activities have spent so much effort in removing from notions of the national, the literary, and the historical; it attempts to keep before itself the contingent constructedness of these terms, their varying specificities, and their investments in particular relations of power. One of the more obvious effects of this is the principles applied to the selection of the texts used to convey my argument. While the final principle has been what the texts have been able to generate out of their resistance to the appropriating form of my argument, I have also tried to illustrate how much different material, even from my rather conventional field of focus, there is to consider. Religiously following the established canon would have led not only to extensive and space-consuming reworkings of material more than adequately dealt with elsewhere, but also, it turns out, to serious distortions of the area that is the subject of this study.

These problems combine in an otherwise excellent essay by that deservedly prominent scholar of the South African novel mentioned above, Stephen Clingman. Because 'Revolution and Reality: South African Fiction in the 1980s'(1990b) launches itself from a three-part identification similar to my own of the 'temporal preoccupations' of past, present, and future in South African fiction (I should note that I shared this plan for my project with him some time before the appearance of his essay), it becomes a particularly good case for illustrating my point.

The essay uses as its stepping stones to the 'future' *The Story of an African Farm*, *Mhudi*, *God's Stepchildren*, *Turbott Wolfe*, and *The Marabi Dance*, texts all now respectably accommodated in standard accounts of South African fiction. These textual pointers, however, distort the pattern that emerges from an investigation of a fuller spread of South African fiction in English. Clingman, for example, uses *God's Stepchildren* (1924) to represent a general swing away from a preoccupation with the past in South African literature, thereby ignoring the explosion of past-fixated fiction that accompanied the rise of the various nationalisms in South Africa in the 1940s and 1950s. *God's Stepchildren*, commonly considered Sarah Gertrude Millin's most representative text, was not her most popular work in South Africa: her straight historical novel *King of the Bastards*, published in 1950, was. Clingman's account must bypass not only this fact but also the existence of so central and well-known a text as Peter Abrahams's *Wild Conquest* (1950), not to mention the immense popularity of a writer as important as Daphne Rooke and the success of a whole spread of lesser, but in their own way just as interesting, figures (such as, to choose another example from those I have chosen to use, Oliver Walker). The attention paid to the past in these texts is in fact so marked that I have made the literary movement they represent the chief focus of my consideration of uses of the past in the strand of South African fiction that I have made my subject.

As the above suggests, what Clingman's work does recognise (if not fully defend) is an opening up of history to the variety of temporal preoccupations argued for in my account of the uses of history in fiction. His *The Novels of Nadine Gordimer: History from the Inside* (1986) is a model study of Gordimer as an historian of the present (discussed further in Chapter One), and to a degree, the future (discussed further in Chapter Eight). The virtual eclipse of the past (other than the recent past) in Gordimer's writing makes her the most obvious figure to study in any treatment of the present as history, but the very comprehensiveness of the attention that has been paid to her work frees us to turn to other writers who have been less exposed and who have used different methods of engaging with the historical present.

The case of J.M. Coetzee is similar to Gordimer's; the extensiveness of scholarly work on his fiction releases us from having to rehearse all the historiographical issues foregrounded there. More generally too, I have avoided recycling the more obvious arguments thrown up by postmodernism's engagement with history; these have been well catered for by now, and I have preferred to concentrate instead on a particularly telling and under-considered element of these arguments as they relate to South African literature, that is, the deployment of the future in historical fiction. Works by Coetzee and Gordimer are dealt with in so far as they are important contributions to this theme, as are works by other comparatively well-known writers when they illuminate a particular concern of this project, but I must admit to a concern with extending notions of what constitutes South African literature in English. I trust I have been successful in giving enough of a sense of unfamiliar works to sustain the reader's interest and my argument, but much more importantly, I hope my account will encourage exploration beyond the necessary confines of this study and, more especially, the usual parameters accorded South African literatures.

It has also, of course, been my intention to extend the notion of the 'historical' within which we place these texts in a literary history; in order to do this, I must now make my case for opening up historical fiction to the present and the future along with the past. This will involve setting out what I mean by 'resistant form', the linking thread in all the chapters to follow, and defining elements of those works I designate in this study as truly 'novel histories'. In order to do this effectively, I must call upon the reader's patience and approach my definition by working through some of the more important recent debates in which history and South African fiction have been implicated.

1

HISTORICAL FICTION AND RESISTANT FORM

———■———

History is history and it should remain so
– *Dr Hendrik Verwoerd, Durban, 26 August 1963*

HISTORY AND FICTION

In her review of the *Oxford History of South Africa*, Shula Marks criticises this 'apogee of the liberal tradition of South African historiography'(1970:447) for its failure to use the 'abundance of resources [available] to construct a picture alive with real people and events' (Marks and Atmore 1980:1). She is speaking particularly of the section on the eastern frontier, but the implication is for broader application and can be traced to a general trend in the historiography of the time. Marks's review, written in 1970, aligns itself with what Raphael Samuel identifies as a new movement towards 'the recovery of subjective experience' in which the aim was 'to personalise the workings of large historical forces'(1981:xvii-xviii). Thus Marks writes of the hundred years of warfare on the eastern frontier as 'in many ways a dramatic story, punctuated by colourful episodes and personalities' and decries the omission of the 'eccentric individuals' with which the 'frontier… brimmed'. By way of example she lists Van der Kemp, De Buys, Alberti, Ngqika, and Ndlambe, adding, 'one could extend the list indefinitely; their story, however, has still to be written' (447).

Several of these figures had had their stories written at the time Marks was writing, however, albeit not in a form generally taken into account by historians.

De Buys and Van der Kemp had each featured as protagonists in historical novels written by Sarah Gertrude Millin, *King of the Bastards* and *The Burning Man* respectively, and many of the other characters listed by Marks (along with a number more from its indefinite extension) are strongly featured in these novels. The currency of these characters in their fictionalised form was no limited one either; as we shall have occasion to investigate further later, *King of the Bastards* became in its time one of South Africa's best-selling novels.

While the appearance of this cast of characters in novels, and popular novels at that, has perhaps understandably isolated the fact of their representation from professional writers of history, the point of *Novel Histories* is to re-examine the distinctions that tend to preserve this isolation. The general neglect or dismissal of historical fiction by historians, no less than the often rather cavalier deployment of historical material in fiction, suggests a clear demarcation between these two forms of discourse. The line between them has, however, not only been challenged from a variety of perspectives by both literary theorists and historiographers, but, perhaps more fundamentally, is demonstrably a shifting one.

> 'To make the past present, to bring the distant near.' It seems a modest enough task: it is what we have come to expect of any novelist with a pronounced sense of history: 'to invest', as Macaulay put it, 'with the reality of human flesh and blood beings whom we are too much inclined to consider as personified qualities in an allegory'. In defining the duties of the historical novelist which were once those of the historian, the English essayist uses a language which would surely find immediate emotional responses from those of our writers haunted by the African past and who are trying to develop strategies for 'bringing the distant near'.

This opening passage from Lewis Nkosi's essay 'History as the "Hero" of the African Novel' (1981:30) indicates just how easily the 'duties' of the historian and historical novelist may be shared or swapped according to context. The fact is that historical fiction makes different demands in relation to history writing in different contexts. What distinguishes these categories, after all, is institutionalised practice, not formal essences; which is not to say the distinction does not exist, only that it can at times be significantly reassessed. Such reassessment seems especially necessary in South Africa, where much historical revisionism has been and still is practised outside formal historical institutions, often taking a 'literary' form. In fact, southern African writers, who have good reason for displaying a strong awareness of how biased and fragmented authorised history writing and historiography can be, often claim that a central preoccupation in their work is, as Bessie Head puts it, 'a search as an African for a sense of historical community' (1984:278). They echo in every genre Matsemela Manaka's definition of the role of theatre, which, he says, 'should reconstruct a people's history and cultural values' ('Matsix' 1981:33; see also Matloatse 1981).

The novel form has an important place in the construction of the type of group identities referred to in these quotations, and I begin my study with what I hope is a useful exploration of why this is so. I move rather quickly from this to a 'phase' of the time span with which I am concerned in which the historical novel 'proper' was a dominant form. I should remind the reader at this point that this study is not a survey constructed strictly around 'periods' and neat transitions between them. I would not be the first to note, however, that no matter how discrete or isolated one's analysis of a particular cultural production is, it always involves an implicit theory of historical periodisation of one form or another. The first stage in a brief schematic outline of my sense of the broad transitions that frame my argument is, as I mentioned in my Introduction and will argue in Part One, the flourishing of historical fiction in the 1940s and 1950s, largely generated either by or in response to the increasingly militant nationalisms emerging at this time. The past is a crucial weapon in the armoury of social definitions of this sort – with, of course, all the potential double-edged dangers of any weapon.

The electoral victory of Afrikaner Nationalism midway in this period gave official versions of the past such strength that opponents to the rapidly evolving new state shifted their attention to the effects in the present of policies authorised as much by manipulations of the past as utopian future visions. Such strategies emphasised the present as history, the subject of Part Two of this book, and the 'historical novel' moved into the background as the work of writers in English charted the events of the day with an immediacy born of the almost instant recognition of their 'historical' significance. The general context of South African fiction, with its implicit or explicit high political profile, makes it difficult to claim the present for history in an exact chronological way; it could easily be argued, and often has been, that South African culture is defined by its allegiance to the 'historical', a term, as I observed in my Introduction, which signifies not so much change over time as an extreme awareness of the present as history. The second 'phase' marked out by my study is, then, not organised around a temporal period, but a discursive strategy that is particularly telling with regard to 'the present as history' – that is, the detective story. I have used this fictional mode to set off the present against the past for, if the present remains pervasive as history in South African fiction, novels which used the past as a setting become by and large limited to 'popular' writing by the first half of the 1960s. The historical form became an ever slighter exploitation of the past as little more than an exotic location for romantic – in the weakest sense of the word – plots.

Reactions against this emptying of history in any real sense from the historical novel began taking place in more serious forms in the early 1970s (although the romantic historical saga remains one of the most popular forms, locally and internationally, of South African fiction). With the first successful postmodernist experiments in South African fiction, a new literary interest in history emerged. This was generally characterised by a sceptical, or at least problematised, attitude towards our ability to know or use the past, and an important effect of this was a tendency in the mid-1980s to turn towards the future as a literary-historical strategy. Here we must return to the pressures of an historical moment, and link our analysis to a specific set of material conditions. Frustration with endlessly battering at what a seemed a particularly intransigent political situation led to an exhaustion with protest that focused on the iniquities of the present or analysed the past as the cause of those iniquities. These works projecting the past and present into the future make a strong case for considering the future as valid historical territory, as I do in Part Three.

In each of the texts I have used to illustrate these shifting temporal allegiances, the underlying or overt thrust is historical revisionism – even if the reasons for and methods of resorting to the strategies of fiction vary widely. Revisionist historiography in South Africa has shown itself to be slowly but increasingly aware of this point, even if, naturally, it is still the use of the past in literature that forms the main area of their interest.

The social history movement, of which Shula Marks was to become a leading figure, has had particularly good reason to develop the connections between history writing and fiction. Both in content and form, as Marks's comments quoted above suggest, the writing of social history comes close to modes that intersect with structures commonly associated with fiction – or, to be more precise, a certain mode of fiction: realism.

SOCIAL HISTORY AND LITERARY REALISM

During the period with which this book is concerned, social history became an increasingly important element in 'oppositional' thought and tactics. Part of its strategy was to renew interest in narrative, biography ('life history'), and human experience as a way of bringing home the lived effects of the dehumanising structures of segregation and apartheid. This is neatly summarised in Charles van Onselen's introduction to his *Studies in the Social and Economic History of the Witwatersrand, 1886-1914*, in which his professed aim was to write 'an analytically informed chronicle of the warm, vibrant and intensely human struggle of people' (1982:xvi). The implications of this statement underline the ways in which, in both content and form, social history continues to share literary realism's interests: its selection of subject matter privileges the average, the ordinary, the everyday ('the history of the person in the street', as Belinda Bozzoli puts it [1987:xiv], or the much-vaunted 'view from below'), and its mode of representation favours the creation of a sense of actual experience (the 'referential illusion' in which, as Roland Barthes has demonstrated, 'the historian tries to give the impression that the referent is speaking for itself' by 'absenting himself' [1970:149] from his writing and treating language as if it gives transparent access to the real). It comes as no surprise, then, that sessions concerned with culture – in which the literary was often, not unproblematically, given a prominent status – became a standard feature of social history forums like the History Workshop at the University of the Witwatersrand. In particular, creative works were celebrated for their representation of the experiences or perspectives of groups or individuals ignored or marginalised by orthodox history, finding favour to the degree that these representations were considered 'authentic' in terms of the political criteria of social history.

Nicholas Visser, a literary scholar, was asked to give one of the Keynote Addresses at the 1990 History Workshop at which for the 'first time ... a full 'cultural' component [was] deliberately and fully incorporated into the proceedings' (1990b:69). He expressed the hope that 'the various disciplines might be made mutually enriching' (77), but other academics present on this occasion were more cynical about the interaction between the disciplines of history and literature. David Attwell, in his account of this History Workshop, stated that literary or cultural scholars who work within the confines of social history 'are always going to play the role of handmaiden to the more powerful, more coherently marshalled, more politically cogent discourses of history' (1990a:84). In this he followed J.M. Coetzee, who, in a talk he gave at the 1987 *Weekly Mail* Book Week, said of 'the novel and history in South Africa today' that there was 'a tendency, a powerful tendency, perhaps even a dominant tendency, to subsume the novel under history'. 'Speaking as a novelist', Coetzee objected to 'the appropriating appetite of the discourse of history' and 'the colonisation of the novel by the discourse of history' (1988b:2).

If, as we have seen, history for Lewis Nkosi was once the 'hero' of a dominant genre within the African novel, then history – at least in certain important forms – would seem to have become something of a villain for writers and academics concerned with defending the independence of literary discourse. It is important to note, however, that Coetzee's position on the relationship between history and fiction was not a claim for some sort of aesthetic ahistoricism; his early novels in particular are overtly concerned with historiographical issues, exploring as they do different manifestations of what is considered to be history at varying moments within history. What was at issue in 'The Novel Today' were the all too often unquestioned foundations of 'history' as it was conceived within the emergence of social history as the dominant mode of southern African historiography; more specifically, it was social history's claim to a privileged grasp of reality, reflected in the emphasis we have seen it places on the mode of realistic representation, that was a problem for Coetzee. The nature of his objections in this regard remain clear:

> I reiterate the elementary and rather obvious point I am making: that history is not reality; that history is a kind of discourse; that the novel is a kind of discourse, too, but a different kind of discourse; that inevitably, in our culture, history will, with varying degrees of forcefulness, try to claim primacy, claim to be a master-form of discourse, just as, inevitably, people like myself will defend themselves by saying that history is nothing but a certain kind of story that people agree to tell each other – that ... the authority of history lies simply in the consensus it commands. The categories of history are not privileged, just as the categories of moral discourse are not privileged. They do not reside in reality: they are a certain construction put upon reality. I see absolutely no reason why, even in the South Africa of the 1980s, we should agree to agree that things are otherwise. (Coetzee 1983b:4)

It is only an apparent irony that the point ultimately made here is that history and literature find an ever-deepening intimacy as the horizons of the questions set for them are pushed back. The reference to a particular historical situation in Coetzee's concluding sentence in the above quotation draws our attention to the historicity of history, to the fact that the concept of 'history' has a history – indeed, many histories, once one acknowledges the multiplicity of what may be called 'history' – and operates in certain and often conflicting ways in specific places at specific times. Obviously this has implications for the varying relationships between, again, the many discourses identified in differing specific ways as 'literature' and the particular 'history' or 'histories' with which they intersect.

Thus the willingness of the social historians to grant literature an important place within their project has not remained necessarily and automatically the progressive gesture it has been assumed to be in the work of, say, Stephen Clingman. Already the subject of some passing criticism in my Introduction, his work will be used again in this chapter, largely because he is a literary critic who has shown some of the real advantages – and potential limitations – of having close ties with social history.

In his contribution on 'Literature and History in South Africa' included in the special 'History from South Africa' issue of the *Radical History Review*, he asks 'what is the legitimate use of fiction for historiographic purposes?', and his answer turns upon a hypothesis that fixes literature in a relationship with history that is highly contestable in Coetzee's terms. 'If literature is to have a real historical value,' Clingman writes, 'we must regard it in the inclusive sense, having to do with its larger significance in embodying the ways of life, patterns of experience, and the structures of thought and feeling of communities and classes at large' (1990a:147). The problem here is not that literature is read back into history; it is that the initial hypothesis governs, limits even, the effectiveness of the ways in which this might be done. Clingman's next question illustrates the effect of the logic of granting the initial 'if' of his first question. He asks 'what kind of evidence' literature offers the discipline of history, and answers 'that fiction writes out, within its hypothetical and potential frame, the normally hidden issues, complexities, and deeper perturbations of society' (149). Although he emphasises that 'fiction is never simply historical "illustration"' (149), this typically social historical view of fiction being, in the final analysis, 'evidence' for history is exactly what Coetzee wishes to resist in 'The Novel Today'.

If the novel aims to provide the reader with vicarious first-hand experience of living in a certain historical time, embodying contending forces in contending characters and filling our experience with a certain density of observation, if it regards this as its goal, for the rest – for what I will call its principal structuration – depending on the model of history – then its relation to history is self-evidently a secondary relation. (Coetzee 1988b:3)

And so Coetzee rejects the type of novel which 'operates in terms of the procedures of history and eventuates in conclusions that are checkable by history (as a child's schoolwork is checked by a schoolmistress)'. The type of novel which interests Coetzee 'operates in terms of its own procedures and issues in its own conclusions', 'evolves its own paradigms and myths, in the process ... perhaps going so far as to show up the mythic status of history – in other words, demythologising history' (3). This is the programme that overtly informs Coetzee's first novel *Dusklands*, of course, a novel which systematically explodes the standard assumptions of history writing as much as historical fiction, but it is to a point that begins with a specifically literary historical question that we must now turn in our consideration of the relationship between fiction and history in South African literature. Fortunately the extraordinarily pithy address by Coetzee which we have been looking at will continue to serve us here.

THE 'HISTORICAL NOVEL' AND 'CONTINUOUS HISTORY'

In the course of his argument in 'The Novel Today', Coetzee does away with a generic distinction once crucial to the meeting of history and fiction within one form: 'we are not – I should make it clear – talking about what used to be called "the historical novel"'; this he goes on to define as 'the novel that self-consciously and on the basis of explicitly historical research sets out to re-create on its own terms a given time in the past' (2).

While Coetzee would no doubt favour the emphasis placed on 'its own terms', I would like to concentrate on two phrases – both temporal – which are important in his brief setting aside of 'the historical novel': 'used to be' and 'in the past'. These two references to the past are distinct but related. To begin with 'in the past': standard definitions of the historical novel give the historical aspect of their category an exclusively past tense. Avrom Fleishman in *The English Historical*

Novel, for example, is happy to go along with the common assumption that 'most novels set in the past – beyond an arbitrary number of years, say 40-60 (two generations) – are liable to be considered historical, while those of the present and preceding generations ... have been called "novels of the recent past"' (1971:3). The very pressures of history on fiction alluded to by Coetzee above have, however, forced scholars of South African fiction into being more defensive about the temporal distinctions involved when seeking to preserve the classical concept of historical fiction. Ian Glenn, for example, says of Daphne Rooke: 'She is the most serious historical (as opposed to political) novelist of South Africa' (1987:2), where 'historical' takes the weight of the past and 'political' the burden of the present. Jacques Berthoud makes the same point about Nadine Gordimer, defining her work as 'more political than historical. If she is an historical writer, as she claims to be,' he continues, 'then the term requires qualification. ... [I]f the past, as it is usually understood, enters into [her stories], it does so by virtue of the attention she gives to the present' (1989:82-83).

In their distinction between 'political' and 'historical', Glenn and Berthoud follow a particular sense of the word 'history', one which Raymond Williams calls the 'established general sense' which has 'lasted into contemporary English as the predominant meaning'; that is, history is 'an account of real *past* events', and 'the organized knowledge of the *past*' (1983:146, my emphasis). This generally acknowledged sense of 'history' coexists somewhat uneasily, however, with 'history' in another more modern and controversial sense. Says Williams:

> ... it is necessary to distinguish an important sense of history which is more than, although it includes, organized knowledge of the past. ... One way of expressing this new sense is to say that past events are seen not as specific histories but as continuous and connected process. Various systematizations and interpretations of this continuous and connected process then become history in a new general and eventually abstract sense. Moreover ... history in many of these uses loses its exclusive association with the past and becomes connected not only to the present but also to the future. (Ibid.:146-47)

This distinction has proved crucial to the invalidation of the historical novel as a discrete genre, and lies behind the other reference to the past in Coetzee's comments upon the form: '... what used to be called "the historical novel"'. Here he is referring to a pervasive contemporary practice which, having severed 'history' from its exclusive association with the past, concludes that the novel form's general fidelity to the continuous process of history makes the isolation of those novels engaged with the past in a specific genre or sub-genre quite superfluous.

Such a manoeuvre regarding literary form depends upon a particular sense of 'history', one we may trace back to Georg Lukács. He initiated the form of Hegelian Marxism in which history, rather than economics, the class struggle, the state, or social relations, became the primary element in the methodology of Marxism, and it is this perspective which leads to his rejection of the validity of the genre which is his subject in *The Historical Novel*. For Lukács:

> One could go through all the problems of content and form in the novel without lighting upon a single question of importance which applied to the historical novel alone. The classical historical novel arose out of the social novel and, having enriched and raised it to a higher level, passed back into it. The higher the level of both historical and social novel in the classical period, the less there are really decisive differences of style between them. (1981:290)

This is because 'the ultimate principles are in either case the same. And they flow from a similar aim: the portrayal of a total context of social life, be it present or past, in narrative form' (290).

The 'total context' referred to here includes pre-eminently, as the connectedness of present and past suggests, a unified sense of 'history'. The very attribution of a specific genre to the 'historical novel', claims Lukács, rests on a failure to grasp this connectedness: '... the social reason for creating the historical novel [as] a genre or sub-genre in its own right is ... the separation of the present from the past, the abstract opposition of the one to the other' (289).

Stephen Clingman's *The Novels of Nadine Gordimer: History from the Inside* is an exemplary study of a South African novelist's use of history which depends upon just such a refusal to separate past and present. This work is saturated from the outset with a Lukácsian historical perspective:

> ... Gordimer's novels prove what Lukács pointed out some time ago: that there is no separable 'historical novel' as a genre. Gordimer's novels, mostly written in the present, establish deep links with broader

and more continuous processes because it is here that they find the meaning of the present. (Clingman 1986:224)

In doing without the generic category of the historical novel, Clingman develops, as the subtitle to his book makes plain, an even stronger sense in which Gordimer is an historical writer. He sees Gordimer's fiction as 'historical' precisely because in it 'history' is no longer tied exclusively to the past; the various ways in which Clingman defines Gordimer as an historical writer have in fact very little to do with the past. Gordimer's 'historical consciousness' lies for Clingman in her 'close observation', and 'in this observation [her] eye is fixed resolutely on the present' (8). She is also an historical writer for Clingman because for her 'social and private life are seen as integrally related' (8); here history enters as externality, with no hint of association with the past: 'the exploration of history and character, of external and internal worlds, becomes entirely indivisible' (8-9).

Gordimer is historical for Clingman at another level because 'her aim is to deliver the kind of fictional judgement whose vindication might be the verdict of history' (12). In order to achieve this, the future must be added to her historical perspective: each of Gordimer's novels, says Clingman, 'ends with a vision, and it might properly be called an historical vision. It is a vision of the future, from the present...' (13). In this, Clingman goes beyond Lukács's merging of past and present and identifies the future – which Lukács explicitly excluded from his historical concerns – as an important aspect in the 'totality' which embodies Gordimer's 'specific historical consciousness...' (13). Here we have, then, a full sense of history as a 'continuous and connected process'.

This is a strong case for maintaining the distinguishing category of the historical even in the absence of a specific association with the past. Crucially, however, it collapses the distinction we saw Glenn and Berthoud making between the 'historical' and the 'political', which turned upon maintaining the distinction between past and present. As long as the past is merged with the present in such a way as to keep us firmly focused on the present *as history* (which provides the logic and central theme of *The Historical Novel*), it remains a powerful literary-historical and critical perspective. There is a danger here, however: in holding the present continually before us, we risk effacing the past in one of its most potentially useful senses.

At the level of setting, this is the effect of Gordimer's view of history on her fiction; her fictional locations are determinedly present-tensed, as we have noted, even when they include the future. The past only appears in passing. Against this we may set the first five novels of J.M. Coetzee; their temporal settings almost militantly avoid the present, chiefly finding their fictional locations in the past and future. Such a strategy may be seen as arising from a desire to approach the present from a point of difference, cutting it loose from a continuous temporal process within which it is guaranteed a position of dominance.

These observations regarding temporality are not divorced from Coetzee's arguments against the authority of history writing. For if the 'historical' as a generic category is abandoned on the grounds that the past as a point of reference is simply subsumed by a narrative constructed in the present, how then can the past serve as a point of difference from which to challenge the present?

Paul Q. Hirst indicates that it cannot. To link the present and past within the discipline of history at all is illegitimate from a materialist perspective, Hirst claims, because it depends upon a 'philosophy of history', which is an idealist category. 'If philosophical ... grounds ... are rejected then historical investigations need to base their pertinence on some other claim, for example, current political or ideological relevance', he writes, concluding, 'whether historical investigations are pertinent or not becomes a matter of politics' (1985:89).

The past, here, is essentially an issue in the politics of the present. This is a common current truism, impossible – indeed dangerous – to refute. And yet, may we not find reasons *in the present* for conceiving of the past as something *apart* from the present? Without a doubt, stressing the historicity of the present moves us quickly into the politics of reconstructing the past. Making this move too quickly, however, risks erasing certain tactical reasons for preserving the historical as something other than, different from, the present.

I wish to illustrate the point I am trying to make here by returning to the problems inherent in the kind of approach adopted by the social historians. When Luli Callinicos uses Ngugi wa Thiong'o's 'I talk about the past mainly because I am interested in the present' as an epigraph to the second volume of her *A People's History of South Africa* (1987:7), she evinces some of the danger inherent in an historiography which authorises the past in the terms of the present. For implicit in such an attitude is an act of totalisation all the more problematic in this case for its apparent absence.

A major complaint made against the revisionist South African historians of the 1970s and 1980s was their failure to produce an overview of South Africa's history from their perspective, and this now dominant South African mode of radical historiography has still proved notoriously incapable of providing an overt single narrative for itself. Against this it may be argued that its main achievements, and they are many and various, have been accomplished by the initiation of an array of new methodologies and new objects of study only possible outside any 'inclusive' overviews.

This is nowhere more manifest than in the form that the writing of social history takes. One of the most typical forms of social history publication is the presentation of the selected proceedings of its workshops (see, for example, Bozzoli 1983; Bonner *et al.* 1989). In these, rather disparate papers are collected together and given coherence of a sort by an introduction which attempts to forge a thematic unity by picking out issues the papers hold in common and listing them under large and general categories. It is often questionable to what degree the papers directly address these broad issues, for what we are really presented with is a series of micro-studies more concerned on the whole with the details of their particular cases than the large-scale implications the introduction wishes to spell out. The discreteness of the papers works against the totalising perspective that their introductions try to impose. What remains is the essay-length, work-in-progress feel that has characterised this movement from the first.

This continued reliance upon the workshop form must be understood in relation to the specific nature of social history's revisionism, which lay in its commitment to the breaking of the monolithic structures informing the dominant form of history writing it was combating.Born in response to the general overview of South African history represented by the two-volume *Oxford History of Southern Africa* edited by Monica Wilson and Leonard Thompson, its method of attack lay in developing highly detailed and specific case studies which discredited the large-scale claims of a more generalised historical approach. The resonations set up by particular cases were left to undermine broader patterns by implication, rather than by articulation into competing overviews. An early victim of the new radicalism was the major liberal explanatory concept of the frontier; more recently, in a new reformist spirit which has often scandalised the revisionists themselves, Julian Cobbing's attack on the way in which a monolithic and politically-compromising mythology surrounding the 'mfecane' informs even the most detailed and radically-orientated micro-studies is perhaps closest in spirit to the original methodological thrust of revisionism (Cobbing 1988a,c).[1]

---

1. Cobbing's critique of the mfecane has been developed in a series of unpublished papers written since 1983; these are listed in 'The Mfecane: Beginning the Inquest', p.1n.

What was once oppositional about social history now verges on the orthodox, however, and as it does so, its very successes in the political sense have begun to emphasise its potential limitations as history.

Major figures in the revisionist movement have been associated with recent comprehensive South African histories, and if these have tended to be in a 'popular' mode – *The Reader's Digest Illustrated History of South Africa* (Saunders 1992), for example – this may be seen as part of its initial programme of keeping academic history within the reach of a larger audience. Yet the real failure of this now firmly established school was not its failure to produce a comprehensive history of South Africa; its deeper failure has arisen from its determinedly anti-theoretical stance, a stance developed originally through its desire to purge itself of the structuralism that dominated the early revisionist enterprise from which it emerged. When forced to defend itself at a conceptual level, social history claims a 'realist' perspective (defined as a dialectical meeting of empirical evidence and theoretical and conceptual categories – see Bozzoli and Delius 1990b:21), but critics note that the distinction this is meant to establish between social history and a full-blown empiricist methodology is barely evident in much of its practice. And the increasing tendency of revisionists to treat the 'realism' of their approach as a guarantee of the 'reality' of their findings – signalled by their readiness to announce their ever-more centralised projects as 'The Real Story' (the subtitle of the *Reader's Digest* history, for example) – is a truly worrying manifestation of their position within present power relations and the truth-claims this allows.

The issue, then, is not one of micro-studies versus overviews; what is evident is that the methodological deployment of increasingly detailed and specifically focused studies, while of strategic significance in particular circumstances, is not an adequate defence against the production and maintenance of generalised assumptions left to hover, often without being directly addressed, behind the details in hand and the apparent variety of studies that produce this detailed information. Social history, in form so differentiated, works at crucial levels from a totalisation it has resisted foregrounding; all too often it is a medley of practices constituted as a field by a set of all too often unspoken assumptions.

Its emergence over a more structurally-orientated revisionism has, for example, reinstalled a fundamentally humanist approach – I use this term in Foucault's sense of 'making human consciousness the original subject of all historical development and all action' (1972:12) – as the only one adequate to the historical material of South Africa. It is this humanism which serves as a base for the realism of the social historian's enterprise, its culturalist emphasis, and the experiential leanings of its research priorities. Behind the myriad subdivisions of its micro-studies, indeed, as a very condition of their existence, lies a particular sense of history as a single, continuous whole.

HISTORY AND DIFFERENCE

In *The Archaeology of Knowledge*, Foucault specifically links 'continuous history' (chronological, linear, teleological, progressive, narrative, and related forms of totalised history) with the construction of the subject at the heart of humanism, and rejects both on the grounds of their appropriativeness. 'Continuous history,' he writes,

> is the indispensable correlative of the founding function of the subject: the guarantee that everything that has eluded him may be restored to him; the certainty that time will disperse nothing without restoring it in a reconstituted unity; the promise that one day the subject – in the form of historical consciousness – will once again be able to appropriate, to bring back under his sway, all those things that are kept at a distance by difference, and find in them what might be called his abode. (1972:12)

Continuous history is, then, as Mark Poster puts it in *Foucault, Marxism and History*, 'a means of controlling and domesticating the past in the form of knowing it' (1984:70), and the problem with this is that the historian (and, we may add, the historical novelist) achieves control over the past 'without placing himself or herself in question' (75). The chief advantage of Foucault's method of stressing discontinuity in the historical process is the challenge it presents to the position of the historian. 'Foucault,' says Poster,

> attempts to show how the past was different, strange, threatening. He labors to distance the past from the present, to disrupt the easy, cosy intimacy that historians have traditionally enjoyed in the relationship of the past to the present. He strives to alter the position of the historian from one who gives support to the present by collecting all the meanings of the past and tracing the line of inevitability through which they are

resolved in the present, to one who breaks off the past from the present and, by demonstrating the foreignness of the past, relativizes and undercuts the legitimacy of the present. (74)

It is on such terms that it seems to me strategically – politically – necessary that we reclaim the historical from the present, and the way in which this is best done is by reminding ourselves that, while we may acknowledge that the categories of the historical and the political are radically implicated, the acts of *politicisation* and *historicisation* are not identical. Again, this can be demonstrated by returning to the question of the contemporary status of the 'historical novel'. For the legacy that the now apparently defunct issue of the nature and status of this genre has left us may be put in the form of this central question: how can a work of fiction make of history something both resistant to being simply appropriated by the present and yet relevant enough to relate meaningfully to the present?

FROM HISTORICAL NOVEL TO HISTORICISING FORM

Fredric Jameson, the American Marxist theorist whose influence was strong in South Africa in the 1980s, goes along with Lukács in allowing that '… in our own time it is generally agreed that all novels are historical, in that in keeping faith with the present their object is just as profoundly historical as any moment from the distant past' (Jameson 1971:350). His attraction in the historically-charged circumstances of South Africa lay in his attempt to preserve the 'Real' (in Lacan's sense of 'that which "resists symbolization absolutely"'– Jameson 1981:35) in the form of History ('History is what hurts, it is what refuses desire…' – Jameson 1981:102) against the post-structural assault upon the 'referent', and his readiness to dismiss the 'historical novel' as such is an important indicator of how he went about this. For if Jameson was prepared to let 'history' as a passive generic or disciplinary distinction go, he preserved in his cultural enquiry the vital activity of *historicisation*. He shifted, then, from distinguishing between past and present as a basis for idealist definitions of the historical genre or discipline, to connecting past and present (and future, it is worth adding) in a quite literal 'new historicism'. Jameson's revival of historicism in the old-fashioned sense of a belief in large-scale laws of continuous and totalising historical development provides a way, I believe, for rethinking the place of the historical within fiction.

The entire structure of *The Political Unconscious* (1981), the great work of what we may now identify as Jameson's 'middle period', finds its origin in tackling what he calls 'the old dilemmas of historicism'. Chief amongst these is the 'unacceptable option, or ideological double bind, between antiquarianism' and 'modernizing "relevance" or projection' (17 and 18). How can one methodologically accommodate within one practice a reading which aims at, as Catherine Belsey puts it, 'a knowledge of history, albeit the unconscious of history', and a reading which is 'of the present and for the present' (1980:140)? Jameson's answer is, as is well known, that these different emphases must be linked within a single historical narrative, and the narrative he puts forward as the most fundamental is that of 'the Marxian notion of the mode of production' (1988b:168). So grand a narrative is positively scandalous in an age characterised by, as Lyotard would have it, an 'incredulity towards metanarratives' (1984:xxiv), but the historicist approach which Jameson's deployment of narrative allows him is not meant, finally, to appropriate and contain all that is potentially Other to it; its real thrust is to cross distance without flattening difference. In historical terms, what Jameson is looking for is a way in which the past may be read from the present without appropriating it for the present; as he puts it in *The Political Unconscious*:

> only a genuine philosophy of history is capable of respecting the specificity and radical difference of the social and cultural past while disclosing the solidarity of its polemics and passions, its forms, structures, experiences, and struggles, with those of the present day. (18)

We must, of course, be suspicious of the 'unity of a single great collective story' told by Jameson to support his particular 'philosophy of history'; we must, along with Robert Young, ask of its 'single vast unfinished plot': 'Whose narrative? And whose unfinished plot? In short, whose history is Jameson's oft-invoked "History itself"?' (Young 1990:113). But I do not think it has been sufficiently acknowledged that these questions are implicitly allowed for in Jameson's project even as it stands in this period of his work (they have certainly been explicitly taken on in his later writings); structurally, the effect of Jameson's narrative (or philosophy, or history) is to allow, even call for, a radical challenge to itself. The structure Jameson presents is intentionally a self-critical one, even as this critique depends upon what produces it. I do not mean to associate Jameson with classically deconstructive procedures far from so much of what he attempts, but it is difficult not to see claim and critique contained in one and the same movement here. Even as Jameson clears a way to the past, that past is presented as potentially inimical to the terms by which it is approached.

In an essay published not long before *The Political Unconscious*, Jameson writes that an important ramification of his historical vision is that

> We will no longer tend to see the past as some inert and dead object which we are called upon to resurrect, or to preserve, or to sustain, in our own living freedom; rather, the past itself will become an active agent in this process and will begin to come before us as a radically different life form which rises up to call our own form of life into question and to pass judgement on us, and through us on the social formation in which we exist. (Jameson 1988b:175)

'It is not only the past that judges us...,' Jameson continues in terms extremely useful to my project, but 'the future as well...'; this is because, in Jameson's account of history, 'only the Utopian future is a place of truth ... and the privilege of contemporary life and of the present lies not in its possession, but at best in the rigorous judgement it may be felt to pass on us' (176).

In spirit, these passages capture the strategies employed by the best exemplars of what I shall define as 'resistant form'. To the extent that the works I call 'future histories' are realised concretely enough in their difference to 'pass judgement' upon the present, they represent a genuinely historical achievement. In much the same way, it is precisely the degree to which the past is recreated in all its difference from the present that allows the most effective of the historical novels of the 1940s and 1950s to call the present 'into question' and become, in this, truly 'historical'. As far as the present is concerned, it must be grasped as poised between a fully-realised conception of past and future and shot through with its own historicity; those novels concentrated on the South African present of which they are a part that achieve this must be included, too, in our redefined sense of what constitutes the 'historical novel'.

It may be seen from even this brief summary of my position that *formally*, the historicised perspective is an identifiable literary practice as much as it is a critical/ historical one. A work of fiction may be considered as 'historical' if it calls up the past, present, or future as a point of resistance to its own production of any of these moments; if other temporal periods are allowed to exist in the work in all their difference from itself; if the very act of creating a particular moment in history in a work is powerful enough to hold at bay the appropriation of that moment by that act of creation.

RESISTANT FORM

I have stressed the formal nature of what I have ransacked from Jameson's project because I wish to avoid the empirical and ontological implications of taking his claims literally. This act of flagrant bad faith at least allows me to foreground the effect of his structural formulation, and extend this to something of a general definition for historicised structures. The totalising nature of Jameson's Marxism – the politicised 'content' of his theory, as it were – leaves him open to the kind of critique mounted by Robert Young noted above, which he summarises in saying: 'it is hard ... to avoid the conclusion that [Jameson's] insistence on socialism's development as a global totality involves a form of neo-colonialism: "we Americans, we masters of the world" know what is best for everyone else. The attitude does not change whether the prescription be capitalism or socialism' (Young 1990:112).

If, however, we take seriously the historicising *form* of Jameson's argument, even his Marxist content is open to its own formal logic, that of historical interrogation. Generative of Jameson's conclusions his content may be, but these conclusions turn out to have much in common with theories as radically opposed to Jameson's as Foucault's; entirely incommensurable as theories, Jameson's and Foucault's accounts share an ultimate interest in history as resistant to the position from which it is produced.

Is, then, the true issue at stake that of totalisation versus difference? It seems to me not; rather, we must follow Young in his early summary of his theme in *White Mythologies: Writing History and the West* when he concludes that

> ... both historicism or entirely differentiated histories are in themselves impossibilities: history will always involve a form of historicism, but an historicism that cannot be sustained. It is thus a contradictory (quasi)concept – a phantasm – in which neither the elements of totalization nor difference can be definitively achieved or dispatched. This means that history can be theorised not so much as a contradictory process but as a concept that must enact its own contradiction with itself: 'this difference is what is called History'. (84)

32

The quotation is from Derrida who, in engaging with Levinas's view that the primacy of History forms part of the imperialism of the same, writes,

> ... history is impossible, meaningless, in the finite totality, and ... it is impossible, meaningless, in the positive and actual infinity; ... history keeps to the difference between totality and infinity ... (1978:123)

What is really at stake is the ability of a form to resist the content it produces and, indeed, itself. History as a form, then, remains a 'phantasm', a necessarily totalising structure that resists all but its own most radical implications of difference. Broadly described as such, all histories need no other defining features; projects of the present all histories are, but if they are to be 'histories', their most meaningful effect must be the way in which they resist that present, the very politics which produces them, and in so doing force it to question itself.

To come back to the present of this project: the validity of such an historical method for contemporary South Africa lies in its insistence on the way in which the position of the historian – and the point of this book is to extend this to the scholar and writer of fiction – must be open to the interrogation of his or her subject. This is an attitude it is important to encourage in the process of attempting to know a still divided community. The resulting sense of a community created out of difference may be read directly into current attempts to transform the signifier 'South Africa' from a term of deeply contested geographical significance to a national one that is able to encompass fractures of region, ethnicity, gender, and class. 'History' is constantly and urgently mobilised by the different factions created in such a project, and if it is not to be merely subsumed into the prevailing and all too often bloody and vicious present-mindedness, we must find terms upon which it can challenge the present and force the different positions within the present to examine the specificities of their positionality. To do this, history must be accorded a force of its own and treated as valid in itself, as it were, and not simply something entirely open to the manipulation of the present.

This is the essence of historicising form, to the resistance it may provide, and I would wish to preserve it as a model for a particular and vital fictional *activity*. This activity has been developed out of debates regarding critical approach, but my aim has been to identify the way in which fiction itself may be seen to carry out this function – without making the fictional simply evidence for the historical, or the historical merely something subsumed in the fictional. The 'historical novel' as a category defined by its subject matter (the past) gives way in this account to the *process* carried out by fiction as an *historicising form*.

And fiction becomes an historicising form when it so operates upon its material – no longer bound to a particular temporal location, but open to the past, present, and future – as to turn it into history; that is, to make of its historical material a moment of resistance that leads to an intervention with its own moment of production or consumption. In this way, the history a work depicts is no mere reflex of that work's own history, but acts upon its construction within that history in the very act of its construction. This for me is truly 'novel history', something clearly divorced from the kind of formal domestication that characterises many – if not most – of the works we are accustomed to calling 'historical novels'.

As far as the historical 'content' of each of the works we will consider in this book is concerned, that will be left to their own structural effects. Given my theme of resistant form, I do not feel it necessary to propose some totalised version of South African History against which to establish or deny a generic continuity between the works considered in this study, attempting to categorise them as 'historical novels' or not in terms of their subject matter. At one level (that of selection for inclusion in this study), it will be enough that in making their subject some element of the communal life of southern Africa, past, present, or future, they enter into a contract with the reader that requires him or her to recognise sequences or events formalised outside the text in question as 'history'. At another level (that of the evaluation of these texts as historical fiction), what will be crucial will be the way in which they fail or succeed in turning their material into history on, as we saw Coetzee would have it, their own terms. Rather than forcing each work into relation with a monolithic conception of history, my method shall be to determine the grounds upon which the work in question conceives of itself as historical and then read it against the principle of resistant form. This will bring us into contact with history as determinate practice and move us away from essentialist definitions by their very nature opposed to serious historical considerations. Our first move in such an endeavour must be to consider the specificities of history, nation, and form woven into this study subtitled 'past, present and future in modern South African fiction'. We shall begin to do this by looking at one of the founding texts of modern 'South African' nationalism, Sol T. Plaatje's *Mhudi*.

PART ONE

---■---

USES OF THE PAST

2

HISTORY, NATION, AND FORM

SOL T. PLAATJE

■

Getting history wrong is part of being a nation
– Ernest Renan, quoted in Hobsbawm 1990:12

IMAGINING A COMMUNITY

The following letter, published in the *Sunday Tribune* of 22 May 1994, was the 'winning letter' of that issue, and earned a Parker ball pen and pencil set for ME Jones of Durban:

> I would like to extend my heartfelt thanks to President Nelson Mandela for a gift I didn't even know I wanted, until May 10, 1994.
>
> As part of probably one of the smallest minorities in this vast country (I am white, suburban, thirty-something mother) I have never understood, let alone had any feelings of, nationalism and patriotism. I have never known what it is to identify with and feel part of a larger whole.
>
> For the first time in my life I am moved when I hear our anthem being played, or see that multicoloured horizontal Y fluttering in the breeze. I have been moved to tears more often this week than in my entire life; and those tears have been of profound joy at finally having a country to claim as my own.
>
> I would like to give a big thank you, from the bottom of my previously cynical and unpatriotic heart, to Mr Mandela, the African National Congress and all those wonderful South Africans who made it happen, for giving me a country to love.

The depth and intensity of my national pride and love has taken me completely by surprise, but what a warm, wonderful, heart-stirring feeling it is.

In the same issue of the *Sunday Tribune*, 'An Open Letter to Nelson Mandela' by Breyten Breytenbach (dated Berlin, 17 May) appeared. Its concluding paragraphs read:

> I must tell you of a final private paradox ... For the first time in more than 30 years I feel myself truly liberated from the perceived responsibility (and the self-blinding temptation) to raise a political voice.
>
> Henceforth my contribution (and that of others of my ilk) will be: that our loyalty is a vigilant opposition; that any collaboration in the big project of constructing a South Africa in worthy accordance with the new realities born of dreams and of struggle will be predicated on principled criticism; and that the assistance we can offer you, as father of the nation, is to treat you as a garden politician risking the mundane corruption of power inherent in all politics; that we shall oppose you through civil society; ... and that we shall grasp the freedom to be creative, each in her and his mother tongue, fully proud of our differences and of that which we share.

Ms Jones's letter would suggest that it is not enough, on the global evidence at present apparently so plentifully available, to reject nationalism out of hand. It would be easy to satirise her views on nationalism, easier still to see them as hopelessly naïve, and qualify their all too recognisable impulses within oneself with the sort of critical edge that the smaller political groupings in the 'new' South Africa try to construct for themselves in their attempts to remain viable. And if the aesthetic in South Africa has become almost defined by its oppositionality, then a position like Breytenbach's is perhaps the most obvious one to adopt; here the artist, if not transcendent, is still characterised as being in some way distant from the messy reality of power politics. Shifting his allegiances away from the oppositional movements that once received his support as they approach orthodoxy, he remains the ever-growling watchdog.

Marxism has not, as again global evidence would seem to indicate, provided a successful foundation for nationalism. If its virtues – unable to be translated into nation-building – have nevertheless often proved themselves as a basis for oppositional strategy, then it may be seen as the archetypal watchdog. Perhaps this is why Marxism has habitually been dismissive of nationalism, but we must ask, then, whether important elements in the contemporary crises of certain 'Communist' states may well be traced back to this. As long ago as 1977 Tom Nairn identified nationalism as 'Marxism's great historical failure' (1977:332), and it is possible now to see something prophetic in Fredric Jameson's claim in 1981

> that a Left which cannot grasp the immense utopian appeal of nationalism (any more than it can grasp that of religion or of fascism) can scarcely hope to 'reappropriate' such collective energies and must effectively doom itself to political impotence. (1981:298)

Aligning the appeal of nationalism with that of fascism and religion is a clear indication of the caution with which Jameson feels the power of these concepts must be handled; indeed, Jameson's later work on postmodernity identifies the 'internationalism' in this, for him, latest stage in the development of a world history as its most positive feature. It is this attitude that prompts Simon During amongst others to question whether postmodernism and post-colonialism can exist in anything other than an antagonistic relation. For During, 'post-colonialism is the need, in nations or groups which have been victims of imperialism, to achieve an identity uncontaminated by universalist or Eurocentric concepts and images'(1990:114). The effect of this definition is that the 'new post-colonial nationalisms' appear as the 'strongest enemies of postmodernity' (116); in doing so, however, they reveal in turn the complicity of postmodernity so defined with the neo-imperialism that effects its influence. A result of such a complicity is that the principles by which one evaluates particular nationalisms return to the holders of, as During puts it in his conclusion to this essay, 'those concepts of justice and reason that totalising denouncers of our postmodernity assure us are in their safekeeping' (130). In the light of such an observation, we must be as cautious about the source of the certitude and rectitude informing the position Breytenbach adopts in his letter as he is of an emergent nationalism. In a country like South Africa, where a persuasive nationalist appeal takes on in the present the force of necessity in relation to a violent legacy of institutionalised ethnic and regional divisions, nationalism as a positive phenomenon – given even the slight embarrassment we may feel before the terms of Jones's letter – is still to be taken seriously in ways that the assumption of an 'international' or 'universal' adjudication finds it difficult to admit.

It would be unfortunate to give the word 'still' in this context the force of simple historical lag. The now-established consensus regarding 'Negative Nationalism' – Anna Rutherford is confidently non-specific when she writes, 'just as the old imperialism was intent on repressing other discourses, so too is the new nationalism, not only in Africa, but in the settler colonies as well' (1992:iii,iv) – can only in the most obvious ways be invoked as a warning for a South African present and future. 'History' in the singular has been a victim of our growing awareness of the specificities of (especially) colonial contexts, and this should prevent us from reading apartheid as just a temporary delay in the enactment of a monolithic narrative of African liberation – a narrative with a far from happy end, and one in which the belated emergence of South Africa as a 'new nation' coincides with the exposure of nationalism as, in the words of Simon Gikandi, 'not the manifestation of a common interest but a repressor of desires' (1992:380).

How, from such a perspective, can South Africans take the urgent project of national reconstruction seriously? How can we accommodate in one act the now commonly traced trajectory of the nationalist enterprise from the utopian to the dystopian, from idealism to disillusionment? It is in relation to such considerations that I would like to read *Mhudi* (Plaatje 1975 [1930]) as an expression of a nationalist project from the past without patronising it.

By this I mean that I wish to avoid the sort of appropriating historicism which creeps back into Gikandi's – in many other ways – fine attempt to 're-configure' Africa as a 'theoretical problematic' (377). For Gikandi, 'In the colonial period, narration, and related acts of cultural production, were predicated on a simple ethical assumption: it was the duty of the African writer to recover the African political unconscious, a fundamental history which colonialism had repressed' (378). It is the naïvete of this 'simple ethical assumption' which leads to the next stage in Gikandi's history – 'the so-called literature of disillusionment' (378). Disillusionment is the result of remaining within an 'African problematic ... defined by its Manichean relationship to the very colonial structure it sought to negate' (378). The attitude expressed to nationalism is a key indicator of this condition: 'If we accept the basic assumption that the desire for national independence is generated by colonial independence,' says Gikandi, 'then this desire and the forms it takes are still functions of the colonial episteme.' Thus Ngugi, for example, is unable to grasp that 'In the post-colonial situation ... the divinity of the nation has collapsed', and so, like his character Matigari, he is 'a prisoner of the emancipatory narrative he promotes' (380).

There is a literary-historical narrative here as appropriatively linear as the historico-political one Gikandi praises Farah for expunging in *Maps*; as a result, despite the apparent contest between these narratives, they share the effect of diminishing a more valid historicist activity. We lose the historical specificity of texts when we read them too strongly in terms of what came after (*pace* Walter Benjamin[2]); we flatten their difference in simply accommodating them in a direct line to our present. There is often more validity in a text's relevance for us when we reconstruct its sense of not knowing what comes next – for this is our present condition, and the condition of the text's production matches ours when we read for the break that this structural similarity represents. In the case of *Mhudi*, our present needs call for a reading which can reconstitute it as a complex practical appeal for nationalism – not in the sense of any one-to-one act of tracing simple and simplistic 'relevance' between the text and ourselves, or between one period and another, but rather creating from the text's very difference a resistance to – in this case – the predetermined disillusion that emerges out of Gikandi's account of the national project. This is the essence of the historicising activity spelled out in Chapter One, in which the critical approach, no less than what one is reading for, both exemplify what I have dubbed 'resistant form'.

Gikandi's account does not depend upon a one-dimensional rejection of nationalism; at several points he acknowledges that certain writers have 'recognised that the nation in Africa was an invented community' (381). *Maps*, however, is exemplary for Gikandi's argument because in it Farah attacks Somalian nationalism for not recognising this and representing itself as a 'natural entity': 'Other African nations may at least accede to their arbitrary invention in the halls of European imperialism, but not Somalia ...' (386). So, it is the foundationalism of Somali nationalism that becomes Gikandi's central example of 'negative nationalism'; this is a pity, because in closing in on this quite obvious object of attack in our age of anti-essentialism, he touches on and then bounces off the far more subtle issue of writers supportive of particular national projects who not

---

2. It is not that I wish to side with Fustel de Coulanges against Benjamin on this point (see thesis VII of the *Theses on the Philosophy of History*); it is just that I have difficulty aligning Benjamin's comments here with those regarding the monad in thesis XVII.

only acknowledge, but *foreground* the constructed nature of nationalism – and its historical contingency. In these cases, the fundamentalism of the 'simple ethical assumption' of the colonial period is a predicate of Gikandi's argument, not of all narratives from that period. Certainly as far as *Mhudi* is concerned, there is nothing simple – ethically and otherwise – or even assumed about nationalism.

Firstly, *Mhudi* not only concedes the constructed nature of nationalism, it formally *enacts* it with a degree of complexity we must spend some time tracing. Before we do this, however, we need to note that concession or acknowledgement here is not in itself enough; the question of what significance is given to nationalism's constructed status, and what implications this has for the discourses involved in its construction, has to be taken into account.

In stressing the 'element of artefact, invention, and social engineering which enters into the making of nations', E.J. Hobsbawm concludes that 'nationalism comes before nations. Nations do not make states and nationalisms but the other way round' (1990:10). In this he is in agreement with other major contemporary theorists on nationalism: Ernest Gellner, for example, makes much the same point when he writes, 'Nationalism is not the awakening of nations to self consciousness: it invents nations where they do not exist'. This is a claim Benedict Anderson quotes approvingly, with the proviso that we do not, as Gellner does, assume that nations are thus 'false' communities; 'all communities,' says Anderson, echoing the evocative title of his book, 'are imagined communities' (1983:15).

HISTORY AND NATION

Even if the constructedness of nationalism is non-pejoratively accepted, one of the crucial elements in the process that goes into the making of nations is, it would seem, harder to accept as a construct. Gikandi talks of the recovery of a 'fundamental history' as central to the 'simple ethical assumption' of colonial nationalism, and it is common for theorists of nationalism to observe, as Johan Degenaar does, that 'a love for the past of the volk ... projects a national consciousness backward in time, true to the precept that a nation, of necessity, creates its own past' (1987:237). Tom Nairn takes the common rather blighted view of this:

> ... it is through nationalism that societies try to propel themselves
> forward to certain kinds of goal (industrialisation, prosperity, equality

42

with other peoples, etc.) *by a certain sort of regression* – by looking inwards, drawing more deeply upon their indigenous resources, resurrecting past folk-heroes and myths about themselves and so on. These idealistic and romantic well-springs adhere to every form of nationalism. It is a perfectly banal fact about nationalist history that such soul-searching quite easily becomes sheer invention, where legends take the place of myths. Indeed, this fabrication of an imaginary past was a prominent feature of that original 'progressive' national-liberation struggle, the Greek War of Independence of the 1820s. (1977:348; original emphasis)

It is out of this perspective that our epigraph comes, or, as Renan has put it more accurately if less pithily elsewhere: 'Forgetting, I would even go so far as to say historical error, is a crucial factor in the creation of a nation, which is why progress in historical studies often constitutes a danger for [the principle of] nationality' (1990:11). From here it is a short step to seeing nationalism as the enemy of history.

Yet there is a sense in which an adequate national vision can be seen as an adequate historical vision. For the opposition set up between these modes of discourse usually depends, as is clear in the quotations above, on the assumption of the 'reality' of history as against the 'constructedness' of nationalism. While this may now be a commonly dismissed assumption, we can demonstrate just how difficult it is to disentangle the two modes if we pay attention to the 'historical novel', a discursive form radically implicated in the construction of both 'nation' and 'history'.

In arguing for the 'modernity of the vocabulary' of nationalism, and against the assumption 'that national identification is somehow so natural, primary and permanent as to precede history', Hobsbawm comes up with an array of surprisingly late first uses of 'the modern concept of "the nation"' (1990:14). People only 'began systematically to operate with this concept in their political and social discourse during the Age of Revolution, and especially, under the name of the "principle of nationality" from about 1830 onwards' (18). This dating, supported by Nairn above, makes the chronological alignment of nationalism and the genre of the 'historical novel' a rather obvious one. Georg Lukács stresses this fact in his account of 'the rise of the historical novel': 'The appeal to national independence and national character is necessarily connected with a re-awakening of national history, with memories of the past, of past greatness, of moments of national dishonour ...' (1981:23), he writes, going on to say, 'Such was the historical basis upon which Sir Walter Scott's historical novel arose' (29).

To what degree the historical novel may be aligned with Nairn's 'sheer invention' on the one hand or Anderson's 'imagination' on the other depends upon the particular example at hand, but the above points provide a general framework within which to consider the fact that the first two novels in English by black South Africans, and the first novel in the vernacular, were historical novels intimately related to specific moments of nationalism in South Africa; Sol Plaatje's *Mhudi* (written 1917; first published 1930) joins Thomas Mofolo's *Chaka* (1910) and Peter Abrahams's *Wild Conquest* (1950) as a serious attempt at projecting in fictional form its national ideal through history.

'SOUTH AFRICA' AS A NATIONAL CONSTRUCT

These general introductory comments regarding nationalism have to be transferred carefully to the South African situation, but the major points do seem to hold. For example, Marks and Trapido (1987:2) feel compelled early in their account of 'the politics of race, class and nationalism' to make the same point in the South African context that Hobsbawm stressed in the European context: 'It is not often realised how recent "national" identifications in South Africa are.' They go on to explore this point in relation to its particular circumstances, claiming that 'both black and white nationalism can in large measure be seen as responses to late-nineteenth-century industrialisation, imperialism and British "race patriotism"'; more specifically,

> for all the peoples of South Africa, new ethnic identities emerged around 1910 when the state was being constructed as a single entity out of the British colonies, the conquered Afrikaner republics and African kingdoms in the region.

What is crucial in this account is the plural within the singular:

> That this unification did not lead to a single pan-South African, pan-ethnic nationalism was the outcome of a history of regional divisions, the racism and social Darwinism of the late nineteenth century and

the specific political-cum-class struggles which were being legitimated by the discourse of nationalism.

Far from serving as an overall uniting factor, nationalism in the South African context accentuated differences; the transformation of 'South Africa' from a geographical expression to a political one highlighted the contrast between 'state' and 'nation'. Anderson's definition of the nation – 'it is an imagined political community – and imagined as both inherently limited and sovereign' – has, we see, as one of its chief features the idea of limits: 'the nation ... has finite, if elastic boundaries, beyond which lie other nations' (1983:15,16). The South African state has been infamous, of course, for seeking to exploit the 'national' limits within itself, but even oppositional positions maintain the concept of competing nationalisms:

> For much of the twentieth century, an exclusive form of white Afrikaner nationalism, with its explicit objective the capture of the state by the white Afrikaner 'nation', has confronted its counterpart, a pan-South African black nationalism, which has sought the incorporation of Africans into the body politic. The exclusivism of Afrikaner Christian nationalism with its roots in late-nineteenth-century European nationalism has been confronted by a black nationalism which, despite strong Africanist underpinnings, has in general espoused the nineteenth-century liberal values of multiracialism. (Marks and Trapido 1987:1)

A telling example of Afrikaner nationalism's 'exclusivism' is, as Isabel Hofmeyr has illustrated, the way in which it has retroactively created a tradition of a homogeneous language for itself (see, for example, Hofmeyr 1987). On a different scale, one of the best illustrations of black nationalism's 'inclusivism' is *Mhudi* – a work for which Plaatje also had to construct a 'language', both at the linguistic and the generic levels.

The point here is that different perspectives within the same historical moment produced radically different national constructs – the one dominating and divisive, the other utopian and reconciliatory. In relating this observation to our time, we have to translate it across some strange reversals: the respecters of otherness, the institutionalisers of difference, those who refused to absorb ethnic, linguistic, and regional divisions into their identity, turn out, of course, to represent (in the dominance they clearly wished to maintain for their position in relation to the others which they were instrumental in defining) the tyranny from which the valorisation of difference is meant to free us. But the opponents of this position, the champions of inclusivism, the proposers of integration, the advocates of incorporation, re-emerge in our time – after a long period in which such ideals had little rhetorical or practical purpose – to be faced themselves with charges of tyranny. In part, we must acknowledge that the transition from oppositionality to dominance will always carry this risk, but the more important questions, those of how unity is to be established without becoming authoritarian, difference accommodated without appeals to exclusivism, tolerance established without becoming a liberal complacency – when even consensus models like representative democracy no longer carry an automatic legitimacy – haunt our attempts to think anew the nation.

PLAATJE'S NATIONAL PROJECT

Plaatje's efforts to imagine a national community faced equally powerful, if very different, challenges, and the very form in which he carries out his project is a mark of the specificity of his historical moment. Choosing to write an 'historical novel' (its generic appellation is significantly tricky, as we shall see, especially in relation to the pan-South Africanism of black nationalism) during the formative period of South African nationalism duplicates the development of the historical novel in the context of emerging European nationalisms. Plaatje wrote from the heart of the early black nationalist movement. He was, as is well known, a founder member of the South African Native National Congress, which was formed in reaction to the formation of the Union (a classic example of nationalism being forged against the creation of the state). It is a commonplace observation that the early ANC was a limited middle-class movement, but as at least one school of theorists on nationalism have shown, the middle class has had an important role to play in the development of nationalism.

> The arrival of nationalism in a distinctively modern sense was tied to the political baptism of the lower classes ... [A]lthough sometimes hostile to democracy, nationalist movements have been invariably populist in outlook and sought to induct lower classes into political life. In its most typical version, this assumed the shape of a restless

middle-class and intellectual leadership trying to stir up and channel popular class energies into support for the new state. (Nairn 1977:41)

While the colonial context of the organisations with which Plaatje was involved meant that perhaps as much energy was poured into trying to convince their former colonial rulers to include them within the coming political dispensation as into mobilising their own excluded constituencies, the history of the ANC from its inception up until the 1940s and 1950s is clearly one of drawing nearer to populist movements. Plaatje's period of activity conforms to the earliest and most inclusivist phase of black nationalism, in which the prime aim was not the replacement of but, in the words of Marks and Trapido given above, 'incorporation into the body politic'.

To the degree that *Mhudi* manifests this aspect of its moment of production, its inclusivist national ideal is cut off from us by a range of political options that have emerged since then – the key moments being the shift away from the attempt at improving the political structures in place (by the extension of their benefits to all) towards the total transformation of these structures, and, more recently, the then difficult to imagine take-over of these structures by groups once considered permanently marginalised by them. But our interest is in Plaatje's intervention as it stands without this 'knowledge', this sense of history which, blinkered by its own hindsight, can only see Plaatje's text as a short-sighted exercise in national definition; what formal shape did his attempt at redefining South African nationalism take in its present construed *as a present*?

Plaatje's expressed intention in his first 'novel' (the only one to be completed and find its way into print) was 'to interpret to the reading public one phase of "the back of the native mind"' (1975:17) as part of the hoped-for process of incorporation – although by 1917 a real note of pessimism is evident in such a project. Given that 'reading', even more than writing, meant 'white' reading in terms of any sort of broad audience, Plaatje was involved in a kind of cross-cultural activity in *Mhudi* that links this text in awkward ways to the important connections often made between nationalism and a common print-language.

THE NOVEL AND THE NATION

Anderson, for example, makes much of the relation between 'the birth of the imagined community of the nation' and 'the basic structure of two forms of imagining which first flowered in Europe in the eighteenth century: the novel and the newspaper (1983:41-49). For these forms,' he says, 'provided the technical means for "re-presenting" the kind of imagined community that is the nation' (30). Fundamental to the formation of an 'imagined community' are the secularisation of religion, the demise of the dynastic realm, and a change in the apprehension of time in which chronology and calendar take over from a simultaneity of past and present. The novel and newspaper are vital to the creation of the last of these conditions (although they are involved in all three). This they achieve by providing a sense of a shared, simultaneous world in which one's relationship with others is guaranteed without first-hand knowledge or contact. Through the book, and the newspaper considered as 'book' (after describing the ritual of reading a newspaper Anderson asks, 'What more vivid figure for the secular, historically-clocked imagined community can be envisaged?' [39]), 'fiction seeps quietly and continuously into reality, creating that remarkable confidence of community in anonymity which is the hallmark of modern nations' (40).

If *Mhudi*'s mode of address is across competing exclusive nationalisms, we cannot expect it to embody any 'remarkable confidence of community'. Indeed, from contemporary reviewers of *Mhudi* onwards, the divided form of the work has been noted, usually negatively. Stephen Black, in his *Sjambok* column 'The Telephone Conversations of Jeremiah', says *Mhudi* 'is composed of two parts ... Sol Plaatje, the Bechuana writer, and all the white authors whom he has been reading' (quoted in Willan 1984:363), and Martin Tucker speaks of Plaatje's '*attempt* at blending African folk material with individually realised characters in the Western novelistic tradition' (quoted in Couzens 1973:12; my emphasis). These assessments refer as much to the overall style of the work as to its structural divisions between the individualised story of Mhudi and Ra-Thaga and the more historical accounts of the Matabele[3] kingdom; Janheinz Jahn, for example, who has written of Plaatje's 'padded "Victorian" style' (quoted in Couzens 1971:188), has elsewhere characterised *Mhudi* as 'weak in comparison with other works, for Plaatje tries to individualise his characters in the European fashion and thus the African pathos of the dialogue becomes empty' (quoted in Couzens 1973:2).

Some recent accounts are more positive about the obvious formal divisions in the book; Brian Willan credits Plaatje with full control over precisely the same

---

3. I have followed Plaatje's use of the Sotho term 'Matabele' (a term signifying 'destroyers') for the Ndebele. Plaatje spells this 'Matebele' throughout Mhudi, and I have used this spelling when quoting from the work.

cross-cultural elements noted above:

> *Mhudi* was the outcome of a quite conscious and deliberate attempt
> on Plaatje's part to marry together two different cultural traditions:
> African oral forms and traditions, particularly those of the Barolong,
> on the one hand; and the written traditions and forms of the English
> language and literature on the other. (1984:352)

'It was the kind of cultural borderland that Plaatje delighted in exploring,' says
Willan later, going on to place whatever limitations are involved in this attempt
firmly in the work's reception: 'the tragedy was that so few people were in any
kind of position to appreciate to the full just what it was that he was doing'
(353).

A significant element of what has been missed in the reception of *Mhudi* is
the degree to which its formal divisions register the constructed nature of the
national project to which it is committed; a nation requires an act of the
imagination to be brought into being, and this imaginative act as Plaatje
represents it is no idealist one: its medium is the historical event, a process of
material engagement that is marked by a firm sense of political, technological,
and environmental struggle. If the strategy of Plaatje's text – as suggested by
the commentaries given above – may be called 'hybrid', this is not in the
sometimes offensive sense of two or more ethnic, regional or cultural
essentialisms accommodating each other's differences; it is an intensely historical
fluidity in which each of the oppositions creates the other beyond an economy
of species. This may best be illustrated by considering *Mhudi* from the perspective
of literary classifications that allow for notions of formal hybridity. All the
above attempts at distinguishing the different formal elements in *Mhudi*
('Bechuana writer'/'white author', 'African folk material'/'Western novelistic
tradition', 'European characters'/'African dialogue, African oral forms and
traditions, particularly those of the Barolong'/'written traditions and forms of
the English language and literature') bear out – even in their often muddled
distinctions – Edward Said's observation that 'the modern history of literary
study is strictly bound up with the development of cultural nationalism'
(1992:14), and so such considerations lead us quickly from the scarcely
suppressed botanical and biological sources of the concept of hybridity to its –
not unrelated – national application.

GENERIC INSTABILITY AND THE NATIONAL PROJECT

Formally the dispute about the literary mode of *Mhudi* remains unresolved. Nowhere is this clearer than when even the most sympathetic critics try, and usually (revealingly) fail, to place the work generically.

Willan ends his account of 'Plaatje's only English-language novel' with the parenthetic comment, 'if novel is the right word for it' (1984:365); he had earlier decided to take Plaatje's subtitle *An Epic of Native Life a Hundred Years Ago* seriously and call the work an 'epic' (352). This was primarily to free the work from the realist expectations of its earlier commentators against which it was bound to fail. Willan, however, also feels compelled to defend *Mhudi* against the author's other categorisation of his work, which would have served the same purpose; Plaatje described it as 'a love story after the manner of the romances ... but based on historical fact', a description Willan dismisses as 'modest' (349). The degree to which the romance form is considered beneath a serious work of fiction (the ghost of Rider Haggard presides here) can be measured by Tim Couzens's concern to answer 'the question whether *Mhudi* is something more than a love idyll with black heroes or an historical romance'; he rejects the romance option on terms entirely opposite to Willan's, arguing 'that *Mhudi* is a sensitive political *novel*' (1973:4; my emphasis). Couzens at times uses 'epic' too, but only loosely when compared with Willan's more strict use of this term (see Willan 1984:352).

Couzens establishes his argument by convincingly demonstrating that Plaatje calls up the past for a very immediate present purpose (1973:1-19); this is Couzens's 'model theory', in which he claims Plaatje uses the 1830s as a model for South Africa after the imposition of the 1913 Native Land Act. Couzens also ably argues for *Mhudi*'s defence of traditional custom and its corrective view on history, both elements that bear out his claim for a political reading. But for Plaatje the political resonates within the national, and it is this which the generic status of his cultural experiment chiefly expresses.

The key to some aspects of the divided nature of *Mhudi* lies, as Couzens has shown, in the way in which Plaatje uses proverbs to express the two-sidedness of arguments; Couzens quotes Plaatje from his collection of Sechuana proverbs:

> The reader will here and there come across two proverbs that appear
> to contradict each other; but such anomalies are not peculiar to

Sechuana ... The whole truth about a fact cannot be summed up in one pithy saying. It may have several different aspects, which, taken separately, seem to be contradictory and have to be considered in connexion with their surrounding circumstances. To explain the connexion is the work of a sermon or essay, not of a proverb. All the latter can do is to express each aspect by itself and let them balance together.

Of this Couzens says:

It seems to me that he extends this idea into both the theme and technique of the novel. Although the book is clearly an epic praising the Baralong [sic], through the technique of shifting perspective, we come to have a certain sympathy for the Matabele ... The technique, then, in the novel, is of shifting perspective; that both sides are given through this technique is a reinforcement of one of the major themes – that there are two sides to every argument. (1973:7)

Couzens here paraphrases one of the most important moments in the novel, when Mzilikazi resolves a moment of extreme conflict between two of his advisors with the following idiomatic passage:

'You see a man has two legs so as to enable him to walk properly. He cannot go far if he hops on one leg. In like manner a man has two hands; to hold his spear in the one and his shield in the other ... For the same reason he has two eyes in order to see better. A man has two ears to hear both sides of a dispute. A man who joins in a discussion with the acts of one side only, will often find himself in the wrong.
'In every grade of life there are two sides to every matter.' (1975:50)

I have quoted from the Sechuana Proverbs, Couzens's article, and the novel at some length not just because I believe Couzens's defence of *Mhudi* to be persuasive, but also because I think it does not fully account for the work's historical perspective.

While the proverbs of a single nation may, in Plaatje's view, only appear to contradict each other, some of the contradictions in *Mhudi* are in fact real and unresolved. While the differing historical perspectives do 'balance each other' as Couzens claims, the essential formal division of the book has another equally complex side to it: the 'African' and 'European' emphases largely correspond to the two elements Plaatje himself identifies in the book, the romantic and the historical. I propose returning to Plaatje's own description of his work and taking it seriously. In doing so I will argue that Plaatje's use of the romantic is a telling element in a fictional project which struggles to construct, in relation to history, an adequate national vision.

Mhudi clearly polarises between the 'love idyll' of Mhudi and Ra-Thaga on the one hand and the 'historical' material on the other. Although the two poles interact in terms of plot – indeed the progress of the plot is towards bringing the two together – stylistic features keep them largely separate. In his earlier assessment of the novel Couzens states 'there is no doubt that *Mhudi* is marred by "poetic" phrases like "native gallantry", "bucolic girl", "an even set of ivories" and "serried ranks"' (1971:189); he plays down the harmful effects of what he calls these '"poetic" archaisms' in his later assessment, pointing out that 'these tend to be absent when Plaatje reaches the more significant moments in his narrative' and 'the phrases often seem to be used with that distinctive sense of irony which is seldom far from the surface in all of Plaatje's writing' (1973:4). Both defences need to be taken further. Firstly, it is as the work approaches its 'historical' material that the '"poetic" archaisms' give way to the more strictly plain and referential prose, marking the romantic and the historical as distinct. Secondly, 'sense of irony' is at times an understatement for what is often broadly humorous, both in style and incident.

The meeting of Mhudi and Ra-Thaga, for example, is hilariously portrayed (and three of the four examples given by Couzens as examples of '"poetic" archaisms' appear in this scene), although it is centred on a moment of real danger. The lovers are left wandering alone in an empty landscape in the aftermath of the horrific destruction of Kunana, the capital city of the Barolong, by the Matebele. They come together when Mhudi runs into Ra-Thaga while fleeing from a lion; the scene in which Ra-Thaga, to prove his gallantry, chases the lion (accompanied by Mhudi who will not be separated from the first person she has met in months), is extremely comically portrayed, and is followed by many other comic scenes; an example (again involving a lion, the most dangerous natural threat they face) is when Mhudi awakens to find Ra-Thaga holding a lion by the tail in order to protect her. We are told she yielded to the humour of the picture of her husband having a tug of war with the lion; highly amused, she gripped the situation, stepped forward in obedience to Ra-Thaga, and summoning all her strength, she aimed a stab at the lion's heart. The infuriated animal fell over with a growl that almost caused the earth to vibrate. (57)

The point is that these moments of high danger in the isolation of the wilderness are controlled and defused by humour. Comedy, which is widely spread throughout the novel, upholds the romance mode and keeps realism at bay.

At times Plaatje fails to control the border between this mode and the more pressing danger of the historical world; this just draws attention to the fact of their separation. There is an awkward moment of conjuncture just after Mhudi and Ra-Thaga's first meeting, for example, where Mhudi meditates, "'My man, my man, ... my stranger man, whom the spirits have sent to save me from loneliness, starvation, and the lion's jaw, *I would willingly pass through another Matebele raid and suffer hair-breadth escapes if but to meet one like you*'" (31; my emphasis). Given the brute horror of the raid described a few pages before, which is brought back to us in Mhudi's description of how she came to be there ("'My father and mother are slain, also my two sisters and little brothers – tiny little children'"), Mhudi's wish comes across as an uncontrolled and uncomfortable swing in tone that allows us to measure the distance normally maintained between the two styles that make up the work.

Again: in the midst of the crucial battle scene Plaatje reminds us that the natural world is also caught up in the fighting; this is an interesting point in itself, and can be related to the way in which the war disrupts the idyllic world in which we have seen Mhudi and Ra-Thaga so happy (and never in any real danger). But Plaatje suddenly strikes a very odd note given the realism and seriousness with which the battle is portrayed:

The very bees hived in hollow tree-stems swarmed forth to enquire what the matter was. Meeting the charges and counter charges of the two armies, they probably demanded the reason for the upheaval. Of course, neither the Matebele nor the invaders understood the language of the bees, who failing to get a satisfactory explanation proceeded to attack the intruders in mass formation. (128-29)

Plaatje goes on to illustrate the way in which the bee stings add particularly to the Matabele's suffering, as they are 'undressed', but the humour again jars with the depiction of the suffering in the Matabele defeat.

These moments register a collision of romance and history in *Mhudi*. Plaatje's failure to integrate these modes is a crucial part of the degree to which he fails in writing a work of historical fiction. This must be measured, however, in terms of the specific historical problem which engages him in this work, which is a national one. That the modes of romance and history are employed in *Mhudi* is ultimately a reflex of its nationalist project. Couzens is alert to the significance of the historical period Plaatje chooses for his setting:

> Plaatje returns to a time when (in the face of a common enemy, the Matabele) there are the beginnings of inter-tribal unity, when the seeds of the alliances of 1917 were first sown, when the possibility of a nationalism transcending tribalism was first conceived (linked naturally to Plaatje's interest in the South African Native Congress). In this period of the 1830s Plaatje discovers 'a sense of pride and independence of spirit' whose incarnation is the heroine, Mhudi. (1973:11)

Certainly Plaatje uses the concepts 'tribe' and 'nation' in a manner consonant with the discourse of nationalism. *Mhudi* opens with a general historical account of the 'Bechuana tribes', then moves in towards a closer focus on 'the Barolong, the original stock of the several tribes' (21). The breeding metaphor here is meant almost literally and, interestingly, is very soon followed by an apparently random anecdote that picks it up and emphasises it:

> Barolong cattlemen at times attempted to create a new species of animal by cross-breeding between an eland and an ox. One cattle-owner, named Motonosi, not very far from Kunana, raised two dozen calves all sired by a buffalo. The result proved so disastrous that Barolong tradition still holds up his achievement as a masterpiece of folly, and attempts at cross-breeding thereafter became taboo. (23)

This serves to drive home the biological determinism which forms the metaphorical base for the closed tribal ethos, something that must be transcended in a national project. But the tribal rejection of 'hybridity' modifies the terms upon which groups translate themselves from the tribal to the national; when, in the next paragraph, Plaatje moves the metaphorical to the literal, he shifts his argument from the essential (biological) to the historical (chronological and geographical):

> These peasants were content to live their monotonous lives, and thought nought of their overseas kinsmen who were making history on the plantations and harbours of Virginia and Mississippi at that time; nor did they know or care about the relations of the Hottentots and the Boers at Cape Town nearer home. (23)

The Barolong are for obvious reasons ignorant of their relationship with the developing American nation; yet the familial overtones of 'kinsmen' arise out of some sort of more general set of relations dependent on, as Anderson has noted of national relations, connections in time ('at the same time') of which the tribe is unaware. Anderson, as we have seen, makes time an important part of nationalism. The development of a national time scale involves a breakdown of 'Messianic time' ('a simultaneity of past and future in an instantaneous present') and the emergence of 'homogeneous, empty time' ('marked … by temporal coincidence, and measured by clock and calendar') (1983:30); the terms of course are Walter Benjamin's. Caught within a pre-national time, the Barolong significantly are not 'making history', as the young American nation is; nor are they part of the historical conflicts 'nearer home'. Couzens may well claim that

> in *Mhudi*, the whites appear only a third of the way through the book, and the course of South African history has already been as much determined by interaction amongst the blacks as anything the blacks could do in the future. In other words, the blacks *made* history in South Africa as much as, if not more so than, the whites (1973:8; original emphasis),

but it is necessary for the tribe to become a nation before it can 'make history'. The issue is one of nationalism, not race, and is a marked strain in nationalist discourse:

> Conceptually opposed to 'tribe' and 'tribal' are the categories of 'nation' and 'civilisation'. Both these evolutionary levels are thought to be

achieved when opposition or disunity among various 'tribes' has been overcome. Similarly, 'tribalism' (the ideology of division into 'tribes') is superseded by 'nationalism' (the quest for the political independence of nations). 'Tribe' is also often juxtaposed to 'state'. In popular understanding 'tribes' are by definition not 'states', since they are neither 'nations' nor 'civilisations'. (Boonzaier and Sharp 1988:70)

These definitions underlie the apparently casual distribution of the words 'tribe' and 'nation' in the first chapter of *Mhudi*. The divisions amongst the Bechuana are marked as tribes, but anything that is common to them all is 'national': 'hunting' we are told, is 'a national enterprise' (21). The definition is applied more strictly the closer we approach historical time: 'one hundred years ago there descended one Mzilikazi, king of a ferocious *tribe* called the Matebele'; 'Mzilikazi's *tribe* originally was a branch of the Zulu *nation* which Chaka once ruled with an iron rod' (23, 24; my emphasis). What distinguishes the Zulu from the Matabele at this historical moment is the inter-tribal character of the Zulu 'nation'; this is a status the Matabele have reached with their subjugation and absorption of many other tribes by the present time of the novel. Under the historical pressure of the Matabele attack (which causes the various units of the Barolong to unite), the Barolong fleetingly aspire to a post-tribal status in the battle; 'the two nations were at grips', we are told (25). This is perhaps an extremely minor example (yet significant in the context of my argument) of the important prophetic element in *Mhudi* (discussed at length by Couzens; see Couzens 1973, 14-18; 1975:14-15), for it is in uniting against the Matabele (most importantly with other 'tribes', including the Boers) that 'the possibility of a nationalism transcending tribalism was first conceived', as Couzens says in the quotation given above.

The revisionist movement that this period of Couzens's work represents was intensely concerned with bringing the excluded perspective of black experience into the writing of history; what they did not take into account was the appropriating nature of the discourse of history. This is one of the most telling 'limits' of social history to which I refer in my first chapter; the confidence of this loose 'school' of history writers (with whom Couzens is closely associated) in the progressiveness of its political alignments comes across in its conviction that its representation of the past is neutral, in the sense of being able to express the truth as it stands for all. Nowhere is this clear in its assumptions about history and nation. A condition of entering the realm of history is emergence into the national, and 'the emergence of the "nation state"' is the first of what Robert Pippin lists as the identifying features of 'the modern social and intellectual tradition' (1991:4). But 'the modern' has had a firm geo-historical specificity; in the words of Simon During, 'the West is modern, the modern is the West' (1991:23). The magnanimity with which South African historical revisionism of the 1970s included blacks in the making of 'history' had its not necessarily unconscious drawbacks; During continues his claim in this essay with the observation that 'By this logic, other societies can enter history, grasp the future, only at the price of their destruction' (23). *Mhudi* registers this in the way the tensions of its formal elements spring apart as the text works towards its conclusion.

The romance of Mhudi and Ra-Thaga's idyllic relationship cannot survive translation into the world of competing nationalisms which unfolds in *Mhudi*; this is caught in the scene in which Mhudi proves more perceptive than her husband about what the Boer way of life involves. Ra-Thaga has been trying to convince Mhudi that she should share his love for the Boers but 'she could not master an inexplicable dread that lingered in her mind'. Left on her own amongst the Boers one day, she begins to be won over – until she witnesses the extraordinarily cruel treatment of a 'Hottentot maid'. The incident evolves from something minor, or, as Plaatje puts it, 'The episode which began rather humorously developed quickly into tragedy' (101). There is no place here, just as there was no place in the scenes of a jarring mix of comedy/romance and history, for the comedy which informs the love relationship and allows for its romance mode.

From this point on the possibility of love or even friendship between Barolong and Boer is severely restricted. Mhudi does pronounce 'Phil Jay "the only humane Boer at Moroka's Hoek"', but, as several critics have pointed out, the only basis for her continuing relationship with him and his wife would be as 'ayah' (161) to their children (with Ra-Thaga no doubt in some equivalent position). The parting between the two couples is remarkable in fact for the other ways in which it reproduces the conditions of the white perspective on black/white relations in the 'nation' to come. Phil Jay has given Ra-Thaga a cast-off wagon as a gift, and it has taken Ra-Thaga's reminder to Annetje that they have children of their own to convince her that they cannot stay. The two couples finally part upon a joke, but one that falls hopelessly flat:

'But can't I persuade you to come back after a good long rest and bring your boys with you?'

'Oh no, Nonnie,' protested Ra-Thaga emphatically, 'you White people have a way of writing down conditional promises and treating them as debts.'

'Well, well,' said Phil, 'it wouldn't be Ra-Thaga if he missed a joke. But this is no time for humour for I tell you I shall feel this wrench.' (164)

One cannot help but feel Phil's assumption that Ra-Thaga is joking is taken a little too quickly. Mzilikazi's prophecy of the Boer's betrayal of their contracts with their black allies looms over the conclusion of the novel, after all, as the one prophecy not fulfilled in its pages but in the chronology of political events between the setting and the writing of the work.

The contribution made by the whites to Mhudi and Ra-Thaga's relationship is presented in tellingly ambivalent terms, terms which can be related to the issue of nationalism that concerns us.

The couple are last seen travelling home in their wagon. The modernisation this has brought to their life-style is spelled out in both practical and visionary terms:

> Gone were the days of their primitive tramping over long distances, with loads on their heads. For them the days of the pack-ox had passed, never to return again. The carcass of a kudu or any number of blesbuck, falling to his musket by the roadside, could be carried home with ease, leaving plenty of room in the vehicle for their luggage. Was it real, or was it just an evanescent dream?

This wonderful technological advancement has a curious effect on their final conversation in the novel, however; the noise of the wagon keeps threatening to drown their voices:

> These pleasant thoughts occupied their minds in the gathering darkness while the old waggon meandered along and the racket of the waggon wheels on the hard road made a fierce yet not very disagreeable assault upon their ears.
>
> 'Tell me,' said Mhudi, raising her voice as the waggon rattled along, 'why were you so angry with me when I found you at the front? Promise

me,' she went on, 'you will not again go away and leave me; will you?'

'Never again,' replied Ra-Thaga, raising his voice above the creak-crack, creak-crack of the old waggon wheels. 'I have had my revenge and ought to be satisfied; from henceforth, I shall have no ears for the call of war or of the chase; my ears shall be open to one call only besides the call of the chief, namely the call of your voice – Mhudi.' (165)

The ringing conclusion is constructed around the aural sense ('I shall have no ears for', 'my ears shall be open to'), the very one being assaulted by the sound of the wagon. This builds in intensity as the passage continues, despite its not being 'disagreeable' at first, with the onomatopoeic 'creak-crack' enacted and repeated just before Ra-Thaga's resounding promise; Mhudi's name only just emerges above all that has come before because it is shouted over the noise of the rumbling future – bequeathed by the whites – that carries the couple. Given that Plaatje, in his Preface to *Mhudi*, expressly cites the *oral* sources of his corrective history – 'while collecting stray scraps of tribal history,' he writes, 'the writer incidentally *heard* of "the day Mzilikazi's tax collectors were killed"' (17; my emphasis) – this near-obliteration of the *aural* takes on a special significance in relation to the clash of histories in *Mhudi*.

Stephen Gray has argued at length that the Lovedale text of *Mhudi* I have been quoting is a seriously distorted version of Plaatje's 'original intentions' (1979:172). One of the great acts of sacrifice in southern African literary history is Gray's rejection of this version, upon which his own Quagga Press edition was based. Meant to be No. 1 in the Series, the African Fiction Library, of which Gray was general editor, the Quagga *Mhudi* became both its first and last text; the series foundered because Gray and Couzens discovered the very different original typescript of Plaatje's work after their publication and before Heinemann offered to buy their typesetting for the African Writers Series. They talked Heinemann into publishing the earlier version, and thus lost the profit that would have kept their series going.[4]

It seems hard in the shadow of such a story to hold to the Lovedale *Mhudi*, and if I do so it is not primarily because Gray's account of the way in which

---

4. *Mhudi* (London, Edinburgh, Melbourne, Sydney, Auckland, Singapore, Tokyo, Madrid, Paris, Athens, Bologna: 1978). The current edition available in South Africa (Johannesburg: 1989) follows the Lovedale text.

Plaatje was bullied into making the changes he did by some hypothetical missionary press editor is highly conjectural at best. It is not, either, in the belief that the first published version is better than the draft – indeed, Gray's case for the greater coherence of the draft is overwhelmingly convincing, especially with regard to the crucial structural alteration made by Plaatje to the way in which the narrative is conveyed to the reader. Plaatje, for reasons we do not know (despite Gray's superbly imaginative reconstruction of the struggle between author and press), excised the narrator to whom he, in the draft, plays scribe; 'Half-a-Crown' was originally presented as not only the oral source for the story Plaatje transcribes into print, but the direct descendent of Mhudi and Ra-Thaga; in fact, Ra-Thaga's very name makes little sense in the Lovedale version: it means 'father of Thaga', and thus in all likelihood even more pointedly refers to the literal erasure of the narrator (identified as the son of Mhudi and Ra-Thaga in Chapter 5 of the original text) obscured by the demeaning '"European" nickname' (177) 'Half-a-Crown' in the typescript.

This point makes mine regarding the obliteration of the oral in *Mhudi* even more poignant, and I am tempted to cite it in support of my argument even as I finally – for purely strategic reasons – reject it. For it seems to me that we should, even as we take account of what the two different versions of the text reveal, respect Plaatje's decisions to go into print with the version he did, and not treat him as a purely passive victim of the mode of production available to him. If we take the Lovedale Press text seriously, the fact that the story of Mhudi and Ra-Thaga is not passed on by an immediate descendent reinforces the sense of a break, a rupture, in the continuous history of their nationhood. It reminds us of how the past has to be actively reconstructed by someone removed from it, and it underscores the lack of a harmonious coming together of the elements of the text that is one of the most important factors in the version of *Mhudi* produced by Plaatje in 1930.

MHUDI AND MODERNITY

It is a truism of southern African literary history that no sustained modernist tradition was produced here in chronological relation with the metropolitan modernist period (*Turbott Wolfe* is read as the exception which proves the rule). This maxim is probably the product of an often limited conception of modernism, one that suits primarily metropolitan concerns and therefore rather unsurprisingly tends only to identify certain metropolitan texts as 'modernist'. In opening up *Mhudi* to consideration as a 'modernist' text, the aim is not to subsume it under that category, but to challenge the category by extending its geo-historical range.

For if modernism, as Pippin would have it, is chiefly characterised by a 'dawning sense of a failure in the social promise of modernisation – individual autonomy and collective rationalisation' (1991:36), then *Mhudi* again qualifies for a literary-historical category, a generic status, that goes beyond the empty formalisms of essentialist and ahistoric genres. The tensions and clashes of romance and realism, epic and novel, may be read back into a specific moment – a modernist one – and the ways in which that moment is defined in material terms. These terms include the political consciousness of a common culture, for, as many theorists have observed, nationalism is specifically a product of industrialisation, in which economic growth demands a unitary social system. Intimately connected as it is, then, to modernisation, it is not surprising to find responses to nationalism woven into texts we call modernist.

Mhudi's conclusion is classically modernist in its ambivalent attitude to the modernisation that the colonising technology represents; the overt celebration – worthy of a Futurist's aesthetic reaction to the aeroplane – is, as we have seen, compromised by the negative effect of that technological advance on the very people being carried along on it into the future. Taking into account that the dominant experience of modernity in South Africa was the kind of 'neurotic obsessiveness' that Horkheimer and Adorno identify in modern subjectivity – 'control, manipulation, exclusion of any deviance from the imperatives of systematic regulation of others and the environment, bureaucratic management, a subjugation of every issue to the demands of technical, efficient regulation, etc.' (see Pippin 1991:152) – in other words, apartheid, the apogee of a developing systematising of segregation – entering 'history', grasping the future, is a near-destructive act for the protagonists of Plaatje's historical vision. Yet the entry is made, and turned into an achievement; '*Mhudi*' is the last word, above chief and enemy, beyond 'history' and 'nation' in exclusive terms, while *Mhudi* creates out of its very formal disparities a sense of what the loss of 'history' and 'nation' in an inclusive sense means.

For what *Mhudi* represents is the failure to achieve the 'confidence of community' that Anderson perceives as essential to the nation. Although linked in a new sense of national time, there is so obviously no sense of community between Matabele, Boer, and Barolong (despite the alliance between the latter two), and even the hopes of the beginnings of community in the friendship between the couples are allowed to fade. Caught between the two nations emerging at the conclusion of the book, Mhudi and Ra-Thaga are threatened with being overwhelmed by the one while travelling to the other. This is not a failure of the personal before the national in abstract terms; we have seen Mhudi and Ra-Thaga perfectly integrated in a community of their own. It is a failure of the two emerging nations, for which the 'model theory' prepares us, to make a place for the couple. In generic terms, the romance cannot be integrated into the historical, given the national divisions that characterise the historical.

FORM RESISTED

If the novel form provides, as we saw Anderson believes, 'the technical means for "re-presenting" the *kind* of imagined community that is the nation' (1983:30; original emphasis), then critics are quite correct to hesitate before calling *Mhudi* a novel. Plaatje cannot conjure up from the historical material available to him the grounds for an imagined community; the only realm of harmony remains within the romantic mode, and this cannot be blended into the realist historical mode. Competing nationalisms hold apart the elements of their fictional embodiment, preventing the integration of the disparate styles of the work into any single generic category. Yet *Mhudi*'s apparent failure on essentialist formal terms is a mark of all that is celebrated in the modernist work – if this category is kept alive as signifying an intensely historical and historicised concept; it is a work filled with a sense of the absence of the ideals of modernity, awkwardly negotiating the material reality of modernisation, but pushing through both to embody in the lived sense of its form the potential achievements of both.

Mhudi may not be a success in the terms of the classical 'historical novel', but it is most certainly one of the very finest '*novel histories*'. In attempting to bring the issues of the past into a vital relation with the present, Plaatje founders to a degree upon the limits of a present that was for him all too present. But this is because the national vision he strives for is simply not available to him, and he has too strong a sense of the terms of its failure to force upon those terms the utopian form which alone could embody the ideal of a truly inclusive nationalism. And so out of the very fractures of his fictional endeavour comes the judgement history delivers to the present; in the breakdown of form, the reader can sense the urgency with which Plaatje believed that the present should be resisted in its divided nature.

The grounds for this resistance prove to be history and nation not as essences but as imaginative acts – processes and constructs – that are capable of taking us beyond the disillusion of our (and their) failures. What *Mhudi* registers about a specifically 'South African' nationalism – that it must be forged out of the absence of the traditional criteria (a common linguistic, racial, or cultural heritage) used to define a nation state – is as important for our national moment as it was for Plaatje's, because it goes against the foundational ethnographic logic of nationalism in general: ethnos is replaced by narrativisation, and, most importantly, the collective story that forms the basis of a nation is an open-ended one. The past perfect of Ms Jones's letter ('… to Mr Mandela, the African National Congress and all those wonderful South Africans who made it happen …') will, then, perhaps always be premature, but the verb at its heart – the performance of which must include the kinds of activities Breytenbach envisages as his contribution to the national project – implicitly recognises that a sense of national identity has to be *created*, communally, continually, and critically.

For, while we may well empathise with the attempts of Johan Degenaar to replace the concept of 'nation' with that of 'democratic culture', it is the very emotional appeal which he cites as a major reason for rejecting nationalism that gives it the specific potential to counter the many other threats to the pluralist democracy that is no less an ideal of an inclusive nationalism than the alternative he presents. And when the symbols of nationalism are produced in texts as subtle, complex, and challenging as *Mhudi*, they are cast in a form capable of resisting the appropriations, emotional and otherwise, of the present.

3

REWRITING HISTORY
AND NATION

PETER ABRAHAMS

———■———

Creating nations is a recurrent activity ...
— *Anthony Smith 1986*

PERIOD AND FORM

In 1958 one S. Kierson presented a bibliography entitled 'English and Afrikaans Novels on South African History' to the University of Cape Town School of Librarianship in order to qualify for the Diploma in Library Science. That this topic should have been chosen at all, along with the evidence the study presents of what seems to be a remarkable number of historical novels produced in the period just prior to its submission (even allowing for a general growth in South African publishing), suggests the high profile historical fiction enjoyed at the time. While the bibliography is the work of a student and we cannot trust it to be exhaustive (Kierson leaves out Daphne Rooke for example), something of a pattern may be formed from a survey of its contents.

Of the 143 Afrikaans historical novels listed, 91 were published in the 1940s and 1950s; of the English, 30 out of 72. As far as the Afrikaans figures are concerned, we can note a definite and direct correlation between the production of historical fiction and the emergence of modern Afrikaner nationalism as a dominant political force. While the connection between historical fiction in English and nationalism is often more oblique, it remains clear that a relatively large amount of historical fiction in English was also produced as part of a complicated range of responses to the rise of the various nationalisms in South Africa dating from the late 1930s to the late 1950s. Given the variety of writers choosing, or finding themselves limited to, English as their medium of expression, such a range is not surprising, and the case studies that follow are meant to indicate some of the more prominent ways in which history in fiction was used, implicitly or explicitly, in support of one sense of social identity or another.

A focus on the novel form keeps us within severe limits as far as this theme is concerned, of course, but the novel was an important indicator of attitudes to history at this time. Without wishing to force a point, we may loosely, borrowing Lukács's famous phrase, call this the period of the 'classical historical novel' in South Africa. This definition is for Lukács not based on content – 'the historical novel does not become an independent genre as a result of its special faithfulness to the past' (1981:201) – or, as we have seen in Chapter One, on form, but rather upon the historical circumstances that generate it. Granting the many and obvious differences between South Africa in this period and the Europe with which Lukács was concerned, it is still possible to identify in the former as he did in the latter a particular 'awakening of national sensibility and with it a feeling and understanding for national history'. But if 'history' was to become in South Africa a similarly new 'mass experience' (2) at this time, and the novel a significant means of expressing this, it was certainly not, as we shall examine in detail later, a unified experience. Thus, although all the works focused on in the rest of Part One of this book come from or relate to this period, I have attempted to select examples that are representative of the competing political voices that may be heard in the uses of history in fiction in English.

The sorry state of South African literary history makes it difficult to establish exactly what was happening to literary uses of history in the other languages and mediums of expression of southern Africa, but it seems likely that the combined effects of modernisation and cultural marginalisation had begun to seriously erode fiction produced in the vernacular, and along with this, the relatively high proportion of historical fiction previously evident there. Certainly if we take Isabel Hofmeyr's superb case study of oral story telling in Mokopane or Valtyn (a Ndebele-Sotho chiefdom in the Transvaal [1993]) as a specific example of the general impact of colonialism and capitalism on such communities, then historical storytelling was seriously eroded along with the communal spaces in which it was produced, the gender roles that controlled it, and the vital structural element of chieftaincy which generated it.

I have tried to capture at least some of the transformations of the concept of history evident in the interactions between tradition and modernity in my account of *Mhudi*, and this theme will continue to be important as we consider the ways in which, during the period of the 'classical' South African historical novel, Peter Abrahams reworks much of not only the story but also the form of Plaatje's work.

ABRAHAMS AND SOUTH AFRICAN NATIONALISM

Wild Conquest is a product of Peter Abrahams's '"nationalist" phase', says Michael Wade (1972:6); the inverted commas, however, are important. Published in 1950, the novel shows little of the resurgence of nationalism evident in South African black politics of the 1940s. We are forced to remind ourselves that Abrahams left South Africa in 1939, and even if this did not mark an immediate break on his part with the national liberation movement, it reinforced the distance from it that he had already begun to feel before leaving.

Black nationalism, indeed black politics in general, had a low organisational profile in the 1930s; state coercion and co-option took its toll on the black intelligentsia, and the famine of 1931-34 in South Africa combined with the world depression 'tended to damp down both rural and urban activism, so that the 1930s saw a remarkable diminution in African political militancy' (Marks and Trapido 1987:44). The state onslaught against communism hindered any integration with nationalist movements, and the conservative wing had taken over the ANC, with the result that, as Karis and Carter put it, 'by the mid-1930s ... the African National Congress became nearly moribund' (1973:81). This is the period towards the middle and end of which Abrahams was cutting his political teeth, and so it comes as no surprise, in some ways, to find his commitment to organised radical politics somewhat thin. Even a few years later, during what Walsh calls 'the ferment of 1939-1950' (1987:327), Abrahams's presence at the Manchester Pan-African Conference of 1945 as one of the two ANC delegates was the result of his being unable, as Publicity Secretary for the Conference, to organise any representatives from South Africa (Walsh 1987:338-39). His fiction too – especially *Wild Conquest*, the historical novel in which he so overtly confronts the issue of nationalism – bears evidence of yet another failed moment in the history of South African nationalism.

Wild Conquest is dialectical in structural intent (of which more later), but the dialectic comes to nothing. This is perhaps indicative in itself of the other ideological framework Abrahams was shedding at the time of its writing. In South

Africa, as in many other countries representing the 'Last Wave' of nationalism (see Anderson 1983:104-28), Marxism and (black) nationalism had come to an accommodation – not without moments of suspicion, of course, but an accommodation nevertheless. The arrangement these two movements were to reach in South African history – which features many of the complexities traced by Nairn in his account of Marxism's necessary collusion with nationalism where 'quite abstract internationalism' has to be counterpoised with 'a pragmatic support of nationalist struggles' (1977:353) – finds no place in the novel as part of its historical interpretation, however. The tripartite division of the book invites the expectation of a progressive unification of opposites on dialectical materialist terms: Section 1 is entitled 'Bible and Rifle' and Section 2 'Bayete!' – what one could call the opposing 'nationalisms' depicted in this are to be resolved in Section 3, one would think, given that it is entitled 'New Day'. The final line of the novel, however, reads, 'Over the land was the shadow of a new day' (309). Not only are the dialectical expectations of the form frustrated, they never really inform the divisions in content, which are, I will argue, essentially nationalist in nature. The dialectic, which is Marxist and failed in form, is purely national in content, where another, but not necessarily related, failure takes place.

In *Wild Conquest* the grounds for our measuring of this failure are drawn from another ally in the history of the South African nationalist struggle – Christianity. Each of the three sections of the novel is prefaced by a metaphysical passage which counterpoints the action to follow. Each preface draws closer to revealing the 'truth' missed by the protagonists, a 'truth' finally revealed by a Christ-like figure in the last preface. He speaks in terms that explicitly transcend the national struggle the novel depicts:

> *Out of the hills a man came ... From the many nations he came and the touch of many lands was on him. His eyes were the eyes of all the people.*
> *He came down from the hills and he said:*
> *That ye might have life, and that ye might have it more abundantly.*
> (263; italics in the original)

This represents another cultural dimension not foreign to the black nationalist movement in South Africa. The ANC was founded in close alliance with Christianity, and prayer was still an important element in ANC meetings long after Abrahams left – so much so that Karis and Carter considered it necessary to include in their documentary history of the period 'a typical example of Christian prayer on behalf of "the African race"'from the opening of the ANC Conference of December 1949 (1973:102, 336-37).

Black political movements were able to contain this variety of discourse fairly comfortably on the whole, whatever contradictions they apparently retained. In the words of Hobsbawm:

> ... contrary to common assumptions, the various principles on which the political appeal to the masses were based – notably the class appeal of the socialists, the confessional appeal of the religious denominations and the appeal to nationality were not mutually exclusive. There was not even a sharp line distinguishing one from the other, even in the one case when both sides tended to insist on an, as it were, ex-officio incompatibility: religion and godless socialism. Men and women did not choose collective identification as they chose shoes, knowing that one could only put on one pair at a time. They had, and still have, several attachments and loyalties simultaneously, including nationality, and are simultaneously concerned with various aspects of life, any of which may at one time be foremost in their minds, as occasion suggests. (1990:123)

The question is why Abrahams was not able to accommodate these ideological factions, particularly in *Wild Conquest* – why, in that novel, the dialectic should fail the nation, the nation contradict the dialectic, metaphysics repudiate in transcendence the dialectic and the nation; why, ultimately, *Wild Conquest* should have to recruit history against the nation.

We must be careful at this point not to read back into the novel the current (and somewhat suspect) consensus regarding 'Negative Nationalism' referred to in Chapter Two, or to read it simply as an early expression of Gikandi's 'so-called literature of disillusionment' also discussed there. When considered seriously in relation to the moment of *Wild Conquest*'s production, the short answer to the question posed above is that Abrahams's anti-nationalism is the result of a romantic individualism characteristic of major strands within certain oppositional South African movements.

When, for example, Abrahams chose to call his autobiography *Tell Freedom*, he had a particular freedom in mind – as he makes plain at the point of departure from South Africa which forms the conclusion of this work:

> Perhaps life had a meaning that transcended race and colour. If it had, I could not find it in South Africa. Also, there was the need to write, to tell freedom, and for this I needed to be personally free ... (1954:311)

Stephen Gray claims, as part of a tightly woven and larger argument, that 'what [Abrahams] commits by way of achieving autonomy and independence is actually betrayal and treachery' (1990:110). Radical readings of Abrahams's career must confront this point; the two full-length works on Abrahams available so far both attribute his individualism to the influence of the other discourse that dominated his career, the tradition of liberal humanism. Michael Wade puts Abrahams's increasingly isolated individualism down to a developing liberalism in Abrahams, while Robert Ensor identifies liberal humanism as the dominant controlling element in Abrahams's work from the very beginning.

However we take this element in Abrahams, it translates itself into the fact of his self-sought exile, which influenced his work in a way of interest to us here. For Stephen Gray, *Tell Freedom*, published in 1954, is 'frozen at 1939':

> He seems to let none of the intervening developments touch this. Trade-unionism, for example, which he deals with on p.260, creates 'a new social and political consciousness in the making', but does not affect *Tell Freedom*. The Defiance campaign of June, 1952, which drastically affected the attitudes and rhetoric of everything to follow in South African history, is cursorily mentioned in *Return to Goli* (184), but it is not allowed to impact on his vision of the past in any way. Other factors are excluded: for example, Abrahams leaves out the whole of World War II. Aged 35, his private self is now more important to him than his social being. (1990:108)

Wild Conquest is a step on the way towards this. History and nation are rendered pessimistically in order to allow 'Peter Abrahams' – the identity adopted by a subject once more concretely located by the signifier 'Lee de Ras', his family name (see Gray 1990:114) – to fly by those nets.

This, as I say, is the short answer. How is it written into an historical novel by a 'coloured' South African writer?

We enter here a discursive impasse not yet transcended in South African politics. Revisionist historians may well refer to the existence of a 'so-called coloured community' as 'one of the enduring myths in South Africa' (see Saunders 1992:393), but some have illustrated the falsity of this myth by stressing, as did the Black Consciousness movement, the community of purpose shared by a 'black community' which included Africans, coloureds, and Indians, while others point to the lack of real difference between coloureds and whites in terms of languages, religions, and cultural values. Davenport notes that the mid-nineteenth century identification of the admixture of Khoisan and freed slaves with surviving freed blacks as 'free persons of colour' produced a legal identity 'which many of [the Cape Coloured people] continued to regard as artificial' (1987:34); as this nevertheless became 'the basis of a very meaningful classification during the second half of the twentieth century' (34), the Group Areas Act and the Population Registration Act enforced what Audrey Brown calls numerous 'creative strategies to survive in a world of scarce resources, bad schools and a lack of job opportunities ...' (1995:9). Amongst these was a fairly common swapping of ethnic identity signification: 'Mthimkulu became Grootboom and Ndlovu was changed to Olifant and never mind the fact that you could not tell one from the other' (9). Current tensions regarding the political identity of the 'coloured' community – illustrated nowhere more clearly than in the liminality of an ethnic signification not quite retained yet not quite erased by the appending of scare quotes to a term which still resists reinvention – have generated movements like the Kleurling Weerstandsbeweging vir die Vooruitgang van Bruinmense, movements which employ all the rhetoric of a separatist nationalism (including appeals to originary historical foundations), but Abrahams must be placed quite carefully in relation to the history of such impulses. If *Wild Conquest* may be read at one level as his attempt to locate his 'racially mixed descent' in relation to the power blocks of Afrikaner and black nationalism, we must take into account the particularities of his position.

In assessing the limitations of *Wild Conquest*, Wade makes much of 'the widely encountered difficulty in African literature of producing satisfactory African characters' (1972:92); Abrahams 'is much dependent, as a writer, on direct personal knowledge of situations for their successful portrayal in fiction', says Wade, and he 'had little experience of "traditional" or tribal African life' (72). On these grounds, it seems, Wade goes on to claim that 'Abrahams's characterization of the members of the slave community is much more successful (particularly in the case of Johannes, their leader) than anything he manages with the Matabele' (93-94). Whatever national identification Abrahams may have felt with the founding of the coloured community, an irony emerges as we come to assess the 'coloured' characters as successful *historical* representations in *Wild Conquest*. Wade praises 'Johannes as a source of wisdom, particularly when he attempts to define freedom' (94), and he goes on to quote at length, without further comment, from the speech in which Johannes does this. Before we approach this speech, we must go back to *Tell Freedom* and the one large-scale national liberation event in South Africa in which Abrahams was directly involved.

When he moved to Cape Town in 1938, Abrahams experienced the beginnings of the resurgence in black political life that was to burst forth in 1939. He was somewhat bemusedly swept up in the radicalisation of coloured politics that had begun in the 1930s (Lodge 1983:39); in particular he found himself affiliated through the contacts he was given in the Cape with the National Liberation League, an organisation his Marxist friends in the Transvaal would naturally have steered him towards. The founders of the League were not Marxists, but the Communist Party, who, seeking as always a base for mass action, typically became involved with this sort of national movement which promised to provide the popular support the Communist Party could not raise itself (Karis and Carter 1973:108). In 1938 the League launched the Non-European United Front in response to the threat of segregationist legislation aimed at the coloureds which followed on the removal of Cape blacks from the voters' roll in 1936. The Cape ANC joined the Communist Party in an event 'extraordinarily representative of radicals of all races' (ibid.), and while the protests arising out of this gathering were successful in postponing the planned legislation (Lodge 1983:39), the whole affair was riven underneath its unity by dislike and distrust between non-communist coloured radicals, white communists, Stalinists, and Trotskyists. It is this Abrahams most remembers (he does not even report on the limited success of the occasion in *Tell Freedom*), and this that he uses as a base for his mixed feelings at being involved at all. His ambivalence is nowhere better caught than in this anecdote from the demonstration given in *Tell Freedom*:

> The procession formed. The toughs of District Six flanked their leaders.
> I strayed out of the tight little group. A huge giant grabbed me and
> lifted me bodily. He pushed his fierce face close to mine.

'Damn you! Stay there! You're a damn leader now!'

My laughter angered him so much, I thought he was going to swipe me into kingdom come. (281)

It is however upon Abrahams's account in *Tell Freedom* of the speeches delivered at this event in 1939 that we must concentrate. Here is some of his impressionistic amalgamation of them:

> speaker after speaker stirred the vast throng to a new realization of the misery of their lives in such a fair and pleasant land ... Look at this land on which the warm sun shines. Look at the vineyards and the orchards; look at the wheat-fields and corn-fields; look at the vegetable gardens. Who work in them? You, the dark people of this land. Who get the rewards of your labours? They do, the white people. Nowhere else on earth do white people do as little real work and live as well as they do here. Do you know why? It is because they have slaves to do the work for them. You sow and they reap. You sweat and they have beautiful homes. You hunger and they are well fed ... (280)

and so on. Here now, from *Wild Conquest*, is the old slave Johannes explaining freedom in 1835 to his fellow slaves:

> The morning sun had climbed to a point almost directly overhead and beat down hotly on them and the valley and on everything in it. It threw a hard and brilliant light over the land and some shaded their eyes as they looked. The blue of the sky was bright.
>
> 'Look at it,' Old Johannes said. 'Do not look at the house only. Look at the house and the earth and the trees and the beasts. All that you see belongs to the Jansens, to Kasper Jansen and his family. Yet we, all of us, we built the house and tilled the earth and got rid of the weeds and planted the food and looked after the cattle.
>
> 'Think, my people. Would it be so wrong for that to belong to us? We made it.' (12)

Beneath the more overt dramatisation and personalisation of fiction as opposed to autobiography, the passages are remarkably similar: in both the audience is lifted up to view a landscape, dominated by sun; both contain the injunction to 'look'; both are agricultural in emphasis (Abrahams does lightly touch on the more pressing issue of industrialisation later in the *Tell Freedom* passage, but the central focus remains agricultural); both stress the principle of labour and its just reward of possession of the product of labour by those who produced it.

Mphahlele complains that in *Wild Conquest* Abrahams has

> introduced 'a new will into times past', thus bending history to a point in order to tell more of the truth than the historian. This 'unhistorical will' operates within a short space of time in history, so that the characters produced short-lived unhistorical effects (1962:178),

but the 'truth' that is told is enveloped in a more complex web of 'unhistorical effects' than Mphahlele has allowed for. What is illustrated in the comparison of these two passages is just how directly Abrahams draws, in 1950, upon a personal political experience from 1939 for his recreation of an historical moment from 1835. He imports more than just a particular 1930s political line into the 1830s; he imports all the traumatic associations he had felt then and resolved in a particular way by the 1950s.

Wade holds that *Wild Conquest* 'in a sense hinges on Johannes' definition of freedom' and that the work fails 'precisely because he has not integrated part one of the book structurally or thematically with the rest of the novel' (1972:97). Certainly the slaves do not appear again, but Old Johannes's meditation does; when the slaves have driven the whites from the valley and appropriated it for themselves (there is no sense of the dispossession to come; as a result it is difficult to read this victory as ironic or even provisional), we are told:

> A wordless prayer, a prayer of feeling and desire and hope rose up deep within the old man and flowed over the children of the ex-slaves and over the ex-slaves and over the burning house and over the valley and the mountains till it reached the skies.
>
> Wordlessly it said: 'That ye might have life, and that ye might have it more abundantly.' (47)

This is, as already shown, the grounds for the metaphysical resolution reached in the novel's prefatory passages to each section, the passages that play off against the failure to be found in its narrative sections. If Old Johannes is able to reach such resolution through the politics of the National Liberation League and the Non-European United Front of 1939, what has happened to the contradictions, limitations, and failings of these political movements registered in *Tell Freedom*? They have been defused in *Wild Conquest* by a metaphysical solution which is not literally meant, but is a metaphor for the humanist values that dominate *Tell Freedom*. Abrahams's account of his relations with Marxism in *Tell Freedom* is, as Gray points out, 'concluded in the pluperfect before begun' (1990:110):

> They had called their explanation Dialectical Materialism. They had called the creed by which they lived Marxism.
>
> Marxism had the impact of a miraculous revelation. I had explored this new creed with delicate care ...
>
> And I had tested the new creed called Marxism against the reality of my experience and the darkness of my land. And only by the Marxian theories of economics and imperialism had the racism of the land made sense. Marxism had supplied an intelligent and reasonable explanation for the things that happened ...
>
> Though Marxism had offered a reasonable explanation of the world in which I lived, the factional abuse and counter abuse disturbed me. And I had still to find, under the political creed, something that would take in human feeling, love and laughter, poetry and music, and the dear warmth of pure, motiveless friendship. Had Marxism any room for the compassionate humanity that pervaded the life and teaching of Christ? (250)

Christianity is rejected earlier in *Tell Freedom*, not because of any internal failing on its part, but because it could not translate into the real world (238-39). Again, it is centrally represented in the autobiography by the principle that 'Christ came that we might have life and have it more abundantly' (238), and the fact that the problems of history and nationalism should be consumed into this formulation suggests that they can only be resolved in some sort of ideal state. Old Johannes cannot reappear in the novel, for the resolution he has found is written out of history by the end of the novel. It exists only outside the narrative – an historical narrative, after all – hovering above and beyond it in the prefaces. Here a cosmic perspective reigns:

*Poised in space, held between nothing and nothing, there floats a golden
ball. Not only is it golden. It is blue as well, and red, and green, and
brown, and gray. Touch gold and blue and red and green and brown
and gray – touch them with love and there is poetry.*
    Such is our earth. (3; italics in the original)

The lyricism which pervades these passages contains an important clue to what
Abrahams is trying to achieve in them; the epigraph to *Wild Conquest* consists of
two extracts from Blake's 'Songs of Innocence and of Experience', and Abrahams
is much given to quoting the Romantic poets in his works. (Ensor says that for
Abrahams the English Romantic movement was 'the apex of liberal-humanism'
[1990:53]). His is not the Romanticism of the early days of the French Revolution
or the Greek War of Independence, however; it is Shelley at – in Abrahams's
interpretation at least – his most universal and transcendent:

Sceptreless, free, uncircumscribed, but man
Equal unclassed, tribeless, and nationless,
Exempt from awe, worship, degree, the king
Over himself; just, gentle, wise: but Man.

This extract appears in both *The Path of Thunder* and *Return to Goli* and is a
key indicator of Abrahams's values: he uses the quotation to represent the third
and highest 'level of living' (above the 'basic struggle' and the 'security of the
group' – which includes nationalism) in *Return to Goli* (26). From such a level
man can appear 'tribeless, and nationless', the two most important categories in
Wild Conquest; what is more, the one division Shelley does not list can also be
overcome. The chief advantage of seeing the earth from such a height is that its
colours can run together. What is achieved naturally from this perspective becomes
only the thinnest of hypothetical hopes in the historical world. The narrative of
Wild Conquest opens with a jarring confrontation between national and historical
colour:

The visible parts of the man's body had been burnt to a reddish brown.
His fair hair had lost its original color and turned a reddish-brown
too. Indeed, he was all reddish brown, even to the whites of his eyes.
The sun and air and rain and earth had transformed him into as near

earth-color as possible. Perhaps in a thousand years his children would be so transformed by sun and earth and air that they would have flat noses and full lips and kinky hair and dark, very dark copper-colored skins. And perhaps his daughters of a thousand years hence would have the broad heavy hips and pointed breasts and round black eyes of the African women. Perhaps. (4)

'Perhaps' is a word that resonates throughout *Wild Conquest*, from the dedication which echoes Mkomozi's dream, 'Perhaps, in the ages to come ...', to most of the major meditations in the novel (see pages 76, 144, 211, and 308). It generally denotes a hesitant and tentative attitude on the part of Abrahams to any positive outcome of the history with which he is dealing. 'Perhaps' is of necessity aimed at the future, but in its final appearance at the conclusion of the novel it has to do with the preservation of the past in the future; here Abrahams is a little more hopeful, possibly because there is a degree of self-referentiality here that gives him some control. Mkomozi is speaking to Mzilikazi after the defeat of the Matabele:[5]

> 'That was our city. Now it is nothing. But, perhaps, one day, in the future that is to be ... One day, in that future, a story will be told of our city. Perhaps an old man will sit in front of a fire. And round him will be little children. Their hands will be out to the fire. And perhaps one child will say:
> '"Tell us a story, grandfather."
> 'And the old man will say:
> '"Once upon a time ... in the long ago ... there was a city. It was called Inzwinyani ..."' (308)

It is at this self-reflexive moment in the novel, when Abrahams blends in with the old man of the first preface who whispers universal truths mortal men cannot understand, that we should be reminded that Abrahams is not the first to tell the story of Inzwinyani in novel form, that he in fact has been dependent in his telling of its story on a prior telling. Abrahams 'chooses the same period and setting as *Mhudi*,' as Ursula Barnett points out, 'and in fact leans heavily on its background and part of its plot' (1983:118).

5. As with Plaatje's work, I have followed Abrahams's use of the Sotho term 'Matabele' for the Ndebele.

Abrahams, very much the product of an urban environment, was in real need of an historical source for the 'tribal' sections of *Wild Conquest*; conventional 'white' history could not provide him with the perspective he needed (this after all was part of the logic of writing the book as a 'corrective' history in the first place), and to whatever degree he was in touch with contemporary black thought at the time, he was likely to find little help, or even interest, there. That the idea for a story like *Wild Conquest* even occurred to him as viable at all at this time suggests his distance from South Africa, a distance we can roughly measure by looking at one of the 'popular' ways in which *Wild Conquest* was distributed and received.

Wild Conquest and Drum

Wild Conquest was published in instalments in *Drum* magazine not long after its publication in novel form (it appeared in the magazine from May 1952 until January 1953 in abridged form – an 'exciting, new story by the famous Coloured writer, Peter Abrahams'); in this it followed on Alan Paton's *Cry, the Beloved Country*, but *Drum* was also beginning during this time to produce the wealth of short stories for which it became famous, and the serialised novel largely gave way to these. The first issue after the *Wild Conquest* serial ended featured two short stories ('Dangerous Love' and 'Crime for Sale') instead of the usual format in which one short story and one instalment of a novel made up the fiction section. Arthur Mogale's 'Crime for Sale', a racy, urban, modern, Americanised 'detective' tale, was obviously tremendously popular, for it produced a sequel in the next issue called 'Hot Diamonds' which turned into something of a serial itself, running over the following few issues. *Drum* would occasionally return to the serialised form (*Tell Freedom* was produced as a serial from April 1954 onwards), but (largely because of *Drum*) black writing of the period became dominated by the short story form.

It is not just in form that *Wild Conquest* stands outside of what was to become the main stream, however. The *Drum* short story, along with everything else in the magazine, was aggressively and determinedly urban and modern – Mogale's stories typified the genre.

It took some time for *Drum* to realise that this was the image to project. First called *African Drum*, the early issues had tried to appeal to a romanticised 'tribal' audience; Anthony Sampson tells us that 'the first numbers contained African poems and stories; articles on "Music of the Tribes" and "Know Yourselves", recounting the history of the Bantu tribes ...' (1983:16). In trying to find out from staff and potential buyers why *Drum* was not achieving a bigger circulation, Sampson (soon to replace Bob Crisp as editor) and Jim Bailey (the owner) discovered that '*Drum* was at cross-purposes with its readers' (21); as one potential reader so graphically put it: 'Tribal music! Tribal history! Chiefs! We don't care about chiefs! Give us jazz and film stars, man!' (20), or, in the words of another, '... we're trying to get away from our tribal history as fast as we can' (21).

Such attitudes severed the usual connection between nationalism and history, a separation that is all the more significant for its obvious rejection of the 'retribalising' policies of the then newly-rampant Afrikaner nationalism. In September 1951 *Drum* dropped the 'African' from its front cover (though it still appeared on the first inside page), and in April 1952 it dropped it altogether. *Wild Conquest*, an historical novel steeped in 'tribal' history, appeared in something of a transitional period, and must have seemed a little out of place as far as the new image of *Drum* was concerned. Sampson talks of the instalments of *Cry, the Beloved Country* in his memoir of the period (1983:16, 19), but says nothing of *Wild Conquest*. This is striking, because Abrahams, who was a friend of *Drum*'s first black reporter, Henry Nxumalo, was a high-profile figure in *Drum*'s pages: in October 1951 it published 'A Letter to My Mother' from Abrahams, along with a brief interview with her about him, and in March 1952, no doubt in preparation for *Wild Conquest*, 'A Letter to You From Peter Abrahams' appeared; this was an open letter in reply to the 'pile' of letters ('nearly a hundred') Abrahams had received from *Drum* readers.

Ironically, history, both 'tribal' and otherwise, did not come easily to someone of Abrahams's background. As far as 'white' history is concerned, he was very much 'a victim of the authorized version', as Wade puts it (1972:75). By this Wade means that Abrahams was writing some time before the publication of the *Oxford History of South Africa* (1969), and with the history of revisionism subsequent to this now also between us and the novel, it is all too easy to 'counterfactualise' Abrahams at almost every turn: in the novel slavery is the key issue in the origins of the Trek, the Trekkers had a fully-articulated vision of themselves as the Chosen People, racism is almost organically inculcated in a frontier situation, and so on, and so on. There is little really to be proved in demonstrating point by point where Abrahams is at fault from a modern perspective (without stating a lot of the obvious), and besides Abrahams's utilisation of his main source for the 'black' sections of the novel – *Mhudi* – is by far the more interesting problem.

MHUDI AND WILD CONQUEST

Wade (1972:85) is very specific in isolating to what degree Abrahams is textually dependent on this source, giving us page by page comparisons and demonstrating 'how Abrahams reworks his raw material' (201). For Wade the material is very raw indeed, as he considers *Mhudi* to be 'not a literary success, technically or stylistically speaking' (200-201); it is in his view 'more the raw material of fiction than fiction itself' (206). In dismissing the 'faults' of *Mhudi* as simply crudities in construction, Wade limits his comparison between the two texts.

One of the ways in which Plaatje influenced Abrahams was with regard to dialogue, Wade feels (201). The suggestion is that this is as much a hindrance as a help; he has already told us that 'in the sections of *Wild Conquest* which describe the Matabele, his diction grows stilted and archaic, vocabulary becomes simplified and sometimes pseudo-biblical' (78). It is true that Abrahams tries to achieve the atmosphere of Plaatje's writing while missing (as indeed Wade does) the levels of complexity that inform Plaatje's prose. Abrahams may well write, 'you descendants of hammersmiths' (135) where Plaatje writes, 'you menial descendants of mercenary hammersmiths' (25), but what goes missing along with the now seemingly inflated adjectives is what Couzens calls 'the concept of decorum' (1973:4) arising from Plaatje's deliberate attempt to approximate Biblical and epic language – a vital part of his depiction of the tribes with which he is concerned. In his introduction to his *Sechuana Proverbs* Plaatje writes: 'the similarity between all pastoral nations is such that some passages in the history of the Jews read uncommonly like a description of the Bechuana during the nineteenth century' (quoted in Couzens 1973:4). The point is that Abrahams has nothing with which to replace this. Writing out the tensions of Plaatje's linguistic moment results in a curiously empty prose in Abrahams, and nowhere is this so clear as in the dialogue he creates.

Wade puts this down to Abrahams's 'inability to become involved in the fate of characters very different in situation and preoccupation from himself' (1972:206), but we can, I think, extend this point. Abrahams, stripped and consciously stripping himself of an 'imagined community' has, precisely, trouble imagining communities. Where language is meant to identify a national affiliation it fails in Abrahams. The search for wisdom involves the stripping away of community, as can be illustrated in the rewriting of the following passage from *Mhudi* in which Gubuza, one of the Matabele leaders, speaks:

'Gubuza has sat at the feet of many a wise man; I have been to Zululand, to Swaziland, to Tongaland and to Basutoland. I know the northern forests, I know the western deserts and I know the eastern and southern seas. Wiseacres of different nationalities are agreed that cheap successes are always followed by grievous aftermaths. Old people likewise declare that individuals, especially nations, should beware of the impetuosity of youth.' (47)

Abrahams rewrites this as follows:

'I was born in Zululand. Lately, I have been there again, not as Gubuza, Commander of the king's armies, but as an ordinary man with no name. I have been to Swaziland, to Tongaland and to Basutoland. I know the northern forests, I know the western deserts, I know the eastern and the southern seas. I have made these journeys, not on a whim, but in search of wisdom ... Wise men of different tribes and nationalities are agreed that cheap successes are nearly always followed by the shadow of tragedy.' (173)

Wisdom, in both passages, is trans-national. Where, however, in the central metaphor of Plaatje's passage, nation and individual are interchangeable as far as the application of wisdom is concerned, in Abrahams the division between nation and individual must be made before wisdom can be achieved (Gubuza must relinquish his national status and travel as an 'ordinary man'). And the wisdom that is achieved is not finally translatable into national terms: the nation has already acted too hastily and without the benefit of wisdom (they are discussing the raid upon Kunana, an act of destruction that will rebound upon the Matabele and result in their near-destruction as a nation), and later not even Gubuza will be able to apply his own wisdom and resist attacking the Boers and their allies. As Wade asks, 'The question is whether Abrahams justifies his forcing of the Matabele warrior into the mould of the modern humanist political sage' (209).

Wade goes on to illustrate accurately how Gubuza handles his retreat when tribal opinion goes counter to the opinion he gives here: in *Mhudi* he retreats into 'caution, the sincere conservative's trustiest weapon', while in *Wild Conquest* he becomes 'a rationalist prophet set against the background of witchcraft and ignorance' (209, 210). The point that needs to be made is that Plaatje can trust his sense of community enough to make of it a viable retreat, while Abrahams must attempt to push beyond communal lines and establish a place of transcendent value. These opposed attitudes can only too clearly be related to contemporary national concerns. Wade says of *Wild Conquest*, 'The novel ... marks the beginnings of Abrahams's alienation from those forms of African nationalism or Pan-Africanism orientated towards the traditional past in Africa' (97); with this we must agree, but without putting too much weight on the qualification Wade gives to the nationalism Abrahams is rejecting: it is not just the 'traditional past' that is the issue, it is nationalism itself.

This brings us to the real point of Abrahams's dependence on Plaatje, which is a deep structural one. I claimed in Chapter Two that *Mhudi* is riven around the issue of nationalism, that the work carries within itself the unresolved national factions Plaatje was trying to address through his account of history. This is reflected in the two dominant styles of the book, but only indirectly; history and romance, broadly aligned to the national and the personal, relate to specific sections of the book, and only occasionally, and usually uncomfortably, come together. Their increasing convergence results in the romance mode of Mhudi and Ra-Thaga's story, never fully accommodated within the historical mode, being threatened by that mode, especially as it becomes dominated by Afrikaner nationalism. There is then a duality of the national and the personal, but they are not cast in a *necessary* opposition. A specific historical failure of nationalism prevents the integration of the national and the personal.

Abrahams picks up this structural polarity from *Mhudi*, but inscribes it into monolithic and trans-historical terms. Nationalism and individualism become permanently opposed terms, beyond any historical resolution. What can be written into an historical relationship is the opposed nationalisms, and it is these that he puts in a dialectical relationship. In doing this he has echoed the structure of *Mhudi*, but entirely altered the nature of its opposed but related terms. The divisions in *Mhudi* prompt the dialectical form of *Wild Conquest*, but take on there a very different content.

THE DIALECTICS OF INDIVIDUALISM

It does seem presumptuous to call in as venerable and contested a concept as the dialectic to explain the division of *Wild Conquest* into three related parts, but as a model of thought it pervaded the Communist Party discourse of the time in special ways – significantly to do with history – with which Abrahams would have been familiar. It underlay the two-stage theory of revolution, whereby a black bourgeois democracy was to be achieved before a socialist society could emerge. The formal adoption of this policy by the South African Communist Party began in 1930 in line with its promulgation by the Sixth World Congress of the Communist International of 1928 (see Legassick 1973). Abrahams found convincing too, as we saw in the quotation to do with his initial admiration for Marxism given above, the Communist Party's analysis of imperialism. Through this he would have been familiar with the concept of internal colonialism, whereby South Africa was seen as a 'special' case of colonialism in which two nations occupied the same territory with the one oppressing the other in that territory (see Lerumo 1971:27). Still dialectical in intent, this also easily aligned itself with the African Nationalists' formulation of social relations in terms of opposition between two homogeneous nations.

It is natural then for Abrahams to use the historical dialectic and to cast it in national terms. The Boer ('Bible and Rifle') and Matabele ('Bayete!') sections of *Wild Conquest* come together in conflict in the battle that dominates the partially ironically named final section, 'New Day'. The way in which Abrahams portrays the battle, however, differs significantly from historical record, particularly the account from which Plaatje, his prime historical source, was working, and we must consider this before we can continue.

The significance of Abrahams's use of Plaatje is not restricted to what he lifts, but what he leaves out as well. He makes of the battle a one-off affair, with the Boers breaking the Matabele in a single contest of strength, and the Barolong appearing at the last moment to do a little mopping up. Abrahams here compresses historical time and elides events of real significance to the nature of the conflict. Plaatje's account can be most easily followed if we look at a succinct version of the events he wrote for *The Annual Yearly Register: The Black Folks' Who's Who*:

> About 1834 the first party of emigrant Boers under Sarel Cilliers made acquaintance with the Barolong and passed on with their voortrekking expedition. They soon came into contact with Mzilikazi's vanguards at Vechtkop, in the Heilbron District. Here they had to resist a vigorous attack by the Matabele who relieved them of every head of their livestock. This fight marked the beginning of the tragic friendship of

Moroka and the Boers. Word reached Moroka that the Boers, having lost all their cattle, were now exposed to starvation and further attacks. The chief nobly rose to the occasion. He sent teams of oxen to bring the Boers back to Thaba Nchu. On their arrival he levied from among his people gifts of milch cows and goats and also hides to make sandals and shoes for the tattered and footsore trekkers and their families, whom he settled at a place called Morokashoek. If South Africans were as romantic and appreciative as white people in Europe and America, Morokashoek would be a hallowed spot among the voortrekker descendants, and efforts would surely be made to keep the memory of the benefactors of their ancestors ...

In a couple of years the Boers had recuperated and, being reinforced by other Boer parties from the south and from Natal, the Barolong, combined with the Boers under Potgieter, drove the Matabele from Bechuanaland ... to Rhodesia. (Quoted in Couzens 1975:9-10)

These are the events as Plaatje dramatises them in *Mhudi*. They are made central to the plot (Phil Jay and Ra-Thaga meet while the Boers are at Thaba Nchu, thus bringing the two nations into individual focus), and of course what is summarised here is the theme of Plaatje's historical revision: black generosity is met by white ingratitude and betrayal on a national scale (Plaatje goes on in *The Black Folks' Who's Who* to trace the way in which the alliance between Barolong and Boer was disastrous for the former). The Barolong are also given a major and leading role in the battle. Abrahams could be forgiven for following the 'authorized version' of these events had he no other source, but to go against his major source in this way is certainly significant.

The clue to its significance lies in the way in which the parts of the dialectic are conceived in *Wild Conquest* as opposed to the relation of the stylistically divorced oppositions within *Mhudi*. In *Mhudi*, as Couzens's 'model theory' makes plain, the historical opponents of the Barolong/Boer alliance on the one hand and the Matabele on other translate in modern terms into the oppressed blacks versus the oppressive whites. The modern terms however are not written *back* into history. Plaatje preserves the historical significance of black history in which the whites are a minor if emergent fraction. *Mhudi* predicts their emergence, but keeps the Boers in their correct historical perspective at the time. Literal history is not yet divided along racial lines, even if, as a metaphor, its significance relates to the racial divisions to come. Plaatje thus preserves the integrity of the past while allowing it to serve a modern metaphorical function.

In *Wild Conquest* the terms of the modern opposition are literally written back into history – too literally, with the result that the past is distorted for both sides of the opposition. The battle must be portrayed as a black/white conflict and Abrahams emphasises this by eliding Moroka's support of the Boers. Black nationalism becomes equated with the Matabele, and Afrikaner nationalism with the Boers, in a one-to-one fashion, with no hint of the real and material co-operation that took place between Boer and black. Black nationalism therefore takes on the associations of the worst excesses of the Matabele, and Afrikaner nationalism those of the Boers. Nationalism is presented, in other words, in solely exclusive terms. Abrahams half-heartedly tries to soften this equation by building in good and bad characters (Anna, Elsie, and Paul; Dabula, Gubuza, and Mkomozi) on both sides. But 'good' and 'bad' become equated with 'individual' and 'national' respectively, so whatever is positive on either side is automatically written out of the national equation. And given that the dialectic is only a national one, it is a foregone conclusion that the good and wise will die because of – or be defeated by – the nationalisms that define the elements of the dialectic. Finally it is not a matter of the historical opposition of nationalisms that is important for Abrahams, it is the transcendent truth, illustrated in the failure of the national dialectic, that only in individualism is there any value. In its Hegelian form at least, the contradictions of the dialectic were surpassed in a higher and unified truth; in Abrahams, it is a truth higher than material history that he seeks, and above all a truth higher than the necessary oppositions of nationalism. In the words of Mkomozi in the central speech of the novel:

'Who made the army? Who created the lust for blood? You did, Gubuza. You and Mzilikazi. When you built this nation and forged this empire, you created a lust for blood ...

'It is not only our people who are in darkness, who are bewitched by false medicine men and false prophets, it is not only our people who are made drunk by words and blood, it is not only our people who are stirred to a frenzy of madness by the tom-toms.

'It is so everywhere, among all nations. The darkness is everywhere. The lust for blood is everywhere. The false medicine men, the false prophets, are everywhere. And they wax powerful and call for blood and are followed by the people. It does not matter if they use tom-toms or other methods to fill the people with a frenzy of madness. The darkness is everywhere. So mourn not, Gubuza, Mzilikazi, mourn not for the Matabele. If you must mourn, mourn for our world that is in darkness, where the false doctors hold power over the simpleness of people.' (210-11)

The malleability of the people, the malevolence of their leaders, the bloodlust that is the logic of nationalism, these are finally world-truths; the higher, cosmic truth governing the dialectic surpasses its component parts of nationalism and history, and it is this that is the deep concern of *Wild Conquest*. Ultimately this higher truth is erased from its own dialectic, leaving the dialectic to fail on its historical terms. History, it seems, is not the real subject of this 'historical novel', for the nationalism that is its ostensible historical subject is not, finally, an intimately historical phenomenon. In *Wild Conquest*, nationalism is a trans-historical negative. The important issue is the degree to which individuals can escape both nation and history, in the process domesticating these modes of existence into the ideal, and ultimately (in Abrahams's terms), idealist category of the individual.

The logic of such a position may well be found in the alienation of exile; it is also understandable given the historical weight of the ethnically-defined nationalism being generated around him. Yet it nevertheless represents the failure of the form in which he cast this exclusivism to register it as historical.

The necessary destructiveness Abrahams saw in all forms of community for his individual characters is a product of the very essentialisms he wished to escape. *Wild Conquest* represents Abrahams's most concentrated exploration of his historical identity, and there he found a subject divided at the most literal biological level. In abandoning the racism written into his given name, Lee de Ras felt it necessary to pursue a freedom beyond the nationalisms constructed on and constructing his racial heritage; this freedom could consist, however, only in its writing itself out of nation and history altogether. What is lost in the process is a sense of the contingency of the terms around which Abrahams's historical novel is constructed. This loss is especially telling when it comes to the issue of nation, for if nationhood is to carry a truly historical meaning, it cannot be based on ethnicity any more than class or any other of the classical material divisions of a society – it is, surely, the medium of negotiation between all these shifting divisions, defining a society, yes, but much more importantly helping it to work. As the pressures for a specifically coloured caucus grow within the supposedly non-racial ideals of the new South Africa, the failure of *Wild Conquest* to produce a history capable of working against the pressures of its production reminds us of how necessary it is, at times, for us to create a past that can resist the present.

4

THE CHANGING PAST

OLIVER WALKER

---■---

It is not the future which is unpredictable, but the past
(After Jorge Luis Borges)
– Christopher Saunders (1988:1)

The question of nationhood in South Africa, like almost every other question, must, as we have seen, engage with the complicated histories that make up race in its various constructions. Indeed, while still in exile, the 'national question' was for the African National Congress little more than a euphemism for the fundamental issue of race in their policies for everything from membership and leadership to future government.

Among the many reasons for discrediting ethnic nationalism is its marginalisation of those considered racially hybrid. When Martin Woollacott writes that 'the legacy of empire was the mixing and muddling of peoples' (1995:27) as part of his analysis of the new moral role of the Commonwealth, he brings to the surface the dangerous assumption beneath some of even the most 'progressive' positions on hybridity: that is, the necessary prior existence of 'pure' categories (in this case of race) for 'mixing' to take place. Assumptions of this sort repress the constructed and changing nature of any and all categories, and are especially dangerous (given their prominence in essentialist arguments) when it comes to questions of gender and race.

If Peter Abrahams was unable to find a meaningful logic in South African history for his identity as one of 'mixed race', this is probably because biological essentialism has been so written into the codification of 'South Africa' that the mixing of race has been variously presented as everything from the nation's originary tragedy, as we will see in the next chapter, to its ultimate solution – the subject of this chapter.

An anecdote in *Tell Freedom* illustrates perfectly the inverse results of any optimistic attitudes towards race on its own terms in South Africa which will also serve as a useful transition from Abrahams to the writer who is the focus of this chapter.

> Early in 1938 I had been 'discovered' by the European press. Oliver Walker of the *Daily Express* had written a feature article, 'Coloured Boy Poet'. He had used some of my less 'revolutionary' poems. The face of a skinny, soulful-looking young man had stared at the whites from their papers. I had gone after a clerk-and-messenger job shortly after the feature appeared. The white man had said:
> 'I know your face. You're the Coloured poet.'
> 'Yes, sir.'
> 'Well, we don't want you.' (251-52)

On a national scale, the clash of gazes here captures perfectly the way in which the 'coloured' is typically central to the frame that marginalises him. From an individual perspective, the ironic effect of the patronage extended by Walker is telling with regard to his particular interest in the historical role of those of 'mixed race' in South Africa.

Walker wrote two novels on the legendary 'miscegenator', John Dunn. More accurately, he wrote the story of the 'white chief of Zululand' twice, on both occasions using him as an historical model for the solution of South Africa's racial divisions. The subject of this chapter is the way in which the telling of this story changed in relation to the contexts in which it was told. I have indicated this by deliberately echoing the title of Ken Smith's study of 'trends in South African historical writing' (1988) in my title for this chapter, and choosing as its epigraph an epigraph from another study of South African historiography that also emphasises the past as the product of an *activity* in the present. My argument regarding 'resistant form' centres on the conviction that this is not, or should not be for certain types of understanding at least, a one-way activity. The point of this chapter is not only to illustrate the old chestnut that the past is ever-changing in relation to the present, but to argue for something beyond the simple acceptance of relativity in these matters. This was the first piece I wrote in the project that has become this book, and it still exemplifies what is, for me, the basis of the search for the defining element in any really *novel* history: what I came to call its 'resistant form'.

JOHN DUNN

Before turning to Walker's treatment of Dunn, it will be helpful to indulge in a little simple historical narrative.

John Robert Dunn was born in 1834, either at Algoa Bay or Port Natal – his parents were moving from the eastern Cape to Natal at the time. At the age of five John witnessed Dingane's sacking of the settlement (in which his grandfather was killed) from the brig *Comet*. The family remained in the area after the threat of further attacks had passed and Dunn's father, Robert Newton Dunn, became a successful hunter, trader, and storekeeper. In 1839 he built a house overlooking the bay, which he named 'Sea View'. He took John with him on hunting and ivory trading expeditions. In 1847 Robert Dunn was killed by an elephant and 'Sea View' sold to settle his debts. His wife and daughters returned to the eastern Cape. Largely uneducated, but competent in Zulu and skilled with a rifle, John earned a meagre living guiding hunting parties (he had killed his first elephant only seven months after his father's death). Later he took employment in the service of a Durban merchant as a transport rider conveying some wagons to Potchefstroom. Upon his return he was refused payment on the grounds that he was under age and that no contract with a minor was binding. Disgusted and broke, he left the settlement to live a semi-nomadic life in Zululand; in this he was joined by Catherine Pierce, the fifteen-year-old daughter of an English settler and a Malay woman. He met Chief Mpande during this time, and made a positive impression. Two years later he was befriended and taken in by Captain Joshua Walmsley, a Border Agent, with whom he and Catherine remained for some years.

After intervening in the civil war between Mbulazi and Cetshwayo (on the losing side) in 1856, he later won the respect and friendship of Cetshwayo and was invited to stay in Zululand. This he did, becoming a key figure in Cetshwayo's reign and integrating himself in the Zulu political economy by acquiring the land, livestock, followers ('clients'), and wives (forty-nine in all, with whom he produced at least a hundred and sixteen children) necessary for success in it. He further enhanced his position by exploiting his contact with the Colony (where he was a controversial but at times influential figure) as a labour recruiter, trader, gun runner, and political and military go-between.

The Anglo-Zulu War, which he did much to try and prevent, shattered the basis for his transfrontier existence. After an attempt at neutrality he was drafted into the invasion and played an important role in the defeat of the Zulu army. In the disastrous Settlement scheme he was again an important figure: he was an architect of partition and a major benefactor of this policy as he recouped his losses by being made chief of the largest and wealthiest of the thirteen districts into which Zululand was divided. With the restoration of Cetshwayo (which he now of course strongly opposed), the resulting Civil War, and the ultimate annexation of Zululand in 1887, Dunn became increasingly peripheral to events. He died in 1895.

A study of John Dunn well-versed in the contemporary debates in southern African historiography appeared in 1985. In the Preface its author, Charles Ballard, writes:

> John Dunn's career in Zululand has escaped the serious notice of most southern African historians. No substantial biography or thesis has dealt with this romantic and little understood figure whose political, economic and military activities spanned three crucial decades (1857-1887) in the history of Natal and Zululand.

At this point one might feel inclined to venture again the point raised in Chapter One concerning Shula Marks and the figures she claims are under-represented in history writing, but in the next sentence Ballard acknowledges that 'Dunn's life has also formed the subject matter of two historical novels'. These are, however, then accorded a brief and complete dismissal:

> His career is sensationalised in Oliver Walker's novels *Proud Zulu* and *Zulu Royal Feather*. Both books are riddled with Walker's fanciful accounts of Dunn's sexual exploits with his African wives; this reflects the author's not unnatural desire to sell copy instead of portraying Dunn's domestic relations in a sensitive and more accurate manner. The publishers, with Walker's approval, described *Zulu Royal Feather* as a 'frank portrait of an epic sensualist who believed that in propagating so freely he was fulfilling the Lord's plan'. Such sensational

descriptions of important individuals have twisted historical fact out of all proportion, and have made the historian's task of debunking popular myths a much more difficult one. (Ballard 1985:10)

Anthony Delius, in a review of *Proud Zulu* written in 1951, shows more insight into the publishing industry by pointing out (with reference to a 'blurb-writer's' description of the book as a 'lusty saga') 'that no author can be held responsible for the excesses of his publisher's *isibongo*' (1951:5). His point holds true for both novels, for neither is fairly represented by its dust-jacket synopsis, but the question remains as to whether these novels may be usefully considered in relation to the historical construction of their subject.

The point is not whether Ballard's thorough book could have gained at a referential level by a closer consultation of Walker's work; quite obviously its research and factual accuracy are better history in this sense. But Walker's novels remain interesting and in some ways unique examples of the way fiction may operate, and fail to operate, as the kind of *historicising* medium I am arguing for in this book.

Firstly, the dates of publication for *Proud Zulu* and *Zulu Royal Feather* are significant: 1949 and 1961 respectively. Although, as Ballard and Andrew Duminy tell us, 'a steady stream of books on the [Anglo-Zulu War] began to appear almost before the last shots had been fired', they also point out that the 'first contribution by a professional historian' only appeared in 1948, and then was focused on a single battle – Sir Reginald Coupland's *Zulu Battlepiece: Isandlwana* (Duminy and Ballard 1981:xvi). If we add to this the fact that the next professional historical attention to be paid to the subject was in 1965 (three chapters in Brookes and Webb's *History of Natal* and Donald Morris's popular history, *The Washing of the Spears*), Walker's novels do take on at least the virtue of making publicly accessible the fruits of much original research. Walker certainly felt that the research he did was an important part of *Proud Zulu*, as is made plain in his correspondence with Dr Killie Campbell. In a letter to her dated 17 October 1945, he writes of a visit to her Africana library:

> ... I was foraging around to see what you had on John Dunn. I must say I was rather disappointed in one way: in another I was pleased because the absence of a full-size, full-blooded portrait of the man confirms my own urge to fill that gap. (KCM 4635 MS CAM 1.04 Folder 14, 17.10.45)

The real extent of the importance he attached to the historical accuracy of his novel becomes most plain, however, when he feels threatened by competition from another writer also working on Dunn. Walker's 1947/48 letters to Killie Campbell are full of defensive claims as to his prior right to source material in her possession. The threat was real as the other writer, Carel Birkby, was already well established as an author, with many popular travel and war books to his credit, as well as some light historical works such as *Thirstland Treks* (1936) and *Zulu Journey* (1937). Walker dreaded the sort of treatment Birkby would accord Dunn, primarily on the grounds of how little effort Birkby tended to put into historical research:

> I have spent many hours not only in your library, but in the Gubbins here in Joburg, and in the Cape Archives following up various clues. I emphasise this research because I feel it would be most unfortunate and undeserved if someone like Birkby comes along and produces a slick, superficial pen-picture of Dunn based on 'John Dunn's Notes'.[6] The whole subject warrants extensive and sober treatment and analysis in its historical context ... which is the method I have adopted. (KCM 4819 MS CAM 1.04 File 16, 10.3.48)

Walker could further have legitimately added to his sources at least the oral evidence gained in his interviews with Dunn's descendants and his scrutiny of the Pietermaritzburg Archives, but further defence proved unnecessary as Birkby's challenge was withdrawn; he went on to take up the biography of the Pagel circus family instead (see Birkby 1948).

Of course research is not virtue enough in itself if accuracy and interpretation are at issue. Walker's Dunn novels, however, are nowhere near as inaccurate in terms of the evidence available as Ballard implies in his haste to reject them on the grounds of their imaginative reconstruction of events and characters. It is interesting, although of course not decisive, to note that *Proud Zulu* is sometimes to be found catalogued under 'History' and sometimes under 'Literature' in South African libraries. *Zulu Royal Feather*, on the other hand, is invariably found under 'Literature'. Many other works share a similar ambiguity of status, and

---

6. The reference is to the brief autobiographical notes made by Dunn which were published as *John Dunn, Cetywayo and the Three Generals*, ed. Duncan Moodie (Pietermaritzburg, 1886). Dunn had embarked on a much fuller autobiography, but the only draft he possessed of it was lost when his homesteads were destroyed in the Anglo-Zulu War.

while one would not want to make too much of the accuracy of library cataloguing systems, the point is obviously relevant to the institutionalisation of history and literature.

More significantly, Anthony Delius, in his review of *Proud Zulu* mentioned above, criticises the novel on grounds diametrically opposed to Ballard's. He comments on 'the immense industry and exact discernment that went in to the accumulation of the historical material', but goes on to complain that

> there seems to be in Mr Walker's handling of his theme a war between fact and fancy, a desperate desire to be factual and a distrust of the imagination which he occasionally has to use. (1951:6) [7]

The discrepancy between Ballard's and Delius's readings of Walker's work could be explained away as simply a result of the differing perspectives of their historical contexts or professions, but more can be made of it, starting with the subject matter of the two novels. For the second important point Ballard's dismissal of Walker's two novels does not make is that the 1961 *Zulu Royal Feather* is, as I mentioned above, a rewriting of the same material covered in the 1949 *Proud Zulu*. What we have is two treatments of the same material by one author at different times, and this fact goes some way towards explaining the discrepancy in reception. Simply, the complaint Delius has to make about *Proud Zulu* does not apply in the same way to *Zulu Royal Feather* and Ballard's criticism of Walker is more accurate when applied to *Zulu Royal Feather* than to *Proud Zulu*.

PROUD ZULU AND ZULU ROYAL FEATHER

Indeed, Walker falls foul of the sort of criticism levelled by Ballard largely because he appears to be trying to redress in his second novel the causes for Delius's negative critique of his first. Delius's main criticism of *Proud Zulu* is one that is typical of the dominant mode of literary criticism of the time, one that has since been identified by Michael Vaughan amongst others as arising from the 'aesthetics of liberalism' (1982:119-21). I do not want to argue for or against the aesthetic criteria involved here, or make of them a test of the quality of the work; I wish simply to test the appropriateness of Delius's invocation of them in the case of

---

7. This review seems to have been the only serious critical attention the novel drew - which suggests that Walker would have taken special note of it.

Proud Zulu. For Vaughan a liberal aesthetics is, in crude summary, a concentration on the character as an individual, within the conventions of realism. Central to this conception is the autonomy of authentic characterisation, especially from overt didactic intention, and it is on this score that Delius primarily takes Walker to task. He writes:

> ... the deepest reason for Mr Walker's failure in this book is his inability to sustain his own interest in even the characters he most likes, Cetewayo [*sic*] and Bishop Colenso. His attention throughout the book is continually straying back to the characters he most dislikes, the great body of smugly superior white South Africans to whom he is reading a lecture in history. The development of his characters is only secondary to his castigation of his invisible audience of latter-day chauvinists. And when a novel's characters are developed as a by-product, and not as the main product, of the author's interest they become as awkward, half-animate and improbable in the main as Mr Walker's are. (7)

The issue of present-mindedness, for historian or novelist, is as we have observed a vexed and complicated one, but if it appears in the form of a simplistic morality tale for the present at the expense of the past it is no doubt a severe failing. Delius's dismissal of Walker as a 'propagandist in a hurry to undo an ancient wrong' (5) is not, however, an adequate explanation for Walker's treatment of character in *Proud Zulu*, nor is it entirely valid. Character is not subordinated so much to lesson as to the historical context in which it is situated. Delius notes in passing the latter as a secondary fault: 'often one feels even through the tough, matter-of-fact journalese the beat of a human crisis approaching ... but the beat falters and dies ...' (6). Walker is accused of promising to lead the reader 'deep into the maze of humanity enmeshed in its own nobility and infirmity' (6) and then retreating to mere action. In this Delius repeats one of the oldest criticisms of the 'historical novel', common ever since contemporary criticisms of Sir Walter Scott. What is missed in these is that character may legitimately merge with larger concerns in some novel forms, and is not necessarily in these cases employed for the sake of expressing 'human' depth or psychology. The reader is directed towards a broader social spectrum for which the protagonist's career is a central prism or – to shift metaphors to the one used by Walker himself – 'peg'.

Walker seems to have surprised himself in coming to precisely this perception of his protagonist in *Proud Zulu*, as comes across in his once again revealing correspondence with Killie Campbell. On 10 March 1948 he wrote:

> ... I discovered, once I was interested, that it was a very big subject ... much bigger than John Dunn who is really a picturesque peg on which to hang a very important historical theme. (KCM op. cit., 10.3.48)

And again, on 26 April 1948:

> Dunn himself is really only a peg to hang the greater story on ... the decline and fall of the Zulu military code and race superbity [*sic*] as expressed and symbolised in the line of Shaka. (Ibid., 26.4.48)

Indeed, when his publishers asked him to change his original title 'White Zulu' (because they 'reckoned this could have a detrimental effect on sales in South Africa'[8]) to 'Proud Zulu', he agreed, although not for their reasons. On 8 July 1948 he wrote to Killie Campbell:

> Re the Dunn book and its new title. This I should have explained has no reference to Dunn himself. '*Proud Zulu*' shifts the emphasis of the story to its proper place ... i.e. the Fall of the House of Shaka. I concurred to this suggestion of the publishers because, quite deliberately, I made the Zulus the real centrepiece of the tale with John Dunn as a linked figure. (Ibid., 8.7.48)

That this shift in emphasis during Walker's research and writing of the novel parallels in its own small way that of the historiographical perspective of the liberal Africanists, which, despite the existence of small radical tradition of strongly Africanist history writing, only became a forceful movement in the 1960s. Unfortunately Walker, by the time he came to rewrite the Dunn story in 1961, lost sight of this strength in his earlier version. He was partially dissatisfied with *Proud Zulu*; as he wrote to Killie Campbell, he felt he had 'pushed it along rather rapidly because of the intrusion of Birkby into the same field' (ibid., 13.4.48). But the changes he later chose to make in rewriting it as *Zulu Royal Feather*

8. Quoted from a letter from Peter Walker (Oliver Walker's son) to myself, 15 June 1988.

result in a far less satisfactory form for the events in which Dunn was involved – certainly as far as historicising form is concerned.

It is possible that *Zulu Royal Feather* was altered directly in response to Delius's critique (or at least some of it; the 'history lesson' was to remain, although in altered form, as we shall see), but even if this is not so, then it was done in accordance with a similar general sense of a more acceptable charactercentric novel form. A related aim also appears to have been to remodel the serious research done for *Proud Zulu* along the lines of the popular historical sagas which came in the wake of the period of the 'classical historical novel' in South Africa. These efforts considerably weaken Walker's original conception of the Dunn story.

To illustrate: *Proud Zulu* opens with

> Like the seeds carried by birds rumours of the impending fight between the Zulu princes were scattered far and wide through the Colony of Natal in the weeks before the armies clashed (Walker 1949:13),

and the first page continues in this vein, establishing the pervasive fear in the area at the prospect of war between Mbulazi and Cetshwayo. It is many pages before we are brought to the actual clash, however; Walker chooses rather to continue building the tension, interspersing it with flashbacks on Dunn's life up to this point, filling us in on his past whilst maintaining the intensity of the action in hand. At first the flashbacks are presented as Dunn's memories, sparked off by the present situation, but before this becomes too restrictive the third person narrator brings them in as it seems appropriate until past and present tense conjoin in November 1856. Our first 'close up' of Dunn, then, is his intervention in the feud over succession as he fights on the side of Mbulazi (ostensibly to protect the settlers at the Bay, but as Walker suggests through Captain Walmsley's suspicions, probably to gain further favour with Mpande, who supported Mbulazi.) With Cetshwayo's victory at the Ndondakusuka battle, Dunn's plans seem to have gone seriously awry, especially as the settlers claim to have lost many cattle through his interference. Dunn saves the situation by risking all on a visit to Cetshwayo, which results in his not only retrieving the settler's cattle, but, in the process, being taken up by the prince he had opposed.

All of this is used to skilfully prepare us for what is to follow: his involvement in Zulu public affairs, his negotiating role across the frontier, his later 'betrayal' of Cetshwayo, and so forth. At the same time he is established for the reader as a character, but by emerging to all significant purposes out of the history in which he participates.

Zulu Royal Feather, on the other hand, opens with an extended fictional recreation of the elephant hunt in which Dunn's father dies. This is followed by a melodramatic compression of *Proud Zulu*'s 'month or two' (14) before he kills his first elephant into one day, with the added poetic justice of the elephant in question now being the one that killed his father. We learn nothing of any extra significance in this episode (his precocious hunting skills and courage are in fact established more effectively in the compact and low-key account in *Proud Zulu*), nor in the spinning out of his early life in Port Natal (the recreation of which is unfortunately dominated by the lengthy representation of the trader who cheated Dunn of his remuneration as an unabashed villain of Victorian theatre proportions). It is some fifty pages before we come to Walker's rewriting of his original effective opening sentence, now reduced to the thin straining after effect that characterises the much-purpled prose (which we will analyse in more detail later) of the second novel: '... rumours of a big fight brewing flocked round his head like evil birds' (Walker 1961:52).

Apart from losing the effective dramatic tension of the first chapter of *Proud Zulu*, an important reorientation of protagonist in relation to action has taken place in *Zulu Royal Feather*. The success of the opening of the first novel is due to its 'epic' quality, that is, in the Lukácsian sense of character being generated in concrete interaction with the broad sweep of historically significant event. Here we must engage a little more fully with Lukács's theories regarding history and the novel. In his materialist transposition of aspects of Hegel's theory of history to literature, the 'typicality' of the 'world-historical individual' becomes a model for the relationship of protagonist to context. The extent, then, to which individualising features and features of the historical moment coincide naturally is, for Lukács, a key evaluative issue. It is this which, in his analysis of the historical novel, he praises most highly in Scott: 'Scott endeavours to portray the struggles and antagonisms of history by means of characters who, in their psychology and destiny, always represent social trends and historical forces' (1981:33). Again, 'Scott's greatness lies in his capacity to give living human embodiment to historical-social types. The typically human terms in which great historical trends become tangible had never before been so superbly, straightforwardly and pregnantly portrayed' (34-35).

While the concept of typicality is problematic and open to abuse – as illustrated in Zhadanovite socialist-realism – (for a discussion of typicality see Clingman 1986:9), it is useful for our purposes here, for in *Zulu Royal Feather* it is precisely the relationship foregrounded by the concept of typicality that has broken down. The character of Dunn is no longer as closely individualised in concrete relation to the social and historical circumstances of his situation. This second novel is an attempt at a modification of *Proud Zulu* that has failed to generate a successfully different form. Walker wishes to personalise the 'epic' form, but succeeds instead only in a synthetic foregrounding of the protagonist. Without genuinely altering strategy, he falls instead into the fault of the bulk of light 'romantic' historical novels; that is, without an adequate narrative relation between character and context, he depends increasingly on gratuitous (in terms of the needs of the form) charactercentric motivation – motivation, what is more, which is no longer produced by a sense of the past as something foreign to the present. The 'human' qualities Walker injects into his narrative in order to give it a greater contemporary appeal betray the sense of the past which his original account of the Dunn story managed to convey. The surest indication that a breakdown of this nature has occurred is an increasing reliance on sentimentality and sensationalism to carry the narrative.

For Lukács it is the changed relationship of the hero to the events portrayed that marks the essentially anti-Romantic nature of the novel form (1981:33-35). The literary effect of anti-Romanticism has an interesting parallel in historiography which we may illustrate from examples close to the present topic (and which we will explore in a very different way in the chapter on Daphne Rooke).

Ballard in his study of Dunn warns that 'the historian of romantic bent must guard against the inclination to exaggerate the historical significance of individuals and minimise the effects of environment'. His awareness of historiographical debates around these issues is illustrated by his concern not to depict the individual as swamped by apersonal abstract forces either, however, so he presents his approach as

> both thematic and biographical; the various and, at times, seemingly unrelated subjects mentioned ... are held together by the continuous thread of Dunn's personality and participation in events related to a wide range of themes. (9)

Unfortunately, the main weakness in Ballard's book is precisely its failure to carry out his intention of evoking a sense of Dunn's personality strongly enough for it to serve as an organisational device. Nevertheless the intention carries the point here, especially if we relate it to Colin Webb's plotting of the ideological significance of various interpretations of the Anglo-Zulu War: he traces the movement from 'orthodox' to 'liberal' to 'radical' in terms of their weighting of specific individuals over general forces and vice versa (1981:1-12).

Walker's two novels can also be considered in relation to these poles. They present something of a unique case study on the topic of the protagonist in relation to environment in fact, for, while neither novel is free of the faults or virtues of the other, they do tend to polarise over this issue – with a corresponding degree of success and failure. Walker's technical ability as a novelist is admittedly modest, but when deployed in the careful control of narrative in the 'epic' sense noted above it is effective, sometimes extremely so. He collapses into sensationalism and sentimentality (not to mention poor prose) when he over-extends himself in the pursuit of 'human interest'. This is not simply a result of his limited talent; the increasing reliance on what becomes merely cheap effect in *Zulu Royal Feather* is a necessary formal reflex of the attempt to establish character and motivation in the absence of the epic logic that informs the more successful sections of *Proud Zulu*. A related failure in history writing would be the 'glamour and tragedy' so often associated with literature on the invasion of Zululand that Jeff Guy criticises in *The Destruction of the Zulu Kingdom* (1979:xx). Similar distortions arising from similar formal issues in fictional and historical texts underline again the proposition that the problem of adequate historicisation – in the sense defined in Chapter One – is common to both literary and historical works.

Since the main reason Ballard gives for rejecting the novels is 'Walker's fanciful accounts of Dunn's sexual exploits with his African wives' (10), we can follow through on this point by comparing the two novels' handling of Dunn's taking of his first black wife.

In *Proud Zulu* Dunn's first feelings for Macebose, her initial rejection of him, Cetshwayo's intervention, Catherine's fury, and Macebose's surrender and pregnancy are to a fair degree interspersed among significant historical events, such as Dunn's advising of Cetshwayo on the planned attack on the amaTonga, his first agreement to engage in substantial gun trading, a meeting at the Bay with Shepstone and Fynney, and so on. While his relationship with Macebose is still given enough attention to be of interest in itself, it fits naturally (for whatever sexual spin it is given) amongst several other steps towards Dunn's increasing absorption into the social, political, and economic life of Zululand. It prepares us for Dunn's later use of marriage relations for the consolidation of his territory, for example, and as such presents gender relations no less than sexuality as vital aspects of a past very different from the present in which it is reconstructed. Basic 'human' (that is, trans-temporal and 'universal') features take on a specific historical logic that mark them of their time and place.

In *Zulu Royal Feather*, the account is extended in detail and incident (little to any pertinent point and including a completely fanciful assassination attempt on Dunn by Catherine's brothers in defence of her honour) on the one hand, and compounded (it is less interspersed and where it is, the events breaking it are of far less significance: a hunting expedition, a visit from a missionary) on the other. The result is that the affair gains a higher textual profile, but loses its coherent place within both the development of Dunn as an historical figure and the narrative. In this *Zulu Royal Feather* slides towards inauthentic spectacle of the 'romantic' historical novels beginning to dominate the South African literary market at the time of its publication, the popularity of which depended strongly on overtly 'dehistoricised' (that is, contemporary) representations of sexuality.

It is such manoeuvres that give Ballard just cause for his criticism (although seeing even *Zulu Royal Feather* as 'riddled' with sex remains, I think, an exaggeration). Admittedly, of the necessary resources for political and economic power in pre-capitalist Zululand, Walker does tend to give more visibility to wives than land, clients, and livestock, but these other elements are substantially present in the novels and specifically related, as are the wives, to Dunn's position in that society. His polygyny was too, the chief reason for his notoriety in the Colony – except during time of war when his gunrunning tended naturally to predominate – and this comes across in the novels as part of the reason for its high profile. The fact remains that Ballard does have a case, but significantly, as I have tried to show, more especially against *Zulu Royal Feather*. It is important to see the misuse of the sexual dimension (and the argument cannot be separated from larger feminist issues) as another vain buttress in support of a characterisation that has lost its narrative logic.

Reference has been made to the deterioration in prose style that accompanies the narrative deterioration. Essentially we find the same symptoms writ small. In the interest of brevity one example will suffice. A major source for sections of the Dunn story is Dunn's short autobiography entitled *John Dunn, Cetywayo and the Three Generals* (referred to above by Walker as 'John Dunn's Notes'). Here is the source sentence from Dunn's account of a hunting trip in which he is describing the experience of a Captain Watson:

> On reaching the spot he could not see anything of his quarry until, suddenly, he heard a growl in the long grass close beside him, and at the same instant the Lion sprang at him.

In *Proud Zulu* Walker makes of this:

> Before Watson could begin the search there was a snarl from the tall tambootie grass at his back, and the wounded lion sprang. (44)

By the time the sentence is rewritten for *Zulu Royal Feather*, it has become:

> Before Watson could decide which way to take, a thunderous belly-snarl came from the tall tamboekie grass at his back and the black-maned lion was upon him. (102)

It is difficult to tell how much of the rewriting was done for what Walker felt to be superior aesthetic effect and how much was done to convince the publishers that the second version was a significantly different book; much of the reworking is almost arbitrary, such as 'could begin to search' and 'could decide which way to take'. The rest demonstrates the point in hand.

The addition of adjectives and adverbs is a feature of the second novel and a common source of cheap effect: the 'growl' of Dunn's account, for example, evolves in its search for effect to a 'snarl' and then a 'thunderous belly-snarl'.

Added detail and even altered spelling are significant: the 'long grass' of the autobiography, no longer supported in the novels by an autobiographical presence, depends for its authenticity on being specifically identified as 'tambootie'. The gain in detail becomes a support for the strategy of verisimilitude, one which escalates yet again: it is promoted from this quite acceptable (according to the *Oxford Dictionary*) alternative spelling (which has in any case a nice regional air to it) to an attempt at the dominant spelling, 'tambouki', which it does not quite make.

Events are heightened: the lion's attack in the novels is now more dramatically from the rear, and in the second novel it gains even more in speed: the 'spring' becomes invisibly fast so that sans verb it is immediately 'upon him'.

These examples, innocuous enough in themselves perhaps, but crippling when compounded over the length of a novel, illustrate the way in which Walker pads up his prose as his narrative strategy weakens. This is no casual attempt on Walker's part, for the controlling authority of the text over its material and the reader is at stake. As its grip on the logic of the past slips, the narrative becomes increasingly reliant on upping its linguistic stakes in the language of the present, with heightened effect replacing historical density.

But how do we define the 'historical' in this case? Whatever devices may be employed to establish the textual authority of Walker's novels, their chief source of authority remains, as it does for all 'historical' or 'documentary' works of fiction, their grounding in a specific kind of 'fact'. Lukács, as we have seen, denies any essential formal distinction between novel and historical novel (1981:40). Credible as this is for his argument in *The Historical Novel*, it does miss the significance of the particular contract that historical fiction sets up with its reader: its appeal to the authority of its basis in institutionalised 'historical' fact. Whatever fictional construction it shapes around the facts it uses, whatever interpretation it gives to them, whatever new facts it introduces, these are supported by the claims of the form to historical reference. This is a claim that is distinguishable from that of realism's reference to 'reality', for it takes on the sanction of a discipline that has codified reality in a particular and persuasive way. We are presented with, to paraphrase Barthes's concept of the 'reality effect', an 'historical effect' that serves as a guarantee for the authority of the text.

We may agree then with Lukács that the novel/historical novel distinction does not lie in any essential formal difference, but add that a distinctive text-reader relationship is entered into in the historical novel. This does not mean, of course, that all historical novels achieve the historicising effect that is the central concern of this book – indeed, it should be obvious by now that surprisingly few of the works treated in Part One as representative of the 'classical' South African historical novel manage this. But the 'historical novel' as an individually definable category has rarely been what Lukács argues so forcefully against, that is, a formally identifiable genre; rather, it has been set apart from other novels by virtue of its concern with material generally codified within another institution of knowledge. The place of the past in this is itself a product of a rather loose conception of 'the historical', and as such it has become a defining feature of the particular contract between text and reader that we call the historical novel.

This contract is always contestable, and should particularly be so for the historical novel, if only because of the popular attraction of 'true' stories. But if this holds for a specific literary form, how much more so should it hold for the discipline against which that form is identified – for in both history and historical fiction the apparently direct reference to the past is created by the demands of the form in which it is couched. Reference is informed by the formal requirements of the work. At even the most basic level, structural devices such as plot, narrative, characterisation, theme, and so on produce the effect of reference as much as attempt to make it.

The narrative mode of the form chosen by Walker in the novels under discussion is a case in point. He uses free indirect discourse in both, largely aligning the third person authorial stance with Dunn's consciousness. There is evidence to suggest that this standard literary device is particularly telling in this instance. On the occasion of the death of Dr Killie Campbell, Walker wrote an article in one sentence of which there is an interesting potential confusion of subject: 'she did not altogether approve of some of my investigations into John Dunn, the White Zulu chief. For her I [and here, given Dunn's reputation, he could just as easily have meant 'he'] was a "bit of a scallywag", a let-down among the pioneers.' I will claim that this slip underlines the extent of Walker's identification with Dunn, and that Walker's choice of the perspective of this particular historical figure on the events of the time, rather than that of an invented minor figure (*à la* Scott), or another actual figure (Shepstone say, whose biography he was at one time interested in writing[9]), is an important indicator of his sense of his own (changing) position in the events of his time. The shift in the significance of the narrative mode of the novels can therefore best be explored if it is analysed as the author's projection of himself into South African history via his protagonist.

This will help us too in understanding more fully the relation of the Dunn novels to each other, and extend the above rather standard observations regarding reference into the real area with which this book is concerned. For, if we draw the usual conclusions regarding the positionality of all reference, we should not be able to adjudicate between Walker's varying identifications of himself with Dunn. At best we would only be able to treat them as equally telling histories of the

9. Walker wrote an obituary for Dr Killie Campbell, 'A Gracious Historian: Tea and Sympathy with Dr Killie Campbell' (*Star*, 2 Oct. 1965), in which he mentions 'her great favourite among Natal's heroes was Sir Theophilus Shepstone. But I never felt that she regarded me as quite worthy of the subject when I expressed a desire to do his biography. (I had been over-critical of him in *Proud Zulu*, the book she helped me to write.)'

present. These they certainly are, but my point in establishing them as such through the fairly detailed biographical account of Walker that follows is a necessary part of illustrating from this case study the significance of 'resistant form'.

FROM LIFE HISTORY TO HISTORICAL FICTION

It has been fairly difficult to piece together a picture of Walker (the 1986 edition of the *Companion to South African English Literature* [Adey *et al.*:206] does not indicate that he is dead, for example: he died in 1965) largely because his work has not earned him the stature necessary to ensure a close record, but also perhaps for a reason that underlies more literary and historical lacunae than we should like to admit: Walker had a reputation for being, in the words of a colleague of his, a 'thoroughly unpleasant' person.[10] Bernard Sachs's 'pen-portrait' of him in his *Personalities and Places* (1965) captures a popular contemporary sense of the man. It opens with: 'Oliver has a good pen – and a bad temper' (48) and continues in the same vein, admitting his abilities but concentrating on his arrogance, 'very highly developed Ego' (52), and, in Sachs's view, anti-Semitism. Walker's editor on the *Star*, too, writes in his memoirs and Walker's obituary that he 'caused me more problems than all the rest of the staff put together'.[11] Be that as it may, I have perhaps over-indulged myself in recreating this man, partly as an act of recovery for one of the sidelined literary figures of South Africa, but primarily because one of the most important lessons social history has taught us is the estranging effect of accumulated detail. We must establish through this our difference from our subject if are not simply to appropriate Walker in our tracing of the place of the present in his retellings of the past. As in the briefer case of Dunn above, I will set my analysis against a rather simple life history.

Oliver Walker was born in Birmingham in 1906. He lived in Cardiff, London, and then Bristol, during which time he started work as a journalist – culminating in a sub-editorship on the *Bristol Times and Mirror* – between playing in dance bands, serving as steward on a tramp ship for a trip across the North Atlantic, and working as a grain clerk. The first two parts of his 1952 novel, *Shapeless Flame* (1951), draw heavily upon this period of his life, while in the third part its consumptive protagonist travels to South Africa.

10. Grateful thanks are extended to Percy Baneshik of the *Star* for an interview which was most helpful in tracing Walker's career.

11. Horace Flather reproduces his obituary from the *Star* word for word in his *The Way of an Editor* (Cape Town, Johannesburg, London: 1977), 145-46.

Walker himself came to South Africa in 1938 to work on the short-lived *Daily Express*. This newspaper had begun as the *Sunday Express*, under the chairmanship of Tielman Roos. Roos believed he had been let down by the press (with whom he had sided against Smuts on the issue of the gold standard) when they supported Smuts for the premiership Roos felt should be his in the Fusion government. He thus called 'for a forthright, outspoken Press, the policy of which would not be dictated by the mining groups' (Smith 1946:148), and launched the *Sunday Express*. After Roos's resignation a similar policy was continued by I.W. Schlesinger when he brought the paper in 1935 as a base for his African Associated Press Ltd. As part of Schlesinger's aggressive expansionism, the *Sunday Express* became the *Daily Express* in late 1937, and Walker was one of the journalists recruited in the process. By March 1939, however, a combination of rival newspapers bought out the Schlesinger group's newspapers (with the controlling share going to the mining groups Roos had sought to challenge), and Walker moved on to work briefly with other newspapers (the *Natal Mercury* and the *Sunday Times*).

Walker's experiences while with the *Daily Express* serve as a basis for his thinly-fictionalised autobiographical novel *Wanton City* (1949). Here actual characters, events, and organisations are fairly transparently translated into fiction: the Argus Group, for example, loses its association with the hundred-eyed guardian giant to become, as befits the representative of a press monopoly, the mono-visioned Cyclops Group, and the *Daily Express* – most aptly, given its short existence – becomes the *Comet*. (One must wonder at the second example's association with the vessel that served as the Dunn family's refuge during Dingane's raid; a similar vehicle for salvation during difficult times, and one of several signs of Walker's merging of himself with Dunn?) At times real names are even kept; Walker identifies the character most closely associated with himself as Peter Random, but when he includes the championing of the poetry of 'a coloured boy ... from the Vrededorp slum zone' (125) mentioned above, he refers to him as Peter Abrahams.[12]

In 1944 Walker was 'doing a war-time propaganda job for the State Bureau of Information' (Walker 1949:7) when he was seconded to the Native Affairs Department where he was meant to write a defence of their policies for international consumption. Sent on field trips all over South Africa for this project,

12. It is further worth mentioning in passing the remarkable structural similarity that Gordimer's *A World of Strangers* bears to *Wanton City*. Walker reviewed the Gordimer novel in the *Star* (2 July) when it appeared in 1958, but remains strangely silent on this.

he finally produced a damning indictment of the whole system which, never used by its sponsors, appeared as *Kaffirs Are Lively: Being Some Backstage Impressions of the South African Democracy* and became a Book Club Choice going into several editions. The title, a pun upon the London Stock Exchange term for South African mining shares (known then as 'Kaffirs'), indicates Walker's awareness of the growing radicalisation of black resistance in the late 1940s. The book is dedicated to 'the Kafferboeties, Liberals and other Christian gentlemen of Africa in whose applied humanity lies the only hope for the peaceful progress of a great Continent' and its theme is well-summarised in the following:

> Let others sing the praises of the white man's energy, his enterprise, his ingenuity, his business acumen, his financial genius, which have made the Rand gold-mines what they are in the economy of the country and in the minds of the 'Kaffir' share-buying public of Europe and America. I am concerned here with the human factor: the myriad unnamed, unknown, 'boys' of a score of great African tribes ... who have made this great industry possible, and in the making of it have destroyed themselves and the social structure of family life which is the foundation of African life as much as it is of any society, white, yellow, brown or black. (20)

Walker left the Department of Information soon after his Native Affairs experience, and from October 1946 until April 1950 was employed by the Institute of Race Relations as editor of publications and publicity officer, while also writing a column ('Leaves from my Diary') for *Trek* magazine. He then joined the *Star* as a sub-editor, but within a year was appointed music and drama critic. Amongst his achievements here was his praise and support for the early work of Fugard, especially *The Blood Knot* (*Star* 5 Sept. 1961). Walker was a highly controversial critic; throughout his fifteen and a half years in this position letters pro and con his bitingly witty and strongly-worded reviews appeared often. His wit made him something of a radio personality (on shows like 'Nice Work'), and it is much in evidence in his continued non-fiction publications. In October 1950 he produced a scathing account of the barely eighteen-month-old Nationalist government entitled *White Man Boss: Footsteps to the South African Volk Republic*, taking care to do so under the pseudonym 'Adamastor' as *Kaffirs Are Lively* had been declared 'undesirable' by the Publications Control Board. The spirit of the Cape is a deliberately apt choice for one who dedicates his book to those who 'fight for the maintenance and expansion of those political rights for civilized non-Europeans which their forefathers conceded without any cause for regret in the pre-Union days of the Cape Colony'(Walker 1950:6). Like *Kaffirs Are Lively* and the later *Kaffirs Are Livelier*, *White Man Boss* is written in an energetic free-style: impressionistic, opinionated, swinging wildly and with enormous panache at every social ill he can identify, but reserving special virulence for the exclusivism underlying, as he saw it, all forms of Afrikaner nationalism. One can understand why Walker spent so little time with the Institute of Race Relations, for his opinions as expressed in these works are of anything but the bland, empirical, and non-political type normally associated with it as it was then.

Walker was involved with the War Veterans' Torch Commando, and wrote a biography of its National President in 1953 as a direct attempt at intervention in the elections of that year. *Sailor Malan* was accurately reviewed as

> a happy and timely study for every South African reader on the eve of the general elections in which the issue seems to be the antithetical values of the two Malans: the Malan who flew like a legendary knight in shining armour against the Nazis, and the Malan who found virtue in the ideologies of his country's enemies. (*Star* 12 March 1953, unsigned)

Although the book is also critical of the Torch Commando (primarily for its begging of the 'colour question'), it nevertheless joins with Walker's other writing in linking him firmly with that rather motley grouping it is so difficult to generalise about, the liberal movement in South Africa. The central principles the Torch Commando held in common with the liberals (as identified by Janet Robertson in *Liberalism in South Africa, 1948-1963* [1971:53]) are firmly present in *Sailor Malan*: the sacredness of the constitution, the value of democracy, the priority of individual liberties, the importance of the rule of law, and anti-totalitarianism in general and fascism in particular. On this last point, however, Walker shows the fairly typical Torch Commando disregard for the concern with white political unity that preoccupied so much liberal thinking, wholly rejecting Afrikaner nationalism and identifying it with Nazism.

Beneath the outrage of his writing in this period there is an underlying optimism that ties in with the liberal hope of a Nationalist defeat in the 1953 election. Horace Flather, editor of the *Star* at the time, captures the liberal mood following the Nationalist victory when he writes in *The Way of an Editor*: 'only once did I feel so deeply about a political matter that for a brief moment ... I contemplated suicide. It was the result of the 1953 election' (176). The effect of the continuing entrenchment of Nationalist power and erosion of the validity of the liberal position is evident in Walker's work, as is made plain in his later publications. A short story ('The Baas Comes Home') contributed to *Africa South* in 1957 uses the return of a bitter Boer soldier after the war to depict the intense racism of those who are, the story makes it clear, eventually to come to power, and the helplessness of those (white and black) who oppose them. This attitude is expressed even more overtly in his sequel to *Kaffirs Are Lively*, *Kaffirs Are Livelier* (1964). Here his journey through Africa and inquiry into Black Nationalism and Pan-Africanism assure him that 'if "Kaffirs" were lively in 1948, they are 100 per cent livelier in 1964' (16), but his hopes for South African internal opposition are not nearly as high. Praise for Michael Scott and (more guardedly) Patrick Duncan throughout indicates his being now even further left of mainstream liberalism, but there is an increased sense of frustration arising from the lack of an effective political role. The book is dedicated, in significant contrast to the dedications of his previous books, to 'All exiles, voluntary and enforced, from their African homelands'. It was banned in February 1965, the same week as Walker's banning from the Brooke Theatre in Johannesburg by its management in response to his continually sharp reviews (triggered by his damning of *How To Succeed in Business*). Walker died of a heart attack at the ninth hole of the Kyalami golf course on Christmas Day of that year.

His fascination with the figure of Dunn is an important element in his career and it continued to the end of his life. (His last work, published posthumously in 1967, is an account of the life of one of Dunn's sons, Tom, entitled *The Hippo Poacher*.) The reason for this seems to lie in the point suggested above: Walker's interpretation of Dunn's position in South African history corresponded strongly with his sense of his own position. As a protagonist Dunn provided Walker with a point of personal access into his adopted country's past that paralleled his view of his place in contemporary events. Charles Ballard's description of Dunn's political position sums up what apparently, from the textual evidence of the novels, attracted Walker to this historical character:

> The turbulent period of the Zulu Civil War and its crucial prelude, the
> Ulundi interim, may be attributed to the interaction and confrontation

of three 'mainstreams of historical forces' which are found in Zululand in the 1880s: 'the one with its source in Zulu history, the other in imperial Britain, and the third in the settler communities on Zululand's borders'. John Dunn failed to straddle these forces successfully and fell from power in 1883. (189)

This picture of Dunn as a victim of his political and cultural transfrontier situation could be, for Walker, transformed (with comparatively little modification of the 'historical forces' involved) into an allegory for the liberal position in South Africa. What is more, the metaphorical significance of Dunn's precarious balancing act, and his fall, proved itself capable of accommodating a substantial reinterpretation between *Proud Zulu* and *Zulu Royal Feather*. In the first novel, Dunn is inscribed into a play of power with which liberals of the late 1940s could easily identify. A significantly different interpretation of their position is registered in the second version of the story Walker wrote.

Proud Zulu is dated March-April 1948. At this time the liberal's hope of successfully straddling the opposed forces in South Africa had not seemed an impossible one. A month before the shock Nationalist victory liberals still appeared to have several serious political options; some trusted in the possibility of reform within the United Party, for example – although after Smuts's revelation of his proposals for the reform of the Native Representative Council in September 1947 this is more an indication of the often-noted optimistic element in liberalism than anything else. Even after the defeat of the United Party, many liberals saw hope in the possibility of a central political representation under Hofmeyr, but this was soon shattered by his death. The ultimate formation of a Liberal Party after the 1953 election was, as Paul Rich claims in *White Power and the Liberal Conscience* (1984c:114), primarily interesting in that it was a last desperate attempt to regain the political influence liberalism was losing on all sides. E.J. Hobsbawm has written that 'some forms of class consciousness, and the ideologies based on them, are, as it were, in tune with historical development, and others not' (1971:13). Walker, along with many others, clearly became increasingly aware of the degree to which his convictions were out of touch with his political environment. We have seen that the effect of the increasing disintegration and marginalisation of the liberal position is strongly registered in Walker's non-fiction. It is equally plain that by the time he came to rewrite his 'lecture on history' in 1961 it could no longer have the same theme and form it took in 1948.

The manuscript of *Proud Zulu* kept in the Johannesburg Public Library bears the typed title 'White Zulu' with what was to become the published title pencilled in. We have discussed above some of the significance that may be attached to this change, but a further reason for Walker's decision to move away from giving an overtly colour-orientated impression of the work comes through in the text. A strong element in the overtly didactic Preface and Epilogue is the status of the coloured community in South Africa. Dunn's founding of a substantial line in this community (one that remains entitled to a land grant of, at present, eight thousand acres – 'Dunnsland' – in KwaZulu-Natal) becomes for Walker a sign for the hope of a non-racial solution to South Africa's problems: 'More than likely they are,' he writes, 'as Bernard Shaw forecast, the mould in which future generations of South Africa will be cast' (260). The ideal of living beyond racial frontiers is made manifest in Dunn's life story; he is presented as a trans-frontiersman in this sense much as in any other, with his progeny being a concrete symbol of the conquering of racial borders. The Preface to *Zulu Royal Feather* restates this biological solution to racial issues even more strongly and literally:

> Stock-breeders have discovered that hybrid strains stand up to Africa better than pure breeds out of Europe. It may therefore be that John Dunn 'builded better than he knew' when he founded the dynasty that bears his name. (7)

This hope echoes hollowly in the Epilogue to the novel, however, when Walker closes it with a quotation from the then contemporary Dunn patriarch, Domenic, that gives a painful sense of the psychological and political complexity of the Dunn line's situation:

> 'For how many generations are they going to visit the sins of the father upon his children? Have we not been punished sufficiently for what our father did? We are the fruit of this country which is a white and black country. Is it God's will that we should be outcasts even in the land of our birth?' (320)

Walker's involvement in the Torch Commando, and his observation of its dilemma regarding coloured participation in a movement ostensibly founded largely to protect coloured constitutional rights, would have been experience enough to explain the forced and desperately over-stated note given in 1961 to any continued hope, at a literal or symbolic level, of the coloured community's serving as an example to other racial groupings of transcended racial divisions.[13]

The change of each novel's attitude to the subject they share is most obviously shown in the alteration of the account of Dunn's death. In *Proud Zulu*, despite the frustrations of Dunn's last years, we are left with a sense of a man who has lived fully and dies satisfied. The text ends, after a representative fragment of Dunn's actual praise poem, with a brief dialogue between two representatives of settler society, Sigurd Sivetson (instructor of Dunn's children)[14] and Mansel (the Commandant of Police):

> 'Is it true – has the chief gone home?' said Mansel, using the Zulu formula.
> 'Yes,' said Sigurd, pulling his horse's head round, 'The Chief is resting.' (256)

In *Zulu Royal Feather* this sense of fulfilment is absent. Once again we are given a brief interchange following on the praise poem, but this time it is between two of Dunn's chief clansmen, Mahlengeni (Dunn's oldest *imbongo*), and Sigananda (an *induna*):

> While Mahlengeni's voice was gathering force from the emotions roused by many memories Sigananda left the stoep and stood by the praise-maker. When Mahlengeni paused for loss of breath and voice Sigananda said solemnly: 'The sun has set for us, old man. Now we shall eat dung.' (315)

This comparison makes it plain that there is a strong shift from combined black and white eulogy in the one novel to black pessimism isolated from white concerns in the other.

---

13. V.A. February's failure to pick up and use Walker's 'Dunn' novels in his *Mind Your Colour: The 'Coloured' Stereotype in South African Literature* (London and Boston: 1981) is surprising and disappointing; the works are central examples of the issues with which he deals.

14. Sigurd Sivetson was alive, although old and ill, at the time of the writing of *Proud Zulu*. Killie Campbell had interviewed him, but Walker's efforts to meet him failed; Campbell then sent Walker her notes from the interview. See KCM 4703 MS CAM 1.04 File 15, Walker to Campbell, 25 Nov. 1947 and Campbell to Walker, Nov. 29, 1947.

The most significant shift between the two novels is, however, not at the overt level of plot and tone; it comes across rather, as I have tried to show, in the degree of historical difference Walker is able to generate; this is particularly evident in the recasting of the relationship between Dunn and the events in which he participates. Walker's intentions in changing this aspect of *Proud Zulu* are no doubt an interesting reflection of the marketing of fiction and critical norms of the time, but, more importantly, the alteration is indicative of the changed relation of the author to contemporary events.

PAST AND PRESENT

There is an interesting paradox here. The liberal position has been noted for its inability to motivate and sustain mass political activity and this is often traced back to its ideal of individualism. Much of the liberal literary aesthetic has been related to a similar source, particularly its tendency to regard autonomy (be it social, historical, political) as the quality that invests character with authenticity. Yet it was while his faith in mainstream liberalism was at its strongest that Walker produced the version of the Dunn story that most affronted this tenet of the liberal aesthetic of the period. The very integration of character and event that is the strength of *Proud Zulu* led to the type of criticism represented by Delius's review. Later however, although considerably disenchanted with the possibilities for liberalism in South Africa, Walker attempts, and fails, in *Zulu Royal Feather* to implement a form of characterisation identified with a liberal world view. This is not to suggest that work embodying a liberal ideology is necessarily and always a failure in the way depicted in these two novels. Walker certainly does not seem to understand precisely what is involved in his rewriting; he operates rather on a vague notion of a popular critical norm (and commercial principle) that reveals the powerful hegemonic pull of a prevailing aesthetic – one that is extremely damaging to his original conception of Dunn's story.

The point to be made here is that ideology stems from a lived sense of the world as much as from consciously held views, and that this can be a crucial factor when trying to trace the complex mediations between ideology and expression. In Walker's case, he was able to write a novel in which the integration of protagonist and context relates more to his own sense of positive political involvement than to the principles of his political stance: hence *Proud Zulu* is in form in many ways an atypical liberal work from a liberal at a period of intense liberal involvement. Out of this sense of firm oppositionality within the present, Walker is able to produce an effective sense of the past in its pastness. This in turn serves, through the difference it conveys to the present, as a concrete vehicle for a form of resistance to that present. The history embodied (textually) in Dunn reminds us of the materiality of the common allegiances that segregation denied.

In *Zulu Royal Feather*, Walker's sense of the marginalisation of his ideological position comes through in the awkward and unsuccessful rewriting of the relation of his protagonist to his historical context. With the erosion of his political position in the present comes his inability to validly call up the past as a mode of resistance to that present. Rather, the weaknesses of that present become inscribed in the past, and reduce it to a shallow picture of itself alone. History here loses the rich novelty that gives it its value for the perspective from which it is perceived.

Walker's uses of John Dunn tell us finally, then, more about Walker than about Dunn. We have considered the argument that history no less than fiction should be read for what it tells us of the moment of its production rather than its grasp of the past. But the contrast between Walker's two tellings of the Dunn story illustrate that we need not give an entirely free reign to the relativity of presentism, in fiction or history. The fact that we are able to identify moments in *Proud Zulu* where Walker manages to generate out of fictional form a vitally historicised perspective, and contrast these with his failure to do so with the same material in *Zulu Royal Feather*, tells us much not only about the present as history, but also about ways to evaluate uses of the past as history.

Walker's rewriting of Dunn's story loses much of his first version's ability to capture historical events in their difference from the present, and, in only an apparent irony, in so doing it diminishes its effectiveness as a medium for grasping the present. As it loses touch with the past through the way it formally accesses it, it becomes a rather thin representation of the present. And a corollary of this is that the past is so diluted as to become little more than a measure of its construction within the present. History, then, if it is to have an historical significance for the present, must be able to create the past powerfully enough, as Fredric Jameson resonantly puts it, 'to come before us as a radically different life form which rises up to call our own form of life into question and to pass judgement on us' (1988a:175). It is not enough to tell the history of the present through the past; it is the challenge to the present that the past may represent that is its most powerful form.

With this in mind, we will now return to the two historical novels which were used at the beginning of Chapter One to illustrate the ways in which fiction and history have been too firmly compartmentalised as forms of rhetoric. In examining the career and work of Sarah Gertrude Millin we shall pursue further the question of resistance in the relationship between the present and the past in the writing of history in fiction.

5

THE PRESENT
IN THE PAST

SARAH GERTRUDE MILLIN

————■————

An instructor is one who explains the causes
of a thing ... and the most knowable things are
first principles and causes, for it is through and
from these that other things are known.
— *Aristotle, Metaphysics*

When Fredric Jameson observes that 'the emergence of the historical novel was itself only a symptom of the increasing historicism of the novel in general' (1971:350), he is of course summarising Lukács's thesis in *The Historical Novel*. However much the kind of historicism I am proposing in this book may run counter to the structural terms of Lukács's historicism, his identification of the effect of the form originated by Scott at a particular historical moment is now generally agreed upon. James C. Simmons, in *The Novelist as Historian: Essays on the Victorian Historical Novel*, traces, for example, how seriously the early historical novelists took their influence upon the institutions of history to be. He suggests, even, another literary category for them, one meant to stress what we would now probably call the 'cross-disciplinary' nature of their enterprise: '... there developed in the 1830s and 1840s the concept of the historian-novelist. Writers such as Bulwer, Macfarlane, and Palgrave saw themselves in competition, not with their contemporary romancers, but with the formal historians of their day' (Simmons 1973:37). Further,

for them the historical romance became a vehicle for the popularization
and commercialization of the most recent findings of historical research.

115

These writers were not content to go to history for an exciting backdrop nor to portray an age merely through a representation of its costumes, manners, and architecture. The historical novel in their hands became a vehicle for the exegesis of the historical period, an exegesis from the perspective of an historian, not a romancer. (35-36)

If I may continue with my rather loose association of the 1940s and 1950s in South Africa with the period of the 'classical' historical novel in Europe, then the writer of fiction who perhaps most earnestly set out to influence the way in which South African history was written was Sarah Gertrude Millin.

It will be necessary in this chapter, as we have done with Oliver Walker, to situate the production and reception of Sarah Gertrude Millin's historical intervention through fiction carefully in order to establish its significance. We shall also make it our concern in this case to turn some of the issues we have been tracing in historical fiction back upon not just history writing in general as we have been doing, but more upon the discipline to which this book will most probably be seen as a contribution – for better or worse: that of literary history itself.

BLOOD AND POLITICS

In arguing against the kind of firm distinctions that usually exist between history and historical fiction, I put forward the proposition that historical fiction is often produced in response to ideological and social motivations similar to those that prompt historical revisionism. Certainly Smuts, in his Foreword to Sarah Gertrude Millin's *King of the Bastards* (published in 1949), saw the work as an act of historical revisionism:

> In our preoccupation with the Great Trek, the earlier phase of our history has been neglected. Here it stands, freed from the obscurity in which it has been buried for so long. We can now form a juster opinion of our beginnings, and of the formative forces which have shaped this history of ours. (1950:v)

Given the ideological use to which the Great Trek had been put in 1938 and the role this had had in his recent political defeat, one can easily understand Smuts's desire for a rethinking of the role of historical origins and parallels in contemporary politics. Whether it was wise of him to associate himself so closely with the historical perspective provided by Millin in *King of the Bastards* and its sequel is another question.

Millin had prided herself on what she saw as her political prominence in South African and international affairs. To the degree that this existed, it was achieved mainly through her friendship with Smuts and Hofmeyr. The defeat of the one and the death of the other left her with little political significance even in her own eyes. Hofmeyr's death in particular, however, had a further effect upon Millin: it removed the comparatively liberalising influence that her political associations had had on her thought. After 1948 Millin slid increasingly into the conservatism that would begin to turn her into an ardent proponent of the Nationalists she had previously vehemently opposed. The two historical novels with which she chose to return to fiction writing after a break of some eight years already make this clear, as we will see below, but we must first consider the route by which Millin came to these novels.

Millin's decision in the late 1940s to write fiction again after a long break was not unrelated to the frustration of her hopes in the political realm. The career of political writer that had preoccupied her during the war had shown signs of faltering even before 1948: that her mammoth five-volume *War Diary* was not a success was beginning to be obvious by the time the second volume was published in 1945. The strong degree of calculation with which she approached the relaunching of herself as a novelist is as a result understandable.

Millin's most prominent success as a writer had been her 1924 novel, *God's Stepchildren*; indeed, this is her only work to remain fairly constantly in print, and it is the novel that virtually invariably marks her place in standard literary histories. Given the implicit racism with which Millin handles its subject – the destructive effects of miscegenation – the work occupies an odd place indeed. Works are situated within the canon of the dominant poetics of recent years by virtue of their formal and moral exemplary nature; Millin's novel and, for that matter, her career, would thus normally be – as they in fact for some time were – simply excluded. As southern African literary history began to take itself seriously, however, it became difficult to ignore the single most prominent writer between Olive Schreiner and Nadine Gordimer. Millin thus enters the canon in much the same way as South African literature entered that most anachronistic of world literary categories, Commonwealth literature: as a decidedly dishonorary member. Invariably she is included on the grounds of reception rather than literary merit, and earns her place as the best English-speaking representative of her local audience's essentially racist character. Michael Wade puts this general argument most succinctly : '... it is fair to say,' he says of Millin's themes,

> that it is difficult to imagine a set of preoccupations more representative of the dominant obsessions of the white group in southern Africa in the period covered by Mrs Millin's novelistic activity – because in some ways Mrs Millin herself becomes a symbol, an embodiment of a certain ineluctable level of truth about South African society ... (1974:92)

Yet – and this is a point usually missed by literary critics – this is far too monolithic a conception of Millin's career if seen in terms of the reception of her work. *God's Stepchildren* did not make much of an impression in South Africa in 1924, or, for that matter, in the metropolitan centre with which South Africa had its strongest cultural ties: it did not sell well in Britain despite being critically well received there. It was in the United States that it scored its resounding success, becoming there, in a slightly cut and revised form, both critically acclaimed and a bestseller. While this established Millin's international reputation, however, it had little effect on her status in South Africa as a popular writer of fiction.

The work that did earn Millin a degree of recognition in her own country was her first work of non-fiction, *The South Africans*, which appeared in 1926 and was revised and enlarged in 1934 and again, under a slightly different title, in 1951. An impressionistic account of the country's history and society meant to explain the nation to the international community, it was, in only an apparent irony, enthusiastically received in South Africa but only very cautiously regarded in Britain and America. Whether this was because the misconception that seems to have attended much of the reception of *God's Stepchildren* – that the work exposes the tragedy of society's treatment of miscegenation, whereas it in fact treats miscegenation itself as a 'tragedy'[15] – could not have developed around the clear and overt racist distinctions that structure her 'factual' account of South Africa, is unclear. What does seem obvious is that, in attempting to revive her career, Millin drew upon (she actually combined) her greatest successes to that date.

---

15. Millin's rather suspect use of tragedy is discussed below.

After *God's Stepchildren* and *The South Africans*, the next high point in Millin's career (this time in Britain) was her biography *Rhodes* (1933). It is not surprising therefore that Millin should have decided to employ the form of historical biography in her return to fiction. *God's Stepchildren* had had an historical element: in it Millin had traced the effects of the 'sin' of miscegenation through the Biblically-sanctioned four generations of a family. The original sin was magnified in its being not a casual sexual encounter, but a deliberate act on the part of a missionary who aimed, superficially at least, to give physical substance to his philosophy of racial equality. This missionary, the Reverend Andrew Flood, was based loosely on Dr Johannes van der Kemp. Millin refers to the historical Van der Kemp in *The South Africans*, where another major figure in the history of miscegenation which so appalled and yet fascinated her, Coenraad de Buys, also appears. What better point from which to make a come-back? – develop the historical link between Van der Kemp and De Buys, fill their histories out into individual stories, and weave these strands into the warp of South African history given in *The South Africans*.

Perhaps this creative strategy was not initially so clear cut, but certainly in the wake of the success of *King of the Bastards* (Millin's vehicle for the story of De Buys) upon its release in 1949 a definite publishing campaign linking all these works takes shape: in 1951 *God's Stepchildren* was reissued with a new preface by the author, and in the same year Millin released *The People of South Africa*, the third version of *The South Africans* referred to above. Nineteen fifty-two then saw the publication of *The Burning Man*, the sequel to *King of the Bastards*. Much of the same historical and biographical material used in *King of the Bastards* is reworked in *The Burning Man*, this time from the perspective of Van der Kemp. Indeed, whole sections of the first novel are simply repeated in the second, while both works feature pages and pages of historical background lifted word for word from *The South Africans*.

Whatever literary limitations such an approach to publishing may suggest, South African readers proved ready for this barrage. As we have had occasion to note before, '*King of the Bastards* was then one of the bestselling novels in the history of South Africa', Millin's biographer, Martin Rubin, tells us, continuing, 'and its success is an indication of how Sarah Gertrude typified her white countrymen's views on colour' (1977:28). All the works mentioned in this project are in fact saturated with the brand of biologically-based racism that is the speciality of Millin's factualisation and fictionalisation of race. Rubin does favour bland one-to-one generalisations about the relation between the attitudes of Millin the writer and her South African readers; his thesis is, after all, that Millin is representative of these attitudes, as is indicated by his sub-title: *A South African Life*. While the connection he claims may be simplistic, it does at least raise, if not answer, some questions all too often left untouched by critics on Millin who simply treat *God's Stepchildren* as a representatively South African text. Why should *King of the Bastards*, universally adjudged by these critics to be far inferior to *God's Stepchildren* – even at the level of readability – as a literary work, have found success where *God's Stepchildren* had not? More significantly, why do critics continue to treat *God's Stepchildren* as *the* indicator of South African racism in literature?

David Rabkin, for example, writes that '*God's Stepchildren* was immediately popular, recognised by South Africans as the plausible and articulate ejaculation of their racial nightmares' (1978:79). In fact, Millin was bitter and resentful at her own country's indifference to her international success in the 1920s. 'While papers like the *New York World*, *Times*, *Post*, and critics like Mencken, Bromfield, Stallings were comparing me to the best they could think of,' she wrote, 'in South Africa I was referred to as "among South Africa's lesser-known writers" – though who the better-known writers were I can't think; or I was classed with anyone who had ever written a book at all, even an unpublished book' (1941:161).

We must be careful, then, of even the more carefully stated correspondence Stephen Clingman makes between the importance which race assumed in the South Africa of the 1920s, as evidenced by the proliferation of racial legislation in this decade, and the social significance of *God's Stepchildren* (see Clingman 1988).

Racism is protean in its forms, and its variations are obviously significant. That Millin's conceptualisation of race was predominantly biological is without doubt; one of the finest accounts of her work, J.M. Coetzee's essay 'Blood, flaw, taint, degeneration: The case of Sarah Gertrude Millin', traces in some detail the intellectual history of Western European racism upon which Millin draws. Coetzee makes it plain that he is concerned with 'the poetics of blood rather then the politics of race' as it is through the former that 'Millin's imagination works' (1980:42). Further, he feels free to trace this mythico-biological emphasis in Millin's work 'without regard to chronology and with minimal regard to context' because 'Millin's ideas on blood and race, and the complex of feelings that underlay these ideas, changed little between 1920 and 1950' (50). Quite so; but the same cannot be said of her audience.

Writing of the development of the concept of segregation in the South African context, Paul Rich states in *White Power and the Liberal Conscience* that

> the important point about segregationist ideology was that it did not incorporate in any significant manner the tradition of European biological racism, which was easily available to a settler regime seeking to defend its ostensibly 'racial' identity. It could perhaps have done so, for the phase of late nineteenth-century expansion of European imperialism certainly acted as a powerful fillip to the tradition of race-thinking which went back to the eighteenth century.(1984c:124)

Rich proposes a distinction between conceptualising segregation in biological and territorial terms to account for this:

> ... the general conclusion can be made that South African racial ideology did not need to employ in quite the same manner theories of biological racial inferiority as in the American instance, since the concept of territorial racial separation acted as a form of cultural and ideological buffer (5),

a point which would help explain the extremely popular reception of *God's Stepchildren* in the United States, and serve as a clue perhaps to the reasons for its muted reception in South Africa in the 1920s.

The few instances of the use of biological determinism in support of the ideology of segregation before Union were, Rich notes, 'of a second-hand variety, resting on the claims of the American race theorist, Robert Bennet Bean, Professor of Anatomy at the University of Virginia, that Negro brains were inferior to Caucasian ones' (5). South African segregationist thought did allow itself the comparative luxury of developing a racist cast of a more biological bent, but this was only after settling the more materially pressing claims of territorial domination. After the 1913 Native Lands Act and the 1923 Natives (Urban Areas) Act had solidly established rural and urban segregation, space could be made for inter-racial mediation – an area of course where South Africa's liberal tradition, safely paralysed politically, could be drawn in. To follow Rich again:

> If white racism *per se* could produce no new categories of analysis [for race-thinking], the compensating influence from the liberal

tradition of missionary interest in African societies, and the experience
of cultural and social mediation between African and white settler
societies, ensured a fund of expertise which the nascent settler state
could not ignore. (124)

Hence the growing inclusion of some major strands of liberal thought, whatever
its original orientation, in the construction of an ideology of segregation suitable
for a modern industrial state.

Millin's work of the 1920s would appear to be in line with exactly this
development, her own shift from the cautious liberalism of her earlier years to
her later overt segregationism finding its crucial ideological hinge on the issue of
biological racial determinism. The poetics of blood is a powerful weapon in the
ideology of race, which in itself is a persuasive way of accounting for the politics
of segregation, and it is true that it is in this respect that Millin may have found
what Wade calls, in a different context, 'liberalism's true voice in the situation'
(1974:107). The evidence of literary reception would suggest, however, something
of a cultural lag in the popular recognition of these issues. While other factors –
such as the status of local publications in South Africa in the mid-1920s, and the
all-out assault launched by Millin and her publishers in the 1949-1952 period –
must be taken into account, the reception *King of the Bastards* and *The Burning
Man* received on publication is a significant indicator of a distinct cultural shift in
white English-speaking South Africa. This would suggest too that the literary-
historical emphasis on *God's Stepchildren* has led to an underestimation in social
history of the significance of the later historical novels.

It is perhaps worth wondering whether this underestimation is a result of our
being still too used to perceiving our literary history from a metropolitan
perspective. Neither of the historical novels did well internationally, especially in
the United States. 'After *King of the Bastards*,' writes Rubin, '[Millin's] American
publisher, Harper, had refused to renew her contract and [*The Burning Man*] had
appeared under the seal of G.P. Putnam's Sons. After the almost universal
condemnation of *The Burning Man*, however, no New York publisher would
accept any of her fiction' (1977:230). Without wishing to claim that the overt
racism of the novels was the only factor in this, the resurgence of liberalism (in a
more internationally accepted sense) which accompanied America's involvement
in the Second World War did, according to Rich, challenge the 'caste explanations
for race relations [which] had been much in vogue in the 1930s in the United

States' (1984c:130). This resurgence would make it less likely that such overtly racially saturated works would be sympathetically received there. However, American indifference or hostility cannot exonerate the failure of South African literary history to deal with works which, whatever their fate in the United States, were enthusiastically welcomed in South Africa.

MORALITY TALES FOR THE IMMORALITY ACT

It is to the historical form of these novels we must now turn in our examination of their significance. Much of their popularity is likely to have been due to this element; as mentioned earlier, the increase in nationalist sentiment in post-war white South Africa had prompted an increase in historical awareness, one of the cultural manifestations of which was a greater interest in and production of historical novels. Certainly Millin's historical perspective lent itself to popular consumption as it drew upon, confirmed, and even helped foster many of the most ingrained biases in popular white conceptions of South African history.

Her choice of narrative period for her paired novels is telling in itself in this respect: the Eastern Cape frontier of the late eighteenth and early nineteenth centuries reverberates through conventional histories of South Africa as the crucible of Afrikaner nationalism. Its twin themes of conflict between black and white and resistance to British imperialism find vital originary moments in the events of this period. Millin's choice of protagonists is equally revealing: De Buys, the voor-Voortekker, and Van der Kemp, who precedes John Philip in prompting the antagonism believed to have caused the Trek itself, are excellent contrasts around which to polarise such an account of South African history. What makes them irresistible to Millin as central representatives of the actual and potential 'tragedy' of that history is their common bond in miscegenation, always her own strongest theme.

To return to Smuts's Foreword to *King of the Bastards*; he applauds the shift of historical emphasis back a generation or so, but what is the result of this shift? 'The tragedy of colour which is South Africa stands revealed for all to see it [*sic*]', writes Smuts, who then invites us to contemplate it 'in wonder and awe, but not in despair' (v). This is an invitation the novels ignore; Millin never achieves anything like a sense of wonder or awe in her depiction of De Buys, or for that matter, Van der Kemp – indeed, this is quite obviously never her intention. Their lives are simply morality tales for the Immorality Act. For those who break the law sanctioned by nature itself there is only despair, and not of the tragic sort either.

It is true that Millin does make a half-hearted attempt to work De Buys up into something of a tragic figure, just as she had attempted to give a Hardyesque sense of tragic inevitability to *God's Stepchildren*. The attempt fails for the same reason in the later novel as in the earlier one: as David Rabkin points out, 'the essence of [Millin's] proposition about miscegenation is that it is a voluntary act of evil' (1978:91). We will see that Millin tries hard to account for the complicity of her protagonists' own agency in their fall, but all references to a tragically determined fate eventually founder on this point. This makes the type of tragedy invoked by Smuts especially inaccurate.

Following A.C. Bradley's definition of tragedy, Smuts writes of De Buys: '... what he might have been and achieved, under a better star! But there was a twist in him, as there sometimes is in great men ... His story reads like a Shakespearean tragedy moving to inevitable doom ...' (vii). Nothing could be further from the achieved effect of the novel, whatever Millin's intentions. De Buys's greatness remains a matter of his physical size throughout the work, and all too quickly even this becomes only an ironic counterpoint to the stature he can never regain in white eyes – and only briefly retain in black eyes before the 'magic' of his whiteness wears off – after 'going native'. While Smuts prefers to keep De Buys's 'tragedy' in the realm of the metaphysical and the aesthetic, Millin spells out its physical base bluntly in her explanatory notes to *King of the Bastards*: '[De Buys] might have come to be regarded as the greatest amongst his people, but for this one thing: his women were black: his families were the coloured rabble that ended as the Buys-volk, kept apart from other people in a land of their own' (viii).

King of the Bastards opens in a contemporary setting, 'the summer of 1948'. With the 26 May behind them, the 'council of the Buyses' discuss (yet again, we are told) whether or not the 'Buys people' should 'try for white'; they, indeed like Millin herself, have little idea of the increasingly bitter resistance to such a plan that lies ahead of them, but this would be, for Millin at least, incidental to their situation as it already stands. For if there is any tragedy in De Buys's story, it is here. One of the Buyses has suggested breeding their whitest children with whites, but, 'throughout their talk, none had spoken of the tragedy of Honoratus' daughter, the whitest in all the nation of the Buyses' (3). Neither has Millin at this point, but with this absence hovering in the background, she launches into Coenraad de Buys's history. After some 336 pages of his history, she concludes with a return to the contemporary scene where the Buyses are now about to vote on their proposed racial course; the outcome is not given, and the futility of voting at all is illustrated by a return to the unexplained reference haunting the story we have been told:

> Throughout their talk, none had spoken of the tragedy of Honoratus' daughter, the whitest of the Buyses – of what befell her when Louis sent her forth to bring back a white bastard for the descendants of Coenraad de Buys, *King of the Bastards.*
>
> Nor is this the place to speak of it,

writes Millin abruptly, before Louis Buys says, 'Let the people vote' (338). The strategy behind this refusal to fulfil the expectations she has set up is obvious: Millin refuses to spell out the tragedy of Honoratus's daughter in order to let the history which it frames flood in. The past echoes in the unspoken present.

What then is the explanatory nature of the history that Millin has to tell?

Firstly we should establish that Millin took her history fairly seriously. There is evidence that she engaged in a fair degree of research to write her historical novels; in her explanatory notes to *King of the Bastards* she mentions consulting 'the records in old registers, the words here and there of officials and missionaries' (viii), and Smuts writes of her 'buil[ding] up his great figure ... from sentences here and there in old records' (vi). The vagueness and paucity of sources claimed – stressed by the repeated 'here and there' – is unfair, however, at least to the travel writing of the period: she lifts, from Barrow and Lichtenstein especially, passages and even pages liberally. She certainly uses Van der Kemp's Diary of 1799-1801, and possibly A.D. Martin's biography *Dr Vanderkemp*, published in 1931. She even goes to Amsterdam to do research for *The Burning Man.* She seems, oddly enough, to have missed the one substantial publication available on De Buys, *Coenraad de Buys: The First Transvaler*, which A.E. Schoeman published in 1938, based on a thesis written for the University of Pretoria. She did, though, gather first-hand oral evidence from De Buys's descendants, which, as the final passage of *King of the Bastards* makes clear, was of seminal importance for the novels:

> 'They talk. But who will build for them, what will become of the world, when I am gone – old Michael de Buys, the son of old Michael de Buys, the son of Coenraad de Buys. WHITE MAN?'
>
> Those were the words that, spoken to the writer, begot this tale. (338)

What is more, in her notes Millin is overt about stating which sections of the story have 'some basis in fact', and which must 'be considered as romancing' (x). Like all historical novelists, the most telling parts of her re-creations are the perhapses and maybes of historical record. We must credit Millin with being honest in this regard, although it is difficult to remain patient with the significance she gives to these lacunae. In her interpretation of the facts available she remains solidly grounded in the 'settler school' (characterised by the tendency of the early historians to see the history of southern Africa virtually entirely from the perspective of the settler) of South African history writing – particularly with respect to blacks and missionaries – but she uses the gaps in the records to drive home this interpretation with a vengeance. In *King of the Bastards* this reaches its apogee in her account of De Buys's activities in Zululand. Millin writes in her notes to the novel:

> A white man is said to have taught Dingiswayo European ways of fighting and trading. Since the white man is not known and Coenraad disappeared into Zululand for a while, the liberty has been taken of making Coenraad that white man. This is the only deliberate inaccuracy in the novel; but for a gap of four years, it might not have been an inaccuracy, and who really knows about those four years? (ix)

Who, indeed! It is by no means certain, amongst all the other uncertainties here, that De Buys did go to Zululand. Preller claims he did, but Schoeman can find no evidence of this other than that if he did he could not have gone during the dates Preller gives (see Schoeman 1938:68). We are here in the heartland of some of the most deeply ingrained South African historical myths, however, where counter-factualisation carries very little weight. In her novels Millin gives support to nearly all the ten major myths that Marianne Cornevin lists in her *Apartheid: Power and Historical Falsification* (1980): whites and blacks arrived in South Africa at the same time, blacks were migrants until they met the whites, the Voortrekkers advanced into uninhabited land that belonged to no one, only the advent of the whites saved the blacks in the Orange Free State and the Transvaal, and so on, but she becomes truly offensive in her version of the myth that the black's original political ideas were always inspired by the whites. For, if Millin does not entirely agree with the myth that all Zulu leaders were bloodthirsty despots, this is only because she feels they lacked the ability effectively to be despots. Which is where

De Buys comes in: he, we are told, 'knew what the Amatetwa did not know; what any white man knew, but hardly a black man' (121). Dingiswayo must learn then from De Buys how to trade (with the Portuguese), fight ('there was a thing no African understood, and that was the drilling of armies into regiments' [122]), and nation-build ('"there are small peoples all around you whose power is nothing because they are separate. Let them come together under Dingiswayo of the Amatetwa. Thus a very great nation will be made"' [121]). In the narrative that follows, Chaka [sic] learns these lessons from Dingiswayo, and Mantatisi and Moselikatze [sic] learn the most destructive of them at least from Chaka. And so we have Millin's account of the 'Mfecane', with Coenraad de Buys now standing at the head of a genealogy of spilled as well as mixed blood. In an ironic counterpoint to recent rewritings of this 'event' in South African history, where Julian Cobbing has replaced black bloodlust as the central causal principle with white-inspired slave-trading, Millin situates a white man as the prime historical agent simply because, for her, blacks are incapable of significant historical agency.

De Buys gains little reward for his contribution to black culture, however; trekking in his old age into the northern Transvaal, he finds not the 'empty land' claimed by the Voortrekkers, but the devastation that is in the process of 'emptying' it. Thus his contribution to South African history, in this respect no less than in those of his sexual exploits, comes crashing ironically down on his own head. Having been crucially instrumental in setting off the process of destruction sweeping across southern Africa, he now becomes its victim. The poetic justice involved is no melodramatic coincidence, however: the 'idea [of introducing De Buys to the Zulus] was,' Millin tells us, 'to bring the Zulus into what is, in effect, the story – running parallel with Coenraad's – of the black man's total decline in South Africa' (ix-x). And it is with regret that she ponders, 'perhaps one should not have given up the idea of linking Coenraad with Mantatisi'; after all, how could so important an area of black history (even in its destructiveness) have been allowed to happen of its own volition?

What force could elevate a white man to such a pivotal position in black history? The answer is, as is always the case in Millin's 'tragic' view of race in South African history, the failure to recognise and maintain racial boundaries. De Buys has not only lived beyond the frontiers of white settlement, he has internalised the frontier in his sexual relations and can thus never again live on one side or the other. While an outlaw, it is his family of mixed blood which prevents him from ever properly taking up the various offers of pardon from different Cape governments; he and his 'farcically mongrel' (98) brood are rejected by family, society, and church when he attempts to resettle in the colony. Millin does not hesitate to project a fully developed apartheid mentality back on to the Eastern Cape frontier – indeed, it is precisely her own contribution to the past that she has projected forward into 1949. The double manoeuvre of inserting contemporary racial attitudes into the past and then finding the origins of those contemporary attitudes in the past is the defining move of her historiographical procedure. In this, of course, she was in no way alone, as the seminal work of Martin Legassick has helped expose (1980, esp. 65-67). Freed of this trope, Legassick is able to cite De Buys specifically in support of his thesis that contemporary South African racism cannot be directly attributed to earlier frontier attitudes.

Millin's racist preoccupations are driven to even more ludicrous lengths, however. 'Colour consciousness', we are told in *The South Africans*, is a 'profound feeling' that can only be overcome by one other biological force: sexual desire (255-56). And for sexual desire to choose to satisfy itself across racial lines it must be perverted in some way, which is how we come to the founding 'flaw' underlying the whole panoramic saga of Coenraad de Buys.

De Buys's mother was married four times, an historical fact which leads Millin to a conclusion for which there is no evidence whatsoever: she murdered her husbands (a 'deliberate inaccuracy' she fails to mention as such). Millin, as we have seen, had a predilection for repeating material, and the research on the symptoms of strychnine poisoning she had done for her novel based on the Daisy de Melker case, *Three Men Die* (1934), finds a new use in Christina de Buys's method of removing her husbands. The young Coenraad is meant to have discovered and observed his mother's murderous ways (his father was Christina's second husband), and as a result has been put off white women for life. We are laboriously and unconvincingly reminded of this throughout the novel.

Why does Millin invent this melodramatic and sensationalist account of De Buys's preference for black women? The novel is written some ten years before E.H.Erikson's *Young Man Luther* made psychohistory a controversial genre, and Millin's comment on the 'good wizards' of tribal life ('They were what are today called psycho-analysts ...' [129]), suggests no great love for the profession. To appreciate more fully the actual strategy involved here, we must defer answering the question until we have considered Millin's representation of Van der Kemp.

To what degree De Buys is aware of the source of his taste in sexual preference is never quite stated. That he recognises it as a folly that will determine the coming to nothing of all his potential is, though, the only rag of respect left him in the reader's eyes. Van der Kemp is denied even this insight. In both *King of the Bastards* and *The Burning Man* (1952) he is a pathetic figure, rejected ultimately even by De Buys for his failure to recognise his sexual hypocrisy. A central passage from *King of the Bastards*, which becomes word for word the opening passage of *The Burning Man*, has Van der Kemp introduce his black wife to De Buys with the words:

'How much have I learned from you, my friend! Do you remember your words to me? "You do not, as I," you said, "live with them and through them to prove there is no difference between black and white!" How deep a lesson that was to my groping mind!'

De Buys responds, 'Verdomde hypocrite!' and continues:

'I taught you this! Where was I when you were running around the brothels of Leyden? ... And I will tell you, you lie when you say you learned from me to show there was no difference between black and white. You knew me, what I was – a sinner, an outcast. And I will tell you, the whole thing is you are still the man that danced in the brothels of Leyden; and a worse man, with the madness of age, not youth, on you; and not any more a wild soldier, but a Christian minister teaching the way of God is for an old man to satisfy himself with a little black girl.' (*King of the Bastards*, 186-87; *The Burning Man*, 1-2)

The reference to Leyden is meant to remind us of the lust that is the constant in the life of this vacillating protagonist. Throughout the novel he is referred to as a 'divided man' in every other respect; this is the thematic refrain around which the work is constructed, to the degree that it could just as well have been entitled *The Divided Man*. It is significant, however, that it is not.

We first meet the young Johannes van der Kemp rejecting his brother Didericus (just appointed Professor of Ecclesiastical History at Leyden University) as a 'superstitious man in the Age of Enlightenment and Reason' (6). Shortly after, he is rejected by his mistress as 'no genuine child, like me, of the Age of Enlightenment and Reason' (22) because he is unable to break completely with the religious and moral conventions of the time. He is continually finding himself in situations of divided allegiance, as in this typical passage summarising his position during the French invasion of Holland:

> ... in this ..., as in other passionate things, Johannes was a divided man. On the one hand, his thoughts marched with the French Revolutionaries and he felt for the down-trodden; on the other, he could not forget his allegiance to the Stadtholder and the traditions of his class. (51)

Yet he must remain in Millin's characterisation a 'burning' rather than a 'divided' man; this is because intellectual confusion of itself could not provide the essential ingredient needed for his failure within the novel's paradigm. Johannes's rational argument with Didericus in the opening scenes, for example, is reduced to mere intellectual posturing before his brother's damning reference to his 'dissipated existence' (5), and all Van der Kemp's other struggles pale before his difficulties in controlling his sexual passions. And so the significance of the title comes to the fore; as Millin quotes in her explanation of the title: '"burn" means here ... "to be perpetually haunted with lustful desires"'. It is essential to Millin's thesis that it must ultimately be Van der Kemp's lust, rather than any intellectual confusion, that condemns his potential abilities.

Van der Kemp is cast in the same false tragic mould as De Buys: a man of great potential (as too in the case of De Buys, this is a potential claimed rather than ever really demonstrated in the novel) destroyed by a flaw in his character. He is exceptionally talented in many areas – medicine, theology, philosophy, and science are mentioned – but throws away careers in all of them. The flaw that causes him to do this is damaging enough in Europe, but there at least it is limited to the personal realm. Transported to Africa in a religious fervour it will have a far more destructive effect, all the more so for being wrapped up in European ideals that have no place in Africa.

That the tragic flaw at the heart of *The Burning Man* is not the confused Enlightenment philosophy of its protagonist can be demonstrated by considering Millin's attitude to the swiftly changing rulers at the Cape in the period covered by her novels. Of these, Millin has most sympathy with the short-lived Batavian government. This sounds incongruous, given her attitude to the principles of the Revolution as applied to South Africa, until we see her depiction of Commissioner De Mist and Governor Janssens. Both had known Van der Kemp in Holland, and we are given extended scenes of their meetings with him. (In the case of Janssens, these substantially follow Lichtenstein's first-hand accounts gathered while he served as Janssens's medical attendant.) We can note in passing how close Millin's interpretation of South African history is to ongoing hegemonic historical attitudes, for what emerges from her re-creation is extraordinarily close to the ambivalent attitude Dean, Hartman, and Katzen find expressed in mid-seventies school textbook accounts of these figures. Boyce, they quote by way of an example useful to us here, writes of De Mist and Janssens in his *Legacy of the Past*: 'Both men were firm believers in the principles of the French Revolution – liberty and equality – nevertheless they were practical men and able administrators' (1983:99). 'Why "nevertheless"?' ask Dean *et al.*, continuing,

> Why should believers in equality not be practical and able? Van Rensburg *et al.* [in *Active History*] have almost the same thing: 'Liberals as they were, they nevertheless believed in strong government, and though much attracted by the ideas of equality and brotherhood, they were shrewd and practical men.' (63)

For Millin, no less than the historians in question, the word 'nevertheless' refers to the two officials' tendency to take local conditions into account – which certainly covers the crucial area of race. In the novels, De Mist and Janssens are depicted as remaining 'practical' chiefly in their withdrawing of the initial support they had given to Van der Kemp's religious settlements. This was in fact largely just a side-effect of their decision that reconciliation of the trekboers to the government should become the central focus of their frontier policy (see Ross 1986), and it seems likely that even the trekboers' complaints regarding Botha's Farm, Fort Frederick, and ultimately Bethelsdorp, had as much to do with labour as race. But Millin, as we may expect, makes race the overwhelming factor. Here is her version of De Mist on the difference between Janssens and himself and Van der Kemp:

> '... he is, while we are not, absolute in his requirement of Liberty, Equality, Fraternity. We clap eyes on the savages of the land and our senses recoil from accepting them as our free and equal brothers, or indeed, as our brothers at all.' (257)

Janssens himself is even stronger in his prejudice and rejection of the missionaries:

> 'For my part, I cannot look at our dark citizens – and especially the
> Hottentots – without feeling that to teach such savages the mysteries
> of the Christian religion is mere insanity.' (258).

De Mist regrets the limits of Enlightenment, to be sure, but in the ensuing conversation agrees with Janssens that practical maintenance of order ('Do not feats of the mind, as of the body, depend on control? Is not to be uncontrolled mad?' [258]) is of final importance.

In pure form, then, the principles of the Age of Enlightenment and Reason, in South Africa, become (and remain) in Millin's view as pathetically out of place as the grubby little rebellions of the 'Patriots' of silly and short-lived 'Republics' that punctuate the action of *The Burning Man* and *King of the Bastards*. Pragmatically tempered – especially in terms of race – some good can be allowed of the Enlightenment, but in the sexual realm especially its foolish idealism can reach 'tragic' proportions. Here, principles of equality, not to mention liberty and fraternity, unleash their full destructive power in disregarding racial divisions.

Nothing marks Van der Kemp as more misguided in Millin's eyes than his belief that he had 'reconciled religion with science. All men are the children of God. That is religion. All men belong to the same – the human – race. That is science' (262). The only undivided position Van der Kemp is able to come to in his life is in fact a false one. The truth lies rather in the words of the mature, sensible, practical, and good Cape resident, Mrs Matilda Smith, to Van der Kemp: '"Here the difference in race is so strong that only" – she paused; he waited – "only the power of sex seems able to overcome it"' (118). Mrs Smith shows questionable taste in becoming attracted to Van der Kemp – whom Millin obviously finds loathsome even physically – but Smith's opinion is sanctioned by being, as we have seen, directly that of the author.

Van der Kemp will later reject the Christian, if slave-holding, Mrs Smith in marriage in favour of his unconverted 'little black girl', thus loading irony on irony on to St Paul's injunction (quoted in the note to the title of the novel) that 'it is better to marry than to burn'. And so we see the divisions in Van der Kemp multiply into both marrying and burning. But a 'burning man', tortured by an implacable sexuality into his ultimate degradation, he must finally be. Millin can conceive of no intellectual, religious, or moral force – no matter how divided against itself – powerful enough to be so 'tragic'.

EXPLANATION AND HISTORY

This brings us to the most remarkable trick Millin has played on us throughout these historical novels. Its essence is that these are not, even in the terms they themselves suggest, historical novels at all. By this I mean they do not finally explain anything in historical terms, although this is what they purport to do. Millin engages another time in order, ostensibly, to analyse the origins of aspects of her own. The whole thrust of the novels, emphasised by the contemporary framing sequence that begins and ends *King of the Bastards*, is meant to make of the lives of Coenraad de Buys and Johannes van der Kemp historical causes of presently felt tragic effects. Explaining in terms of cause and effect, however, turns out to be more problematic than Millin, and perhaps we ourselves, have allowed.

It is fortuitous that the man whose most original and influential ideas dealt with the problem of causality should date from the period in which Millin's historical novels are set. Hume is in fact the philosopher Millin has Van der Kemp most admire. What is perhaps surprising about this philosopher, who is, of course, famous for his scepticism regarding causality, is that he initially found fame as an historian: after all, from Herodotus to Montesquieu to Voltaire, history was conceived of as the organisation of past experience in terms of cause and effect. Even mid-twentieth century arguments concerning the role of causation in historicism left E.H. Carr unruffled in his conviction that 'the study of history is the study of causes' (1987:87). More recently, however, causality has become suspect again in the detotalising historiographical strategies of writers like Foucault. For Foucault causality is a primary feature of linear, progressive history – be it Marxist, liberal, positivist, even empiricist – in its attempt to control or domesticate the past in the form of knowing it. He wishes to challenge the concept of 'continuous history' because, as we have seen in our introductory chapter and will consider again when we come to the work of Daphne Rooke, it is intimately related to the appropriation of all that is 'different' (including the past) by the unified 'subject' who is at the centre of discourses of power.

Such a perspective can, of course, be seen as a radical challenge to structures in power at present, or as implicitly conservative attempts by those same structures to prevent those oppressed by them from claiming a sense of subjectivity within history. No concept is innocent of context. In our analysis of Millin, however, its usefulness is evident. The causal links Millin establishes with her subjects draws them into an historical continuum in which they are made, as causes, to carry the blame for present ills. In the process she obscures the present material causes for those ills. By refusing to allow a difference between colonial and capitalist racial practice, she obscures the causes of the latter behind the effect of the former. In the process she loses the material motivations of the past as much as those of the present. As we have seen, she reads apartheid attitudes into the Eastern Cape frontier, and then, with the most surprisingly convincing (if the standard myths of South African history are anything to go by) sleight-of-hand, finds in the Eastern Cape frontier justification for apartheid attitudes.

Along the way Millin appropriates black history into white (via, as demonstrated above, Coenraad de Buys), making its most striking features knowable in ascribing their cause to a white instigator and architect, but leaving them their inherent villainy by making that cause its victim as well. It is not surprising that at the very moment she was pandering to white historical tastes by producing a string of colourful anecdotes about tribal history that reinforced the worst stereotypes of an otherwise ignored historical past, urban blacks were turning away from tribalism with a vengeance. At the very time Millin was producing these novels, *Drum* magazine, for example (as we have mentioned earlier and must return to at more length later), was drastically shifting its emphasis from the rural, tribal, and historical to the racy urban present (see Sampson 1983, esp. 29).

Yet Millin's use of causation in her historical appropriation is suspect in more than its chauvinism. When we say that one thing causes another, all that we actually observe, Hume demonstrated in *Treatise of Human Nature* (I, III, vi), is 'that like objects have always been placed in like relations of contiguity and succession' (quoted in Culler 1983:87). Causation, and in particular the temporal priority we accord to cause, is an interpretation of this relationship, as Nietzsche claims in his analysis of the trope that governs causality in *The Will to Power* (*Werke* 3:804):

> The fragment of the outside world of which we become conscious comes after the effect that has been produced on us and is projected a posteriori as its 'cause'. In the phenomenalism of the 'inner world' we invert the chronology of cause and effect. The basic fact of 'inner experience' is that the cause gets imagined after the effect has occurred'. (Quoted in Culler 1983:86)

This tropological inversion governs much history writing, as it does Millin's historical novels; the 'cause' (race attitudes of the late eighteenth-century and early nineteenth-century frontier situations) is imagined – here literally, in the form of the novels – after the 'effect' (mid-twentieth century apartheid). The normal hierarchy of cause and effect, Jonathan Culler reminds us, 'makes the cause an origin, logically and temporarily prior. The effect is derived, secondary, dependent upon the cause ... If,' however, he continues (following Nietzsche), 'the effect is what causes the cause to become a cause, than the effect, not the cause, should be treated as an origin' (1983:88). Which is precisely the figurative operation Millin has applied to race: in her novels contemporary racism 'causes' the racism she writes into the past, while ostensibly being an 'effect' of it. Claimed to be the 'origin' of contemporary racism, her depiction of racial attitudes in the past in fact finds its origin in contemporary racism.

All this is bad history, but – for our sins – history of sorts it remains. We have, to be thorough about Millin's causal chain, to go back yet a step further to find the originary moment when history itself disappears. The lives of De Buys and Van der Kemp may serve as causes for the present, but what, as it were, caused them? From what origins do their tragedies stem? Millin goes to great lengths to situate her protagonists historically, but how does she account for the crucial individual twists that make them what they are?

In *The Burning Man*, Van der Kemp asserts:

> 'I speak as a scientist no less than a missionary, when I say that history
> rather than nature makes one individual different from another.' (177)

The novels show him to be misguided as both a scientist and a missionary; *The Burning Man* and *King of the Bastards* are quite centrally designed to disprove, apparently in the laboratory of history, this statement. The experiment is entered into – in accordance with the assumption governing the terms in which it is carried out and therefore also its foregone conclusion – under conditions appropriate to the natural sciences, for Van der Kemp is wrong in that he has precisely inverted the necessary priorities of Millin's convictions. History has little, if anything, to do with the ultimate origins (in nature) of the tragedies the novels trace through time.

As I have been at pains to establish, the flaws that mark De Buys and Van der Kemp and through them and the history of which they are a part are, finally (as far as history is concerned), simply contingent. Lost in a murky pseudo-psychological, quasi-biological, ahistoric swamp, the origins of Christina de Buys's husband-murdering tendencies which had so telling an effect on her son Coenraad, and Johannes van der Kemp's ever-burning lust, are as quirkily unexplainable as any other historically irreducible given. As ultimate causes then, they are ahistorical and lack all explanatory power in historical terms. The source of the tragedy of mixed blood flowing through South African history, and more importantly, the cautionary metaphor for maintaining racial purity it actually is in Millin's work, slips away over the horizon of history, leaving its irrational stain as unexplained – in these terms – as ever.

Georg Lukács condemns those historical novelists who 'make history private, [who] turn it into an exotic, colourful panorama based upon some eccentric case of psychology' (1981:340). This is an excellent description of Millin's failure, although Lukács is speaking of another place and time, and other reasons for this failure. What makes it all the more intriguing that Millin should fail in this way is that it goes against her own enterprise. She genuinely seems to want to write history, but there is for her no history of race. It is a trans-historical given, and any attempt to explain it historically must then remain, at best, tautological. In much the same way, she genuinely wants to write a tragedy, but there can be no tragedy of race without a history to define it; all that is left otherwise is contingency, which is to say, farce.

No amount of rewriting alters the basic givens in Millin's writing; she is able to endlessly rework her ideas, transpose bits of text from one work to another, work up a sequel to a successful novel, and use history in her fiction all with ease because her fictional foundations remain – fundamentally ahistorically – constant. As a result, nothing in the past, or, for that matter, in the present or the future, is capable of being innovative. Nothing new can come of the passing of time, for eternal givens prevent the emergence of anything truly novel. Millin's historical novels erase not only history, but the generative power of originality that is inscribed into the very name given to the fictional form in which she works.

FICTIONAL AND LITERARY HISTORY

We may, in conclusion, draw together the arguments of the first two sections of this chapter. Millin presents racism in monolithic terms, identical across all South African history. As a result her historical novels lose any real historical sense, for their subject is treated ahistorically. Literary critics have tended to see Millin's career in monolithic terms, as a unitary expression of white South African racism. In doing so, have they not risked losing, in the case of Sarah Gertrude Millin, some of the nuances of a truly historically-based literary history? In both cases a sense of the past as effectively differentiated from the present is needed. Success in this represents the real achievement of literary and social history as much as historical fiction. The past must be called up in all its difference if it is to become what Jameson calls an 'active agent' (1988a:175) in its recreation. Or, as Jameson puts it elsewhere and we have quoted before, it is only in 'respecting the specificity and radical difference of the social and cultural past' that we may disclose 'the solidarity of its polemics and passions, its forms, structures, experiences, and struggles, with those of the present day' (1981:18). The truth of Jameson's paradox rests in the fact that a simple blurring of the present into the past does not constitute bringing present and past into a genuine relationship. The past only comes alive in relation to the present when it is constructed as resistant to the present; only when this is achieved can the present and the past be aligned in such a way as to reveal whatever community of interests they may share in a meaningful way. Setting up false similarities between present and past is to undercut real historical activity. This is demonstrated in Millin's failure to truly historicise her material through the strategies she uses in her two historical novels. Formally, they are more than willing servants of the present, and in not calling up the past through fictional structures capable of resisting that present, they lose touch with the past which is the ostensible object of their creation.

6

ROMANCING
THE PAST

DAPHNE ROOKE

■

What romance means is the capacity for a true
conception of history, a power of making
the past part of the present.
– *William Morris*

Literary histories are often inclined to use the terms 'historical novel' and 'historical
romance' almost interchangeably. If any distinction is attributed to these categories,
it is usually used to emphasise the distance between 'literature' and 'history' as
far as factual accuracy is concerned; 'romances', as we saw in our study of Plaatje,
are considered not only to take more liberties with what *actually* occurred in the
past, but also to relate the past to the present less seriously than 'novels' do. The
generally dismissive 'historical' attitude towards uses of the past in fiction explains
the running together of 'romance' and 'novel'.

It should be clear by this point in my argument that it is necessary to bring the
assumptions behind terminological distinctions (or lack of them) of this sort to
the surface – not in order to claim or reclaim for them any defining characteristics
intrinsic to the form they describe, but rather to examine the significance of how
they are deployed in specific times and places.

'Romance' was given a particular place in our analysis of Plaatje, and elements
of this will serve to link it as an appropriate term for our consideration of its very
different status in the work of Daphne Rooke. What will chiefly be held in common
between these two very different senses of 'romance' is their potential for serious
consideration within the activity of historicisation.

REGION AND ROMANCE

'Natal,' Shula Marks reminds us, is 'the smallest and least politically influential of the four provinces of what became the Union of South Africa in 1910' (1986:10). This state of affairs, noted here by one of the region's most influential historians, has not surprisingly been reflected in the histories of South Africa. The editors of *Natal and Zululand: A New History* comment upon the fact that it was not until 1965 that any substantial historical works on south-east Africa were produced. In doing so they even find it necessary to point out that this is because the region – now known as KwaZulu-Natal – has been 'greatly neglected', and not because it deserves to be 'dismissed as an unimportant sideshow in the history of southern Africa' (Duminy and Guest 1989:xvii).

South African literary history has taken a similar shape. The country's most famous novel may well begin and end in the obscure valley of Ndotsheni in then-Natal, but the bulk of its action must migrate to Johannesburg to be of significance. Literary reputation too, regardless of its region of origin, must prove capable of migrating to the metropolitan centres to be established. The work of the novelist who may best lay claim to being *the* KwaZulu-Natal writer has, until recently, not been deemed worthy of such recruitment. Daphne Rooke, of whom a *Guardian* reviewer in the mid-sixties wrote, 'Gordimer, Lessing, Rooke, and the greatest of these is Rooke', has, until the recent Chameleon Press re-issue of some of her books, been all but dismissed or ignored by the South African literary establishment. It is of at least passing significance for my argument here that her most popular and famous work, *Mittee* (first published in 1951 and recently reissued in the Penguin Classics series), is not set in KwaZulu-Natal; this despite the fact that a case can be made for seeing as the core of her real achievement as a writer a set of four novels intimately concerned with KwaZulu-Natal: *A Grove of Fever Trees* (her first novel, originally published as *The Sea Hath Bounds* in 1946), *Ratoons* (1953), *Wizards' Country* (1957), and *A Lover for Estelle* (1961). Between them, these novels represent perhaps one of the most searching literary explorations of a region in South Africa, yet they have drawn little comment in general and none at all from a regional perspective.

Tellingly, this may be for reasons not unrelated to the marked historiographical suspicion surrounding the more visible moments of KwaZulu-Natal's history: that is, the way these lend themselves to romanticisation. Of the two works published in 1965 which Duminy and Guest say mark 'Natal's' emergence into

South African history writing, only one is a 'serious' history, Brookes and Webb's *A History of Natal* (1965); the other is a 'popular' history, Donald R. Morris's *The Washing of the Spears* (1966), which is usually dismissed from overviews of the literature on KwaZulu-Natal because of its 'amateur', romantic treatment of its material. Mackeurtan's (1930) and Lugg's (1948) earlier works on the region are largely discarded by historians for much the same reason, and the event that will most concern us here, the Anglo-Zulu War, is notorious for the flood of highly romanticised, mostly amateur, historical writing it unleashed.

The 'romantic' exists, of course, in weak and strong forms, although distinctions in this regard are notoriously controversial. It is difficult to relate the undeniable historiographical weaknesses of the abovementioned historians of KwaZulu-Natal to the common literary comparisons made by reviewers between Rooke's work and that nineteenth-century English novel most peculiar in its romanticism, *Wuthering Heights*, but it is the contention of this chapter that we must renegotiate the similarities and distinctions that emerge from just such a relation – especially in so far as the rendering of history is concerned.

'Romanticism' is applied to *Wuthering Heights* in a variety of senses. Most often critics wish to establish, along with Elizabeth Jennings in her Introduction to the Pan edition, the novel's 'Romantic quality, its kinship with Byron and Keats' (1967:7), but in so doing they also have to deal with what critics like Derek Traversi call 'the commonplaces of romantic inspiration' which 'play a great part in [the] novel' (1958:260-61). *Wuthering Heights*'s 'true significance lies in the transformation of this romanticism through the operation of an intensely personal imaginative power' (261), claims Traversi, going on to defend this by noting that all tendencies towards romantic sensationalism in the novel, all its potentially melodramatic elements, are controlled by and yet also inform a concrete realism. It is to a similar mix of genres that Lily Rabkin refers when she points out that Rooke's 'study of intense passions in a naturalistic setting is not a new literary device' (1952:37); Rabkin is attempting to defend Rooke's work in the face of the indifference or antagonism it met at the hands of contemporary local reviewers by placing it in a recognised tradition, but in 1948, just four years before this defence, F.R. Leavis had in one stroke both defined and marginalised that particular tradition.

I have no wish to engage in some belated anti-Leavisism, but *Wizards' Country* did appear in the middle of an ongoing debate regarding generic distinctions that is relevant to the reception of Rooke's work. In *The Great Tradition*, Leavis explains his now-(in)famous relegation of the Brontës to a 'Note' at the end of the introductory chapter by telling us that he has 'said nothing about *Wuthering Heights* because that astonishing work seems to me a kind of sport' (1962:38). A 'sport' 'deviates strikingly from the type of its species' (*OED*), and it is in this biologically-based sense that Leavis refers to what he perceives as a mating of romance and realism in Emily Brontë's novel; in it, he says,

> she broke completely and in the most challenging way, both with the Scott tradition that imposed on the novelist a romantic resolution of his themes, and with the tradition coming down from the eighteenth century that demanded a plane-mirror reflection of the surface of 'real' life. Out of her a minor tradition comes ... (38)

Less than a decade later, and in the same year as the publication of *Wizards' Country*, Richard Chase argued in his *The American Novel and its Tradition* (1960 [1957]) that if situated in terms of an American 'great tradition', *Wuthering Heights* would find a place well within the mainstream. It has now become something of a commonplace for critics, especially those working outside established realist (and metropolitan) canons, to challenge Ian Watt's claim (also first made in 1957) that the 'lowest common denominator of the novel genre as a whole' is 'its formal realism' (1974:37), on the grounds that such a definition leads to the pejorative evaluation of those prose works which cannot primarily be characterised as striving only for the fictional effect of realism. From the time of Nathaniel Hawthorne, at least, these critics remind us, writers and scholars have felt the need to distinguish works which 'claim a certain latitude' ('Romances') from those committed to the mimetic fidelity expected of a 'Novel' (Hawthorne 1851:iii). More modern versions of this debate, of course, valorise the kinds of 'hybridity' which cross traditional generic strains – especially the realist and the romantic – but this was not the atmosphere in which Rooke's work was received.

I must stress the issue of reception at this point, because what is at issue, as I mentioned above but must re-emphasise here, is not some generic essence 'in' the work, but how specific generic assumptions allow the work to be – or not be – accommodated within particular critical practices. To return to the 'effulgence' of which the compilers of the *Companion to South African English Literature* (Adey *et al.* 1986:170) accuse the anonymous reviewer who placed Rooke above Lessing and Gordimer: Lessing has gone on to be taken up by an international audience now more involved with her extra-terrestrial and futuristic visions than her Rhodesian roots, but Gordimer's status as the premier southern African novelist has largely depended upon the reception of her work on essentially realist terms. Rooke, on the other hand, has slipped out of sight because she has worked in a form that has not lent itself to this formal reflex of both the national and international perspective on South Africa.

Paul Rich opens his essay 'Romance and the Development of the South African Novel' with an identification of precisely such a dominant critical focus: 'the critical evaluation of English South African Novels has been mainly dictated by the norms of literary realism' (1984b:120). He goes on to question, however, 'how far this tradition can be seen as defining the history of the South African novel' (121). He persuasively argues for an acknowledgment that South African fiction (including Gordimer) 'has developed as much out of [the] romance genre as it has out of literary realism' (122), a fact which he says is emerging all the more clearly since the historically-provoked crises in the conventional realist genre in South Africa. In reacting against realism, 'what is beginning to emerge in South African fiction is a partial restoration to the romance mode through the idiom of literary post-modernism', says Rich (133). While he is interested in pointing towards this development, his main concern is to illustrate the important romantic strain which has been present in South African fiction from its inception. Most centrally however, he looks forward to a progressive purging of this anti-historical influence: 'romance formulas remain deeply embedded within the South African literary experience and it may, indeed, take generations of urban living before the nostalgia for the pastoral and idyllic is finally driven from its heart' (135).

In this Rich joins the ranks of those critical of the elitist and idealist tendencies of South African post-modernism (see Rich 1982). Another tradition of criticism in South Africa, perhaps best represented in the work of David Attwell, has argued for post-modernism's serious engagement with the historical (see Attwell 1990b, for example). While these critics have not marshalled their case around the issue of romanticism, it is perhaps worth reviving this element in the debate. I do not intend to take up the issue of post-modernism *per se* here, but I do think it is significant that it is only in the wake of its challenge to the dominance of realism in southern African literature and criticism that these practices have proved more accommodating to the romantic elements within themselves. What is needed is a reading of romanticism back into the historicity it is normally assumed to write itself out of or negate. With this concern before us, I believe the case of Daphne

Rooke may still prove a crucial one to the rewriting of a southern African literary history. Whereas Rich highlights the romantic strand within works canonised into a dominant realist tradition, Rooke's novels have been, I would argue, entirely marginalised from any such canon largely because of their romantic orientation. This orientation is intimately intermingled with historical concerns, and as such, makes Rooke's work a prime site upon which to argue for a revaluation of the romantic and the historical.

Ian Glenn, representing the recently renewed interest in Rooke, has called her 'the most serious historical (as opposed to political) novelist of South Africa' (1987:2). This is a formulation we have had occasion to consider earlier in this book. Here, however, it is not just Rooke's status as an 'historical novelist' that I wish to consider, for it is impossible to divorce the issue of romance from her approach to the historical. Indeed, I believe it is precisely her 'romanticism' that has hindered others from reaching Glenn's accurate evaluation of her work earlier. Before turning to a closer assessment of Rooke's work, it will be necessary to consider some contemporary conceptions of the relationship between romanticism and history.

Romanticism and History

Post-modernism's heightening of our awareness of romanticism is not arbitrary. Hayden White has identified an important strand of romanticism in post-modernism, significantly within its historical consciousness; when he claims, for example, in 'Foucault Decoded: Notes From the Underground', that 'Foucault represents a continuation of a tradition of historical thought which originates in Romanticism' (1986:256), it is on the grounds that what Foucault and the Romantics hold in common is a desire to defamiliarise the past. For Foucault this involves, says White, an

> utter unconcern for the staple conventional history of ideas: continuities, traditions, influences, causes, comparisons, typologies, and so on. He is interested, he tells us, only in the 'ruptures,' 'discontinuities,' and 'disjunctions' in the history of consciousness, that is to say, in the *differences* between the various epochs in the history of consciousness, rather than the similarities. (234)

This is obviously in itself a radical break with the discipline of history as it has been constituted since the nineteenth-century revolution in historical consciousness. It is worth quoting White's characterisation of conventional historiography at some length for the clear sense it conveys of the opposition conventional historiography presents to the emphasis upon *difference* favoured by Foucault:

> Since historians always deal with a subject matter that is strange, and often exotic, they often assume that their principal aim should be to render that subject matter 'familiar' to their readers. What appears strange at first glance must be shown in the course of the narrative to have had sufficient reasons for its occurrence and therefore susceptible to understanding by ordinary informed common sense. Since all things historical are presumed to have had their origins in human thought and practice, it is supposed that a vaguely conceived 'human nature' must be capable of recognising something of itself in the residues of such thought and action appearing as artifacts in the historical record … Hence the essentially *domesticating* effect of most historical writing. By rendering the strange familiar, the historian divests the human world of the mystery in which it comes clothed by virtue of its antiquity and origination in a different form of life from that taken as 'normal' by his readers. (256)

I have quoted White on Foucault, rather than Foucault himself, because we may trace a shift in White's own attitudes on these issues which is revealing for our purposes. The quotations given above are from an essay originally published in 1973, and then again in the 1978 collection *Tropics of Discourse*. As its title suggests, all the essays in *Tropics of Discourse* are gathered around the concept of history as an essentially narrative enterprise, identifiably so in even the most unlikely cases (Foucault for example) in terms of the four governing tropes White finds at a deep structural level in all his examples. This is a useful and often illuminating exercise, but there is something cumulatively irritating about the way in which each analysis in the volume predictably ends in the production, like a rabbit from a hat, of these tropological structures. They come across as, ironically (given that White's subject is the representation of history), alarmingly ahistorical; their effect is also pre-eminently domesticating: the most dissonant material is shown to be comprehensible in terms of the fixed rhetorical structures of metaphor, metonymy, synecdoche, and irony.

However, when White approaches a similar topic (although not in relation to Foucault) in his 1982 essay 'The Politics of Historical Interpretation: Discipline and De-Sublimation', he is far more open to the reflexivity of his own radical insights. Discussing the transformation of historical studies into a discipline, he demonstrates that a necessary feature of this process was the subjugation of the utopian impulse which springs from perceiving the past as truly *different* from the present. In making the past explainable, the discipline of history *domesticates* it or, in Enlightenment terms, reduces it from the 'sublime' (in which awe, even revulsion, prompts a utopian reaction) to the 'beautiful' (in which all difference is reduced to an aesthetically acceptable pluralism). This is a feature of all modern philosophies of history, even those apparently most diametrically opposed to each other. For in this sense even

> Marxism is anti-utopian insofar as it shares with its bourgeois counterpart the conviction that history is not a sublime spectacle but a comprehensible process, the various parts, stages, epochs, and even individual events of which are transparent to a consciousness endowed with the means to make sense of it in one way or another. (129)

What may one posit in place of this disciplinisation of history? A return, of sorts, for

> prior to the nineteenth century, history had been conceived as a spectacle of crimes, superstitions, errors, duplicities, and terrorisms that justified visionary recommendations for a politics that would place social processes on a new ground. (129)

It is here then we must return to our theme of romanticism, for, says White, 'Romanticism represented the last attempt in the West to generate a visionary politics on the basis of a sublime conception of the historical process' (129). He concludes his article by looking forward to 'a recovery of the historical sublime which bourgeois historiography repressed in the process of its disciplinization' (136).

HISTORY AND IDENTITY

There is an important connection here (despite the critical distance) between this historiographical point and the way in which Georg Lukács accounts for the founding of the historical novel as an historically-situated genre. Lukács denies the common assumption that Walter Scott ranks among the first Romantics. While 'the historical subject-matter of his novels is very close to that of the Romantics proper ... Scott's interpretation of this subject-matter is entirely opposed to that of the Romantics, as is his manner of portrayal' (1981:34). Crucial to this portrayal is Scott's choice of a '"middling", merely correct and never heroic "hero"', a fictional strategy which directly opposes that of the Romantic '"demonic"' hero and represents 'a renunciation of Romanticism, a conquest of Romanticism, a higher development of the *realist* literary traditions of the Enlightenment' (33; my emphasis).

Of course this is premised on Lukács's dialectical materialist contention that the past is the prehistory of the present; it is because of this in fact that his position is such a clear demonstration of the type of domestication of history with which White is concerned. On this view Scott becomes not so much an Enlightenment carry-over as an important precursive signifier of the break that characterises the modern disciplinisation of history – particularly with regard to the essentially realist mode within which it expresses itself.

For our concerns what is important in this argument is the way in which identity is established in the 'classical form of the historical novel' which Lukács says that Scott represents. 'Scott's greatness lies in his capacity to give living human embodiment to historical social types', Lukács maintains (34), claiming that in Scott 'the great historical personality is the representative of an important and significant moment embracing large sections of the people' (38). Identity lies in typicality then; as we saw in our definition of the 'epic' mode in relation to the work of Oliver Walker, the historical subject becomes a subject by virtue of his or her collective representativeness.

I do not wish to take issue with this perspective on formalist or humanist grounds; the problem we encounter here has more to do with the structural articulation of the realist text or, more to our purpose, the discourse of realism in general. In it, even beyond the much-debated issue of typicality, we still see identity equated with narrative coherence, and, perhaps more importantly, narrative coherence equated with identity. The reader, aligned with this identity, inhabits its space as perspective, and thus assumes its position of dominant specularity.

This is precisely the space guaranteed to the historian by the modern discipline of history; the epistemological innocence attached to establishing 'the facts' makes of our knowledge of these facts a domesticating force that neutralises their difference. We feel, as Foucault points out in *The Archaeology of Knowledge,* 'a particular repugnance to conceiving of difference, to describing separations and dispersions, to dissociating the reassuring form of the identical' (1972:12) because this would challenge the control that our sense of self gives us. As we saw in Chapter One, Foucault makes it clear that the obverse of what he calls 'continuous history' is 'the sovereignty of the subject' (12); 'history in its classical form' has so much trouble with 'the notion of discontinuity' (8) precisely because of the attack the latter launches upon the subject at the core of the former. It is 'as if we were afraid to conceive of *the Other* in the time of our own thought' says Foucault (12).

Out of this comes the central observation that the way one conceives of the self is related to the way one conceives of history. The subject and history are intimately implicated, with a threat to the one leading to a threat to the other.

The pressures brought to bear on the self in relation to the past here provide a valuable point from which to return to the work of Daphne Rooke. In a series of novels she almost programmatically explores South African history from a variety of different subjective viewpoints, fracturing it into disparate perspectives. From the mad white male narrator of *A Grove of Fever Trees* to the coloured Afrikaans female narrator of *Mittee,* from the semi-autobiographical English settler girls of *Ratoons* and *A Lover for Estelle* to the quasi-historical Barnato look-alike of *Diamond Joe,* Rooke has splintered her vision of South African history into numerous facets. Her most extreme experiment, however, most clearly revealed the sense of dislocation inherent in such an enterprise. Her account of the writing of *Wizards' Country,* captured in Ian Glenn's valuable interviews,[16] is haunted by the threat this work – as an historical work – presented to her own subjectivity.

Speaking of the South African-based historical novelist Mary Renault, Rooke notes the general difficulties involved in writing historical fiction:

> She made the effort to go back into the past and write about the Greeks which you know takes terrific minding ...

From this Rooke goes on to talk of a breakdown of sorts born of the difficulties involved in her own attempt to recreate the African past in fiction:

16. I am much in debt to Professor Ian Glenn for allowing me free access to this lengthy and important interview conducted at Daphne Rooke's previous residence in Australia in 1989 (unpublished).

And *Wizards' Country* did that – I intended to write a trilogy but after I did that first one I didn't do the other two because I felt you had to twist your viewpoint, your mind to take the Zulu point on it ... (Interview:26)

The problems of a radically different perspective finally become disenabling for Rooke, despite the attractions they present, and are central to her failure to sustain the historical project as originally envisaged:

It was quite fascinating. I left it. I couldn't, I didn't want to do that any more. I couldn't because you can't look at it in that light – you eventually come to look at the same thing from such a difficult angle that it becomes much too difficult. I only did that one book – I've never done another. (27)

Actually *Wizards' Country* was 'another' of sorts in itself: in relation that is, to its markedly different first draft, called 'Yesterday's Child'. Rooke used 'Yesterday's Child' as a working title until relatively late in the creation of *Wizards' Country* (in an article published in *Milady* in February 1956 she refers to *Yesterday's Child* as her 'latest' novel), but the typescript draft that bears this title is different enough to be an intriguing work in its own right. In the tensions between the two texts, what is more, we can return to the theme of this chapter, and map the distance between the beautiful and the sublime, the domestic and the different, the real and the romance.

DRAFT AND NOVEL

Before tracing such tensions, it is worth introducing these works by mapping the key elements that the draft and the novel as it finally appeared have in common.

They share a basically similar plot, which revolves around the story of a Zulu clan (the Tshanini; Tshaneni in 'Yesterday's Child', of which more below) in the 1870s and 1880s. Both are lyrical evocations of the last days of the Zulu kingdom. They are told from the perspective of various events at first seemingly marginal to history; slowly however, these are drawn into the centre of historical events. Cetshwayo's enforcement of the marriage laws first interrupts the life of the Tshanini; later they become swept up in the Anglo-Zulu War, directly involved with the death of the Prince Imperial, and finally virtually wiped out in the civil wars following on the exile of Cetshwayo.

Thematically, both works follow the growth of a protagonist from child to adult through these events. Each is the narrative of a rite of passage, of an initiation into a maturity defined within a clash of cultures.

The setting too remains the same for both works, and is important enough for them both in related ways to warrant some preliminary exploration and comment.

The name Rooke gives the Tshaneni clan in 'Yesterday's Child' is directly derived from the mountain against which Rooke's brother-in-law's farm (significantly, as we shall see, named 'Banghoek') was situated in northern Zululand. She lived here with her mother for a time, and made the same area the setting of her first novel, *A Grove of Fever Trees*. In the Introduction (written from her home in Australia) to the recent new edition of this novel she says, 'Tshaneni is home to me; I think of myself as an exile' (1989:5). She was to return to this setting not only for *Wizards' Country*, but also for the later *A Lover for Estelle*. This is the only location repeated as a setting in her novels, and thus we can assume the particular importance it has for Rooke – an importance which extends beyond nostalgia, and takes us to the heart of the significance of 'Yesterday's Child' and *Wizards' Country* for this essay.

In *Wizards' Country*, Rooke subtly alters the name of the clan, indicating a loosened and more symbolic use of the name. *Tshaneni* means literally 'the place of the little stone', and in 'Yesterday's Child' this refers to the dominant geographical feature of the clan's area ('The Tshaneni clan drank from the waters of Inqaba, generation upon generation. Their pasturelands lay east of the mountains and their boundary was the little stone'[17]). *Tshanini*, on the other hand, means 'the place of grass', grass being the emblem of the clan. In *Wizards' Country*, members of the clan are taught 'to hold grass in awe, for [their] ancestor's name is grass'; they are also taught to 'avoid the smoke of a grass fire for such smoke is death to the Tshanini' (7). Indeed the description of the near-destruction of the clan at the end of the novel is dominated by burning grass. We may be able to read into the change of clan-name something of the significance of the changes to the story that occur between draft and novel, particularly as regards the death of the protagonist of 'Yesterday's Child' as opposed to the survival of the narrator of *Wizards' Country* (this will be discussed in detail later), but I am also told the names are close enough to allow for them to serve as local variants of one and the same place. As Rooke certainly wants to keep the connotations attached to the

---

17. This typed manuscript is among the valuable items brought back by Professor Glenn from his visit to Daphne Rooke. The quotation is from p.2.

geographical reference in both works, we can investigate its shared significance at this stage. I will use 'Tshaneni' to refer to the actual location and 'Tshanini' to refer to the clan in the general comments to follow. When referring to the two works I will keep to the spellings each uses.

The home village of the Tshanini clan, Liyana, is set near the 'Peak of Lightnings' which marks the border between the idyllic pastoral existence of the clan and the area which gives the title to the novel. The 'wizards' country' is an area dominated and haunted by magic, in which witches and wizards hold sway and where the conventional and domestic become subject to the visionary and the terrifying. Assuming from their geographical similarities that the 'Peak of Lightnings' is modelled on Tshaneni, Rooke's 'wizards' country' has a type of basis in reality. Among English-speakers Tshaneni is known as 'Ghost Mountain' and it has a curious reputation; according to T.V. Bulpin, 'at irregular intervals over the years, strange lights and flickering fires are seen among the fissures and cliffs of the summit. Weird noises and strange calls are also heard' (1986:366). This reputation in all probability stems from the fact that Tshaneni served as the burial ground for the heads of the Gasa family of the Ndwandwe people, even after their defeat by Shaka and flight into Mozambique.

These associations can only be strengthened by the fact that Tshaneni was also the place where, as Daphne Rooke puts it in her Introduction to *A Grove of Fever Trees*, 'the last battle between the Zulus and the Boers was fought' (5). She is referring to the deciding battle in the civil war which erupted out of the British attempt to rule Zululand by dividing it into thirteen separate states after the Anglo-Zulu War, a battle which is referred to in some sources as the 'Battle of Ghost Mountain' and in others as the 'Battle of Etshaneni'. This conflict was marked by the enlistment of white frontiersman into the armies of the two principal rivals, Dinuzulu kaCetshwayo and Zibhebhu kaMaphitha. The eight hundred-odd 'Boers' employed by the victorious Dinuzulu as opposed to the handful of whites in Zibhebhu's army give this battle something of the status Rooke claims for it. Certainly she uses this battle as the culmination of the historical events in both 'Yesterday's Child' and *Wizards' Country*.

Tshaneni's real location is near where the Mkuzi River passes through the Lebombo Mountains. In her fiction Rooke moves it significantly further south, south of Ulundi in fact. This brings it much closer to the other major landmark in the two works: Isandhlwana. That a variety of names has been given to this geographical feature is well known (and referred to in 'Yesterday's Child', p.34);

in both draft and novel it is known as 'the little stone', which slips easily over from its other historical name, 'little hand', but more crucially merges it with Tshaneni. None of Tshaneni's associations are attached to Isandhlwana (these remain transferred, as we have seen, to the Peak of Lightnings), but the running of the names into each other brings even closer together the two literally distinct locations and intensifies the symbolic role Rooke gives her setting. The fictional area carries both the magical connotations of Tshaneni and the historical connotations of Isandhlwana.[18]

The move south also places Liyana much closer to the southern border of Zululand, marked by the Tugela (Thukela) River and its tributary, the Buffalo (Mzinyathi). We see then that Rooke goes to some lengths to set 'Yesterday's Child' and *Wizards' Country* geographically at a point that marks the intersection between both the domestic and the magical and the two different cultures that were historically about to clash. Spatially and temporally, then, the works are poised between contending forces that become related by this arrangement.

The differences between the two versions of the story of the Tshanini will occupy us for the rest of this chapter. The best place to start on these is Daphne Rooke's own view of how she sees the draft in relation to the novel, and for this we will return to the Glenn interview:

> I was telling you about *Wizards' Country* and how it started and why I think it is quite interesting is because I have actually got that first draft which is really in the nature of a dream and that is what I put down first and then I took that and turned it into *Wizards' Country* which is something that anybody who picks it up can read and understand but I don't know whether they could actually have followed what I call 'Yesterday's Child'. 'Yesterday's Child' is not as easy to follow as *Wizards' Country* because it is more or less the dream put down in print and then taken and then *Wizards' Country* is then taken from that and made into a commercial book that one can read and understand, although it still remains a difficult book to read. (25)

Put into the terms around which this chapter is constructed, the dream-like

---

18. I was pleased to have the geographic intricacies of the setting for the draft and novel confirmed in an interview I conducted with Daphne Rooke at her present home in Cambridge on 10 June 1992 (unpublished).

'Yesterday's Child' would seem to tend towards the pole of difference, and the more strategically organised *Wizards' Country* towards the pole of domesticity. This is an odd assessment, however, and one which we must question, for a comparison of the novel and its first draft fairly plainly reveals 'Yesterday's Child' to be in fact the more calculated and programmatic of the two versions. Opposing Rooke's assessment as it does, some support will have to be given for this claim; this I will try to do by giving my sense of the novel and its draft, starting with 'Yesterday's Child'.

'YESTERDAY'S CHILD'

In the draft the protagonist is Donisa, heir to the chieftainship of the Tshaneni clan, and we follow his progress from childhood to adulthood or, more precisely (and tellingly, as we shall see later) in this version, from birth to death.

Donisa's story is set in a detailed and faithful depiction of traditional Zulu life. Its anthropological accuracy is based, as Rooke says in the Glenn interview, on her own observations (while living in Zululand) which flesh out later background reading – primarily A.T. Bryant's *The Zulu People: As They Were Before the White Man Came*. 'I read that,' says Rooke in her interview with Glenn, 'but I'd suddenly remember seeing a scene exactly like that' (26). This attempt at constructing a narrative perspective very different from Rooke's own permeates the otherwise conventional third-person omniscient narrative point of view. The narrative takes the form of an apostrophe, addressed to a generalised 'Friend' – the first word of the text, and one that returns at key points throughout the work. This gives it an oral flavour, something that is picked up in its rich idiomatic texture and often startlingly different metaphorical range ('the gardens lay below them like a bowl of green milk' (36), for example). What emerges from this is a marvellous evocation of traditional life, the effectiveness of which depends not so much upon ethnographic accuracy (indeed, much time could be spent detailing Rooke's failures, both personal and historical, in this regard), but upon the way in which the extensive anthropological dressing is drawn into another element which helps in the creation of the quite radically different narrative perspective which is adopted.

This is the effect of a central visionary experience on the perspective of the protagonist. Donisa's life is governed by a childhood experience that continually haunts him, but the vision Rooke gives him is firmly located in her own experience.

It is autobiographical in a more intimate way than the observation of others (as in the anthropological material noted above) and arises out of something intensely personal. In her conversations with Ian Glenn, Rooke makes this vision central to her writing in general (although she never refers to its place within the novels we have selected). She says:

> Small things happened to me, it looks small but it made an enormous difference to my whole life. It was around about that age [six] that locusts used to come over ... The children were incredibly cruel to the locusts. They used to pull out their legs and their wings. You know what children can be like, and one night ... we had been doing this to the locusts and the most awful ear-ache afflicted me ... I made the connection between the terrible ear-ache and what we had done to the locusts. It was an incredible revelation to me. Small as I was, I saw what we had inflicted on the locust. I didn't feel that I had that ear-ache because we had done that. I understood in one flash that what I felt was what the locust felt and it completely changed my life at the age of six and in a way it finished me for ordinary life because from then onwards I always felt one with everybody. I was always conscious, when I was very small and be going to sleep I would think of those who were ill and those who were dying and those who were in pain as if that was myself and identifying myself with that ... I understand that the pain is not really my pain but I feel that I am part of the entire agony of the world and not necessarily of its joy. (29-30)

The remarkable degree of imaginative identification with others expressed here seems at first almost the opposite of the 'general theory of discontinuity' Foucault makes a plea for, but without something of this attitude there is no basis for history whatsoever, even one based on difference. Indeed it is only out of the respect for otherness born of this experience that Rooke is willing to project herself, at such a threat to her self, into the world of difference she creates in her novels.

The experience described above becomes a theme that recurs in many of the novels, from the first, *A Grove of Fever Trees*, to one of the most recent, *Margaretha de la Porte*, although it emerges in different ways.

In *A Grove of Fever Trees* we are introduced, in passing, to an incident from

Zulu life that will become the vehicle for the later fictional naturalisation of Rooke's childhood experience into Zulu culture:

> They [the umfaans] showed me how they snared the cruel hawks that swooped from the skies upon the chickens. A circle of small pointed sticks imprisoned a sacrificial chicken, as bait to the hawk. As it fell in headlong flight upon the helpless bird, it threw itself upon the pointed sticks and died. The umfaans screamed with glee when they trapped a hawk, but I felt sad to see the lovely flight halted forever. (31)

In 'Yesterday's Child' and *Wizards' Country* the snaring of a hawk in this fashion becomes the act that precipitates the painful insight. Another alteration is made, however: the chicken is replaced by a dove, gearing up the significance of the experience and preparing it for the symbolic weight it is to carry in these books.

In 'Yesterday's Child' the trapping of the hawk is drawn out over several pages and described in intense detail: colours, textures, and sounds are heightened to an extreme pitch, and drawn out even more by the tension of a goat's potential disruption of the trap. Its effects, too, are substantially developed, and are dispersed throughout the story. These are constantly cast in the form of a contrast between the public and the private. Much celebration follows on what is in fact Donisa's first successful hunt, for example; it is treated as the first step of his initiation into adulthood, as the childish refrain he repeats upon being invited by his father to sit in adult fashion on a mat at meal times indicates: 'I sat on a mat, I killed a hawk' (20). This public rejoicing is set against a terrible private pain, which takes the same form as it did for the young Rooke (ear-ache) and has much the same effect (isolation):

> He was alone with his pain and he cried out. It was then that he remembered the dove and the hawk. He remembered the cry of the hawk when he split its beak, and knew its pain.
> This was for him the beginning of a great loneliness.
> The doctor cured the pain of his ears: but thereafter whenever he heard a cry of pain it went through his ears like a spear and he heard again the cry of the hawk. So pain was often with him, in the village and on the grassy mountainside. (23)

When Donisa reports his pain to the elders, their limitations are revealed. They warn him against it as possibly the work of a wizard and miss its significance. Just as the pain experienced by Rooke as a child embodied a positive vision that isolated her from those less enlightened ('it finished me for ordinary life'), so Donisa's vision is shown as superior to the traditional, communal wisdom of his clan:

> ... he caught from his elders the wisdom of his fathers. He did not find this wisdom for himself, it was there for him as food was, provided by those who had a duty to him.
>
> But Donisa's knowledge was beyond the teaching of the old people. Friend: Light is light and darkness is darkness. It is because there is light that we know darkness.
>
> He had whispered in his own pain, 'Hawk, you suffered so?' and thus as a child found the very heart of all suffering. (24)

From now on, throughout the novel, the enlightened insight of this vision is counterpointed against the wisdom of his community. We see this again, for example, at Donisa's formal initiation; after being given a detailed account of traditional law as it is taught to him, we are told:

> All these things he learned from his elders, and only little things he learned of himself: except that one great thing, that all living creatures are linked by pain. (30)

It is this awareness that makes Donisa the special object of the Zulu Christian missionary's attention. Zungu is rejected by the Tshaneni clan, 'yet he remained with the Tshaneni for he had come to know Donisa ... here lay the pathway to Liyana: Zungu was a patient man and looked to the day when Donisa would be chief of the Tshaneni' (89). Through Zungu we see Donisa's vision directly equated with Christianity. The missionary feels he has a natural ally in Donisa, and he is prepared to wait on his maturing to achieve his ends. His pragmatic aims never obscure the central point, however: Donisa has naturally come to a knowledge of the Christian faith:

> Such a one, being praised by men, would bring converts, he himself being a Christian: for though he had not seen Donisa for many seasons

he remembered only the boy who had called on the name of Jesu
Kristo, and who knew of himself the great secret, the inner meaning
of all pain. (106-107)

Here we have the key structural polarities representing the key ideological polarities
within the draft. It is in this respect that the work comes across as calculated and
programmatic; it is quite undream-like in the firm outlines that carry its theme:
Donisa's vision represents the essence of Christianity (mildness, gentleness, care
for others) as opposed to the essentially militaristic traditional wisdom (courage,
skill in warfare, sublimation of personal relations). Donisa is torn between the
two as he matures and is drawn into traditional life, especially Cetshwayo's revived
military structures. Donisa's elder brother, Thunzi – handsome, powerful, a soldier
in the king's army – represents in the clan (and the narrative) the idealised figure
of the traditional and militaristic virtues. Thunzi and Zungu, then, become
symbolically contrasted, the poles of the conflict within Donisa:

> He loved Zungu for Zungu of all people knew the mildness of his
> heart: but he feared him because he might take from him Liyana ...
> With manhood so close he saw in front of him a lovely path which
> had been trodden by his people in their generations. Soon he would
> be sent to do service to a great man. He would be as Thunzi who cast
> a shadow ...
>
> To be as Thunzi! this was the longing of Donisa's heart. Zungu
> owned a book and pictures, he had a necklace of beads and a cross: he
> was mild: it was happiness to speak with him. But Thunzi owned a
> spear and a shield, a warrior's headdress of plumes and leopard skin,
> and long fringes of shining white cows' tails. (91-92)

Beneath this polar tension lies a deeper conflict, however, one not as easily
accommodated within the novel's programme. While Zungu and Thunzi
characterise the warring elements within the protagonist, Zungu's most crucial
struggle is with someone equally divorced from the community, although for
radically different reasons: this is Benge, another half-brother of Donisa's.

Benge is a hunchback, an outcast saved from being killed (deformity being
traditionally seen as evil) at birth by his mother and grandmother. Had he not
been deformed, he would have been heir to the chieftaincy, in the place of Donisa.

Marginalised as he is, Benge (in 'Yesterday's Child') is a minor character who only becomes important through his associations with magic and witchcraft and the area in which these are dominant: the wizards' country.

We have already had cause to consider the place of the wizards' country within the novel and its draft. What needs to be added here is the obvious point that this area is in many ways typical of the devices of romantic fiction. In it we find the traditional romantic relation of character to setting; here the setting is hostile, mysterious, portentous, filled with the supernatural power to menace and harm, as is the witch who lives there. Those who enter its realm come under its power. In it even Donisa's vision becomes a nightmarish and self-destructive one as we see when he enters it in a dream after an actual terrifying experience there:

> In his sleep he wandered in the wizards' country. He saw the great rocks piled one on the other, and the trees marked by the lightning bird. A sky more brilliant than any he had ever seen blazed above him and across it was drawn the half-circle of a rainbow. He walked towards the end of the rainbow. When he saw the animal that lived there he would die. But he heard voices: the rainbow faded from the sky, the rocks and trees vanished. There was only the sky left now and he heard the great winds that rushed through it, he saw clouds come spinning across it like purple dust. Now he was the hawk, so high that he could not see the earth. He swooped down out of the sky with a singing of his wings. The feathered mamba reared but he was not afraid of it: he feared only the stakes towards which he hurtled. (62)

The landscape has all the trappings of the sublime; it inspires awe and wonder in a terrifying combination. As such it is the true location of romance within the story. It is the realm wherein realism acquires the latitude which transforms it into romance.

If Donisa finds potential destruction in the wizards' country, Benge finds a home of sorts there for a while. Both he and his mother are driven to this because of their outsider status, the result of Benge's deformity. He is suspected of being a Magic Dwarf, and is thus in constant danger from the community. This means he is associated with witches and wizards by them anyway, for a Magic Dwarf may have certain powers but not freely; he must serve a witch or a wizard. He is (like Benge) ugly, hairy, and small but heavy-shouldered; he raids crops, seduces women, and is loved by children; he can change his form and even kill, but only on the command of his master or mistress. In actuality Benge's worst features are that he can be cruel and malevolent in a petty sort of way, but his associations with the wizards' country make him into something more for both the village of Liyana and the reader. He becomes the figure of romance in the story, associated as he is with the sublime landscape of the wizards' country, but in this draft version he and his setting are only uncomfortably accommodated.

The Zungu/Benge conflict is made secondary to the tension within Donisa between Christianity and traditional life. With his initiation Donisa rejects Zungu and embraces the world of Thunzi, ultimately surpassing Thunzi's military prowess. Circumstances result in Zungu's banishment from Liyana, and he is aided in his flight by Benge, who has also been outlawed upon the clan's killing of his mother and the witch she and Benge have served. Benge guides Zungu to safety on the Peak of Lightnings and in the wizards' country and here gives up his magic and is converted to Christianity. Zungu is forced to accept this outlaw and cripple as his only convert from Liyana (a huge disappointment to him after his designs upon Donisa and through him the whole community) and Benge accompanies Zungu on his return to the white mission station. With the words 'Thus Benge rested in the shadow of Jesu Kristo' (115), the 'Magic Dwarf' disappears from the story.

With Benge go all references to the sublime as it is allegorised by magic and witchcraft in the novel; Christianity absorbs and neutralises these and the realm of romance they represent within the narrative. From this point on the story moves increasingly into the more strictly historical world. As Donisa is pulled into history along with his tribe by the Anglo-Zulu War he has greater and greater success in terms of traditional values. Yet he remains haunted by his vision, constantly fearing the weakness it represents in traditional terms. Donisa is 'Yesterday's Child' in terms of his commitment to the ways of his people, but within him are the seeds of a new way – one ironically linked with the coming destruction of traditional life. It is this ironic link that cannot be adequately handled within the draft, and I would claim the failure apparent here is related to the awkwardness with which romance is built into 'Yesterday's Child'. The degree to which the draft fails as historical fiction is the degree to which it domesticates the historical differences with which it is concerned.

The wizards' country continues to play a role in the story after Benge's exit, but it is no longer charged with the power of the sublime. As the Zulus are defeated, at first the Tshaneni clan and then all the surviving Zulus retreat to hide in the wizards' country; later Cetshwayo himself will flee there as traditional life is defeated. In the final destruction of the Zulu kingdom, carried out amidst the civil war and culminating in the battle of 'Ghost Mountain'/Etshaneni, Donisa himself retreats to the wizard's country, mortally wounded. But the wizards' country is by now stripped of its mystical and magical associations; it is simply an inaccessible region offering retreat and refuge. It has ceased to be a place of tension, alive in the threatening alternative it offers to the domestic life of the Tshaneni.

In the midst of the destruction of his community it is Donisa's childhood vision which returns to him, becoming again the real focus of the tensions of the narrative:

> He tried to remember his life at Liyana before he became a warrior. It was not so long ago ... the dove and the hawk ...
>
> Had that been the secret of his innermost recesses? Had a spirit come to him when he was a boy, and repudiated, become angry with him? How could a man live his life except as life was? He would have been despised and killed if he had given way to the thoughts within him. (167)

With the destruction of the world that stood against his vision, Donisa is left at last to recognise his essential 'spirit' as that of the vision. As his death approaches, the novel climaxes with a final struggle in which the insight he has gained is now free to triumph:

> His spirit rose within him, strong as a spear but serene still. And now knowledge came to him. It came as light comes in broad sweeps that are not seen but are there. His spirit would not leave him. All that he was would sink within its eye and go with it on its far journey. It was mild and lovely and changeless, the seed of Nkulunkulu ... (191)

With this acceptance, Donisa dies. Significantly there is no place for him in the coming (Christian) world he embraces in death. This conclusion is telling: it suggests, despite itself, the lack of any syncretic cultural possibility. Any such direction is foreclosed with the end of the novel, just as it is only in death that Donisa can resolve the tensions within himself. Finally his growth to manhood within a clash of cultures reaches not maturity, but death.

As a protagonist Donisa operates within restricted latitudes. He is caught in a Manichean bind that ultimately destroys him, no matter how much the narrative may wish to push him through it into some kind of transcendence. That this problematic has to do with the treatment of romance in the draft is borne out by the nature of the recasting of the story in its final version.

WIZARDS' COUNTRY

When Rooke chose to turn this 'dream' into a 'commercial novel' she actually worked against the calculated, programmatic structure of 'Yesterday's Child'. Handwritten on the title page of the draft typescript is a new title, never to be used but an important indicator of how she was to go about recasting the work; this second working title is 'The Magic Dwarf', and it points to the remarkable transformation of the text Rooke was about to perform. Formally this involved a shift from the omniscient third-person to the first-person, but what is more interesting is the character she chooses to make the new centre of consciousness – not the originally central Donisa, as one might have expected, but a minor and finally entirely marginalised character: Benge. His awkward placing in 'Yesterday's Child' is rescued not by improving his strategic relation to the other characters, but by making him the containing device of all the relations presented. This effects an almost classic deconstruction of the story (if we keep in mind one of the characteristic and by now venerable manoeuvres of Derrida): by taking something marginal and making it central Rooke unsettles the entire programmatic structure of 'Yesterday's Child' and transforms the work entirely.

The shift from third to first person has its usual effects; it precipitates the novel away from the privileges of authorial omniscience in which, in the words of Colin MacCabe, there is an 'unproblematic taking up of the position of the subject' (1989:139) which 'guarantees the position of the subject exactly outside any articulation' (140). In this we have the beginnings of Rooke's challenge to her own sense of the history she wishes to tell. In adopting the perspective of one of her own characters, she writes herself out of the dominant specularity assumed in the draft, and exposes herself to the latitudes inherent in Benge's perspective. I am not suggesting that the first-person point of view automatically ensures this; quite obviously it is a narrative device as open to authorial control as any other. The nature of the point of view adopted here, however, has further implications, one of which is the alienation Rooke experienced in her writing of *Wizards'*

Country. Her comments in the interviews certainly seem more applicable to the completed novel than the draft, for *Wizards' Country* is finally a far more radical and challenging text than 'Yesterday's Child'.

If, however, the more orderly, controlled draft version seems in retrospect dream-like and foreign to Rooke, this could possibly be because the bulk of her fiction operates in a fashion akin to the strategy adopted in *Wizards' Country*. Nearly all her narrators are first person and, in the words of Ian Glenn in the interviews, tend to be 'strange' and 'disturbed' (27), or – Rooke's own word for it in the interviews – 'deranged' (30). Certainly they are all outsiders in some way. Glenn finds the narrator of *A Grove of Fever Trees* Faulkner-like, but the overall effect of Rooke's work is not classically modernist. We must look further for the full implications of this otherwise not in itself necessarily significant narrative manoeuvre; we cannot simply generalise any formal strategy as it always has a particular, historical effect.

In Rooke's case the primary generic energy set in motion by her fictional strategies is a romantic one. In an era of strident realism in South Africa (Gordimer's *A World of Strangers* was published within a year of *Wizards' Country*) it would be remarkable if her novels were pure romances; as it is we must fall back on that minor tradition identified by Leavis to characterise them, with its blend of romance and realism. Bearing this in mind we may see as Rooke's most representative narrator Fikizolo, the eponymous narrator of one of the only two short stories Rooke ever published (1968).

Fikizolo is, in the most literal of fashions, a 'sport'. He is the offspring of a donkey and a zebra, and his very name (which means 'He arrived yesterday') is a clue to his fictional affiliation with Benge. As a hybrid he is 'born to be laughed at' and 'always ... threatened with death'; he tells us too that 'I had a wildness in me that I could not control' and that 'I was rather lonely' (49). In all this he resembles Benge, but the chief similarity between them is that they both act as points of contact between the ordinary world and the world of witchcraft. Fikizolo is the only one able to identify the old widow as a witch, and thus finally defeat her. He and Benge are conduits between the domestic and the different; they are the means by which the historical realism of their stories becomes shot through with romance.

In the social terms of the narratives in which these narrators feature they are noted not for their generic representativeness, but rather for their difference. Their identity is established upon their atypicality rather than their typicality. The forces they represent are not the literally historical, but neither are they the transcendental to which it is often assumed the romance is limited. For Abdul R. JanMohamed, for instance, the romance is the most significant formal manifestation of the fixed divisions that make up the Manichean allegory of the colonial world (1985). No genre is automatically and always the producer of one effect, however. History is only too capable of drawing out of one formal structure a variety of effects. And the romance is perfectly able to serve as a mode of serious utopian reaction, shattering the basis for the fixing of differences that is inherent in the process of the construction of the subject or of identification generally.

How is this manifested in the case of the redrafting of *Wizards' Country*? What is the effect of redistributing the narrative around Benge?

We can begin to answer these questions by comparing the ways in which the draft and the novel open and close. The first sentence of 'Yesterday's Child' reads, 'Friend: Here is a mountain above a plain, here is a river that goes past many homes'; what follows is a lengthy description of place centred upon the river, plain, and mountain, whose 'constancy' is stressed in contrast to the ephemerality of the humans who inhabit this landscape. The point is emphasised by the fact that once the course of the narrative is run and its characters have lived and died, the novel ends on the same note: 'Come friend: What do we see here? Only a river, a plain and a mountain' (191). The endurance of the landscape, ultimately represented by the river because earth erodes, forms a back-drop to the nostalgia which is the primary mood of the novel:

> Yes, a man does not tread again the paths of his boyhood.
> But he finds in the stream a constancy. He takes pleasure in this constancy. Thus and thus Inqaba ran when I was a boy, he says, and thus it runs now. (1-2)

The timelessness of nature is played off against the chronology of history, providing an act of containment. Brief as the trilogy of mountain, plain, and river is, it is, to invoke another term from the rhetoric which gave us the concept of the sublime as it is used above, recognisably picturesque. In the opening sentence we move into the fictionally framed landscape from its most distant features (the mountain), through its middleground (the plain), to its foreground (the river), which brings us to a human scale (represented by the 'many homes'). In the concluding sentence of the novel this movement is reversed, and we leave the now almost completely deserted foreground of the picture to move out to its more distant features. This is a gesture towards transcendence, but it remains no more than that. As I have tried to show in my reading of 'Yesterday's Child', the narrative cannot accommodate its attempt at transcendence. Its protagonist may well die in a moment of spiritual grace (embracing what is identified as an essentially Christian vision), but in the material terms of the Imperial ideology which imports that grace (Christianity comes ultimately by conquest), Donisa must be physically destroyed. His personal vision cannot become an historical one, only a weak (in the sense of only being possible when written out of any cultural syncretism) transcendental one. The overall vision of the narrative too, remains, in romantic terms, a limited one; it never breaks out of the frame of the picturesque.

The sublime eludes 'Yesterday's Child' precisely because the real zone of creative possibility in the narrative is the one that is finally marginalised: the wizards' country; it is this that Rooke seems to recognise in her recasting of the narrative, and indicates in her final choice of title for the work. This is reflected too in the way in which she rewrites its opening.

Wizards' Country shifts its focus from the landscape of 'Yesterday's Child' to features of the character who has now become its enveloping consciousness (many of these features will be recognisable from the description of the magic dwarf given above):

> A movement in the reeds, a pebble rolling on the stones ... the people stop to listen. Perhaps a magic dwarf is there, come to steal a maiden or to work some mischief in the crops. Perhaps he has come innocently, to frolic with the children. Where is he, who may hide in a shadow? Magic dwarf, hear it on the edge of the wind, in grass, hear it in the crying of the quail. (1)

The next line takes us straight into the perspective of the first person: 'I who am old listen as I listened when I was a boy'. Not only is the new perspective emphasised by the rhythmic repetition of the pronoun, but another important distinction is immediately introduced: the narrator is a survivor; the narrative may still be one of a rite of passage, of a growth to maturity, but it is not a movement from birth to death. The past tense of 'Yesterday's Child' is a perfect past, completed and frozen in death. The first person convention of *Wizards' Country* has as its reflex the necessity of survival – its past tense is one of living recall – but this is more than simply a formal reflex, as we shall see.

The narrative then takes us back into a scene from Benge's childhood. The river features again, but all its heavy metaphorical associations are gone: we are simply introduced to a group of boys swimming until our focus is drawn to the hunchback Benge: 'the other boys swam, but not I, not Benge'. From this first moment Benge takes on the form so typical (from her first novel) of Rooke's best narrators: he is an outsider, yes, but one fascinated by and focused on an idealised insider (typically too a close relation): 'I would lie amongst the reeds and watch my brother, I would watch Thunzi' (1). As in 'Yesterday's Child', Thunzi is handsome, strong, and loved, but he is second in stature to his elder brother, Danisa (Rooke corrects the draft's spelling in the final version), who is, as in the draft, heir to the chieftaincy in the place of the crippled Benge. While Benge's love for Thunzi is returned, his hatred for Danisa is also returned. Immediately then, we find the protagonist of 'Yesterday's Child' moved aside and recast. He is an extremely unsympathetic figure and comparatively marginal to the narrative, representing the side of the community antagonistic towards Benge because of his appearance (he continually refers to Benge as a 'magic dwarf' which, if taken seriously, would lead to Benge's execution).

While many of the main features of these three characters remain in *Wizards' Country*, they are often redistributed differently among the characters. We see them then from radically different angles, and their significance alters in important ways.

The most telling alteration has to do with the visionary experience undergone by the protagonist of 'Yesterday's Child'. Thunzi now has and is haunted by the pain that follows on his trapping of the hawk with the dove; he becomes the one torn between the traditional virtues in which he excels, and the comprehension of the essence of pain which encourages mildness in all things. Along with the change of character, the hunt is given to us in a much more compressed form, and its ramifications are nowhere near as central to the development of the narrative. Thunzi shares with Benge the secret of his pain, but Benge explicitly rejects it; it is a threat, after all, to his vicarious existence in the community through Thunzi (his brother has promised, for example, to father a child for the crippled Benge, as one would do for the dead). It is Thunzi then who upon initiation hides the knowledge of the cry of the hawk, and who constantly has to fight off the threat this represents to his military prowess and status in the community and kingdom. It is Benge who relates the vision to evil and witchcraft, as the elders do in

'Yesterday's Child'. He is shown as self-serving and wrong in this, but the cry of the hawk still never assumes the same weight and associations that it does in 'Yesterday's Child'. In *Wizards' Country* it becomes associated with Thunzi's love for Cece, a sub-plot that weaves its way between Benge's story but is never outside the range of traditional life, even if it is complicated and challenged by it.

The major effect of this is to expel entirely the rather heavy-handed Christian associations given to Donisa's vision in 'Yesterday's Child'. No mention is made at all of this primary domesticating reference: *Wizards' Country* escapes the programmatic historical naturalisation of the colonial clash with the traditional, overseen by the containing authorial consciousness. Instead we stay well within the historical difference represented by Benge's consciousness. The conflict of the vision and traditional life is played down, and the two poles are finally integrated (fairly easily) within the traditional world at Thunzi's death. It is no longer the novel's visionary centre, its overwhelming moral heart; it is now contained within the sublimation of all the elements of 'Yesterday's Child' into a different consciousness.

This consciousness is shaped in relation to the landscape that symbolically expresses it, the *Wizards' Country*. Benge is threatened by this region but also both drawn and finally driven into it. The wizards' country becomes our centre of consciousness for much of the novel, and in this way the romantic is introduced into the narrative in a far more central way. That magical area of shifting latitudes, where bewitchment taken seriously marks the difference from realism, defines the changed sense of the controlling consciousness and makes the new title more than apt for the recast story. What the possessive in the final title stresses now is not past time but a sense of place, the nature of which governs much of our reading. The narrative becomes one of 'once upon a place ...' (*Wizards' Country*) rather than 'once upon a time ...' ('Yesterday's Child').

What is more, the world of historical difference that we encounter in the traditional life of the narrative is no longer achieved primarily by its surface anthropological dressing; there is in fact much less of the Bryant-type anthropology in *Wizards' Country*. Instead we are drawn into a different consciousness, drawn into the bewitchment Benge undergoes, and in this fashion enter the sublime centre of the novel that the wizards' country represents. The world of difference presented is no longer just a matter of idiom and metaphor, no matter how striking; we are now submerged in the perspective of magic, and the difference it represents envelops us in Benge's telling of the tale.

What must be stressed here is that the world of history we thus enter is an imagined one, although this need not be construed as placing Rooke's fictional endeavour entirely outside the methods of more formal historical accounts. Without wishing to claim that Rooke was familiar with her contemporaries in historiography, it is significant that the major historiographical work of the time, R.G. Collingwood's *The Idea of History* (first published in 1946), emphasised the role of the imagination in history writing in a manner not foreign to Rooke's work. Hayden White usefully characterises the place of the imagination in this 'modern historical theory' in a way that brings its relevance to Rooke to the fore:

> It is present above all in the effort, peculiar to the modern concept of the historian's task, to enter sympathetically into the minds or consciousnesses of human agents long dead, to empathize with the intentions and motivations of actors impelled by beliefs and values which may differ totally from anything the historian might himself honor in his own life, and to understand, even when he cannot condone, the most bizarre social and cultural practices. (1982:123)

What is caught here is the blend of identification and difference that we saw in Rooke's own account of the writing of *Wizards' Country*. The empathy of her vision of pain meets with the sense of dislocation involved in trying very earnestly to enter another point of view. The result, in *Wizards' Country*, is that the differences of the society Rooke presents are maintained in their difference, even as they are depicted as ordinary. Making Benge's perspective primary naturalises his perception without domesticating it. While the world which we so enter is not necessarily that of the literally historical, Rooke still uses her imaginative strategies in *Wizards' Country* to serious historical effect. Fiction becomes an historicising form, letting us experience the resistance of a world different from our own and yet finding a way to relate that world meaningfully to our own. *Wizards' Country* thus presents a compellingly novel history to the reader.

In both 'Yesterday's Child' and *Wizards' Country* the movement of the narrative is towards an increasing integration into formal history; the recasting of the story gives this a very different significance in each case, however. In *Wizard's Country* the narrative's progressive integration into formal history parallels Benge's progressive integration into his community. While Donisa's social initiation in 'Yesterday's Child' is hindered by his personal vision (with its 'foreign' Christian connotations), Benge's is threatened by a force both of and against traditional life. The witchcraft emanating from the wizards' country is as much a product of the community as it is opposed to it. It emerges from the belief systems of the Zulu, and if it is an enemy, it is an enemy from *within* those systems. This is important, for the tensions surrounding the protagonist of *Wizards' Country* are generated by the world from which he comes, and must be resolved, historically, on that world's own terms, not those of its material and ideological antagonist.

We may measure continued (deliberate) colonial ignorance in this regard by noting that in the year *Wizards' Country* first appeared the Witchcraft Suppression Act No. 3 of 1957 was passed; this act was intended to introduce uniformity into the individual legislative acts dealing with witchcraft, the first of which emerged from the events upon which the story of *Wizards' Country* is based and the place in which it is set – Law No. 19 of 1891 (Natal). While Milton and Cowling, in their commentary on the act of 1957 (as amended in 1970), argue that 'criminal law has long been used to suppress what have thought to be the undesirable features of these beliefs', Ros Posel clearly shows that 'from the perspective of African people, the proscriptions of such law amount to an overturning of values within their communities' (1993:4). In the light of such observations, we remember that magic is often a positive force in Rooke's novel, and is an important element in freeing Benge from the influence of the witch. The ambiguous role of the supernatural is caught in Posel's comment that 'the identification *by the witchdoctor* of the witch as the source of evil and hence disorder was regarded as a crucial step in the restoration of order and harmony' (my emphasis); as such, witchhunting (the central practice the Witchcraft Suppression Act was designed to eradicate), 'was held to constitute a moral good in African society' (3).

Benge's personal story is one of restoration, and magic is no less crucial than history in this process. The negative side of communal supernatural belief causes him to be treated as a child well into his adult years because of his physical deformity. His initiation into the more positive aspects of the community begins informally but no less seriously when he rescues Thunzi and Danisa on their crossing over into Natal after lovers who have fled Cetshwayo's reinforcement of Shaka's marriage laws. This fictional event follows in broad form an actual event which was to become enshrined historically in the infamous Ultimatum presented by the British to the Zulus and serve as the flash-point of the Anglo-Zulu War. It sets up therefore the relationship between the historical and the communal (integration into the one brings about integration into the other) which is to become increasingly marked with the development of the narrative. Immediately after this however, we are given a long new section (entirely absent from 'Yesterday's Child') in which Benge (as a magic dwarf) seduces and then abandons a woman of another clan, is drawn entirely into a world of witchcraft and wizardry, and is constantly assailed with doubt as to his own position in relation to these things. He fights a long struggle to be free of them, rejects them, but remains haunted by them for much of the rest of the novel. They are only dispelled by the intervention of the larger community – and history – into the narrative. As his brothers, now warriors in the king's army, come home, he is drawn away from the threat and temptation of the world of witchcraft. Finally Usibebu, significantly an actual historical figure (and the one to whom the novel is dedicated), invades the wizards' country while on a mission to the area. He befriends Benge, reveals the very real political motivation behind the actions of the wizards, and guides Benge safely out of the magic zone when he is about to succumb to it again. He then gives Benge his first cattle, which furthers his integration into the community. In passing, but vital to the narrative, Usibebu saves Thunzi's lover, Cece, from the disgrace and threat to her life she has incurred in defying the marriage laws and running off with another lover when Thunzi apparently rejects her. Thunzi, in turn, kills the witch who has haunted Benge and finally draws Benge away from witchcraft and into history.

This movement does not dispel the positive power of the magic that preserves the sense of difference which pervades the novel; if witchcraft's evil and isolating effects on Benge are defeated, he continues to experience the magic that is a part of his community. By the time his clan is engaged in the war against the British, Benge is entirely integrated in both the clan and the war. The pronouns in the following passage contrast strongly with the lonely and repeated singulars of the opening paragraphs and mark his having taken his place in the community:

> We drank those medicines which make a man's heart angry and we were sprinkled with medicines that turn away the weapons of the enemy. We were strengthened by the sinews of bulls. The war torch was laid upon our bodies; the war charm was held before our eyes. (244)

Magic is here an integral part of the community and its rites, and Benge's involvement in it is entirely a communal one; no longer is he the lonely servant of an antisocial and malevolent witchcraft.

During the battle Benge discovers a new communal sense of his own individuality which is represented by his use of his full clan name for the first time: 'That day I took three rifles; I, Benge Tshanini' (255). Again this contrasts with his earlier self, when he tells us 'I was hidden from strangers, nor was the name of Benge Tshanini known to any but those we trusted' (14).

Benge ultimately moves to the historical centre of the narrative when he (along with Thunzi) is selected to kill the Prince Imperial; his engagement in a military operation that is not just reserved for the finest soldiers of the army but one which also historically actually occurred places him centrally in terms of the fiction and its historical referent.

The Tshanini clan is almost completely destroyed (along with the destruction of the Zulu nation in the fragmented power struggle following on Cetshwayo's defeat and the division of the Zulu kingdom) in the battle of 'Ghost Mountain'/Etshaneni. This battle is pervaded with the smoke of burning grass which poisons the Tshanini for whom grass, as their clan-name indicates, is sacred; in the midst of this burning, however, Benge comments, 'How lovely is the grass that withers but never dies' (295) and here the significance of the altered clan-name comes to the fore. The clan will survive the destruction, but with a clan-leader born of the romance at the heart of the story. Thunzi, the heir to the chieftaincy of the Tshanini, is mortally wounded, but upon Thunzi's death Benge takes on the inheritance which his deformity prevented him from claiming. His emergence into full manhood is completed in an ironic reversal which has him surviving to father a child (and found a new community) for the dying Thunzi with Thunzi's now reconciled lover, Cece:

> I said, 'brother, be easy: I once had a son. I will build a village for
> you and you will be remembered.'

In turn, Thunzi accepts in death his vision which, as has been pointed out, is no longer presented in opposition to the traditional way of life; it is now part of the inheritance of the clan:

> Name the village for my beloved, and the child ... give him the
> name of the wind. And teach him what was in my heart, even of the
> . hawk's cry ...'
> The old people say that beneath the earth the dead live again as

they lived above it, the warrior with his spear and the evil person with his poisons. I could not believe this as I looked at Thunzi's face which had the mark of his spirit's passing. It seemed to me then that his spirit was a gentle thing and that the caverns of the dead would be of quietness and of peace.

Our grandmother had strength to pull his shield over him. (298)

The traditional act performed by a venerable member of the community merges easily with the vision now, and Benge is the mature figure finally able to live out the recognition of this. With Thunzi's death Benge must finally live for himself, generate his own line, and stop living vicariously through his brother. In short, he enters full adulthood:

It was not for me any more, the food of childhood. For me there was the stinging switches, the water into which a red-hot axehead had been dipped and the bitter porridge of manhood.

I knew then that it was over, my long bewitchment,

he says, but this new reality, this beginning again, is haunted by the world of the sublime from which it has emerged. Like 'Yesterday's Child', *Wizards' Country* ends on the focus with which it begins, and its final sentence reads:

'Magic dwarf ... hear it on the edge of the wind, in grass, hear it in the crying of the quail.' (299)

Where, in 'Yesterday's Child', Donisa dies, Benge survives to enter history on his own terms. Rooke could not integrate her protagonist in 'Yesterday's Child' into the vision upon which the narrative ends; in *Wizards' Country* she has reworked that narrative, enabling it to accommodate its real sense of difference fully. The picturesque frame is gone, the landscape is inhabited. Personal and historical maturity are achieved, and the sublime force that preserves and carries this through survives as an echo even in its timely exit.

DIFFERENCE AND APARTHEID

Rooke abandons the attempt to domesticate the historical difference that is her concern because the price is a threat to her own sense of identity. Certainly this ultimately disenables her; she cannot continue the project beyond the point she achieves here. This I think is an effect of her historical moment, however, and her achievement in *Wizards' Country* is all the greater for her acknowledgement of it. She was writing as the full force of grand apartheid was getting under way, and the traps that lay before her in exploring historical difference on ethno-national terms are obvious. But the differences she does explore, the history of the Other she does achieve, the past represented in its discontinuity, are all perhaps more materially important than they first seem in the face of the ideology that dominated the period in which this book was written. Perhaps difference needed to be more strongly guarded in a different way, even as it was politically proclaimed in every corner of South African life. For the differences which Rooke's romance reinvokes were not so much destroyed by apartheid as domesticated by it. A passage from Shula Marks and Anthony Atmore's introduction to *Economy and Society in Pre-Industrial South Africa* speaks to this point most eloquently:

In Natal in many ways the British were able to take over at a political level where Shaka had left off. This was not simply because after a long period of civil war, Africans were anxious to re-establish any kind of order; it was also that the colonial administrators were able to take over the centralised powers of the Zulu kings, without introducing a major discontinuity into African life. So long as colonial society remained small and weak, it was forced to work within the modes of thought and control already established in the area. There was thus considerable continuity even at the political and ideological level in African life in nineteenth-century Natal, with Theophilus Shepstone, the Secretary for Native Affairs, taking on, certainly in his own mind, perhaps more questionably in African eyes, many of the attributes of the Zulu kings. Again, as Slater points out, the fact that the land companies were content with extracting rent and did not try to restructure productive relations among the peasantry, contributed to this sense of continuity, and masked the critical changes which were in fact taking place.

It has been argued recently that it was these particular circumstances in Natal, where the forces of colonisation were weak and had to come to terms with existing structures, utilising the pre-colonial forms and ideology for its own purposes of surplus extraction, but not totally restructuring it, which led to the development in Natal of a policy and ideology of segregation which were to provide late nineteenth-century policy-makers with useful precedents. (1980:19)

Those precedents then, so intimately concerned with the domestication of what is different in the traditional life which Rooke depicts as difference in *Wizards' Country*, were to make of the dynamics of Natal history something of chilling importance to the very national issues which have tended to marginalise Natal.

For it has often been noted that the policy of 'separate development' found in the 'Shepstone system' a powerful precedent; like Shepstone's policies, the Bantu Authorities Act, No 68 of 1951 'utilised traditional systems of production ... and ... recognised selective features of the structure of authority' (Guy 1983:41) when it 'stipulated that political control within the reserves was to be exercised through a three-tiered system comprising local, regional and tribal authorities' (Posel 1993:6). The act insisted, in fact, that Bantu Tribal Authorities were 'to be constituted with due regard to Native Law and Custom' (quoted in ibid.), but it is here that 'continuous history' reveals its will to power. For the 'considerable continuity' noted by Marks and Atmore above of course involved, as Cobbing says of the Stuart Archives, '*the selective preservation* of Native Modes of Life'; traditions, as Cobbing argues, are

> seldom if ever things internal to a society which can be retrieved like diamonds from the earth or collected like mushrooms in the field. They are produced on the spot in conditions almost entirely set up by the collector. The product, the tradition, is either exploited outside the society to which it is said to allude, or reinserted as 'history' into it, in both cases for purposes which are frequently extremely devious. (1988b:118-19)

Traditions, then, are all too often the links we forge to manacle the past to our present concerns. This is no less true of 'great traditions' in literary history (which makes Leavisism's programmatic ahistoricism refreshingly honest in this regard), however different the scale of their project, than the more explicitly and viciously exploitative social engineering that formed the context in which Rooke wrote *Wizards' Country*.

The materiality of the past often reasserts itself through the contradictions generated in its domestication, however. This is demonstrated by Posel in terms relevant to our discussion of *Wizards' Country* when she shows that the Bantu Authorities Act and the Witchcraft Suppression Act 'shared a common purpose' (1993:6). The real aim of the Witchcraft Suppression Act was to loosen the hold of the witchdoctors on the chiefs, thus strengthening the power of the local tribal authorities in terms of the Bantu Authorities Act. In the process, however, it became increasingly obvious that the chiefs were no longer primarily answerable to their communities, but rather to the Native Affairs Department. This resulted in, on the one hand, the legitimacy of the chiefs being eroded as they came increasingly to be seen as government agents and, on the other, the related problem of the most dangerous aspects of witchhunting being cut adrift from their traditional controls and becoming an horrific force in the struggles emerging from collapsing communities. In Rooke's novel, a communal effort balancing history and magic frees the protagonist from the 'evil' elements of the wizards' country, and creates an historical base, however tentative, from which to translate the values learned in this into a struggle against a new and even more destructive world.

That struggle, today, is usually inscribed in the terms of 'tradition' and 'modernity', and the region Rooke very much made her fictional home has become one of the central stages on which the tensions between these forces are being played out. KwaZulu-Natal is the area in which the African National Congess's modern concept of the nation faces possibly its greatest test as it attempts to come to terms with one of the most powerful political vehicles of tradition, the Inkatha Freedom Party. Here democracy itself tests its limits in trying to accommodate practices formed within very different systems, and tradition must choose between its chauvinist, regional, and ethnic potential and engaging in a truly national agenda. The civil conflict generated by these tensions can only, finally, be opposed by negotiations within a medium that allows for a subtle, self-reflexive, creative awareness of the differences involved, and it is my suggestion, that, as we saw in Plaatje's representation of the national, the romance form has a place in helping us grasp this.

Rooke's attempt to imagine the past in its difference to the degree that it may challenge her identity rather than be appropriated by it can be measured by the fact that it pushed her to the point of productive collapse (no trilogy, but one powerful work achieved). This means for me that Rooke stands in the margins of southern Africa's literary history much as KwaZulu-Natal does in South Africa's history books – with all the potential to return from the periphery and forcefully remind us of the differences we have domesticated.

HISTORICISING THE PAST

This brings to a conclusion our study of uses of the past. In it we have defined the most successful deployments of 'history' in fiction to be those which allow the past to resist being appropriated by the present. Fiction which recreates the past in its difference powerfully enough to challenge the present shifts us from the rather insignificant category of 'historical fiction' to the more important activity of historicising form.

What these case studies have illustrated too, is how few 'historical novels' – in even the 'classical' Lukácsian sense – may be seen to function as *historicising form*. While, for Lukács, 'the question of the historical novel as an independent genre only ever arises if for some reason or other the proper and adequate connexion with a correct understanding of the present is lacking' (1981:201), for us a form which properly historicises forces us to question whatever 'correct understanding' of the present we may think we have through the relationship we establish with the past. The effect of this is, to return to words of the theorist who has helped give us a vocabulary for the kind of historicisation invoked in this book, that

> the very dynamics of the historical tribunal are unexpectedly and dialectically reversed: it is not we who sit in judgement on the past, but rather the past ... which judges us, imposing the painful knowledge of what we are not, what we are no longer, what we are not yet. (Jameson 1988b:175)

We have concentrated on 'what we are no longer' up to now, but in the chapters to come we will have to take into account 'what we are not' and 'what we are not yet'. For while 'historical' fiction may still be identified by its particular interaction with the institutions within which 'history' is constructed, this need no longer, as far as historicising form is concerned, attach it exclusively to the past. The act of historicising may make of the present, and the future too, *'novel histories'*.

PART TWO

■

THE PRESENT AS HISTORY

7

THE HISTORIAN
AS DETECTIVE

■

This people, plunged wholly in the present,
lives with neither myths nor consolation.
*– Albert Camus (quoted as an epigraph in
Goldblatt and Gordimer 1973)*

PERIODISING THE PRESENT

Of the three temporal affiliations evident in the uses of history in South African fiction, it is least useful to attempt to periodise literature which treats the present as history. The present appears historical, of course, when it is overtly just pre- or post- a phase or moment that lends itself to being identified as 'historically' different from itself as a phase or moment – that is, when the present seems particularly significant in some scheme of development or decline, linear or otherwise, teleological or not. Such conceptions of 'stages' are unpopular at the moment for a whole variety of reasons, but chiefly because they tend, in the words of the grand reviver of the 'periodising hypothesis' whose theories I have raided for my central analogy for historicising form, 'to obliterate difference and to project an idea of the historical period as a massive homogeneity (bounded on either side by inexplicable chronological metamorphoses and punctuation marks)' (Jameson 1991:3). Jameson's continued but increasingly subtle commitment to the all-embracing Marxist model of modes of production registers his awareness of this problem in its bearing the influence of non-totalisers like Foucault, who has presented his 'genealogy' as a way of reading texts against their contexts without reducing them to a single causality, and his 'archaeology' as a way of stressing that each particular historical 'level' or 'general horizon' is first and foremost a discursive formation ('enunciative field')(1972:131).

Analysing representations of the present as history in South African fiction brings me up against the problem of periodisation from another direction. Accepting, as I did in Chapter One in quoting Robert Young's conclusion that 'history will always involve a form of historicism, but an historicism that cannot be sustained', I will hold to my broad outline of a 'stage' in which the present as history moves to the foreground in South African literature in English. But the present as history appears, to use Foucault's terms, as a *continuing* 'practice that causes a multiplicity of statements to emerge as regular events' (1972:130) across the whole range of modern South African fiction. It is present as a force behind the period dominated by uses of the past in fiction no less than it is the medium within which what I will call 'future histories' are generated. It is overwhelmingly *'the general system of the formation and transformation of statements'* (130) if put in the terminology of Foucault's archaeology. As Stephen Clingman says in his *The Novels of Nadine Gordimer: History from the Inside* (a work which we have noted for its concentration upon the historical present), 'If one were looking for a society that has undergone historical experience of a most intense kind, there would be few to compete with South Africa' (1986:ix), and David Attwell, in commenting on how a passage from Nadine Gordimer's *Burger's Daughter* 'throws all of the past into the present' says, 'This History is a hermeneutic pressure that dominates the field, everywhere establishing its own radical priorities' (1990b:100).

The reasons for the high profile of the historical novel 'proper' in the 1940s and 1950s – that is, as I have claimed, primarily (but not solely) the emergent nationalisms of the period – were to culminate, for some time, in the coming into power of Afrikaner Nationalism and its consolidation in the unfolding grand vision of apartheid. The fairly rapid deployment of blatant force to establish this and the spectacular social effects this had certainly seem to have emphasised the historicity of the present. As far as fiction is concerned, this is first evident in the 1950s in the writing of Alan Paton, Harold Bloom, and the early Nadine Gordimer, but it is with the harsh repressions of the 1960s that a host of writers emerge firmly committed to the present as history. This was made more obvious as the 'historical novel' moved into the background as a corollary of the stress upon the present. Works by C.J. Driver, Jack Cope, Richard Rive, Alex La Guma, and, especially, the continuing work of Nadine Gordimer, are written in the firm conviction that the contemporary events they represent are 'historically' significant.

The historicism manifest in such a claim is supported by the parallel it sets up between South African fiction and a development central to Lukács's argument regarding the place of the historical novel within the development of the novel as a genre:

> ... its classical form arises out of the great social novel and then, enriched by a conscious historical attitude, flows back into the latter. On the one hand, the development of the social novel first makes possible the historical novel; on the other, the historical novel transforms the social novel into genuine history of the present, an authentic history of manners ... (1981:200-201)

If Lukács's thesis is accurate regarding the 'social novel' in South Africa from the late 1950s onwards, his claim that the historical novels that came after the 'classical' period of the genre are characterised by a thin use of the past is also accurate in the South African context. We observe in the general production of the South African historical novel a similar reduction of the materiality of the past to a mere exotic location that emerges out of a wish to escape the reality of the present: 'Distance, then', as Lukács puts it, 'is no longer something historically concrete ... Distance is simply negation of the present ...' (278). Strictly historical novels (that is, those which use the past as a setting) become by and large limited to 'popular' writing by the first half of the 1960s, with Wilbur Smith beginning to take up Stuart Cloete's role as the major populariser of the South African past.

Even at the bestselling level, however, we find the historical form of this period becoming distinctly slighter. Whereas Cloete's first novel, *Turning Wheels*, was banned in South Africa from its publication in 1937 up until 1974 'presumably for its realistic and sometimes harsh portrayal of the Afrikaner' (Adey *et al.* 1986:201), Smith's début, *When the Lion Feeds*, was promptly banned on its appearance in 1964 because of its salacity. No doubt grounds too for its popularity, nowhere is the novel less convincing as an historical novel than in its prominent depiction of sexuality. The characters betray little or no evidence of working through the predominant sexual mores of their time, but behave in accordance with popular contemporary ideas of sensuality. This attitude is telling (as we considered in relation to Oliver Walker) because the inability to present intimacy historically is a particularly clear signal of the present's invasion of the past. Popular attitudes to the historical events portrayed in Smith's work are just as obvious, with no attempt to think through them again from the new perspectives creatively allowed by the fictional mode; history is simply used, not explored or redefined, let alone created as a challenge to the present.

Analysis of this form of light 'romancing' may usually be left to a plotting of its rather crude ideological determinants, and while some interesting work has been done in this area (see especially Maughan-Brown 1990), such investigations do not really add much to my specific argument. We move on, then, to consider the present as history, a trope I will treat along the lines suggested by Jameson when, in periodising postmodernism, he treats it 'not as a style but rather as a cultural dominant: a conception which allows for the presence and coexistence of a range of very different, yet subordinate, features' (1991:4). The sheer volume of South African fiction which may be characterised as historicising their contemporary circumstances forced me to look for a 'subordinate feature' that would provide at one and the same time some limits to the field (again, a reminder that this book does not aim at being a survey) and an interesting (preferably under-researched) angle on it.

These criteria are met by the detective genre, perhaps the most novel of the forms for which I will be claiming historiographical significance. The detective story in South Africa has largely been ignored by literary scholarship, yet it provides an extremely useful way into treatments of the present as history. The detective form, as I shall go on to illustrate, is by convention generally present-tensed, but in the most unexpected of ways it is drawn into the cultural dominant of the 'historical' in the South African context.

If detective fiction, in what I will call its best exemplars, does treat the present as history, and our definition of history is a point of resistance from which to challenge the present, the problem which arises in this section is how the form creates within the present the necessary difference from which to 'judge' the present. It is precisely, in my terms, the weaker forms of detective fiction which show themselves unable to do this and the stronger forms which, in the vocabulary of R.G. Collingwood which we shall be drawing from in this chapter, show themselves capable of putting the present 'to the question'. We will be tracing our way, then, from works of detective fiction which show themselves to be typically conservative products of their context to those which, in line with the theme of this book, are capable of producing through their form an effectively historical perspective; in other words, we will be studying the way in which the detective form in southern Africa moves from being a reflex of contemporary historical circumstances to the point where it resists the pressures of its time and produces the present as history.

It will take some time to approach the specifically South African material of this section. This is because I must first examine the connection between historical and detective fiction which emerges from the literary and historiographical implications of the commonly utilised analogy of the detective for the historian. I go on then to use this to structure my critical approach and my selection of material.

COLLINGWOOD'S DETECTIVE

As Georg Lukács was composing *The Historical Novel* in the winter of 1936-37, R.G. Collingwood was completing a series of lectures written during 1935 and 1936 out of which his posthumously published *The Idea of History* (1983 [1946]) was put together. Looming large amongst Lukács's targets for attack was Benedetto Croce, whose ideas Collingwood was at the same time in the process of refining and expounding. Croce, for Lukács, is representative of a general scepticism dominating the intellectual and political life of the period, a scepticism often expressed in the form of a pervasive relativism. This relativism, most obviously seen in the vogue of Einstein's theories in the popular imagination, naturally included a drastic reassessment of post-Rankean historiographic assumptions. A combination of subjectivism and present-mindedness prevailed in historiography, which Lukács makes the special subject of his attack on Croce. Lukács traces a line of 'historical solecism' from Burckhardt and Nietzsche to Croce: Croce's dictum 'All true history is history of the present', says Lukács,

> should not be interpreted as connecting history with the objective
> problems of the present; it is not a conception according to which the
> present can only be comprehended objectively through its prehistory.
> No, for Croce, too, history is something subjective, an experience.
> (1981:214)

Lukács reads Croce's aphorism as a negation – implicitly, what is more, a negation of his own position. The materialist, who defines himself as seeking 'to uncover the real driving forces of history as they objectively worked and to explain history from them' (209), is scandalised by an attitude to the past in which:

> History as a total process disappears; in its place there remains a chaos
> to be ordered as one likes. This chaos is approached from consciously
> subjective viewpoints. (215)

This critique of Croce is not unproblematic (a later Marxist cultural theorist, for example, is able to praise 'Croce's great dictum', pointing out that '"all history is contemporary history" does not mean that all history is our contemporary history' [Jameson 1981:18]), but it has maintained a certain currency. Collingwood, Croce's 'English disciple', has more recently been taken up as prime example of the same sort of subjective idealism Lukács attacked in Croce. He had after all announced a 'Copernican revolution in the theory of history', which he described in *The Idea of History* as:

> the discovery that, so far from relying on an authority other than himself, to whose statements his thought must conform [the common-sense theory], the historian is his own authority and his thought autonomous, self-authorizing, possessed of a criterion to which his so-called authorities must conform and by reference to which they are criticized. (1983:236)

Collingwood's target is of course the positivist's conception of historiography which, he says, 'consisted of two things: first, ascertaining facts; secondly, framing laws. The facts were immediately ascertained by sensuous perception. The laws were framed through generalizing from these facts by induction' (126-27). It is commonly assumed that he attacks positivism from a position of subjective idealism. E.H. Carr, for example, sees in Collingwood a wilful relativism, a 'total scepticism' which 'comes perilously close to treating history as something spun out of the human brain' (1987:20). Paul Q. Hirst, however, has since eloquently defended Collingwood against these charges (not without, of course, some reservations), finding that what is at stake is 'the reconstruction of the past in terms of contemporary significance' a project which is 'neither relativist or idealist' (1985:51). But I am not concerned here with rehearsing the idealist/materialist conflict, or in following literally Collingwood's demonstration of the autonomy of the historian over his authorities. We may touch upon some relevant aspects of this debate as we go along, but our main concern will be elsewhere. I propose to attend to something which may seem initially only marginal in Collingwood's elaboration of his case, but which I believe will be significant for our purposes. This is his liberal use of literary analogies in his discussion of history writing – a figurative strategy that is not just interesting from an historiographical point of view; it will also provide us with a particularly useful way of approaching the uses of history in fiction.

Collingwood's case for the autonomy of the historian in relation to his authorities – that is, the works of previous historians (see 33) – rests on three key historical activities: selection, criticism, and interpolation. The last is most important for us, for it most clearly illustrates Collingwood's ideal of 'constructive history': 'I described constructive history as interpolating, between the statements borrowed from our authorities, other statements implied by them' (240). This is a 'necessary' or '*a priori*' characteristic of history writing (240), one which is 'properly not ornamental but structural' (241). Being 'essentially something imagined' (241), one would think that it is precisely this element of historical writing that brings it closest to the literary; however, Collingwood proposes a firm distinction between the historical and the literary imagination.

He does this by contrasting history writing with its nearest literary form, the historical novel. This genre is dispensed with early in Collingwood's argument: historians must, like historical novelists, go beyond their authorities by way of interpolating implied evidence. Historical novelists may, however, be arbitrary in such constructions (filling up the narrative with 'fanciful details' [240], for example), while the historian may employ 'nothing that is not necessitated by the evidence' (241). This is a commonplace distinction, and need not detain us. (Which does not mean that it is not an uneasy one. F.W. Hayes says the historical novelist must provide only 'what could be proved by evidence and what could not be disproved by evidence' [quoted in Baker 1968:xi].)

Slightly more interesting is Collingwood's use of a more general sense of the novelist to illustrate what he calls the *a priori* imagination. This is no arbitrary or fanciful faculty, and both historian and novelist rely upon it: 'the story, if it is a good story, cannot develop other than it does; the novelist in imagining it cannot imagine it developing except as it does develop' (242). More specifically, the 'historical imagination' is quite simply 'an original and fundamental activity of the human mind', or, in Cartesian terms, an '"innate" idea' (247). Stopping short of any inquiry into whatever social and cultural determinants may be involved here leaves this mental function equally mysterious for the novelist and the historian, making it difficult for us to do more with this point upon Collingwood's terms.

His literary metaphors become really interesting and useful to us when he introduces into his argument an analogy with a popular contemporary literary form, the detective story. 'The hero of a detective novel', he writes, 'is thinking exactly like an historian when, from indications of the most varied kinds, he

183

constructs an imaginary picture of how a crime was committed, and by whom' (243). It is at this point that we must remind ourselves that while the intellectual history of the mid-1930s may have been marked by a grand disillusionment with old absolutes – a disillusionment signalled in literature by the great Modernist texts – it was also known as the Golden Age of detective fiction. *The Idea of History* registers this by providing a short detective story (of Collingwood's own creation) as an extended metaphor for the way in which historical evidence is, as Collingwood would have it in his 'constructive history', constructed.

The story is entitled 'Who killed John Doe?' and, as the name of its victim must already suggest, it is meant to represent an average or typical example of its kind. As such, it reproduces all the essential elements of what had, by the 1920s, already become a rigidly formulaic genre. Rules governing it emerged in works like R. Austin Freeman's 'The Art of the Detective Story' (1924), Monsignor Ronald Knox's 'Ten Commandments of Detection' (1928), and the oath to uphold the form's conventions taken by the members of the Detection Club founded in Britain in 1928 (Symons 1972:9-10). 'The basic formula is this:' writes W.H. Auden, 'a murder occurs; many are suspected; all but one suspect, who is the murderer, are eliminated; the murderer is arrested or dies' (quoted in ibid.:10). To this must be added what members of the Detection Club had crucially to swear: that their detectives would 'well and truly detect the crimes presented to them' without reliance on 'Divine Revelation, Feminine Intuition, Mumbo-Jumbo, Jiggery-Pokery, Coincidence or the Act of God' (ibid.). Collingwood's Detective-Inspector, called in from Scotland Yard by the perplexed local Chief Constable (who has only managed to eliminate some of the suspects), solves the murder of John Doe by strict logical deduction based upon asking the right questions in the right order. It is this that is at the heart of what Collingwood calls his 'fable'.

For the central issue that leads Collingwood to relate historical writing to detective fiction is that of 'the question'. Building on Francis Bacon's injunction to the natural scientist to 'put nature to the question', Collingwood distinguishes 'scientific history, or history proper' (269) from 'scissors-and-paste history' (his term for positivist historiography) on the grounds of the former's active interrogation of evidence and the latter's passive acceptance and mere arrangement of evidence. The point is that authority resides in the questioner, not in the evidence commonly assumed to be his 'authorities'. Collingwood analyses his own detective story at some length in order to demonstrate the nature and manner of correct questioning. We must, for the moment, take the metaphor he develops to express his case literally, and consider the significance of the detective story on its own terms as a genre. This will enable us to tease out the full significance of its figurative role for historiography and also cross over into the literary considerations which ultimately concern us.

It will be necessary for us to spend some time setting up and analysing the conventions of detective fiction. Our aims here will be to introduce the conventions of the form so that we will have some sense of the significance of Collingwood's metaphor, to give an idea of what South African fiction is taking on when it adopts the genre, and to illustrate in some detail precisely how a particular literary form is historically significant, a central concern which will stay with us as we approach the South African material.

DETECTIVE FICTION

Generic distinctions are, as Lukács so lucidly demonstrates when he effectively does away with the 'genre' that is his subject in *The Historical Novel*, empty formalisms unless we avoid the ahistorical stasis which threatens generic divisions once they are established. For all its fixed conventions, the detective genre has a history of change over time. Collingwood himself acknowledges this in drawing upon a transition within the history of detective fiction to conclude his illustration of contrasting historiographical modes. This is a good place for us to begin, and the passage in question is worth quoting at some length. Valorising the interrogative (scientific) method, Collingwood claims:

> It was a correct understanding of this truth that underlay Lord Acton's great precept, 'Study problems, not periods'. Scissors-and-paste historians study periods; they collect all the extant testimony about a certain limited group of events, and hope in vain that something will come of it. Scientific historians study problems: they ask questions, and if they are good historians they ask questions they see their way to answering. It was a correct understanding of the same truth that led Monsieur Hercule Poirot to pour scorn on the 'human bloodhound' who crawls about the floor trying to collect everything, no matter what, which might conceivably turn out to be a clue; and to insist that the secret of detection was to use what, with possibly wearisome iteration, he called 'the little grey cells'. You can't collect

your evidence before you begin thinking, he meant: because thinking means asking questions (logicians, please note), and nothing is evidence except in relation to some definite question. The difference between Poirot and Holmes in this respect is deeply significant of the change that has taken place in the understanding of historical method in the last forty years. Lord Acton was preaching his doctrine in the heyday of Sherlock Holmes, in his inaugural lecture at Cambridge in 1895; but it was caviare to the general. In Monsieur Poirot's time, to judge by his sales, the general cannot have too much of it. The revolution which dethroned the principles of scissors-and-paste history, and replaced them by those of scientific history, had become common property. (281-82)

That Holmes should be expelled from the ranks of the scientific will occasion surprise in many quarters. Perhaps the first of the truisms that comes to mind when one thinks of the rise of detective fiction is its association with scientific method. Victorian England saw the beginnings of the genre's widespread popularity, pre-eminently in the serialisation of Conan Doyle's Holmes series in the *Strand Magazine*. Of these Catherine Belsey says:

> The stories are a plea for science not only in the spheres conventionally associated with detection (footprints, traces of hair or cloth, cigarette ends), where they have been deservedly influential on forensic practice, but in all areas. They reflect the widespread optimism characteristic of their period concerning the comprehensive power of positivist science. (1980:112)

The difference between Collingwood and Belsey on the significance of the Sherlock Holmes stories turns, of course, upon what definition of science is invoked, and it is precisely the positivist element at the heart of Victorian science that Collingwood wishes to expel from his definition of 'scientific' history. Science, for the positivist (as we have seen), 'consists first in ascertaining facts and then in discovering laws' (132-33); Collingwood is prepared to allow this definition to stand for the natural sciences, but not for history. As positivist historians from the time of Ranke onwards have in any case contented themselves with only the first part of the positivist definition of science (sociology made its special area the second), they become lost in a world of increasingly intricate detail – 'the best historian, like Mommsen or Maitland, became the greatest master of detail' (127) – uninformed by a creative and productive interrogation. 'Scientific' history is not concerned with simply ascertaining empirically verifiable facts; its facts 'are arrived at inferentially by a process of interpreting data according to a complicated system of rules and assumptions. A theory of historical knowledge', Collingwood continues, 'would discover what these rules and assumptions are ...' (133), and *The Idea of History* has as its aim just this. Holmes, like all positivists, chooses to appear to operate free of any 'theoretical' constraints or constructions. The detective, like the historian, 'wants only to show what actually happened' (quoted in Marwick 1983:37). The very humility of that 'only' is a screen for the 'rules and assumptions' informing the positivist position.

The positivist attitude towards establishing empirical detail tends to defend itself against observations of this kind on the grounds of the accuracy of its conclusions. It is in these that the details with which it concerns itself take on an overall shape. The manner, then, by which its conclusions are reached naturally foregrounds itself. 'I see it, I deduce it,' says Holmes (Doyle 1928:5), and Watson speaks of 'those deductive methods of reasoning by which [Holmes] achieved such remarkable results' (201); this is a claim which has been repeated in so many ways so often that it has blurred into another truism of detective fiction. Yet as Conan Doyle himself admitted in his memoirs, the 'clever little deductions' which preface many of the cases 'often have nothing to do with the matter in hand, but impress the reader with a general sense of power' (quoted in Knight 1980:86). This is a particularly telling comment, in that it makes plain what is at stake (power) and the significance of the method by which it is achieved.

Stephen Knight observes that Holmes only uses 'deduction' by default in terms of his own claims about his method: '... if Holmes really were finding patterns in facts he would be practising "induction": in reality he has a knowledge of what certain phenomena will mean, and is practising deduction, that is drawing from a set of existent theories to explain new events' (86). In this observation we find a conclusive rejection of positivism. As Collingwood wanted to stress, observation is never in itself objective; the 'rules and assumptions' which make up its 'theoretical' position may simply remain unspoken. Knight gives a more contemporary and concrete expression to this point when he goes on to demonstrate that

Doyle's wish to protect old values, ideas and their social setting is innate to his hero's methodology; the weakness of his own reasoning is clear in misnaming his hero's methodology. The dress of modern materialist science is used for conservative thinking, for a failure to face the real, disorderly experience of data: Doyle's own process and the needs of the bourgeois audience faced with threats of disorder are quite the same. (86)

The transparent medium then, in which Holmes's deductions take their positivist stance, becomes opaque, takes on its ideological solidity, as neutral method becomes loaded attitude. Many commentators agree with Knight that a major factor behind the genre's original popularity was the social reassurance offered by the operation of its form. 'Behind the conscious Victorian and Edwardian adherence to a firmly fixed hierarchical society there lay a deep vein of unease about the possible overturn of that society', writes Symons in *Bloody Murder*, going on to quote Pierre Nordon's point that the Sherlock Holmes cycle is 'addressed to the privileged majority, it plays on their fears of social disturbance and at the same time makes use of Sherlock Holmes and what he stands for to reassure them' (1972:18).

And so the next major truism associated with the beginnings of the popularity of detective fiction emerges: works within the genre are innately conservative. As Foucault demonstrates in *Discipline and Punish*, the 'new literature of crime' is, in the 'disciplinary society', a part of 'the discourse of the Law' (1979:56, 68-69). This is not only portrayed in the status accorded the legal structures of its setting – Dennis Porter notes that 'in a detective story ... the law itself is never on trial' (1981:122) – it is also inscribed in its formal strategies. In its Victorian formulation its scientism is, as we have seen, a reflex of this, as indeed was its rapid attainment of popularity. The continuing popularity of the form brings us to another important point as far as its social significance is concerned.

In *The Pursuit of Crime* Dennis Porter claims that 'detective fiction owes its longevity to its power of grafting contemporary fears to an endlessly repeated formula' (127). Two points of concern to us may be extrapolated from this. Firstly, the 'endlessly repeated formula': this harks back to our earlier comments on the exceptionally conventional – in both a literary and social sense – nature of works within the detective genre. The stylised and static nature of the form, where the realities of the violence and brutality of its content are sublimated, ritualised into the classical proportions of what Dorothy Sayers called 'an Aristotelian perfection of beginning, middle and end' (quoted in Symons 1972:10), naturalises the inevitable punishment following on wrongdoing. The tendency of early detective fiction towards the short story form (compare for example the far less satisfying longer works – the later romances, for example – of Conan Doyle with the elegance and precision of the short stories) reinforces the formal emphasis of the genre, and the way in which this dominates its content.

Secondly, the 'grafting of contemporary fears': this has to do with the way in which the form demands a contemporary expression. It is a significant fact of the classic detective story that it tends – with notable exceptions (the notability suggests how exceptional these are) – to be almost exclusively set in the present. The power of this formal requirement may be illustrated by the fact that Conan Doyle thought little of his Holmes adventures, taking himself most seriously (and this is intriguing for our longer-term aims) as an historical novelist. Yet the period atmosphere for which the first three collections of Holmes stories are famous was not 'period' at the time of their writing. This was Conan Doyle's world, and when popular pressure and financial rewards forced him to keep producing Holmes stories (complete, usually, with their original settings) well past the period in which he first conceived and set them, the aura of the era is far less successfully depicted. Conan Doyle's historical skills and interests could not successfully translate into the detective medium. That this is something of a general rule for detective fiction is made clear in T.J. Binyon's survey of the genre, *Murder Will Out: The Detective in Fiction*, when he lists the 'practice of setting detective stories in the past' under the category of 'A Few Oddities' (1989:125).

This is to be expected, given that what is at stake is the preservation of a particular way of life dominant at a particular time. Eventually the genre was to succumb to changes that no longer accommodated its classic formula, at which point the enormous power of nostalgia transformed the form and its settings into something else. This is all part of a survey of the genre well beyond our interests here, but we may bring ourselves back to the issue in hand by noting that Collingwood's shift from Holmes to Poirot serves precisely to make his metaphor a contemporary one. The pressure of the genre (even when used as a metaphor) is, as I have tried to demonstrate in some detail, towards making the present its subject.

Agatha Christie's stories, like Conan Doyle's, were originally set in the present – a stylised present perhaps, with an implicit leaning towards a rapidly vanishing period which was to increase over time – but even this was directly related to the present she constructed (it is of course a marked feature of the conservatism of her work). Collingwood's deliberate caricature captures effectively the central features of this period. 'John Doe' is no universal Everyman, any more than the story of his murder is a transcendently archetypal detective story: victim and tale both bear very specific marks of a particular type of character in a particular type of detective plot.

Christie's typical South England village settings (we will deal with her use of more distant locations later), rural yet with a convenient town near by and capable too of serving as a commuter base for the metropolis, stocked with characters perfectly representative in appearance and behaviour of their class, profession, or trade, are a product of a combination of urban middle-class idealisation of the country and nostalgia for a world already almost gone. They are simply the board to the game, the two-dimensional space upon which the exchange of a limited range of counters may take place. Emotion is limited to the state of play, and is never engaged with any of the formal elements directly, for their own sake. Given the central convention of murder, then, the victim must be carefully cast so as to fail to engage our sympathy: a criminal him or herself perhaps, or foolish in the extreme or hated by all.

All of this Collingwood recreates in 'Who Killed John Doe?': the village setting, Scotland Yard near enough to lend a hand, a cast of typical village inhabitants, a victim who is a blackmailer, a murderer acting from the best and most understandable of intentions who neatly removes himself from an emotionally messy conclusion by committing suicide.

What is created in Christie's fictional world and recreated in Collingwood's is an environment as solid and dependable and as impervious to the wrongdoing that briefly emerges in it as anything the Victorian age found so comforting in the Holmes stories. The differences between Conan Doyle's and Christie's settings and characters measure the differences between their periods, but still match perfectly in terms of their equal affiliation to their respective dominant classes: the residual aristocratic leanings of Holmes's concerns are replaced with a determinedly upper middle-class perspective in Christie's works.

The contrasting methodologies of their detectives are equally telling. Contemporary detective fiction, Collingwood suggested above on the evidence of Agatha Christie's extensive sales, indicates a popular shift away from what Stephen Knight calls 'the positivistic mysteries of contemporary science' and towards 'the illusion of effective self-help and self-sufficiency' (1980:110). The superior powers and personality of Sherlock Holmes are replaced by detectives or everyday characters far closer to the common abilities available to the reader: 'Poirot's actually simple methods are less illusionary than Holmes's because they are firmly supported by the detective's advocation of simple orderly observation and by the possibility, offered in the clue-puzzle structure, that a reader may solve the problem', says Knight (111). This is central to what Knight goes on to establish as the ideological significance of Christie's work: their celebration of the collective individualism of the bourgeois class and its ability to solve its anxieties on its own terms and with its own abilities.

Collingwood's allegiance to Agatha Christie goes beyond an admiration for Poirot's methods of detection; his story also imports something of the ideological weight of her settings and characters. The obvious parodic elements in 'Who Killed John Doe?' do not finally distance it from the more telling aspects of Christie's conventions, as Paul Hirst makes plain when he identifies a 'commitment to a species of methodological individualism' as 'a central component of Collingwood's doctrine' (1985:55). Hirst is referring to the way in which Collingwood's insistence upon the historian as his own authority can be read as isolating the historian from broader sociological and ideological concerns, a real danger of Collingwood's position. If the historian is entirely his own authority, if the questions that he puts arise purely out of his own perspective, then how are we to account for these questions in historical terms? How are we to question the questioner? Surely not merely upon the terms of the questioner as an isolated individual; social and historical factors must flood into any serious attempt to put the questioner to the question, and this means the questioner is not, to the degree Collingwood insists, his own authority. That authority must be available to us on historical terms.

As we shall see in the study of one of Christie's works to follow, there is a very real sense in which her 'detective' does not push her questions far enough; her solution to the crime at the heart of the story is cut off precisely from the broader historical context of that crime. But the context in which the questions are put is not only an historical one in this sense. As I have tried to demonstrate in my references to Holmes, the very form which gives the questions their validity as questions has to be considered as historically significant. In rejecting Holmes a little too quickly, Collingwood comes close to missing this point. And in presenting 'Who Killed John Doe?' as a permanent analogy for the practice of the historian, he fails, somewhat ironically as an historian, to register the historicity of history, and the material significance of any particular form of practising history. Questions are never innocent of the structures in which they exist, and it is only when these structures are taken into account that a degree of self-reflexivity, the questioner questioning his own questions, can take place. Collingwood's setting forth of the correct method of historical questioning is limited in that it does not take into account the status of its own method; this status is clearly available to us, however, in the metaphors within which it is expressed. This is why we have spent so much time analysing the analogies Collingwood draws between history and the detective form. This is why too we have spent so much time investigating the full circumstances of the development of the detective story; it has been necessary to do this in order to illustrate fully that no genre is innocent, that its very form embodies an historical significance.

In our analyses of South African detective fiction, it will be necessary for us to keep these considerations in mind as we concentrate upon the relationship between the detective story form and its historicising abilities. What we will be looking for in each case is the ability of the writers in question to overcome the origins of their form in the positivist and conservative tendencies of the genre, and to make of it a form which allows for – indeed even creates – a radical historical questioning. Out of this will come a sense of the present as history, as something resistant to merely being appropriated by trivialising forms. The present as history is something that must be produced, achieved through a form which can represent it as a challenge to an unhistoricised sense of the present. There is something of this in Collingwood's idea of the questions that must be put to history, but as I have tried to suggest, his central metaphor for this process is telling with regard to the limits it implies.

One would certainly not wish to push too far the way in which Collingwood's metaphor (the detective story) turns back upon its literal equivalent (the historian's activity), but the match is there to a telling degree. It is the nature of the metaphor which will again primarily concern us here, however, as we focus upon its ability to translate its ideological emphases beyond their initial domestic setting.

AGATHA CHRISTIE IN SOUTHERN AFRICA

Many of Christie's novels play out in exotic settings, but these only concern the plots in the most external of their features. She maintains a fundamental continuity of the ideological features identified above, largely by importing her cast of characters with all the usual trappings of their nation and class into the new location. The variability of the geography barely touches the immediate social relations of the stories.

A prime example of this is an early work which will serve not only as an illustration but also transport us, finally, into the South African historical context.

In 1922 Archie Christie was appointed Financial Adviser to a tour of the Dominions of the British Empire, the object of which was to drum up interest in these areas for an Empire Exhibition to be held in London in 1924. Agatha accompanied him and used the southern African section of the trip as background for *The Man in the Brown Suit* (repr. 1962). The various members of the tour, from Major E.A. Belcher, its leader, to his secretary, are thinly and mostly comically transformed into the cast of characters; the tour, encapsulated in its metropolitan concerns but moving through a series of varied and colourful contexts, provided the perfect model for a Christie plot in foreign climes.

Southern Africa is at the beginning of the novel shamelessly cast as an adventurous location for a bored and frustrated heroine. Anne Beddingfeld is the very ordinary heroine who will prove, true to the Christie formula, the finest of detectives. She is not handicapped in this by maintaining the most superficial and sentimental of attitudes to the strange environment she will later (temporarily, one cannot help but feel) adopt. She tells us, very much in the voice of the young Agatha who, her biographer says, 'longed to travel to the strange and remote places she knew only from explorer's tales and watercolours' (Morgan 1984:87), that she 'yearned for adventure, for love, for romance' and 'went to sleep dreaming of stern silent Rhodesians' (Christie 1962:12); the Rhodesian appears as a constant refrain in the work's preoccupation with a suitable romantic hero. Upon first seeing the 'extra beautiful' Table Mountain she experiences 'Something new, something hitherto undreamed of, something that satisfied my aching hunger for romance' (90). However moving the setting of her adventure is, it never permeates the nature of her story any more than its complement of characters (except for a few very minor ones) admits any local inhabitants. Christie, through her heroine, is quite refreshingly open about this:

> By the way, I should like to make it clear here and now that this story
> will not be a story of South Africa. I guarantee no genuine local colour
> – you know the sort of thing – half a dozen words in italics on every

page. I admire it very much, but I can't do it. In South Sea Islands, of course, you make an immediate reference to *bêche-de-mer*. I don't know what *bêche-de-mer* is, I have never known, I probably never shall know. I've guessed once or twice and guessed wrong. In South Africa I know you at once begin to talk about a stoep – I do know what a stoep is – it's the thing round a house and you sit on it. In various other parts of the world you call it a veranda, a piazza, and a ha-ha. Then again, there are pawpaws ... I was very pleased to meet a pawpaw. I had always vaguely associated it with a hula-hula, which I believe, though I may be wrong, is a kind of straw skirt that Hawaiian girls dance in. No, I think I am wrong – that is a lava-lava.

At any rate, all these things are very cheering after England. I can't help thinking that it would brighten our cold Island life if one could have a breakfast of bacon-bacon, and then go out clad in a jumper-jumper to pay the books. (92-93)

Southern Africa blurs in with a number of exotic locations here, all equally characterised not by any intrinsic interest but only by contrast with the ordinary which is rendered in distinct national terms. The lightness of tone is a true measure of the seriousness of intent, and the level of language at which the foreignness is dealt with remains, quite deliberately, on the surface. Most importantly, it is made clear here that the story, although played out largely in southern Africa, can never be appropriated, at a linguistic or any other level, by that location. Anne will eventually say of the southern African landscape, 'I loved it – loved it more than any place I had ever seen' and her wish that she 'could have a little hut somewhere in the heart of the scrub and live there always – always ...' (127) will come true when she settles with her husband on an island above the Victoria Falls. The 'man in the brown suit' will change from a reference to a clue to a murder in England to her 'son ... lying in the sun, kicking his legs. There's a "man in a brown suit" if you like. He's wearing as little as possible, which is the best costume for Africa, and is as brown as a berry' (190). Yet her naturalisation into Africa is never quite convincing, and we cannot help but feel along with her friend, Suzanne Blair, that it is no more than a long honeymoon. The world of England's upper middle-class society (captured perfectly in Suzanne's last letter to Anne) waits behind the conclusion to reclaim what remains after all its own.

This is true of the romantic geographical descriptions throughout ('Oh, dear,

dear Falls, how I love and worship you and always shall' [128]) which, despite the disclaimer regarding local colour given above, abound in the novel. They give the impression of being transferred quite immediately from Agatha Christie's diary (she kept one of the trip) to the fiction, however, and maintain the atmosphere of travel writing.

Much of the detail of the novel is, in fact, lifted directly from the Christies' own experiences in South Africa. In a letter home, for example, Agatha expresses her delight in the heat and the sunshine of South Africa, especially for the opportunity they provided for what she calls 'bathing with planks'. 'Agatha and Archie slipped away whenever they could to Muizenburg for surfing, or to a white sandy beach, edged with mountains, at a place called Fish Hoek', her biographer tells us (Morgan 1984:90), and Agatha writes home about surfing with quite a professional air: '… swimming is a little tame after surfing. We are going to buy light curved boards (that don't jab you in the middle) and absolutely master the art' (quoted in ibid.). Anne Beddingfeld's account in the novel of her surfing clearly echoes Christie's:

> There was some perfectly entrancing bathing going on. The people had short curved boards and came floating in on the waves … I made for the bathing pavilion, and when they said would I have a surf board, I said 'Yes, please.' Surfing looks perfectly easy. It isn't. I say no more. I got very angry and fairly hurled my plank from me. Nevertheless, I determined to return on the first possible opportunity and have another go. I would not be beaten. Quite by mistake I then got a good run on my board, and came out delirious with happiness. Surfing is like that. You are either vigorously cursing or else you are idiotically pleased with yourself. (94)

Anne emerges from the surf to be kidnapped in Muizenburg, another episode in a plot which surges from wave to episodic wave in a style not yet governed by the tight clue-puzzle structure of which Christie was later to become the master. As Anne is swept into her South African experience, she is carried into more than just an exotic location; she has to ride a tumultuous moment of South African history experienced by Christie and promptly written directly into the plot (and central crime) of her novel. An extract from another of her letters home shows her ability to catch in firm, if short, strokes an immediate sense of this moment and her transitory position within it:

At Germiston a wire was handed in from the Trade Commissioner ...
saying Jo'burg was unsafe, he would meet us on the platform there
and had arranged accommodation for us at Pretoria instead ... All the
Hotels had shut down that afternoon with their waiters etc. on strike
– and there was no meat and no bread, as the bakers had come out,
and the strikers had stopped all taxis and pulled out the drivers. They
were throwing hand grenades in the street ... Today they have
proclaimed Martial law in Jo'burg – and all the bars are shut here. It
seems an idiotic moment for coming to try and talk about an exhibition
that is to be held in two year's time – but we are off to Rhodesia on
Tuesday, so we must do what we can. (Quoted in Morgan 1984:92)

Whether these experiences make *The Man in the Brown Suit* any more a 'story of
South Africa' than its geographic setting does, or whether the history it deals
with remains a sea its detective-protagonist simply surfs over, briefly beaching on
one exotic location after another and 'doing what she can' before moving on,
needs to be investigated.

The immediacy of the diary form (which emphasises the present tense of the
novel) is overtly built into the way in which the story is recounted. Much of it is
related to us through long extracts from the diary of Sir Eustace Pedler, MP. This
is, as only the conclusion of the novel will reveal, a running joke, for it is he who
will turn out to be the mastermind behind all the villainy. References are made to
a mysterious 'Colonel' from the beginning; he has a long career of criminal
involvement, but has always escaped detection (usually by ingeniously setting up
someone else as the scapegoat). The crime in which he is involved which sets off
the story of *The Man in the Brown Suit* is a complicated plot involving South
American and South African diamonds, a plot which has entangled the hero (an
Englishman, but he has settled in Rhodesia long enough to qualify as strong and
silent) who has been made the scapegoat and which draws in, by a series of
coincidences, the impulsive heroine. The actual crime, in true detective fashion,
precedes the novel's action, but its consequences make up the bulk of the story; in
the process however, it blurs over into the 'Colonel's' next criminal project, and
this is the one that will mainly concern us.

Pedler, because he has 'large interests in Rhodesia ... and the question of
Rhodesia joining the Union is one in which [he has] a vital interest', is asked by a
British Government official to take certain secret documents to General Smuts; in

doing so the official talks 'About South Africa and the industrial situation there. About the growing rumours of a strike on the Rand. Of' – and this is crucial – 'the secret causes actuating that strike' (39). Pedler thus boards a ship which ends up, for various reasons to do finally with the criminal plot, carrying all the important characters of the novel on a typical 'passage to South Africa'.

A further blind to our spotting Pedler as the villain is that he is the chief comic character in an often extremely comic book. He hates work, wants only a comfortable life (so he constantly tells us in his crucially unrevealing diary), and yet – ostensibly only because he is forced into it by his secretary – we often catch glimpses of him at work. This is, from the fragments we are allowed to overhear, focused upon the labour situation in South Africa: 'Sir Eustace paused dead in the middle of a complicated sentence on the labour situation ...' (113), and, '"I therefore venture to suggest, that in tackling this problem of coloured labour ..."' (129). Even on board ship when he is meant to be relaxing he invites 'a quaint little fellow called Reeves' to join his table at dinner: 'He's a prominent member of the South African Labour Party. Horrible little man,' he tells us, 'but I want to keep in with him, as he gives me information that I need. I want to understand this Rand business from both sides' (64). Of course he wishes to understand it for nefarious purposes kept hidden from us at this point, and is using the unsuspecting Labour Party member.

Reeves is disliked not only by Sir Eustace; he is damned by the author as well. He is guilty of the worst sin, that is, of having no sense of humour (see page 65; Sir Eustace, the villain, is treated quite affectionately in this regard) and once the Strike has broken out – the Labour Party having publicly backed the South African Industrial Federation's action – proves to lack the courage of his own convictions:

> 'He's like all the rest of these people; they make inflammatory speeches of enormous length, solely for political purposes, and then wish they hadn't. He's busy now going about saying he didn't really do it ... [H]e was just off to Cape Town, where he meditates making a three days' speech in Dutch, vindicating himself, and pointing out that the things he said really meant something entirely different.' (154)

Christie makes no secret of her dislike for Labour politics, then, but much more is implied in her attitude to the historical circumstances that she winds around her criminal plot. She is capable of capturing very real moments and issues concerning the Strike in a rather impressionistic sort of way when she puts her mind to it. Another of the fragments we overhear from Sir Eustace at work runs: 'Tylman [sic] Roos, in his speech at ...' (114); this is in all likelihood a reference related to the Transvaal Nationalist leader's letter in the *Vaderland* urging Active Citizen Force members to disobey the call-up, and could effectively have been used to establish the Labour and Nationalist Party alliance in support of the Strike. It is, however, simply dropped as an atmospheric titbit. Again, Sir Eustace himself puts it to a South African official 'that his government were letting things go rather far' (155), which echoes the popular sentiment of the time that 'the Government had sat idly by while the rising got out of hand'. Whereas Smuts countered this charge by 'contending that before declaring martial law the Government was "bound in the interest of the country to let the situation develop, ... because it was possible that the situation might develop peacefully"' (Davenport 1987:282), Christie has her Government official say, '"There is such a thing as giving a man enough rope, and letting him hang himself, Sir Eustace"' (155), a cliché in which we must take the singular seriously, because it is an individual mastermind behind the Strike that she has the government waiting to catch.

Whenever the Rand Rebellion is mentioned, it is connected not so much with the proportion of white to black workers on the mines that historians have been content to give as its immediate origin; instead, the 'secret causes' mentioned by the British government official come increasingly, and ironically, to dominate each reference to the Strike. Anne, as she realises that she has 'stumbled on a bigger thing' (109) than she first thought, tells us:

> The murder in the house at Marlow was not an isolated incident committed by a solitary individual. I was up against a gang, and ... I was beginning to understand some of its manifold activities. Systematized crime, organized by the man known to his followers as the 'Colonel'! I remembered some of the talk I had heard on board ship, of the strike on the Rand and the causes underlying it – and the belief that some secret organization was at work fomenting the agitation. That was the 'Colonel's' work, his emissaries were acting according to plan. (110)

Our not knowing, along with Anne, that Sir Eustace Pedler is the 'Colonel' leads to moments of intense yet hidden irony in this regard, especially in the extracts from Pedler's diary. Here, for example, he continues his account of the interview with the South African Government official, reinforcing Christie's proposition of there being ultimately a single individual behind the Rebellion:

> 'It is not the strikers themselves who are causing the trouble. There is some organization at work behind them. Arms and explosives have been pouring in ... More than that, Sir Eustace, we have every reason to believe that the man who runs the whole show, the directing genius of the affair, is at this minute in Johannesburg.'
>
> He stared at me so hard that I began to fear that he suspected me of being the man. I broke out into a cold perspiration at the thought, and began to regret that I had ever conceived the idea of inspecting a miniature revolution at first hand,

says the 'directing genius' himself (155). Our clue (the one that would enable us to solve the mystery along with Anne) that he is up to much more than 'studying conditions on the Rand' (156) is that his refusal to be sent to the safety of Pretoria goes clearly against his apparently indolent and cowardly nature.

Eventually Sir Eustace, when he has Anne in his clutches and the climax of the novel is playing out amidst the firing guns and falling bombs of the 'Revolution', expresses himself openly in the terms of a hired agitator. (The hired agitator is of course typically and fervently central to the historical explanations of certain class interests.) Anne and he engage in this telling interchange:

> 'You believe in the success of this Revolution? You've burnt your boats.'
>
> 'For an otherwise intelligent young woman, that's a singularly unintelligent remark. No, my dear child, I do not believe in this Revolution. I give it a couple of days longer and it will fizzle out ignominiously.'
>
> 'Not one of your successes, in fact?' I said nastily.
>
> 'Like all women, you've no idea of business. The job I took on was to supply certain explosives and arms – heavily paid for – to foment feeling generally, and to incriminate certain people up to the hilt. I've carried out my contract with complete success, and I was careful to be paid in advance.' (171)

Purged of all idealism and reduced to purely material interest, the manipulator of the Rand Rebellion stands fully exposed; the strikers are the mere dupes of a superior criminal, not, whatever they might think (and we are given no evidence at all as to what they might think; the class limits of Christie's world prevent us from even meeting a mine worker), active makers of their own history. Strangely, however, Christie's solution is no solution at all, for if Pedler is the material cause behind the Rebellion, we are left none the wiser as to who stands behind him in this chain of responsibility. We are in fact no closer to discovering who has actually instigated the manipulation; the 'Colonel' by his own admission is only a hired hand, and the originator of this historical event recedes ever further into the background of history, never to be unmasked.

Christie's biographer reminds us that this is no oversight confined to a particular work; it is in fact a theme touched on earlier in *The Secret Adversary* and often returned to in Christie's novels: Janet Morgan describes it as

> ... the notion of there being a hidden but vigorous international conspiracy, whose operations, whether traffic in arms, drugs, jewels, works of art or human skills, whether intended to promote a single ideology, none or several, whether fostered via youthful zealots, naïve disciples or cynical experts, were all ultimately fuelled by money ... (1984:109)

This is a central element in the brand of generic conservatism that informs Christie's work, a form of historical mystification that robs any cause or event of which she did not approve of any deeper motivation than the classic criminal one of financial gain. Following the clues in the historical plot of *The Man in the Brown Suit* leads finally to no solution, only a dead end reached at the limits of the form of detective fiction as it is employed here. Historical agency can never be, from this perspective, a mass-based movement, or even the product of genuinely politically motivated individuals. Out of the picture goes the mining industry's position in the political economy, white workers' relation with the state, and the form South African government was to take for the decade after the Rebellion (see Stadler 1987:48) and in comes – Sir Eustace Pedler. Pedler who, as his name indicates, has only something to sell, be it diamonds or rebellion.

In this way Christie grafts genuine (if misguided) contemporary fears on to the formula of the detective story. If those fears are not quite allayed in the conclusion to *The Man in the Brown Suit*, they are certainly quelled along with the Revolution – at least for the time being. The point remains that the novel has engaged with *contemporary* events which, in the pressures of the South African situation, immediately become *historical* ones. The present as history pervades a form normally immune from such considerations. The question is to what degree the form is able to deal with these events as *history*.

Christie has to leave her mannered and static English settings to find a location that will admit the disturbances of historical transition, but in terms of her plot and characters this upheaval must be neutralised and returned to the stable and well-defined social structures necessary to support the 'detective novel of manners' (Porter 1981:160) which dominated the 1920s and 1930s and which her work so pre-eminently represents. The only way in which political and historical events can be reabsorbed into an unchanging social structure is for their causes to be understood and accounted for within the terms of that social structure. Thus criminality in *The Man in the Brown Suit* must ultimately be a matter of individual perversion, not social complexity or structural malfunction. Only in this way can an event such as the Rand Rebellion be accommodated within the classic detective story of the period; only in this way can history give way to the ideological stasis at the heart of this version of the form.

We see then that even when precipitated into overtly historical events, the classical detective genre is unable to make history of them.

In Collingwood's terms, which by virtue of their metaphorical expression are implicated in the same problem, the questions are put, but this does not prove enough to elicit the correct answers. Certainly this has to do with the nature of the questions put, but this then raises the issue of the nature of the authority posing the questions. If the historian is entirely his own authority, what is the relationship between the questions he poses and the material to be interrogated? Can the later not act back upon the former? The problem in our illustration drawn from Agatha Christie is that the questions are not radical enough; they do not find enough purchase in the material with which they are concerned to turn back upon their own authority and question it in turn. The methodology of historical questioning as put forward by Collingwood is, like its figurative counterpart, in danger of being trapped within its potential limits unless it keeps itself open to its own full implications. These implications must include, as we suggested in relation to uses of the past, the ability of the present to put the questioner to question. Only when the present is created in such a way as to 'pass judgement' on itself, as we saw Fredric Jameson would have it, is it too capable of being transformed into history.

DRUM AND THE 'TOUGH TALE'

If *The Man in the Brown Suit* represents the failure of the classic detective story to take root in South Africa, it also measures the terms of that failure; these have essentially to do with history – the present as history specifically, given the tendency of the form to privilege the present. This almost classically apolitical and ahistorical genre, as it appeared in its 'Golden Age' at least, is pressured to take on the weight of history in a context as marked by that mode of existence as South Africa; this is a burden to the form, one which as we have seen in *The Man in the Brown Suit* it takes up with a great degree of awkwardness.

The essentially British detective story which Collingwood uses for his metaphor is not the only model for the genre, however; continuing with our argument that it is the very social conservatism of this form that relates it so specifically to its moment of production, we should expect to see even its formal conservatism alter in relation to context. Many theorists of the form agree, as we have seen above in connection with the detective genre in its classic phase, that it betrays specifically a particular class allegiance, and its 'popularity' must be measured in these terms. Colin Watson's social history of the genre, *Snobbery with Violence: Crime Stories and their Audience*, joins other studies, like those of Julian Symons and R.F. Stewart (1980), for example, in tracing in some detail the ways in which, as Symons puts it, 'the values put forward by the detective story from the time of Holmes to the beginning of World War II ... are those of a class in society that felt it had everything to lose by social change' (1972:17).

Symons goes on to quote the claim by 'Nicholas Blake' (Cecil Day Lewis) that 'detective stories were mostly read by the "upper and professional" classes and thrillers by those with less money and inferior social status' (17), a claim which leads to his thesis, expressed in the sub-title to his *Bloody Murder*, that changes in class dominance were largely instrumental in bringing about a shift in popularity *From the Detective Story to the Crime Novel*.

What Symons calls the 'crime novel' developed mainly in the United States in the 1920s, and the characteristics of the pervasive tradition of the private eye or 'hard-boiled dick' are important to us as it was in this guise that the detective form first really integrated itself into South Africa. In doing so it presented a different set of problems for the relation of the form to history; the one thing it kept in common with its more British counterpart, however, was a determinedly present sense of history.

A product initially of the Depression and Prohibition era, the American detective story developed a much more ambiguous relationship with its social circumstances; in the place of the conservatism of the British detective story we have noted above, the social attitude of the 'crime novel', while varying, was 'often radical in the sense of questioning some aspect of law, justice, or the way society is run' (Symons 1972:175). If the thriller fiction of the years between the two World Wars was dominated by the detective story, the crime novel took over as the more dominant form after the Second World War. Again, following Symons:

> The War was a watershed in the history of the crime story, separating not only the world of housemaids and nurses from that of daily helps and au pair girls, but also the world of reason from that of force. The conscious assumption of the classical detective story was that human affairs are ruled by reason. Crimes were committed by individuals, small holes torn in the fabric of society. The individuals were discovered, the holes mended, by the detective who represented the force of order, and he did this through a process of reasoning ... The War forced upon them [the Golden Age crime writers] the acknowledgement that quite a different world existed, one in which force was supreme and in which irrational doctrines ruled more than one nation. (148)

A nation in which such convictions were likely to flourish was one which, within a few years of the end of the war, turned to a doctrine, if not strictly irrational, then only implementable through the massive deployment of force: apartheid South Africa. That the crime story was adopted as a genre particularly by one sector of this divided society may well be related to the structural nature of force in South African society; certainly class allegiance shifted – albeit in a somewhat convoluted fashion – from the strictly middle-class foundations of the detective story.

The crossover of the genre was facilitated by the forms of popular cultural expression available in post-World War 2 South Africa. The American crime story grew out of the pulp magazine, of which a large number were specifically devoted to the crime story in the 1920s and 1930s; T.J. Binyon lists by way of example: *Detective Story, Detective Fiction Weekly, Clues, Dime Detective, Thrilling Detective, Spicy Detective,* and, most famous of all, *Black Mask* (Binyon 1989:38). Popular sensationalist publishing in South Africa showed a similar trend, so it is not surprising that a new magazine launched in the early 1950s, *Drum*, should serve as a natural point of transition for the form in terms of its means of production.

Ideologically too, detective fiction aligned itself with much of what *Drum* would come to represent. We have had occasion in Chapter Three to consider how telling *Drum* is as far as reflecting the attitudes to history of blacks playing a part within the modernisation process is concerned, and have briefly referred there too to the importance of the detective story in this. Here we will have to push these observations a little further.

As the magazine moved away from the paternalistic 'ethnic' emphasis of its first editor, Bob Crisp, it consciously followed the tastes of the new urban audience to which it was trying to appeal. In the words of one of the prospective readers (quoted in part before) interviewed by the owner of *Drum*, Jim Bailey, and the soon-to-be editor, Anthony Sampson:

> Tribal music! Tribal history! Chiefs! We don't care about chiefs! Give us jazz and film stars, man! ... Yes, brother, anything American. You can cut out this junk about kraals and folk-tales and Basutos in blankets – forget it! You're just trying to keep us backward, that's what! Tell us what's happening right here, man, on the Reef! (Sampson 1983:20)

Right *here*, and right *now*. A key casualty of this attitude, again as we've noted before but which we need to emphasise in this context, was history in any past sense. 'Here' (in which all references to the urban become implicit and immediate rejections of the apartheid vision of removing all blacks from the cities) was matched in political importance by 'now' (which firmly removes the stories from the manufactured 'tribal' past of apartheid with which 'history' had become associated). The early issues of *Drum* had included a series 'recounting the history of the Bantu tribes' (ibid.:16), to which a telling response was:

> Now, take this tribal history business, which you call 'Know Yourselves': we all know ourselves quite well enough ..., I assure you.

And we're trying to get away from our tribal history as fast as we can.
(Ibid.:21)

This was a natural reaction in the face of the retribalising policies of the Nationalist Government (as well as being a characteristic demand of an urbanised proletariat), and is a vital component in the construction of the present as history in black South African writing. In the 1980s Mothobi Mutloatse edited three collections meant to contribute towards the 'reconstruction' of a lost black South African cultural history. The second volume in particular (although this is true of the vast bulk of the material in all three volumes), entitled *Reconstruction: 90 Years of Black Historical Literature* (1981), is remarkable for the fact that the literature in question is – in contrast to the usual usage of 'historical' in relation to literature – contemporary to the historical events it commemorates. A large selection of *Drum* writers are included in *Reconstruction*, represented by their journalism's urgent address to the present.

Drum was to increase its popularity dramatically with its coverage of contemporary historical issues and events. Henry ('Mr *Drum*') Nxumalo's exposure of the conditions of farm workers and convict labour in Bethal in March 1952, a photo-feature on the Defiance Campaign in October 1952, and another exposure by Nxumalo in March 1954, this time of prison conditions, each pushed sales higher until *Drum* began outselling its main competitor, the 'politically non-contentious *Zonk!*' (Chapman 1989b:194).

The image of the investigative reporter is not far removed from that of the private investigator (as even style of dress emphasised), and in South Africa the investigation into what we could call political crimes blurs easily over into more conventional ideas of criminality, just as the usual range of social crimes (theft, blackmail, even murder) can be seen as a reflex of the political situation. A central element of *Drum* was its pervasive use of features on crime in the conventional sense, but only the most tentative of borders existed between this and the topics covered in its investigative reporting and, for that matter, its crime fiction. The fictional private eye, then, hovers on the edge of the socially-significant documentary even as he inhabits a space that is 'politically naïve or, at least, disdainful of politics' (Chapman 1989b:208). This is caught in William 'Bloke' Modisane's penetrating analysis of the ambiguities of his own early writing (which Michael Chapman treats as tellingly typical).

Modisane, initially caught up in the ANC Youth League's Programme of

Action, became disillusioned with what he saw as the compromising alliances entered into by the ANC – the leadership of which now included prominent Youth Leaguers – at the time of the Defiance Campaign, alliances which in their multiracial emphasis went directly against the Youth League's original suspicion of Indian and coloured leaders, and left-wing whites. He angrily 'retreated into a political wilderness':

> I assumed a mask of political innocence and established a reputation for being apolitical. I turned again to my writing, but this time there was a broad omission of the commitment to fight against the prejudice against my skin, to speak out against injustice and wrong. I wrote innocuous stories about boxers with domestic problems, respectable pickpockets, hole-in-the-wall housebreakers, private detectives and other cardboard figures of romanticism, and yet against this background my escapist hero was seldom, if ever, on the side of formal law and order. Like me, my characters were invested with a contempt for the law, their efforts were directed towards flaunting of the law; my heroes were social maladjusts in a society where heroism is measured by acts of defiance against law and order. I did not then recognise the sociological significance of what I was doing, that with a central idea behind them I could use my stories as a reflection or study of our society. (Modisane 1986:139)

In a complex movement the private detective joins other 'cardboard figures of romanticism' in expressing an apolitical retreat that is intensely political; as Chapman says of *Drum* generally: 'Its romance was part of the real world; its reality often manifested itself in acts of romantic possibility ...' (1989b:197). Stepping outside both organised protest against and integral support for the social system, the detective joins other folk-devils becoming folk-heroes in a transformation both radical and reactionary and perfectly suited to the ambiguities of the American 'tough tale'. This can best be illustrated in the work of Arthur Mogale.

Nineteen fifty-three was, as far as the short fiction of *Drum* was concerned, the year of Arthur Mogale (the pseudonym of Arthur Maimane), one of the most prolific writers for *Drum*. He concentrated on detective fiction and his popularity is a measure of the demand for the form. Mogale produced a story or episode for each month of 1953, outstripping the contributions of any other single writer. The first three stories consist of more or less separate 'Escapades', but these are linked by the protagonist they hold in common, *Drum*'s first private detective, O. Chester Morena. His popularity ensured that he went on to appear in two more 'series' ('Hot Diamonds!', four episodes, and 'You Can't Buy Me!', five episodes), each of which grew increasingly integrated into a coherent serial form. Increasingly too, Mogale went on to approximate the standard American private eye plot and setting (with due allowances for geography and race). Whereas Morena begins life as a somewhat loose and anarchic street-operator, by the third serial he is equipped with an office, a secretary who sends in pretty but mysterious woman clients, a fast car, and a semi-formal relationship with the police.

O. Chester Morena announces himself in his first story with an immediacy reminiscent of the voice-over in the popular American detective B-movies which were so important an influence upon the life of Sophiatown that *Drum* represented. An easy translation from the page to the screen in America, the typical first-person reporting voice of detective fiction translates back to the page in South Africa just as easily, mixing in with the tsotsi-taal of the era. After some directly dramatic opening dialogue, Mogale's detective introduces himself:

> Yes ladies and gentleman. This is me. O. Chester Morena, Private Detective, and what not. These uneducated crooks call me 'Chief'. Anyway, that's what my last name means.
>
> Me, I'm smart. I know all the angles. I've been plenty places. They kicked me out of university during my second year, and my father kicked me out of the family. I became a gangster, pick-pocket, robber and all-round crook. But I played it scientifically. Still, after a few years I decided the old saying 'crime doesn't pay' was correct. I joined the police-force in Pretoria – where I wasn't known.
>
> After a year's excellent service I sent in my resignation. After I'd convinced the Inspector I meant it, and told him my plans, he pulled a few strings to get me a private detective licence – and one for a gun.
>
> Of course, you all know such creatures don't exist in Johannesburg. Well I don't exist either – except on paper. (Chapman 1989a:26)

What looks for a moment like a marvellously self-reflective reference turns out to be literal: Morena exists only on paper not because he is a fictional character

South African society would never allow to exist in reality, but because – despite his license – he does not, in these early stories, operate as a private detective; the 'and what not' is crucial. His method of operation is to use his inside knowledge of the criminal world to recycle crime to his own advantage. With a camera hidden in a book he films the criminal activities around him (pick-pocketing in one story, gambling in another) and blackmails the criminals involved with this evidence: hence the title of each of the three stories in this first collection of 'escapades', 'Crime for Sale'.

These first stories, because of the technology upon which they turn, become metaphors which we may use to place the *Drum* detective story. Poised like O. Chester Morena between criminality and legality with no commitment to either, arrogant too in his superior sense of celebratory individualism, they exploit their environment with the same 'nonchalant disdain' with which Chapman (1989b:206) says the thoroughly Europeanised Maimane created his stories. Like the camera in the book, the stories document in textual form a world from which they have separated themselves, appropriating its more sensational elements for their own use. There is a moment at which Morena has to choose between clearing an innocent victim with the police and making a profit from a criminal; his choice is clear: 'I could have helped the poor innocent to put up a case with a witness who never lies – the camera. But the money Cassim was prepared to pay me for burning the film was too tempting.'[19]

As a witness of its times the *Drum* detective story must be read through the key elements of its fictionality, and this will make of it in crucial respects a false witness. Its combination of the documentary realism of its setting and the flaunted individualism of its perspective create a strangely mixed account of its times. As far as treating the present as history is concerned, the form hovers between its potential and its limits.

The classic pose of the private eye may be clearly related to certain class interests within black popular life. Just as the *Drum* writers generally were associated with middle-class aspirations that set them apart from the masses, so the detective's anarchic stance isolated him from the very events with which he was involved. Alienated from the trends amongst the once in many ways elitist black oppositional political movements towards a more mass-based approach, the *Drum* detective, for all his engagement in the popular life of his times, faced a limited future.

19. 'Crime for Sale', *Drum* 3(2), Feb.1953:35. Where the stories have been republished in *The Drum Decade* I have given this reference as it will be more available for the general reader.

Fiction was to give way to journalism as *Drum* went on, but detective fiction was to fade as a form within what fiction was published even before that. The high point of 1953 was never to be repeated, even though other detective stories (one of which we will look at below) were still sporadically to appear. Mogale himself only published one short story in *Drum* after 1953, and this is a sentimental piece that has nothing to do with crime called 'Broken Hearted' (June 1954).

What undercut the detective story as a viable form of oppositional writing? The detective's anarchic stance, as we have seen, was the product of various levels of defiance, and Modisane reads back into that a continuing rejection of the 'law and order' which was to prove such a threat to the world of Sophiatown in which the detective and his brothers and sisters in romance found their medium. Yet his effectiveness as a figure of protest depended upon an isolation and individualism that cut him off from the community of opposition which was beginning to re-emerge. Criminality and justice would equally have to seek a new place in this. The nature of the crime off which the detective lived ('Crime is a business, so I'm in it. So I reckon I ain't got the right to stop people from being criminals as it brings in the mazoola for yours truly, O. Chester Morena.'[20]) needed a deeper analysis than the detective form allowed, and its definition in terms of justice needed to be sharpened for a more communal form of protest to take place. We can look more closely at this by examining one of the later detective stories to appear in *Drum*, one in which the detective again takes his place on the side of law and order. As we shall see, this leads to no greater satisfaction within the limits of the form.

In Mbokotwane Manqupu's 'Love Comes Deadly' (January 1955) the detective is more realistically cast as white; although his name is 'Gray' (which finds its significance in relation to the name of the chief black criminal, 'Chocolate') he, and the law he represents, cannot cross over effectively and equally into the black community. The story opens with a murder in which the victim, Barney, is interrupted in his reading by the murderers. Pulled, like Barney, from text into reality, the story spends some time recounting the reaction of the community to the murder:

> Kitoe, leader of the area's Civic Guards, leaned against the wall and
> said: 'What is the Township coming to?' Then he ordered that some-

---

20. 'You Can't Buy Me!', *Drum* 3(12), Dec. 1953:29.

body be sent on a bicycle to the police-station to tell the police about the tragedy.

'Such things make me cry for Shaka,' Kuzwayo said. 'He would have collected all the men of the age-group of the guilty ones and killed them!'

'Yes,' Kitoe agreed, 'as long as the sentences of the courts are small, crime will march on undaunted.'

'Heavy sentences won't stop crime,' said Moreti, a school-teacher member of the Guards. 'Look at it this way,' he went on quietly. 'You always preach that crime was unknown in our ancestor's day because sentences were heavy. But that is not altogether true: poverty was unknown, and there was no idleness – and so there was no crime.'

'So you say,' Kitoe answered angrily, 'but some of these tsotsis are from well-off homes.'

'It is not the fault of the boys,' Moreti answered, 'for how can a good potato stay good among rotten ones? How can these boys stay good when they are surrounded by evil? Would you be the good man you are today if you had grown up in a place like this, where illicit liquor is sold openly, where prostitution goes on day and night without even the decency of closed doors, where one is killed for no reason at all, where ... Goodness! Why do I have to tell you things you know?' (Chapman 1989a:68)

In playing the past off against the present, the modern community – the older members of which are in transition between the worlds they discuss – bears witness to the failure of the law. This quickly moves from the role of the law in its direct application (sentencing) to its broader social context. At the same time the discussion moves from prevention to cause, and the criminality that was so often the focus of *Drum* takes on its central political expression as it is read as a symptom of a failed social structure. The idealised invocation of tradition is registered as unreal in relation to the all too real effects of modernisation, but the analysis of these effects stops short of attributing them to the broader structural features of apartheid society – in much the same way as the detective story works towards a limited conclusion.

Immediately after the passage quoted above we meet Gray. He is the embodiment of the law, and so the logic of the story requires us to measure him against not just the criminals themselves, but the whole environment producing that criminality. He effectively confronts Barney's girlfriend, Jacqueline, with evidence that implicates her in the murder, disarms her strong-arm accomplice, Chocolate, and chases Jacqueline into the night. There she is run down by a passing car, thus robbing Gray of his arrest; a random action of the community completes the cycle of justice, which remains thus poetic rather than becoming political. As for Gray, his moralising at the end of the story side-steps everything the community brought to the fore about the crime within itself:

> And Gray thought that there was still a lot of trusting Barneys in Johannesburg; and while there are still so many Jacquelines making eyes at the Barneys, Marshall Square will be kept busy. (72)

Again the individual focus prevents a social perspective, and white justice is removed from any understanding of the complicity between the broader structural features that link the individual act of crime with its historical context. This is an issue which the story itself has raised after all, but one which the detective element in that story is unable to confront.

This problem is registered at a stylistic level as well. There is a strange moment when the language of popular resistance emerges for a telling moment in 'Love Comes Deadly'; several critics have noted the enormous disjunction between phrases like 'I'm levelling a torpedo at your spine' (the pulp style which dominates the story) and the way in which Gray imagines Jacqueline behaving in Hell:

> '... a dame like that is liable to start a strike in hell! Lucifer will find himself up against a wench who'll promise a better standard of living to the inmates and lead them in a revolt to overthrow the established government of that joint.' (72)

A veritable chorus of discourses bursts forth here – the distance between 'dame' and 'wench' disturbs even the predominantly American tough style – with the language of organised protest coming briefly (and only comically) to the fore. While the overall intent is obviously humorous, the translation of the terminology of Congress and Communism into the metaphysical is telling here. It underlines the fact that it has no serious place in the world of detective fiction, linguistically or ideologically. This is a world where, in Gray's words, '"Sooner or later the law will catch up with you as it always does ...'" (71), but the full weight of the story works against this unironical sentiment. The law is naturalised in the false comfort of fatalism, not confronted for its limitations which this purely poetic justice makes manifest. The first half of the story, in which the community measures the failure of the law, remains undigested by the denouement of the detective story, haunting it with its picture of criminality beyond the social controls represented by the law. The detective of law and order, like his more anarchic counterpart in the Mogale stories, is out of touch with the nature of the community, and the form that embodies them both is finally silent before the reality which it tries to depict.

The *Drum* detective story, then, remains a reflex of history – the present as history – rather than a form able to resist and interrogate the history – again, the present as history – with which it is so intimate. It registers the social pressures of the present, and so takes on the present as history to this degree, but it is unable to transform these pressures completely through fiction into history in the full sense. By this I mean it does not generate a truly social and material perspective out of the social and historical issues it makes its subject. It does not challenge the present with a sense of its own historicity, and contribute thereby to the recognition that as history it can be altered. The form is valuable in that it is a witness to the present as history, but it is a witness often silent when it comes to the most vital evidence; even more importantly, to continue the forensic metaphor which seems apt in this context, it remains a witness rather than becoming the prosecutor that the crimes which it confronts would seem to demand of it. The evidence is led, but the questions are not put.

THE LAW ON TRIAL: *WILLEMSDORP*

A year or two before Mogale created his detective, Herman Charles Bosman died while revising *Willemsdorp* (1977), a novel which handles the detective figure in a significantly new way in South Africa. *Willemsdorp* examines South African life in all its intensity in a small-town situation: 'The backveld town of Willemsdorp was a place where Life was still spelt with an upper case L. It was Life with the Mask off' (208). In particular the novel explores the effects of the Acts being passed by the newly-elected Nationalist Government (called the Volksparty in the novel, as the United Party becomes the Union Party) on which the edifice of apartheid was being erected.

Willemsdorp is remarkable for being one of the few works of fiction Bosman wrote set in his own times. The writing and the story take place as the various prejudices and previously rather vague laws regulating inter-racial contact are broadened and strengthened: the Prohibition of Mixed Marriages Act of 1949, which made all marriages between whites and other groups illegal, was developed from the Hertzogian precedent banning marriages between Africans and whites, and the Immorality Act, designed originally to combat extramarital intercourse, was given its specifically racial cast in 1950 as the offence was made more serious when indulged in across racial differences. Looming behind these was the Population Registration Act of 1950, which allocated each person to a racial group, but the Mixed Marriages and Immorality Acts brought home such large-scale social schemes in a particularly intimate way.

This is the route Bosman follows, writing his murder mystery straight into contemporary history via these specifically South African laws. The law in *Willemsdorp* is embodied in Detective Sergeant Brits, a grotesque amalgam of skill and prejudice who is all the more threatening for his absurdities. Physically unimpressive, comically dressed, single-minded to a degree at first suggesting dim-wittedness, and communicating in a ridiculous broken English, Brits is a brutally effective policeman not above using torture to extort a confession or considering framing a suspect to achieve a conviction. Told by his superior, who wishes to avoid a scandal, to warn anyone he suspects of miscegenation before arresting them, Brits makes it his task to inform personally every sexually active white male in the town of the situation, leaving himself free to effect an arrest immediately should he catch anyone 'dead to rights'; he thus weaves through the novel as the personification of the new laws and a constant reminder of the threat they pose.

Bosman succeeds here in turning the generic conservatism we have seen as so integral a part of detective fiction back upon itself. He maintains the detective as the representative of law and order, but in his depiction of the detective he exposes the corruption at the heart of that law and order. The law itself is the informing evil whose operations the detective carries out; its distortions are the ones revealed in the actions of its representative. The law, in effect, is finally put on trial.

The one incontrovertible crime in the novel, the murder of the coloured prostitute, is a direct product of the law. Marjorie is murdered by someone fearing the consequences of contravening the Immorality Act. Who this is we never find out, although not even the novel's protagonist, Charlie Hendricks, is free of the reader's suspicion at the inconclusive ending. Guilt there is aplenty; *Willemsdorp* is racked with guilt, be it for miscegenation, dagga-smoking, adultery, achieving status through personal favours or murder itself. But the conviction of guilt is as much personally imposed as applied by the law; the law is internalised, 'moral' before legal, as Hendricks discovers when he analyses his feelings after having sex with Marjorie for the second time:

> Charlie Hendricks remembered the contempt he had felt for his editorial predecessor, Esselen, when the suspicion had first entered his mind that Esselen had had illicit intercourse with Marjorie. There was a lot of hypocrisy about it, and all that, Charlie Hendricks realised. But all the same it was a real feeling. It was something you couldn't get away from. You just felt there was something low about a white man that went to bed with a woman that wasn't white. And even if you yourself were also that kind of white man, it just didn't make any difference. (124)

This is one of the reasons that by the end of the novel Hendricks discovers 'that he was running away from himself. And when it is yourself you're running away from that you can never stop running' (208). The novel concludes with this insight, burying the law within the farthest regions of the self. History is acquitted, in its past or present tense, and the isolated, alienated self takes over.

Bosman's detective follows, though, right into the deepest levels of the protagonist's psyche, prowling the edges of consciousness with as much precision as he reads the tracks in Willemsdorp's unpaved streets. It is he who appears in Hendricks's dagga-dream near the end of the book, and the shape he takes there is that of the archetypal literary detective. Hendricks dreams he has returned to the Wondergat, an ancient digging into which Marjorie's body was thrown; here he is accosted by a man speaking in 'cultured accents. But Charlie Hendricks wasn't taken in by the fact that he spoke like an educated man. He knew it was Detective Sergeant Brits.' Brits arrests him in the perfect English of Hendricks's own self-image and when Hendricks asks him how he knew he would find him there, Brits replies:

> 'Elementary, my dear Hendricks ... Every tyro knows that the murderer always revisits the scene of his crime ... If you want a good book to read, why not try "The Adventures of Sherlock Holmes"?' (205)

Fiction pursues where reality is left behind, but even in the form of the master of the positivist enterprise only a phantom is captured. All the factual detail of the book does not add up to an arrest, all the clues fail to ensure a conviction. At the novel's conclusion, Hendricks is left continuing his flight, and we are none the wiser as to his, or anyone else's, guilt or innocence. In the open-endedness of the plot the law finally evades conviction in its social sense, even if it is not entirely excused; it is the law written into the heart of the lonely individual which moves into the dock, and the lonely individual must stand trial before himself even if the full extent of his guilt is never established.

Brits may well recommend Conan Doyle, but nothing could be further from the tightly constructed Holmes stories than the narrative of *Willemsdorp*. In an ironic reversal (remembering what has been said above regarding Conan Doyle) what fame Bosman has achieved depends virtually entirely upon his marvellously elegant and compact short stories. These, set firmly in the past, convey history in a comic and satirical light that is designed to dismantle the myths of Afrikaner nationalism generated in the 1930s and 1940s. His detective novel, however, proceeds loosely incident by incident and, crucially, comes to no conclusion – in terms of the murder mystery at least. The detective genre which ostensibly throws the story headlong into the present as history – at least as far as it is entangled in the public events of the period – is robbed of the revelation towards which the plot has been apparently working; instead the narrative swerves aside and confronts a different issue, the metaphysics of self-confrontation.

The question of the degree to which this self is socially constructed is cut short, but at least the question is raised in *Willemsdorp*. Our clue here is the detective himself, and his ability to translate himself from the reality of the various Acts to their source in the elusive depths of the South African psyche. The moment of conviction at this level is a long way off in the heady days of a confident and emerging nationalism, as is the acknowledgement that it is the detective himself – the very embodiment of law and order – who carries the guilt and commits the crime, but Bosman has stripped his subject until these facts are ready to come to light, whatever other mysteries continue. As yet the questions he puts do not fully illumine the nature of the problem – while the law is put on trial it is finally situated too monolithically within an individualist perspective rather than in the relation of the individual to material circumstance, to history, in effect – but here we have the beginnings of a resistance to the law. This is not entirely carried through, but it creates enough ground for a hint of the resistance that will turn the detective story into a truly historical form in which the questions put to the present arise out of the present as history.

In the early 1970s Bosman's precedent was to resurface in a rather more limited satirical form in the grotesqueries of Konstabel Els, Tom Sharpe's 'detective' in *Riotous Assembly* (1973 [1971]), just as the *Drum* detective, whose demise was completed by the 'bannings, premature deaths and despair' (Chapman 1989b:222) that afflicted the *Drum* writers, reappeared in the same year in the form of Zondi, assistant to detective Kramer, in James McClure's *The Steam Pig* (1983 [1971]). June Drummond has kept alive the influence of the Golden Age writers in her novels, the best-known of which, *Farewell Party*, also appeared in 1971. Each of these writers continued at some level the engagement of the detective form with history in their respective ways while, in keeping with the urgency of the times and the tendency of their genre, maintaining that engagement through a primary focus on the present. In the work of Wessel Ebersohn, however, the present as history became virtually the central focus of the detective genre.

History as Detective Fiction:
Wessel Ebersohn

Wessel Ebersohn has divided his production to date fairly evenly between thrillers and what he calls his 'straight' novels. While this division has been of some concern to those involved in the marketing side of his work, Ebersohn himself plays it down: 'I don't think ... that my serious writing, I don't even like the term you know, my straight novels and my thrillers are that far apart ...'[21] We will be concerned with one of his novels in which the 'thriller' and 'straight' elements intermingle in a way that is particularly telling as far as the uses of history in fiction are concerned.

Ebersohn has always (with the exception of his third published and first-written novel, *The Centurion* [1980]), written his thrillers directly into the contemporary South African historical situation. This is a technique that has intensified with time, but his very first thriller – and first published work – *A Lonely Place to Die* (1979), apart from introducing his trademark 'detective', Yudel Gordon (who is actually a prison psychologist), already indicated the preoccupation with extreme right-wing activity in South Africa which dominates

---

21. Michael Green, interview with Wessel Ebersohn, July 1991 (unpublished), 44.

the other two Yudel Gordon thrillers published up to now, *Divide the Night* (1981) and *Closed Circle* (1990). *The Centurion*, though a thriller, is also an experiment in science fiction – not a very successful one in Ebersohn's view; 'I'd as soon forget *The Centurion*,' he says in a letter.[22] While its detective figure, like Yudel Gordon, is a psychologist, and much of its action takes place in South Africa, its plot concerns an international conspiracy and stands as a very shaky first attempt outside the mainstream of Ebersohn's output.

Of his two 'straight' novels to date, the first, *Store Up the Anger* (1984 [1980]), is an intensely South African work and will concern us in detail later. The second, *Klara's Visitors* (1987), is the one novel he has not set in South Africa. Cast as Hitler's private journal, it is, however, given a highly satirical link with South Africa in that the notebooks the journal is written in land up in the hands of a 'coloured' ex-serviceman who bequeaths them to his nephew, 'Wessel Ebersohn': 'So look after them for me. Maybe you can straighten them out a bit, work on the plot or something, you know. If the story was speeded up it could be pretty good reading. Introduce a few interesting characters, see what you can do. Maybe you can set the action at home, give it a bit of authenticity,' says Uncle Abdool in his posthumous covering letter with the journal (13), which drives home its deliberately and pointedly farcical local application.

Ebersohn's novels are not just generally set in specifically South African settings; a technique he has returned to is the thin fictionalisation of actual persons and events in South Africa. In *Closed Circle*, the plot revolves around the harassment and assassination of left-wing activists. The novel opens with the dramatisation of three attacks and many others are referred to in the course of the novel, each identifiable in relation to actual historical cases despite changed names and sometimes swapped circumstances. Yudel Gordon is called in to investigate these cases which remain all too obviously unsolved in terms of their official enquiries; here the thriller mode runs into conflict with the historical – the detective convention demands a solution which history refuses, at the time of writing, to provide: 'the problem with *Closed Circle* was that I am aware that there have been many of these sort of killings in South Africa and almost none, in almost no cases have the killers been brought to justice, so I just simply couldn't have the fictitious character brought to justice ...' (interview:13).

Ebersohn here expresses a respect for history which some may see elements of

---

22. Ebersohn to Green, 11 Feb. 1991.

his technique denying. Yudel Gordon does manage to establish, to his own satisfaction at least, a motive that explains why particular people are selected by the hit squads and not others who are just as engaged in oppositional tactics – 'what linked them was audacity. They were people who had not only resisted the workings of the system, but resisted them in the most audacious possible ways' (211) – but his investigation only goes so far as to discover the specific engagement of one high-ranking police officer, and the motives of this man centre on a perverted form of homosexuality which becomes interlinked with his political operations because it is in essence a 'distorted drive for power' (305). Yudel's dissatisfaction at only being able to prove this against Colonel Wheelwright is felt by the reader too at the conclusion of the novel, but the linking of history and sexuality presents other problems for the novel. Specifically, the point at which the fictional detective has an affair with an all too easily identifiable historical character leads to the uneasy suspicion that the author might be treating history without the respect it deserves; that he might himself, in fact, be 'screwing history'.

To what degree, then, should fictionality privilege the historical in the sense of respecting its factual status? This is a question which, generally put, blurs into the mundane; it takes on, however, a specific interest in relation to Ebersohn's most extended use of contemporary history in the novel form: *Store Up the Anger*. Considered for the Booker Prize, it was dropped because, as Margaret Forster (one of the judges) explained, 'nobody denied the power of the book, but the counter-argument ran that it really seemed to be a documentary about Steve Biko rather than a novel. It was goodbye Ebersohn' (1980). From the other extreme, a similar observation has vastly different implications: the Committee of Experts appointed by the Publications Appeal Board claimed that *Store Up the Anger* '"cannot be defended as literature"' because it is '"very obviously based, with only slight efforts at glossing over, on the sensational and broadly documented or rather reported case of Steve Biko"' (Thornycroft 1980). The work then, on these grounds, should remain banned they decided, which it was for a while.

Giving evidence for the appeal against the banning order, Professor John Dugard made central to his argument a precedent set by the Committee in relation to Andre Brink's *Dry White Season*:

> Gegewe die konteks van die Komitee se literêre advies, is die sentrale probleemveld by 'n beoordeling van die roman die vraag na die verhouding van werklikheid: roman-werklikheid. Daar is duidelik

herkenbare en herleibare verwysings na die Suid-Afrikaanse aktualiteit – die skrywer het volgens gerapporteerde verklarings aan die pers (onder meer) hofstukke as bronnemateriaal gebruik. En nou sal die vraag òf ons dit hier te make het met letterkunde en die daarmee verbandhoudende vraag na die kwaliteit van die produk, afhang van die graad en die kwaliteit van die transponering van 'n bepaalde stuk realiteit (boonop resente S.A. geskiedenis) na die wêreld van 'n roman'.[23]

(*Given the context of the Committee's literary advice, the central problem with the evaluation of the novel is the question of the relationship with reality: novel-reality. There are easily recognisable and deducible references to South African actuality – the writer has according to reported testimonies to the press (inter alia) used court reports as source material. And now the question is whether we have to do here with literature and the related question of the quality of the product, depending on the degree and the quality of the transposing of a specific piece of reality (moreover recent S.A. history) to the world of a novel.*)

This takes us into age-old questions of the relation of fiction to reality, actuality, history, and especially recent history. Given its source, however, we should not be surprised to find what after all sounds like a potentially sophisticated approach to fiction and history is deployed in the most limited of ways. In Dugard's summary of the approach implicit in the above, he says the Committee appears 'to take the view that it is impermissible from a literary point of view to rely on contemporary events and characters in a work of fiction. Where this is done, the work loses its character as fiction or literature' (6). Again,

The Committee seems to take the view that if a work of fiction describes socio-political events, which can be identified with contemporary factual happenings, in a sober, unsentimental and unimaginative manner, the work cannot be defended as literature. It then becomes a form of documentary propaganda masquerading under the name of literature. (7)

23. Quoted from the material presented by way of appeal against a banning order by Professor John Dugard, 21 Nov. 1980, 3-4 and repeated on 6.

The objections Dugard makes to this approach can in many respects be easily anticipated; they include the facts that this is 'not a generally held view among literary experts' (7); 'that the historical novel plays an important role in literature' (8); that 'literature' is a debatable category; that while the Publications Appeal Board 'has enunciated standards for works of fiction and documentary works ... there are no standards or guidelines laid down ... for judging ... hybrid works' (8) and it would be unwise (legally) to invent such a category; the novel is a realistic form; and, finally, that *Store Up the Anger* has literary merit. Interestingly, Dugard argues this last point (which makes up much of the 32-page document) on the Committee's own ground, that is, he argues for the 'fictionality' (that is, avoidance of specific referentiality) of the work in order to support its claim to 'literary merit'. Much time is spent detailing exactly where the novel departs from the known facts of Steve Biko's life. This is easy to do, for although the present tense of the novel, the last hours in the life of a political activist in the hands of the security police, is in many respects similar to the Biko case, Sam Bhengu's past – and the novel is made up of interlinking present moments and past flashbacks covering his history – is entirely invented. Ebersohn creates a representative black South African life experience, moving from Bhengu's youth in Sophiatown (Biko was born in King William's Town) through his ever-increasing politicisation as a young man in Cato Manor (Biko studied at Mariannhill before coming to Durban), leading up to his involvement in community projects (here the similarities increase) and his detention and ultimate death (set in Durban in the novel, whereas Biko was held in Port Elizabeth). In short, argues Dugard:

> [*Store Up the Anger*] is clearly not a work of non-fiction. It is a novel dealing with fictitious characters. The fact that some of them may resemble real persons, and that the situation may resemble a real situation does not deprive it of its quality as a work of fiction. It is an historical novel in the best tradition. (10)

Quite simply what prevents this concluding generic classification from being clear is the contemporaneity of the novel's material; it is because it treats the *present* as history, a temporal emphasis stressed in much of what we have quoted from this case already, that it is robbed of its generic defence and considered not to be 'in the best tradition' by the Committee. Obviously the novel's relation to the present increased, at the time, the sensitivity of the material handled, and it is probably this very urgency that makes the 'documentary' as opposed to the 'history' especially damning; the very immediacy of the engagement is what makes it counter-literary in the Committee's view.

There is more than this at stake, however. Interestingly, Ebersohn quite openly goes along with the sentiments expressed by the Committee regarding the documentary, although for exactly the opposite reasons: 'faction [sic] is nonsense. It's either on one side or other of the line – unquestionably' (interview:82); 'it's a lot of bullshit, there's no such thing as faction anyway, you know' (interview:81); '... to write the Biko story? No, I am a novelist, and I was never tempted to write the history of the man, no never' (interview 82). What Ebersohn wishes to preserve here is what Macherey has called the 'necessary freedom which defines [the writer's] use of language' (1978:46):

> It might be said that the language spoken by the work is not answerable to any external meaning or reality; however, ... there is no first, independent, innocent language. To take an elementary example, the Napoleon in Tolstoy's *War and Peace* is not open to refutation by historians. If we are reading properly we know that the name is not quite being used to designate a real person. It derives its meaning only from its relationship to the rest of the text of which it is a part. The writer is able to create both an object and the standards by which it is to be judged. Uninhibited by customary usage and narrow definitions, language wins a remarkable freedom and power of improvisation which has wrongly been considered to be the monopoly of poetry but which actually defines all types of writing. (45)

I realise that there is much in this quotation that is dependent upon a particular view of language which might be contestable in many respects, but what Macherey does foreground here is a sense of language crucially at odds with the common-sense assumptions of the Committee of Experts, particularly as far as reference is concerned; it is at the point of reference to something external to itself that Macherey stresses the 'freedom' of language. 'However, this freedom ... is not indiscriminate', Macherey points out, going on to describe the pressures of convention which restrain it, and preparing his argument for the material pressures behind these conventions (or 'models' as he calls them) which is so important a part of his theme in *A Theory of Literary Production*. What we must focus on is just what 'models' inform the depiction of history in *Store Up the Anger*.

Earlier in *A Theory of Literary Production* Macherey uses a literary metaphor we have come across before in a different context to describe the type of 'normative' criticism which stands in a prescriptive relationship with its object of study and which so informs the type of criticism deployed by the Committee of Experts. In this, 'criticism derives its authority from the model and is determined by the rules which govern access to this model':

> ... such a reading is prompted by a desire to grasp the content of the narrative directly, independently, immediately. The literal narrative is irrelevant because it serves only to hide a secret and can be cast aside once this secret is revealed.
>
> The detective story offers the best example of this disappearance of narrative. It is constructed entirely around the possibility of this prophetic reading which completes the story at the moment of its abolition. We find in such stories, so manifestly concerned with the discovery of a truth, the temptation of a short cut which can lead us directly to the solution of the mystery, the temptation to read the last page first. (18)

The 'model' in question for *Store Up the Anger*, as far as the Committee is concerned, is not a literary genre, it is reality itself. The work in fact disqualifies itself as literature while its real allegiance is to its 'model' in contemporary history. As a 'documentary' it cannot be defended as fiction. Ironically, however, the novel's very closeness to actual events puts it at even a further distance from the truth, as, in the Committee's view, it deliberately distorts its 'model' to no fictional, only a propagandistic, purpose. It is in this way that the normative readers of the Committee cause 'the disappearance of the narrative'; the 'short cut' they take is to history and what is cast aside is the significance of the form of the narrative in which that history is embodied. While *Store Up the Anger* is overtly, as we have said, one of Ebersohn's 'straight' novels, its approach to its historical material, in a very real sense the 'truth' it wishes to tell, involves solving a mystery; in this central respect, then, the novel is, in form, a 'thriller', or, to pick up on the metaphor Macherey employs above and apply it literally, a detective story.

We began this section by examining the way in which detective fiction served as a metaphor for history writing; it is only appropriate then that we come round to this other metaphorical deployment of detective fiction, one in which the genre is now an illustration of a critical approach. It is even more appropriate that, again, we must treat the metaphor literally to tease out its significance in this context. For it is as, literally, detective fiction that *Store Up the Anger* can most usefully be read into its appropriation of the present as history.

In order to appreciate fully the way in which the detective form is significant for the shape *Store Up the Anger* gives to contemporary historical events, we must return briefly to the issues that concerned us earlier in this chapter. What is at stake in freeing 'history' from its usual orientation towards the past; what does it mean to stress the historical nature of the present? These questions will help us to focus on not just the structure of the novel, but also on our consideration of the present as history.

Paul Hirst, as we have seen, admires Collingwood's thought particularly for its 'insistence that historical writing must find its point of departure in the questions we must ask ourselves in the present' (1985:56). It is in this respect that Collingwood's 'idea of history' brings us most firmly back to the present, and makes his choice of a present-orientated genre like the detective story (inadvertently) all the more precise a metaphor for the activity of the historian. Says Collingwood:

> ... since the past in itself is nothing, the knowledge of the past is not, and cannot be, the historian's goal. His goal, as the goal of a thinking being, is knowledge of the present; to that everything must return, round that everything must revolve. But, as historian, he is concerned with one special aspect of the present – how it came to be what it is. In this sense, the past is an aspect or function of the present ... (Quoted in Marwick 1983:83)

This brings us to one final but central theoretical feature of detective fiction – one that remains surprisingly absent from Collingwood's metaphorical use of the genre.

In 1929 Ronald Knox noted in his Introduction to *Best Detective Stories of the Year* that whereas 'the interest of the ordinary romance centres in the question, "What will happen?" ... the interest of the detective romance centres in the question, "What has happened?"' (quoted in Stewart 1980:68). The significance of this shift in tense is emphasised by several commentators on the genre; here is Jameson, paraphrasing Bloch:

> ... the detective story is the very archetype of Oedipal construction in
> the manner in which everything in it, events and sentences alike, draws
> its ultimate value and even its meaning from an event in the past, an
> event necessarily external to the work's structure. (1971:131)

The crime, or at least the circumstances behind the crime, exist prior to the
beginning of the narrative as such. Dennis Porter makes much the same point:

> The effect of the crime is revealed before the statement of its causes.
> This means that detective fiction is preoccupied with the closing of
> the logico-temporal gap that separates the present of the discovery of
> the crime from the past that prepared it. It is a genre committed to an
> act of recovery, moving forward in order to move back. (1981:29)

The degree to which these analyses apply equally to history writing is remarkable,
bringing in a telling reinforcement to Collingwood's relation of the detective story
to history. History works backwards to its subject; it starts its investigation at a
point necessarily after the event. Specifically this reminds us of Collingwood's
point regarding the unavoidable relation between present and past in historical
writing; whereas historical writing in the conventional sense appears preoccupied
with the past it is in fact pervaded by the concerns of the present. Detective
fiction, on the other hand, presents the perfect model for grasping the present as
history as its temporal implications are the inverse of the conventional historical
mode: it is focused on the present but governed by an event in the (recent) past. In
giving *Store Up the Anger* a buried but implicit thriller form, Ebersohn brings the
techniques of detective fiction to bear in his exploration of the present as history.

This sense of the novel is reinforced even by a commentator who wishes to
distinguish it from Ebersohn's more explicitly detective fiction. In her review of
Store Up the Anger, Sally Ramsey says, 'Unlike Ebersohn's earlier novel, *A Lonely
Place to Die* (1979), this is no thriller. Any expectations of mystery or intrigue are
quelled by the dry finality of the opening sentence: "Sam Bhengu knew that he
was dying".' She goes on, however, to describe accurately the structure of the
novel in terms that strongly approximate the detective form, out of which emerges
its relation to history:

> ... the author's superb sense of timing ensures that the whole truth is
> not revealed until the closing pages of the novel when the complete

historical background to the event has been reconstructed, imaginatively and methodically, and each individual motive has been explored. (1980)

Store Up the Anger opens just a few scenes short of its conclusion; the present moment of the novel covers this matter of hours, from our meeting with the fatally injured Bhengu until his transfer to the van that is to take him to Pretoria Central prison. In this time we follow the workings of Bhengu's mind after his acknowledgement to himself of the certainty of his death. A series of flashbacks, usually associatively related to a moment in the present, systematically work through his life from childhood until they converge upon the present again. What is revealed are the influences and pressures which have brought Bhengu to the point of the present. This is crucial, for the theme of the novel concerns the positive responsibility of the victim for his own fate, and is encapsulated in the epigraph taken from Karl A. Menninger's *Man Against Himself*: 'It is true ... that in the end each man kills himself in his own selected way, fast or slow, soon or late.' Bhengu is no passive subject, but – and here the novel echoes the Black Consciousness position of self-recovery and self-affirmation – he is in this position because of his own conscious commitment, one that has grown out of his past. Colonel Lategan tries to turn this responsibility entirely and negatively on to Bhengu in their telling final interchange:

> 'You're dying, aren't you? You're dying and you're blaming us. But we didn't kill you. You killed yourself. Where did you think this would all end? Did you think we'd allow it indefinitely? You've been at it for nearly twenty years. Did you think you could go on forever? It wasn't van Rooyen and Fourie who killed you, Sam. You did it yourself. Any time in those twenty years you could have stopped and you would have saved yourself. That was enough time, wasn't it? Wasn't twenty years enough? You made your own choice. Don't blame us, Sam. It was your choice. You killed yourself as surely as if you'd taken a knife and slit your own throat.' (186-87)

In response to this, Bhengu forces out with tremendous effort his final two spoken words in the novel, two words which in their brevity after Lategan's long speech effectively place the issue of responsibility clearly in the correct perspective: 'You also,' he says (187).

Lategan's stress in his speech upon the twenty years of Bhengu's political activity serves to remind us of the weight of history behind the present moment, a fact underscored as we have noted by the entire structure of the novel. The past informs each moment of the present, contributing cumulatively to its significance as an historical moment. *Store Up the Anger* enacts Collingwood's sense of the historian's engagement with the present: 'he is concerned with one special aspect of the present – how it came to be what it is'.

The detective mode is deployed as a primary structuring device in this. The novel is built around the repeated reference to a clue, a clue we cannot grasp until all is revealed, but one that repeatedly ghosts through the narrative until it takes on its full substance in its shocking revelation of the truth.

A major reason for the inquest into the death of Steve Biko coming to the conclusion that 'the available evidence does not prove that the death was brought about by any act or omission involving or amounting to an offence on the part of any person' (Essa and Pillay n.d.:85) was the failure of the inquest to establish the exact cause of Biko's fatal injuries. *Store Up the Anger* deliberately fictionalises almost every aspect of Biko's life, but at the heart of 'Sam Bhengu's' story is, Ebersohn believes, the truth of how Biko's fatal injuries were administered. In answer to my enquiry regarding this, Ebersohn wrote:

> The method of killing described in the novel was given to me by a former security policeman. The man was a fool who had been goaded into bragging. He was nowhere near Biko at any time and had no first hand knowledge of the matter. All he knew was the method itself and its effects. And of course it matches exactly the marks on Biko and the effects described at the inquest. I believe that it probably is more actual than anything reached in the factual accounts ...[24]

Again, in my interview with him, Ebersohn told me the story of a pathologist who had testified for the state at the inquest and who bought a copy of *Store Up the Anger*. He returned to the bookshop a few days later to buy three more copies, saying, 'I never understood how they did it, but now I know.' 'He believed it,' said Ebersohn, 'that ex-Security policeman believed it – there's a very good chance that that's how Steve Biko died.' (67)

24. Letter to Green, 11 Feb. 1991.

The method in question involves dropping a small sack filled with sand systematically on a particular place at the base of the skull: 'You've got to know how,' says Van Rooyen, the policeman who subjects Bhengu to this torture. 'You mustn't hit too hard. Just let the bag fall under its own weight. And you've got to hit the right place. You can scramble a man's brains without leaving a single mark' (202). The scene in which this violence is perpetrated comes as something of a revelation; the bag is the clue which has been introduced from the second page, and returned to at intervals throughout the novel with a significance dependent upon this still-to-come revelation. The first reference is loaded, but its implications escape us at this point:

> The small sack, no larger than a man's fist, lay on the floor next to the bed. If his hands had been free and if he had been able to move them, he could have reached out and picked it up. It had toppled over onto its side, spilling some of the beach sand onto the floor. It looked innocent now, like a child's toy, used and discarded. He turned his head away. It was not possible to look at the bag, just as it was not possible to look at the policeman. He could not separate them. (8)

This chilling description, linking torturer and instrument, is presented with an almost Gothic sense of mystery, in that we have no idea why the policeman or the sack invoke the terror they do. Bhengu is unable even to name the policeman, although all others are named when we first meet them; Van Rooyen remains nameless for fifty more pages, another clue to his horrific actions. When he is named we are told:

> Bhengu found himself acknowledging the policeman's name, momentarily overcoming his fear enough to allow it into his conscious thinking. He could still not look at the face, but the name drove strongly into his mind until it filled every corner, pervading all of his consciousness, an instrument of torture that allowed no area of relief. (58)

The deed becomes word, but not yet flesh; approaching us across the distance of language, it becomes name before it becomes substance. This is a measure of its terror, which we feel in its effects; structurally all-pervasive, the sack is (if an

Althusserian parallel may be forgiven) until the 'last instance' an 'absent cause'. In terms closer to detective fiction, it is in progressively tracing the significance of the sack that, as Porter put it above, we approach 'the closing of the logico-temporal gap that separates the present of the discovery of crime from the past that prepared it'. In 'moving forward' we 'move back', drawing in all the relevant history behind us, be it the truth behind the sack or – its structural parallel – Bhengu's life history.

Just as each flashback fills in further the meaning of the present as it is presented to us, so each reference to the sand bag draws closer to its full significance. The second time it is noted, it is noted in its absence; Bhengu observes that it has disappeared with the night-shift policemen (of whom Van Rooyen is one) as they go off duty (13). Van Rooyen must keep his actions hidden even from his fellow officers. Later, after Bhengu has engaged in the struggle with his guards in which it will be assumed he 'accidentally' sustains his fatal injury, the bag appears more fully in its effects, although we are not yet completely able to understand the reference:

> He had felt their punches, wild and hard to his body, and he had fought back, knowing that he had no hope of winning, that there would always be too many of them. And he had felt those other blows, not hard, but insistent, continuous, seemingly never-ending until his brain was like a ping-pong ball inside his skull. (96)

As Bhengu comes closer to despair further on in the novel, the sand bag appears as the culmination of the various violences done to him in detention and due to be repeated on endless victims to come: 'The head-shrinker, the isolation cell, the boat rides, the sand bag would again have work to do' (153). Finally, as the sand bag is produced by Van Rooyen, it is again described for us, but, unlike its first description, the details are now given in relation to the way in which the bag will be used:

> Bhengu had heard of the sand bag. Van Rooyen was crouching next to his face and holding it up for him to see. It was small, a little bigger than a man's fist and filled with coarse white sand. Van Rooyen had taken a little out of the bag and let Bhengu watch it run through his fingers. The neck of the bag was narrower and was empty of sand to provide a grip for its manipulator. (200)

Gone is its innocence, its comparison to a child's toy; in the scene that follows its vicious application is graphically portrayed, and its conclusion brings us to the beginning of the novel: 'Something gave inside his head, stopping the pain immediately. It was then that Sam Bhengu knew that he was dying' (205).

The narrative achieves extraordinary control through its drawing together of the detective and historical modes. In following the repetition of the clue to its revelation, and in tracing Bhengu's history to the present moment of his death, the narrative points, what is more, beyond its own conclusion. Temporally we have lived through it the last hours of Bhengu's life; historically we have followed that life from the Sophiatown removals to the Cato Manor riots to the community programmes of the Black People's Convention. That these two time spans have embraced the protagonist's death and a people's defeat is not, however, the emphasis the novel finally carries. Its title derives from Bhengu's meditation on those just joining the struggle in his place:

> Bhengu knew them all. He had known them drunk and sober, brave and cowardly, apathetic and alive to the possibilities of the future. He knew that it was in the unbowed hearts of the young that an anger was stirring, storing up against the day of reckoning ... (116)

As we have seen, however, the novel does not depend entirely upon this utopian vision for the quiet sense of triumph informing its conclusion. In this account of contemporary history the past is just as important as the future. The gentle celebration upon which the novel ends arises out of the sense of personal control Bhengu has wrested from his past and present circumstances; he is able to die upon his own terms, terms that have been established historically and personally:

> It was all right. Before it had been very bad, but now it was all right. He would be able to do it now. All he wanted was to lie quietly until the time came. He knew that he was ready. It had taken time to get there, but he had done it and he was ready.
> ... He knew he could do it now. It was going to be all right. (205-206)

Formally this control is reflected in the control of the narrative, and this grows out of the meeting of the detective and historical forms that makes the present an historical one.

Store Up the Anger emerges from historical material, but its allegiance to history goes beyond adherence to the facts; the freedom it demands from those facts (as in making Bhengu a typical – in Lukács's sense – figure rather than a literal representation of Biko) is used to resist the material from which it springs in order to question it. The question at the centre of the detective form as it is used in the novel – how did Bhengu/Biko die? – is not as important in its correctness as evidence as it is in its being a figure for the questioning that the novel represents. This questioning is carried out in the best spirit of Collingwood. It is guided by the firm focus of an enquiry into the circumstances surrounding a man's death, yet the notion of the responsibility behind this death plays back into the history from which it arises. For its solution does not lie in the life of the man upon whom it is focused alone, but in the entire set of circumstances that make up the history of which he is part. And this includes, as the immediacy of the South African situation makes only too plain – Ebersohn was forced to complete the manuscript of *Store Up the Anger* in hiding after word got out that he was working on a 'Biko' novel – the investigation includes the act of its own creation as history. This is, surely, the most pressing way in which we can conceive of the present as history.

We can draw back from this specific observation to conclude upon a related more general one: as a perspective on the uses of history in South African fiction, the detective genre – in its failures as much as its successes – has proved the present, its special terrain, to be entirely an historical realm. In its failures, detective fiction has illustrated this in the limits it has imposed upon grasping the fullness of historical circumstance; in its successes it has, in Collingwood's terms, put the present 'to the question' (1983:269) or, in a phrasing perhaps more apt in the case of *Store Up the Anger*, put it 'to the torture' (ibid.:270). In Ebersohn's hands, the detective genre is used to similar effect, and in its more literal deployment it also reinforces Collingwood's observations with regard to history and the present. *Store Up the Anger* proves the present, its special terrain, to be entirely an historical terrain. Out of the painful re-creation of an event in the historical present comes the history of the full range of its 'causes'. In the process of revelation that Ebersohn's novel represents, the significance of the past emerges in the present and the present takes on its full force in relation to the past as the structure of the detective story plays itself out. Fiction successfully and on its own terms translates its material into an act of historicisation that resists the appropriation of the past by the present, or the present by the past.

Certainly the more obvious features of the detective form disappear in the process. Yudel Gordon does not preside here, but in his absence the *reader* becomes the detective, moving back into the past with each appearance of the central clue in order to achieve an ever-increasing grasp of what is involved in solving the mystery of the present. And while the guilty are not punished, they are identified; in this process the victim becomes more than that – the dead body is not simply the inert signifier of a crime, but eloquent witness to not only the perpetration of that crime but the history that informs it. Here the formula of the detective story is submerged in the material it investigates; out of this the standard form of the genre, resisted by its content, re-emerges to challenge the limits of its founding conventions and produce a history that is novel in both form and content. The form loses its generic precision along the way, but in this case, as in that of the 'historical novel', we must follow Lukács in rejecting 'the genre theory of later bourgeois aesthetics which splits up the novel into various "sub-genres" – adventure novel, detective novel, psychological novel, peasant novel, historical novel etc.'; Wessel Ebersohn's achievement as a writer of detective fiction is that he takes the genre beyond its 'thoroughly bureaucratic classification' and immerses it in 'the living dialectics of history' from which it is so often isolated (Lukacs 1981:287-88).

'FORM' AND 'CONTENT'

The histories we tell ourselves, as much in their present as in their past form, are, of course, constructs rather than givens, but constructs that are created out of specific materially-based and ideologically-informed tropes and figures. We have concentrated on the contribution of one form of figuration – the detective genre – to remind ourselves, however, that historicisation is not an activity that is relative, even in the somewhat ironic sense, say, of being 'historically determined'. The forms available to us for this activity are materially contingent, but they are also, as I have tried to demonstrate, capable of being employed *against* the pressures that generate them.

To say that form can resist the moment that gives rise to it is to say that it is, as Marx observed of literature so long ago, a mode of production. And if what it produces is to be meaningful, then it too must resist the terms of its production. To return to the metaphor governing this chapter: for evidence to be significant, as much for the historian as the detective, it must be able to alter the terms of its analysis. It is thus not (*pace* Sherlock Holmes) simply so much data revealing a story when observed accurately enough; neither, however, is it simply (*pace* Conan Doyle) a reinforcement for the authority of the particular story in which it appears. Form and content emerge out of their common resistance to each other and their context.

I have tried to illustrate this by reading Collingwood's central metaphor somewhat against itself in taking it 'literally'. This gives the form that is his analogy for the activity of the historian its own historical density, the sort of density with which all form is informed, but it also demonstrates the resistance that form can generate out of the material it produces while both resisting and being produced by it. Out of this has come the shape a literary genre has helped give to a certain history while taking on a specific (and contingent) shape within that history.

PART THREE

---■---

THE FUTURE AS HISTORY

8

FUTURE
HISTORIES

━━━━■━━━━

... the future is a prologue to all history
– Robert Bundy (1976:2)

ERASING THE PAST

'Man's thrust into the future is history,' declares S.J. Coetzee in J.M. Coetzee's
Dusklands; 'all the rest,' he continues confidently, 'the dallying by the wayside,
the retraced path, belongs to anecdote, the evening by the hearth-fire' (1974:121).
In this single sentence S.J. Coetzee erases most of what his historical subject,
Jacobus Coetzee, considered important in his history. He also reminds us that the
past is rarely given shape without a sense of the future, but we must delay our
analysis of this temporal orientation until we have worked through the displacing
of the past that is necessary to bring the future into clearer focus.

One of a proliferation of 'Coetzees' in the novel, 'S.J.' is supposedly the author
of the Afterword to 'The Narrative of Jocobus Coetzee', an account of a journey
undertaken by his 'ancestor' (108) into the interior of the Western Cape in 1760.
Within the extended conceit of the novel, the 'Afterword' was originally the
Afrikaans 'Introduction' to a Dutch version of the narrative edited by S.J. Coetzee
and published in 1951 by the Van Plettenberg Society. This in turn was 'drawn
from a course of lectures on the early explorers of South Africa given annually by
[S.J.Coetzee] at the University of Stellenbosch between 1934 and 1948' (55). It is
here translated into English, as is the text of the narrative, by one 'J.M. Coetzee',
who tells us in his Preface to this new edition that 'S.J.' is his father (55).

This tortuous history of text and affiliation is further complicated by the

235

inclusion of an Appendix consisting of a Deposition 'Related to the Political Secretariat at the Castle of Good Hope on the 18th November 1760' (125) by Jocobus Coetzee and transcribed by 'O.M. Bergh, Councillor & Secretary'. Jacobus, in the ultimate irony of an intricate play on textuality and history, is illiterate, as witnessed by his 'mark' on the Deposition, which is an 'X' (125). This signature is appropriate, because the Deposition is clearly a distillation of his journey into only that which is of interest to the as yet tentatively colonising Cape authorities – a fact noted by S.J. Coetzee, who treats this version of Jocobus's journey with dismissive disdain. Yet, as we have noted, S.J. Coetzee's pronouncement regarding history dismisses, in its own way, almost all of Jocobus Coetzee's own version of his experiences; his 'Narrative' – a metafictional re-creation of both his first and second expeditions – consists largely of what 'S.J.' calls 'dallying by the wayside' and 'the retraced path'.

'The Narrative of Jacobus Coetzee' and its attachments make up the second half of *Dusklands*, a novel which compresses typically postmodern attitudes to history into itself to such a degree as to be almost the final word on the new international literary interest in history which emerged in the 1960s and 1970s. The British novelist John Fowles's popular successes would be one indicator of this interest, and Teresa Dovey (1988:67) has pointed out the similarities between Coetzee's first novel – published in 1974 – and those of the American 'non-fiction' novelists of the period who, in the words of E.L. Doctorow, aimed at composing 'false documents more valid, more real, more truthful than the true documents of the politicians or the journalists or the psychologists'.[25]

Or, especially in South Africa, the historians: in 1976 Anthony Delius had published *Border: A Novel*, described in the *Companion to South African English Literature* as 'a novelistic treatment of a typical 1820 Settler's diary' (Adey *et al.* 1986:66). This is a useful work with which to lead into a brief discussion of some of the general fictional techniques evident in the historical novels which sought to revive history as a serious subject for literature in the wake of the cheapening of the past so common in light historical romances.

Delius's re-creation of the past is, as his novel's title immediately suggests, intended to trace its protagonist's painful and progressive crossing of the 'borders' – geographical, but, of course ultimately, in the South African terms of the 1970s, racial – that divide 'our common humanity': 'how much has my heart made that

---

25. Theresa Dovey cites these words of Doctorow's as coming from an article in the *New York Times*, 'Novelist Syncopating History in *Ragtime*', by Mel Gussow (11 July 1975:12).

crossing to what we all are' (341) muses Captain Alexander Hampton, author of
the journal and ancestor of the by now *de rigueur* descendent who has found
reasons in the present for putting the past into print. Hampton's conviction –
acted out in his taking of a black lover – that 'All borders slide together in the
night, and in the years' (345) has made his journal the 'mildly embarrassing
possession of the Hampton-de-Ritter family' (vi), suppressed for over a century.

Yet the novel's ultimate definition of a border is temporal; time is the real
difference we have to cross in defining our humanity. '"Every man is a border"',
says the baboon become 'sage' in the reverie recorded in Hampton's final journal
entry, and when Hampton asks, '"A border? ... What do you know of us?"', the
baboon replies: '"A country between what's coming and what's going"' (387).
D.A. Hampton-de-Ritter's decision to publish the journal in the 1970s is based
on his belief that the border between past and present is just as porous as those
inscribed in geography and race: 'Captain Alexander Hamilton was a man not
very different from ourselves,' he says in concluding his Foreword, 'and his times
were strangely closer to our own than at first appears' (vi).

These classically liberal sentiments – in the strong sense, given oppositional
strategies in the South African political spectrum of the time – tend to erode the
sort of power available to us from the past that it is the subject of *Novel Histories*
to claim. All the efforts towards authenticity in a novel like *Border* are intended
to emphasise the fundamental sameness beneath them. Laudable as this strategy
is when set against the institutionalisation of difference that defined apartheid,
such universalising tendencies give little scope for arguing against the kinds of
dangerous relativism that those who stress certain types of difference propose –
as we have seen in the case of Sarah Gertrude Millin. Her essentialism of difference
negates history, and it is only in historicising her perspective – that is, positioning
it in relation to the material moment of its discursive production – that we are
able to counter her divisive sense of dissimilarity. Our other option would be to
judge her in ethical terms of our own, extended to her across time on the basis of
some sort of generalised morality – which is precisely the historical attitude
criticised in my analysis of her 'ahistorical' historical novels.

Universalising sameness or difference, then, generates equal difficulty.
Emphasising 'sameness' is not the opposite of emphasising 'difference'; as in all
classic binaries, the oppositions involved share a certain logic. The danger is always
that difference will not so much be erased by the counter claim of sameness as be
appropriated by it. Alexander Hampton exemplifies the most benign attitude to

the crossing of borders, but it is still finally *his* story that is told, with those of the others he seeks to preserve neutralised in the medium of their fundamental similarity (see the interchange with the 'Strandloper', for example [155-61]) as the basis for their being positioned within it.

This may be further illustrated by referring to another mid-1970s South African historical novel, one that found a wider audience than *Border*. André Brink's best-selling *An Instant in the Wind* (1983 [1976]) is constructed around the belief that two individuals separated by race and class are able to find love when taken out of these structures. His pessimistic conclusion, in which that love is betrayed upon the return to such constraints, is meant to add emotional weight to the loss involved. This loss is defined by history. Brink's anonymous present-based re-creator of the past decides to tell the story because he senses in it 'occasional remarks in which one suddenly glimpses an existence beyond history' (14). The historical documents that are his source 'are presently being prepared for publication in annotated editions ... Then history will claim them for itself,' he says, continuing, 'But such history is irrelevant' (14). In determined opposition to the institutionalised history writing of his time and place, the revisionist is insistent that 'the crust of history must be scraped off' (15).

But the terms of this resistance are not sufficient to hold at bay the official history writers; dehistoricised, the past simply becomes even more open to the appropriations of the present. Brink's naked couple, hand and hand in the wilderness, are meant to represent the timeless truth of our human potential, but they remind us, instead, that each invocation of Eden, even, is historically substantial and represents a particular positioning within the politics of the present. In *An Instant in the Wind* history rather than an angel expels the couple from paradise – but the very paradise called up in the novel is itself marked by the history of its moment of production. In this case that moment, for all its utopian attitude to race, has extremely unfortunate implications for gender, for example. Elizabeth, in full knowledge of the ideal – 'All this time we've been nothing but man and woman, two people alone in the wilderness' (246) – and the threat to this the social represents – 'From now on the Cape will try to make us black and white' (246) – commits her original sin in betraying 'Adam' (Brink's naming is not subtle). It is she who accepts that 'One has to learn to live with betrayal' (250), apparently in relation to the actions performed by Adam to keep them alive in the wilderness, which she translates into her social needs upon their return to the Cape.

The sudden twist in the plot when she betrays Adam to the authorities on the last page, effective as it is in catching the reader off guard and shocking him or her into realising the point Brink wishes to make, is not a neutral device. Into its very suddenness and the reader's unpreparedness rushes the whole weight of Judao-Christian patriarchy, crystallised into a moment of contemporary gender relations not fully explained in the historical terms set up by the novel. The issue of individual choice and historical determinism at the centre of *An Instant in the Wind* is inscribed, ultimately, into a myth pattern rather than an historical context, and this pattern, in its locatable current formulation, betrays history into the hands of the present. In trying to evade history, the present simply raises its own profile.

No doubt this is generally what takes place, even in the most insistent acts of historicisation, but the point of *Novel Histories* is that there are moments (in a whole range of texts, despite my concentration upon the literary) when 'the historical' becomes more than that; moments when we glimpse a difference that positively erases our sameness, acts back upon our appropriations, and alters the position from which we produce our pasts, presents, and futures.

To return to *Dusklands*: when Coetzee adopts the trope of playing the past off against the present within which it is recreated, he takes this device further than the two novels just considered do. The first half of *Dusklands* is roughly contemporary to the writing of the novel. Entitled 'The Vietnam Project' and set in the United States in the 1970s, it is the apparently unrelated story of the mental breakdown of one Eugene Dawn, who is, to use Noam Chomsky's term for the bureaucratic strategists behind the military presence in Vietnam, a 'backroom boy'. Dawn's breakdown is prompted by the collapse of his professional and domestic situation; the failure of his marriage is intimately related in the text to the rejection of his analysis of the errors in America's psychological approach to the war. The 'personal' and the 'political' blur and merge in this section of the novel, as they do in 'The Narrative of Jocobus Coetzee'. In Coetzee's representation of this interaction, we find what first appears, for all its self-conscious theorising, a technique that is structurally similar to that just criticised in Delius's and Brink's work. Indeed, this seems to come about *because of* Coetzee's self-conscious theorising. Dawn's strategies for defeating the Vietnamese through psychoanalysis and myth, no less than his interpretation of his own breakdown, draw upon high theory current in an array of disciplines in the 1960s and 1970s. Rather more startlingly, Jacobus Coetzee's 1760 meditations are equally and overtly informed by this range of thought – if anything, they extend it, as the uneducated and illiterate trekboer's inner life wanders through classical, Enlightenment, structural, deconstructive, and a host of other frames of awareness. This forms the medium through which the present and the past are related, associated across their disjunctures in the novel by the pervading theme of the construction of others as Other as the essence of their subjugation.

The similarities between the discursive tactics of Eugene Dawn and Jocobus Coetzee bring out the common genealogy of eighteenth-century colonialism and twentieth-century imperialism. At the same time, however, history is not so much denied as foregrounded as one of its most standard operations is rigorously called into question. Central to Coetzee's analysis of history in *Dusklands* is the conventional historical device of explaining in terms of origins. The tense of Dawn's section is the present definite and Jacobus Coetzee's is the past historic, but no developmental connection from past to present is traced between them. *Dusklands* may begin in the present and switch midway into the past, but Coetzee's Narrative is no more future-orientated than Dawn's story is understandable in terms of its sources. The standard structures of Western history writing – linear, progressive, teleological – give way to the exposure of its enunciative formation, which is revealed as fundamentally evasive. Here Coetzee's interrogation of historicity moves his fiction away from the 'historical' towards the ethical dimensions referred to in my Introduction.

The epigraph to the first section of *Dusklands* is taken from Herman Kahn's introduction to *Can We Win in Vietnam? The American Dilemma.* Kahn's observation that

> Obviously it is difficult not to sympathize with those European and American audiences who, when shown films of fighter-bomber pilots visibly exhilarated by successful napalm bombing runs on Viet-Cong targets, react with horror and disgust. Yet, it is unreasonable to expect the U.S. Government to obtain pilots who are so appalled by the damage they may be doing that they cannot carry out their missions or become excessively depressed or guilt-ridden,

encapsulates the ethical dilemma at the centre of the imperial project in a modern context. The current technologies of representation available to an audience with ostensible democratic sympathies provoke the requisite moral sentiments, but this also prepares us for Dawn's attempts to side-step his familial and historical responsibilities. His opening sentences – 'My name is Eugene Dawn. I cannot help that. Here goes' – thrust us through his account of his actions – replete with playing the games of a number of forms of contemporary analysis (professional, legal, psychoanalytic) – to his utopian conclusion: 'I have high hopes of finding whose fault I am' (49). This final sentence of the first part of *Dusklands* carries us over to the epigraph (taken from Flaubert) to its second section: 'What is important is the philosophy of history'. This tempts the reader to find in 'history' (that is, in the context of the novel, the past as exemplified in Jacobus Coetzee's narrative) the determining 'causes' of actions in the present. The weight of Flaubert's statement, however, resides in its *questioning* of what constitutes 'the historical'; in this, it is a meta-historical observation that does not allow us to follow through on the logic of Dawn's concluding hope any more than we can take at face value Jocobus Coetzee's claim that he is 'a tool in the hands of history' (106). Dawn is no more Jacobus's 'fault' than the two people he sees as responsible for his persecution and blames for his actions: his wife, Marilyn, and his supervising superior, yet another 'Coetzee'.

The latter signifies a cultural anachronism which serves to extend and blur the presence of the implied author of *Dusklands* into the present as much as he permeates the past in the shape of 'Jacobus', 'S.J', and 'J.M.'. It also crosses national and temporal boundaries in a way which reveals them as the constructs of particular histories. Far from leading us towards origins as explanations, the novel leads us into the past as a highly variable textual product, open to the manipulations of a present which is no less a general text. Yet if, as Jameson observes, history 'is inaccessible to us except in textual form', it is also, as Jameson insists and Coetzee's fictional strategy exemplifies, *'not* a text' itself (1981:35); rather, we find exemplified in *Dusklands* Jameson's famous formulation, referred to earlier: 'History is what hurts, it is what refuses desire ...' (ibid.:102). It is in this sense excessive in relation to the texts by which it is always and only accessed. The rupture between 'The Vietnam Project' and 'The Narrative of Jocobus Coetzee', no less than the fissures within these stories (pre-eminently, in the former, Dawn's account of the injury to his son and, in the latter, the two conflicting accounts of the death of Klawer), prove not so much that history is relative to its teller, as that it resists the inconsistencies which mark its production within particular positionalities. In this Coetzee goes beyond the pastlessness of some powerful 'postmodern' perspective on history, in which the resistance to closure becomes equally an erasure of any past other than one produced in the present.

To claim this for Coetzee is not to go against his aim as a novelist which was, as we saw in Chapter One, 'to show up the mythic status of history'. It is to acknowledge that he, along with the best writers of postmodern fiction who engage with the historical, is not so much an 'historical novelist' as an 'historiographical novelist'. His metafiction is also intimately metahistory, problematising our very concepts of history and producing a range of distinctly novel approaches to history. As his next four novels went on to demonstrate, this included deliberately avoiding the currency of the present in South African fiction of the 1970s and 1980s; only with *Age of Iron* in 1990 was Coetzee to return to the historical present he leapt out of in shifting from the first to the second part of *Dusklands*. An essential part of that leap, however, was to examine in detail the 'thrust into the future' that S.J. Coetzee declared to be the true subject of history.

In this Coetzee engaged with a preoccupation common to several important South African writers in the early to mid-1980s. As I contended in Chapter One, the type of protest which concentrated on condemning the present and revising the past seems to have tired in the darkest moments of what Nadine Gordimer was to characterise as the 'interregnum'; exhausted by a material context manifestly finished yet refusing to pass away, some writers projected themselves beyond the repetitions of hammering at the present into a future that called for a different sort of imaginative effort. Some of the various forms this has taken will concern us for the rest of this chapter.

THE FUTURE IN HISTORY AND LITERATURE

We view the present trial as an interim affair. Somewhere in the future lies a date when black and white South Africans will take a second look at these moments of our history. They will evaluate afresh the events now in contention and our role in them. And since the privilege will belong to them, they will pass final judgement. We are convinced that theirs will be contrary to the present one. They will vindicate us.

    – Patrick 'Terror' Lekota, Popo Molefe, Moss Chikane,
    joint statement in the 'Delmas' treason trial[26]

26. Quoted in the *Weekly Mail*, 9-15 Dec. 1988:3.

In his study of the historical novel, Georg Lukács is, as I noted in passing in Chapter One, adamant that the future, especially in its utopian sense, has no serious place in fiction. To quote his firm dismissal:

> What Marx said of legal institutions applies in wide measure to literary forms. They cannot stand higher than the society which brought them forth. Indeed, since they deal with the deepest human laws, problems and contradictions of an epoch, they should not stand higher – in the sense, say, of anticipating coming perspectives of development by romantic-utopian projections of the future into the present. For the tendencies leading to the future are in fact more firmly and definitely contained in what really is than in the most beautiful utopian dreams or projections. (1981:421)

Historiography proves just as unaccommodating when it comes to the future. Fredric Jameson, for whom, as we have seen, the future is decidedly historical, is still cautious about the ways in which it can be seen and used as such. He in fact joins a long line of those who deride the many 'theories of history' available on grounds remarkably similar to those used by Lukács in his rejection of the use of the future in fiction:

> The multiplication of 'theories of history' strikes me ... as the symptom of [a] ... cultural illness: an attempt to outsmart the present, first of all, to think your way behind history to the point where even the present itself can be seen as a completed historical instant...; to name and label the moment you are standing in even before it reaches its ultimate consecration *sub specie aeternitatis* in the history books themselves. (1971:320)

And what inspires manoeuvres of this type? 'Such a mode of thought,' says Jameson, 'springs from a profound horror of time and fear of change; it is a very different kind of mental operation from the Marxist sensitivity to the present as history, which welcomes and rejoices in an ever more intense existential awareness of the historicity of life.'

The historicity of the present, as we have observed, is the central theme of Lukács's *The Historical Novel*, and we may continue to shuttle between Lukács and Jameson on this topic because, up to a certain point, their common insistence on seeing the present as history produces an equal rejection of attempts to colonise the future from the present: 'the attempt to predict', writes Jameson, 'is but one of the symptoms of a failure to think in a situational way ...' (1971:361).

Both literature and history, it seems, address the future at some risk to their integrity. What then are we to make of the emergence of a group of texts intimately concerned with history which take the future seriously as their subject? That this may signal certain types of failure may well be true, but to the extent that this is so, these would seem to be significant failures. For future histories stubbornly come forth, at significant points in particular literatures. These works seek to comment upon the past and present by projecting the implications of the past and the present forward in time. In this they reverse the standard techniques of historical fiction, but remain directly related to them. In any event, attempts to give meaning to the past generally involve, as we shall see in some of the theory and examples to come, an implied or explicit appeal to the future. Hence the term 'future histories'; it designates those fictional forms that explore the future in much the same way as we have seen the classical historical novel explore the past, investigating another time whilst retaining a serious commitment to particular and specific historical conditions.

Margaret Lenta, in her 'Fictions of the future', states: 'fictions which read like attempts to predict and perhaps influence the kind of future which South Africa will have after the revolution have been numerous since the early seventies' (1988:133). Stephen Clingman, while acknowledging that such a tendency started manifesting itself as early as 1972 in Karel Schoeman's *Promised Land* and – as Clingman himself is primarily responsible for establishing – in the latently prophetic strands to be found in Nadine Gordimer's *The Guest of Honour* (1971), *The Conservationist* (1974), and *Burger's Daughter* (1979), is more accurate in identifying this more explicitly as a phenomenon of the 1980s.[27] I argue for a slightly more specific chronological placing of what I have called 'future histories', but it is well worth approaching this through earlier texts like *Promised Land*.

27. See Clingman 1990b, where on pages 44 and 45 he traces the shift from a literary emphasis on the past to one on the future within the forms of social opposition available: he characterises opposition movements in the 1950s as operating within the framework of South African reality; what was sought was an extension of the rights available to all sections of society. The repression of the 1960s forced opposition groupings outside this framework, away from concentrating on its improvement and towards its replacement. He locates the subject of the future within an intensification of these latter attitudes in the South Africa of the 1970s and 1980s: the oppositional interest is now in wholesale transformation of the framework of South African reality.

This will help define another period's concern with the future in displaying features firmly grounded in its own, and it will illustrate why cautions regarding the future expressed by Lukács and Jameson must be taken seriously.

SCHOEMAN: REVERSAL

Karel Schoeman's *Promised Land* (1978) originally appeared in Afrikaans (although it was soon translated into English) as *Na die Geliefde Land* (1972). It deals with the return of a young Afrikaner to South Africa after having lived abroad since his childhood. During his absence the country has been politically transformed, and although this is not spelt out for us in detail, what is clear is that the once-dominant Afrikaner community now exists in a state of marginalisation and repression. The action plays out in an isolated farming community, the original home of the returnee's family. Here he encounters a variety of responses to the new political situation, a strong element of which includes resistance to what is now obviously the government of a new regime; this resistance is largely based upon what proves to be a stifling commitment to the past.

The novel shows little interest in the actual processes by which the future it represents is achieved; *Na die Geliefde Land* is closely related to the classical utopian form in that it basically chooses to ignore the period of transition to the future it presents. The work's protagonist, George, is as foreign in the homeland he revisits as his name is in the Afrikaans text; he is a child of exile, with only the sketchiest sense of the process of change that has made him a foreigner. Carla, a young woman he meets who in her resistance to the state of things is the true child of her time, is simply dismissive of the history of defeat which has made her. It is her compatriots who are fixated on their past – the past as past, that is, not as a path to the present – but this proves only to be a claustrophobic trap, feeding on itself in the form of inspiring useless resistance. The future present of *Na die Geliefde Land* cannot sustain George (he returns to what he now recognises as his home in a 'foreign' country), or, more significantly, Carla, whose commitment to staying hovers between the perverse and the heroic: she is an empty heroine, heroic in attitude, but with no personal, let alone social direction to make that attitude meaningful. Carla refuses the offer of leaving with George, but we are given no clear account of what the significance of her staying will be. Historical agency is reduced to gesture, and inessential gesture at that.

Transition and the active role of people in that transition are not important for *Na die Geliefde Land* primarily because its presentation of the future works on a simple act of reversal; the Afrikaners now suffer the kind of repression they once imposed upon other groups. Positions within the relations of power are directly swapped, the intention being to motivate the present holders of power to recognise the negative effects of that power by placing them within the terms of subjugation they themselves employ. Domination based on ethnic terms, with resistance and culture equally violently suppressed, culminates in the raid on the party held in George's honour before his return. However careful Schoeman is not to characterise the shadowy yet ubiquitous regime in power, the terms of opposition he sets up require us to see it as government by the oppositional groups of the present – a government what is more which is capable of being no more than a mirror-image of the government it has replaced. A by-product of his method this may be, but an unfortunate by-product it is, for it gives a non-progressive political slant to a work which is anything but this in intention. Its binary logic allows for no dialectic of change, and makes the unfortunate title of the English translation more accurately representative of the work: 'Promised Land' reduces the richly ambiguous potential of the original Afrikaans 'Na die Geliefde Land', in which 'na' is able to resonate with its twin sense of 'after' and 'towards'. Like its heroine, 'Promised Land' cannot move towards anything; it retreats in every direction, finding only its own trap of 'after'. It hangs in stasis, no product and no producer. This is no just summary even of the victimisers it seeks allegorically to castigate: they can be, indeed must be, accounted for historically, not simply made present in their negative effects – however monolithic these must have seemed in 1972.

The novel works along dystopian lines, but its historical form of reversal results in a content that cannot call up even in its opposite an effective sense of community with which to challenge the failure of the present. In terms of evaluating works as resistant form we have come across this type of failure before; certain works record the 'history' of their moment with some success, but in failing to generate genuine difference they limit the effectiveness of their resistance to that moment. What is nevertheless valuable about *Na die Geliefde Land*'s failure to represent any kind of dynamic community – in resistance or in government – is just how representative the novel is of the stultifying effects of repression at the time of its writing. One is reminded of how even the most radical work of Athol Fugard, his collaborative plays in the *Statements* collection, poised as they are in 1973 just months before the Durban strikes, do not have available to them the progressive confidence some, at least, expected. Critic after critic has written at length of the way in which *Sizwe Banzi is Dead* in particular, with much of its action set in an industrial environment, depicts a retreat into personal survival rather than advocating the sort of radical communal action which was to so large a degree responsible for finally forcing change upon an intransigent political system.

We must be wary, of course, of the way in which this sort of criticism can lead to the reading of texts out of the materiality of their production. The real question, for criticism concerned to be more than prescription, is how available radical communal action seemed at the specific time of Kani, Ntshona, and Fugard's workshopping. Still, despite the historical evidence which explains why the idea of an inspirational future was so unavailable in this context for Schoeman as much as for Fugard and his collaborators, Fugard himself acknowledges the type of failure that has possibly taken place here. In his notebook entry for 26 December 1968, he wrote: 'How do I align myself with a future, a possibility, in which I believe but of which I have no clear image? A failure of imagination.' He reproduced this comment in his Introduction to the 1981 edition of *Boesman and Lena and Other Plays* (xxv), underscoring the way in which such a reaction to his political context was still current by adding, 'Today's future barely includes tomorrow. At times I see the situation deteriorating still further, to the point where even the thought of a tomorrow will be a luxury' (xxv). At this point Fugard was coming to accept the particular 'failure of the imagination' with regard to the future that he had identified in 1968 by 'trying to live and work in preparation for that eventuality' (xxv); at roughly the same moment, Mongane Serote was revitalising a text that had been stalemated by its context with an energy which, whilst registering the beginnings of a change, still had to work within a mode we can only call utopian. It is to this impulse towards the future that we must now turn.

UTOPIA (ONE)

The true genesis is not at the beginning but at the end
— Ernst Bloch (quoted in Degenaar 1988:14)

Despite, or perhaps because of, Jameson's scepticism regarding textual strategies which include the future, *Marxism and Form* is an extraordinary (in the senses of both unusual and extreme) meditation upon the future. If we ask how this position accords with Jameson's dismissal of 'theories of history' noted above, we will find that the answer is related to the special sense in which utopia is employed in *Marxism and Form*.

In spelling out his 'Versions of a Marxist Hermeneutic' in this book, Jameson states that he is concerned with hermeneutics as 'a political discipline', one which 'provides the means for maintaining contact with the very sources of revolutionary energy during a stagnant time, of preserving the concept of freedom itself, underground, during geological ages of repression. Indeed,' he continues, 'it is the concept of freedom which ... proves to be the privileged instrument of a political hermeneutic.' In this sense, freedom is 'best understood as an interpretive device rather than a philosophical essence or idea. For wherever the concept of freedom is once more understood, it always comes as the awakening of dissatisfaction in the midst of all...' (84). Jameson identifies freedom with the utopian idea, which 'keeps alive the possibility of a world qualitatively distinct from this one and takes the form of a stubborn negation of all that is' (111).

While this 'revolutionary stimulus' (82) may draw its energy from a profound nostalgia (as it does in Jameson's analysis of Walter Benjamin), it is most explicitly associated with the future in Jameson's account of the work of Ernst Bloch. If, for Freud, 'comprehension consists of working back to origins', Bloch's dialogue with Freud is precisely one of finding room alongside this for 'an ontological pull of the future' – 'an unconscious of what is yet to come' (129). To expand upon the epigraph to this section: for Bloch, 'the meaning of Being itself comes into being, if at all, only at the moment when the world passes over into utopia, and when that final utopian destination returns upon the past to confer direction upon it' (131). These somewhat large metaphysical terms take on meaning for me in the way they capture a very real sense of how our understanding works. We need to posit a point of conclusion (not necessarily final; this will prove crucial later) in order for what has come before to make sense; it takes shape only in relation to an end point which then allows for the organisation of what preceded it. In so far as we allow for this before coming to a point of conclusion, such a conclusion may be described as utopian.

The teleological implications here are consciously related by Jameson to their textual source and model: the 'sense in which all plot may be seen as a movement toward utopia, in its basic working through to some ultimate resolution of the basic tensions' (146) is taken to the point where 'the very time of the work may itself stand as a figure of utopian development: "Every great work of art, above and beyond its manifest content, is carried out according to a latency of the page to come, or in other words, in the light of the content of a future which has not yet come into being, and indeed of some ultimate resolution as yet unknown"' (149). For Jameson, such a perspective

> may serve as an object lesson in some of the ways available to a Marxist hermeneutic to restore a genuine political dimension to the disparate texts preserved in the book of our culture: not by some facile symbolic or allegorical interpretation, but by reading the very content and the formal impulse of the texts themselves as figures – whether of psychic wholeness, of freedom, or of the drive towards utopian transfiguration – of the irrepressible revolutionary wish. (159)

And of the duties falling to literary criticism at the conclusion of *Marxism and Form*, pride of (last) place is reserved for 'keep[ing] alive the idea of a concrete future' (416).

The terms of this utopian model translate quite easily into the terms of the 'future histories' which concern us in this chapter. These works were all created in a context of repression and represent attempts at 'maintaining contact with the ... sources of revolutionary energy in a stagnant time'. At a time when the oppressive system in South Africa, although in difficulties, still seemed thoroughly entrenched and opposition was active but all too often stalemated, the responsibility carried by works concerned with the future became more than one of representing the time of oppression; it was also one of keeping a creative way open to the future. Only in the light of a future hope could the struggle towards that future continue to literally 'make sense' in the form discussed above. In so far as these works are the product of a time of oppressive closure that hope may be characterised in utopian terms.

If history, as we have been claiming in this book up to now, exists in its strongest form as a mode of resistance to the present (or of the present to itself), then this utopian impulse – which is precisely a mode of resistance – takes on the shape of the historical in its relation to the moment of its production. Its strength depends upon the difference it is able to set up 'in the midst of all', against 'all that is'. It becomes the work of the future no less than the work of the past or the present in its oppositional sense to produce what we saw Jameson call in Chapter One the 'rigorous judgement' that is the real effect of powerfully told history; the future must remind us of 'what we are not yet'. This it does by embodying within itself, positively or negatively displayed, the criteria by which to evaluate the present state of society. For Jameson the key term here is 'freedom', but the urgencies of the South African situation – the 'political dimension' never far below its surface – demand more content to this potentially empty form. It is precisely the social and historical dimensions generated by the texts which take on the future that concern us – although not necessarily only as reflected in any direct mimetic sense. It is the formal terms upon which these representations of the future engage the present which concern me, especially when they attempt to generate a future out of a present particularly oppressive in its intransigence.

SEROTE: TRANSITION

The history of the production of *To Every Birth its Blood* (1981) carries us from the frustrations registered by Schoeman and Fugard to the period in which the major 'future histories' were produced. The extent of the sense of historical stagnation that dominated the early 1970s is palpable in the first part of Mongane Serote's novel. Nick Visser has convincingly accounted for the major shift that all critics note between Parts I and II in historical terms; working from the dates of composition Serote appends to the text (1975-1980), Visser claims:

> When Serote was already some way into the process of writing a novel
> – and my guess is fairly a long way – the events of June 1976 erupted,
> and he expanded the novel to incorporate them. The novel, in the
> very process of its composition, was opened to the unfolding of history,
> to the unfolding of momentous events as they occurred. (1987:69)

This 'irruption of history' into the text transforms the novelistic strategy Serote employs – here I will follow Kelwyn Sole's modification of Visser's reading (1991) which allows for a greater degree of integration between Serote's narrative methods than Visser allows, while still challenging the neat totalisation Barboure claims (1984) – from the alienated, fragmented, individual perspective that dominates Part I to the socially-integrated multiple perspectives of Part II. Much has been written about this transition, and – as with all the other texts considered in this chapter – I wish to isolate only those elements which characterise the work as a 'future history'.

If Schoeman largely ignores historical transition in his fictional relocation to the future, Serote's strategy implies that it is only possible to situate the past and present that make up much of his novel meaningful by seeing them as transition – that is, in relation to an incomplete but significant foray into a possible future. It is unclear, even unlikely in fact, that the story line of the novel enters that future, but *To Every Birth its Blood* acts as a 'future history' in terms similar to those regarding the utopian given above. Serote's story thus takes us from the confused (and often confusing) past and present of a single protagonist (which is almost classically modernist in its representation of personal breakdown) and integrates this into at least the awareness of a material thrust into a near-future of communal and coherent political action. It is in this future where a guarantee of victory is found in the heroism of revolutionary action, even if the victory itself is not presented as fictionally realised. The chaotic narrative perspective of Part I, the reflex of Tsi's existential collapse, is ordered into an orchestrated pattern of communal narration in Part II by the temporal vantage attained by the novel's concluding orientation towards the future. Nick Visser has noted that 'in the first part of *To Every Birth its Blood* ... the temporal vantage point is uncertain, unfixed, free-floating', resulting in 'the narrative of Part I [being] uncertain, inconsistent, even contradictory' (1987:71). What we must add to this is that the device which ultimately allows Serote the purchase of a conventionally posterior narrative perspective is his positioning of his narrative vantage point in a potential future – a future characterised by at least the motion towards a whole, coherent community in which the individual's place is assured.

This tentative teleology may operate formally along the lines of the utopian, but it is limited in terms of content. It makes of the politically progressive elements in history as it is conceived in the novel (here, essentially, 'the Movement') a natural, organic process: 'like an old tree, the Movement spreads and spreads its roots' (326); 'a force which was slowly, very slowly but very systematically, like water flowing from a dam, approaching every corner of the country'; 'the Movement was like the wind' (272); 'the Movement, like the sea, is deep, is vast, is reflective. It can be calm. It can be rough and tough. Like the wind, it moves and moves and moves' (359). Serote specifically empties this process of any metaphysical, transcendental content (symbolised in this highly symbolic novel by constant references to the sky's inability to provide any solution: see p.342, for example: 'The sky was blue, so blue, it looked transparent, confirming his [Yao's] belief that it was empty, as empty as a deep whistling pit'), as we may expect, but his avowed materialism founders on a contradiction inherent in his text, one which produces a form of idealism – in which politics is taken out of history and transformed into a natural process – which is becoming increasingly troubling as far as the reception of the work is concerned. The problem turns upon an incompletely worked out sense of the relationship between history as (pre)determined process and history as the product of human agency.

Serote stresses human agency constantly in *To Every Birth its Blood*; choice, for each character, no matter how restricted, remains vital, but it is only successful if it accords with the larger 'natural' development of history. This is, of course, an ambiguity at the heart of traditional Marxism, characterised by Coward and Ellis as:

> the ambiguity of showing the place of the subjective moment in the transformation of society when subjective actions are initially posited as simply mirroring the objective processes of history. (1977:8)

Postmodern criticism may resort to resolving this ambiguity within, say, notions of the Lacanian subject (as Coward and Ellis in fact do), but the discursive possibilities available to Serote suggest the narrative strategy sketched above as at least a partial solution: the democratisation of narrative perspective and its accompanying recuperation of the individual self within a communal subject. This strategy is increasingly popular in politically progressive South African literature, but it is as yet insufficiently explored by criticism. The beginnings of a serious consideration of it may be found, however, in a prevalent recent line of criticism on *To Every Birth its Blood*; here I wish to isolate one element within the *reception* of Serote's novel generated from a position *beyond* the point in the future upon which the work anchors its narrative logic. This will help us keep in focus the nature of the utopian impulse the novel depends upon.

Critiques of *To Every Birth its Blood* produced in the late 1980s and early 1990s stress the relation between the personal and political in the novel, especially as these are brought into alignment by the work's developmental strategy. Martin Trump queries the implication in *To Every Birth its Blood* 'that commitment to the resistance movement serves as an antidote to a host of personal ills' (1990b:6), and Kelwyn Sole counters this thrust within the novel with: 'political discipline cannot be a cure for psychic disorder' (1989:39). For Sole, this tendency is a result of the work employing realist and symbolic levels which are 'neither in synchronicity nor complete thematic and logical harmony with each other' (1991:77).

This is a convincing argument, but it does miss the significance of the utopian element in *To Every Birth its Blood*. It was completed in the much darker days of the early 1980s, when successful achievement by progressive forces in South Africa was more a matter of hopeful projection than at the time of Trump's and Sole's critiques. Perhaps we should understand the utopian element as more easily taken into account then, and accepted for what it was (by author and audience), rather than measuring it against more contemporary pressures which require, quite rightly, a harder edge of pragmatism to be brought to bear on the precise nature of revolutionary achievement. Again, this is the degree to which the novel tells us more of its own historical moment than the future it envisages, but in the process its historical perspective, limited though it may be by its idealism, still generates something of a positive utopian element.

The utopian thrust of Serote's novel must be read in the sense of Jameson's political hermeneutic; it is, like the novel's step of faith into the future, its measure of its 'dissatisfaction in the midst of all' and 'stubborn negation of all that is'. It represents the point of resistance from which the novel is able to cast judgement back over the present. The future here becomes an essential element in an oppositional technique, a strategy of protest rather than prediction. Serote's novel is concerned to operate, as Michael Chapman says of Soweto poetry, 'not only as a critique on oppressive systems, but ... as a weapon of transformation' (1982:18); like this poetry, it has 'begun to focus not so much back on a bare Soweto [for Serote, read Alexandra rather than Soweto] existence as forward to a "pre-Azanian" phase of South African history, one wherein the construct of "the people", including the participatory ideals of the black community, has increasingly begun to function as an inspirational myth' (22). Such forms of opposition are dependent upon their formal allegiance to an historically novel future period.

With the emergence of the African National Congress from the thinly-symbolic shadows of 'the Movement' into the glare of the all-too immediate politics of the present, Serote's literary strategy is drawn into the qualifications Jameson attaches to the deployment of the utopian. As he warns us in *Marxism and Form*, 'first and foremost', utopia is 'nothing but a logical possibility', the 'naïve projection' of which 'into the realm of historical chronology can only result in metaphysical nostalgia ... or in utopianism' (38). The negative sense in which 'utopianism' is used here, where it signifies a one-dimensional attempt at prediction, must be marked off from the creative impulse towards the future that characterises Jameson's broader idea of the utopian. *To Every Birth its Blood* is a text which should be read more in the spirit of the latter than the former, but in order to do this, it must be adequately historicised. This involves reading its gesture towards the future back to a point prior to the coming into being of something of the hope upon which its resistance depended. Such an observation may be taken, of course, as a general critical *caveat*, but it takes on a particular type of significance in relation to literary uses of the future as history. Whatever the limits of Serote's representation of the force for change in South Africa, the forward-looking impulse that carried his once-deadlocked 1970s text into completion with it found a real purchase amongst other novels of the early to mid-1980s.

PERIOD

For the gods perceive things in the future, ordinary people
things in the present, but the wise perceive things about to happen.

– Philostratos, *Life of Apollonios of Tyana*, viii, 7.[28]

It is time to attempt a periodising of the most important grouping of texts engaging the future in South Africa. These may be, as I have indicated, linked to the early to mid-1980s, when the most important and powerful fictional 'future histories' (at least within the time frame I have adopted) appeared. While an intense – even, in a broader public sense, an increased – interest in the future continues in South Africa, it shifted from literature to the more overtly socio-political realm by the later 1980s.

Obviously sociological, political, and economic concern with the future in South Africa is evident in texts prior to this, but it resurfaced in a stronger form in the late 1980s and early 1990s: R.W. Johnson's 1977 thesis in his *How Long Will South Africa Survive?* – that the revolutionary situation was steadfastly locked at five minutes to midnight – is reassessed by various thinkers a decade later, for example, in John D. Brewer's collection, *Can South Africa Survive? Five Minutes to Midnight*. This later work fits in with many others published roughly contemporaneously, such as *A Future South Africa: Vision, Strategies and Realities*

---

28. Quoted as an epigraph to C.P. Cavafy's 'But the Wise Perceive Things About to Happen', translated by Edmund Keeley and Philip Sherrard.

(Peter L. Berger and Bobby Godsell (eds), 1988), *After Apartheid* (John Suckling and Landeg White (eds), 1988), *Wat Kom Ná Apartheid?* (J.P. Landman, Philip Nel, Anton van Niekerk, 1988), *South Africa: Future Perspectives* (H.C. Marais (ed.), 1988), and *Negotiating South Africa's Future* (Lawrence Schlemmer and Hermann Giliomee, 1989). Throughout this period the person with perhaps the highest profile when it came to popularising South Africa's future prospects was Clem Sunter, whose publications, videos, and speeches launched from his position as chief scenario planner for Anglo American reached a broad audience within the South African business community.

It is worth noting, in passing, that alternative theatre in South Africa, a more socially immediate medium than prose fiction, shows clear signs of a relation with work of a sociological nature; at least two plays presented in 1989 had the future as their setting and subject: Clare Stopford's workshopped *The Last Trek* and Ian Bruce's *My Father's House*. In terms of the novel, however, a pattern we noted before in relation to uses of the past seems again to be emerging, with the serious fictional interest in the future giving way to a light popular colonisation of the field: Geoffrey Jenkins's 'high-speed adventure thriller' (*Star* 15 Feb. 1989) *Hold Down a Shadow* (1989), for example, is set in Lesotho in 1995 and June Drummond's *Junta* (1989), published in the Gollancz Thriller series, is 'set some years in the future' of South Africa.

Serious 'future histories' in the novel form, then, do seem limited to a particular historical moment within the time I cover in this study (a new clutch of novels concerned with the future started appearing around 1992/93), one in some way cut off by the time the future had taken hold on the wider popular imagination. Serote's *To Every Birth its Blood* and Gordimer's *July's People* both appeared in 1981, to be followed quite quickly by Coetzee's *Life and Times of Michael K* in 1983 and Hope's *Kruger's Alp* in 1984. The one 'future history' published after mid-1980, Gordimer's *A Sport of Nature* (1987), is, I will claim, in essence a reworking of concerns first essayed in *July's People*. At the risk of over simplification, I suggest that the states of emergency of 1985 closed off serious fictional options in this direction, while prompting, eventually, an increase in the non-fictional socio-political concern with the future. It seems as if the very extremities represented by the state of emergency transformed by its intensity the fictional into the more overtly referential. The dramatic developments of early 1990 have reformulated the terms of inquiry entered into by socio-political texts that predate them, however; most of them have rapidly acquired the sense of quaintness, even naïvety, that socio-political prediction is wont to accrue to itself in the wake of the actual developments they have tried to make their subject. It is this, of course, which gives prediction the bad name it has in the social and political sciences.

And literature, or so it would seem from the traditional critical perspective of someone like A.L. Rowse. Of Shakespeare, Rowse writes: 'He was not interested in the future, as secondary artists are – for the past is inspirational and inspires poetry, the future polemics and propaganda' (1978,II:10). This is a misleading formulation of the problem, of course; past and future no more produce their own aesthetics than their own politics, and these two categories are indistinguishable in any serious sense in any event. But creative works that make it their business to evoke the historical future do provoke particular sorts of questions, and central amongst these, no matter how subtly put, is an interest in how – or indeed whether – they can survive being proved wrong, or being made to look obsolete or quaint, by events that follow their production. Aesthetic critiques may wish to play down the element of prediction, or the inappropriateness of the representations of the future, but a criticism which takes the historical claims of these texts seriously must engage itself with such issues; the question is how to pursue this without reducing it to a crude interest in simply what the works got right or wrong.

The answer lies at least partially in understanding what these predictions tell us of the moment of their production. It would be difficult to deny the pressures of the moment in stimulating a concern with the future in the texts that concern us; how, though, does one deal with that impulse when it has been overtaken or bypassed by that future? An emphasis on the literally predictive almost automatically undercuts attempts at evaluation, with the possible exception of the few cases of remarkable predictive accuracy one encounters. The rest of the answer (perhaps its major emphasis, for the question of context could apply equally to the non-fictional focus on the future) lies in the nature of the utopian form and content of these works which makes them, along the lines suggested above, 'future histories'. We have given this some consideration already, but we must at least briefly consider the contextual pressures of the period before we return to it.

Certainly the period from 1974 to 1984 gave new cause for exploring the future through the cracks in the South African state's hegemony: the threatening or achieved independence of neighbouring states, the schoolchildren's rebellion, the major advances made by the black working class, the community struggles and sustained stay-aways, all initiating massive state repression indicative of destabilisation in its own right, made an apartheid future less likely than at any other time in its history. Perhaps not as obvious, at least at some levels, but just as telling, was the failure of the state's monetarist response to the economic downturn of the 1970s. Inflation, rising interest rates, a fall in manufacturing's profitability, and a sharp increase in foreign debt were tackled by devaluing the currency, cutting real wages, and curbing the money supply. Instead of improving, the economy plunged into the recession of 1981. The state found it impossible to free itself of its dependence on imports, and its manufacturing industry was unable to compete in the international market or create markets for itself in the neighbouring states it had destabilised or in the local market it had itself severely limited. With no margin between current wages and the subsistence level to absorb wage cuts, and with the lack of confidence international financiers showed in the face of unrest sparked off by attempts to cut wages anyway, the apartheid economy was in severe trouble. All in all, in the words of Alf Stadler,

> The potentials for a major break in the system were everywhere evident, but it was difficult to foresee the circumstances in which it might take place, or to discern the social and political conjuncture about which it might be hinged. (1987:2)

Given such a predicament, history and fiction have resorted to a range of strategies in attempting to address the future. Historians, on the whole, have tended towards the caution Stadler himself invokes in the work just quoted:

> Rather than make predictions about the outcome of such processes, the purpose of this study was to identify the kinds of constraints that would need to be transcended in order for significant changes to be accomplished. Because it is primarily an exercise in contemporary history, and not of prediction, it is to a lesser extent concerned to identify the forces working for change. (4)

Quite sensibly, Stadler concludes this argument with exactly the sort of observation the novelistic 'historians of the future' choose to ignore: 'The reader of this book will have better knowledge of the outcome of the processes being discussed than the writer did while he was composing it'. The novelists are precisely able to ignore the caution of the historian because their enterprise carries, quite obviously, a different emphasis. Their concern is to make the present meaningful in terms of its possible outcome; the imaginative effort invested in this is not to be measured in terms of their literal ability correctly to foresee the outcome, but rather in their ability to use a particular literary strategy to intervene in the present. That more is involved in this than prediction will be illustrated by an analysis of the conclusions to the two of Nadine Gordimer's novels which may most obviously be designated as 'future histories'.

GORDIMER: TWO SENSES OF AN ENDING

The simple fact that the form of protest taken by *To Every Birth its Blood* can include an element of prediction is in itself significant. It is easy to set Serote's work against the work of white South African novelists and come to a conclusion not far off that reached in a different but comparable comparative context: 'U.S. writers' predominant modern mood is one of despair of a loss of a future, a loss of ambition', writes John Donatich, quoting against this Edmundo Desnoes's point that 'Latin Americans write with greater hope for new political horizons but are burdened with the despair of a loss of history' (Donatich 1988:14, 21).

The relationship between these two perspectives – at least in South Africa – is a more complicated one, however; rather than the neat polarity suggested, what we find in practice is an interrelationship between them. Serote's novel – and indeed the major thrust of recent historical revisionism in South Africa[29] – illustrates that the confidence to reclaim an abrogated past is intimately concerned with a confident claiming of the future. The reflex of this is that a loss of confidence in relation to the future results in an erosion of a sense of the past, a shrinking in from both sides of the linearly extended temporal poles that ultimately encroaches on the present itself.

Nadine Gordimer's *July's People* (1982 [1981]), published in the same year as *To Every Birth its Blood*, apparently approaches the future more confidently in terms of narrative strategy than Serote's work. It is entirely set in the near future, which, like Serote's futurist timescape, is characterised by rapidly escalating violence. While, however, the progress of Serote's narrative towards the future allows for – creates, in fact – an increasingly solid sense of the past (nowhere more clearly represented than in the way the novel takes on its overall shape in

---

29. See, for example, *New Nation/New History*, Vol. 1. Johannesburg: New Nation and the History Workshop, 1989.

relation to the future that makes up its conclusion), the 'past' in *July's People* is evoked only in an increasingly eroded impressionism; it is called up most typically in moments between sleep and waking, melting away as full awareness seeps in. Maureen Smales's surfacing from sleep on her first morning in the hut at July's home is representative of this: 'At first what fell into place was what was vanished, the past' (3). By the time the novel approaches its climax, these dream glimpses of the past – and along with them any grip upon the present – are negated, as the later direct reference back to this moment indicates:

> She was not in possession of any part of her life. One or another could only be turned up, by hazard. The background had fallen away; since that first morning she had become conscious in the hut, she had regained no established point of a continuing present from which to recognize her own sequence. (139)

This passage also indicates the novel's actual attitude to the future; set in the near future which *To Every Birth its Blood* gestures towards, it differs radically from Serote's novel in that it reflects a process of dispossession for its protagonist (mirrored by an ever more assertive appropriation of her family's possessions by her 'hosts'), leading to an epiphany characterised by none of the concrete promise inherent in *To Every Birth its Blood*. This point is in some senses debatable (see below), but the extreme open-endedness of *July's People*'s conclusion narratively presents a future with no future. This temporal stripping prepares us for the change in tense of the final chapter; the narrative up to this point, while set in the narrative present (referential future), is related in that past tense conventionally read as relating the present and accepted as only the product of the formal rupture between the act of narration and the action presented. (See the last sentence of the penultimate chapter of the novel, for example: 'She looked a long time at the closed eyelids' [155].) With the apocalyptic arrival of the helicopter, Gordimer's protagonist finds her presence in the present, signified by the transformation of the narrative into the actual present tense – which, we must not forget, is located in the future ('women put', a 'sun … sweetens', 'the stuff of which these houses were made is alive' [156]; most importantly, the work ends with the stark simplicity of 'She runs').

What exactly the significance of this moment is has already become one of the standard debates of South African fiction. Gordimer's conclusion is by now surely notoriously open-ended: Maureen's baptismal sprint towards the helicopter has been most obviously read as ambiguous and inconclusive (Rowland Smith [1984]), an empty reading most South African critics have felt it necessary to fill. Thus it has been presented as a positive embrace of the unknown future (the Clingman hypothesis [1986, esp. Ch.6]), a futile attempt at escape from that future (the Lenta refutation [1988]), and – with a most pertinent shift from the otherwise consistent critical focus on the protagonist as character to an intertextual reading of the moment of convergence as symbol – an act of social annunciation (the Visser modification [1990a]).

Such variations turn on the future as open or empty, but they all over-ride the primary function of the future in *July's People*: this is signalled by the tense of its concluding section, and it is another manoeuvre in Gordimer's consistent struggle to get a purchase on the *present*. Clingman has recognised this from the first: 'what appears to be a projection from the present into the future in the novel is from another point of view *seeing the present through the eyes of the future*', he writes in *The Novels of Nadine Gordimer: History from the Inside* (201-202; his emphasis), although we must note in the same work the apparent contradiction of: '... it may be that the future that is written here, especially in *July's People*, is the ultimate concern of Gordimer's historical consciousness' (171), and '... the present – an area that, overall, appears to be the greatest concern for Nadine Gordimer's consciousness of history in general' (180). The potential for contradiction in these statements is mentioned only because out of it is generated the rather forced optimism of Clingman's attempt to give a content to a 'future' that is essentially a formal device intended to play back on the events anterior to itself. Gordimer extrapolates impressionistically along lines of most-likelihood (and Clingman's account of how accurate she is in this respect has itself become dated by events subsequent to it [1986:200-201]), but her excursion into the future is more of a rearguard action against the present. Even more so than Serote, she is not seriously engaged with the future *per se*: of all South Africa's writers, Gordimer is most aggressively present-tensed, and her interest in the future is a perspective from which to speak posteriorly of the present.

July's People, then, is an attempt to locate an authentic moment of present/ presence, produced by, yet legitimate apart from, its past and future. It is in this sense, surely, that we are meant to read the penultimate sentence of the novel, a passage seen by some critics as focusing in on a community-stripped individualism of one sort or another:

> She runs: trusting herself with all the suppressed trust of a lifetime, alert, like a solitary animal at the season when animals neither seek a mate or take care of young, existing only for their lone survival, the enemy of all that would make claims of responsibility. (160)

The conclusion of the novel is created as an enactment of what we have seen Bloch call 'an ontological pull of the future', 'an unconsciousness of what is yet to come'. The concluding moment of present tense in *July's People* captures perfectly Bloch's sense of utopia as quoted earlier: 'the meaning of Being itself comes into being, if at all, only at the *moment* when the world passes over into utopia, and when that final utopian destination returns upon the past to confer direction upon it' (my emphasis). Gordimer quotes from Gramsci's *Prison Notebooks* for her epigraph: 'The old is dying and the new cannot be born; in this interregnum there arises a great diversity of morbid symptoms.' In her attempt to make of *July's People* something more than a 'morbid symptom', Gordimer tries to reach beyond the 'interregnum' and in so doing throw meaning back over this sterile period, the present. That this moment of historical transcendence, which is in Bloch's sense thus utopian, is so tentative has been considered extremely telling by some critics.

Criticism of the type levelled by Paul Rich at *July's People* asks more of the novel's open-endedness than it is willing to offer in this respect: 'Gordimer has ultimately been successful in rejecting the cultural foundations of the postmodern urban civilisation and its own heroic conception of historical progress', he writes, 'without being able to grasp any coherent moral alternatives ...' (1984a:381). Underlying this conclusion is a symptomatic reading of the way the future is represented that follows Raymond Williams's point made with regard to utopias:

> The whole alternative society rests, paradoxically, on two quite different social situations: either that of social confidence, the mood of the rising class, which knows, down to detail, that it can replace the existing order; or that of social despair, the mood of the declining class, or fraction of a class, which has to create a new heaven because its earth is a hell. (1979:58)

That I take this observation as significant should be illustrated by my discussion of Gordimer's sense of the future in relation to Serote's; whether the way in which it appears that Gordimer chose to answer criticism of the type levelled by Rich was useful or not does, however, need some discussion. *A Sport of Nature*, published in 1987 (repr.1988), certainly seems cast as an alternative method of fictionally using the historical future, which is why I strongly associate it with a set of texts rooted earlier in the 1980s.

In *A Sport of Nature*, Gordimer emphasises the second half of Bloch on utopia: the novel attempts to proceed teleologically, presenting 'that *final* utopian destination' as returning 'upon the past to confer direction on it' (my emphasis). It attempts too, to refute Rich's challenge by giving content to as yet unrealised 'coherent ... alternatives'. Epic in scope, *A Sport of Nature* presents past, present, and future as contained in the terms of its almost concluding formula: 'the past is not a haunting, but was a preparation, put into use' (396). In the absence of the future (a utopian moment giving meaning back to its past), it creates one, giving a substance to Sasha's scattered notes on utopia (one which he is unable, but at least tries, to give):

> ... *the dynamic of real change is always utopian. The original impulse may get modified – even messed up – in the result, but it always has to be there no matter how far from utopia that result may be.*
>
> *Utopia is unattainable; without aiming for it – taking a chance! – you can never even hope to fall far short of it.*
>
> ... *Without utopia – the idea of utopia – there's a failure of the imagination – and that's a failure to know how to go on living* ...
> (217-18)

... or writing. The utopian conclusion of *A Sport of Nature* permeates back through the work, suggesting its necessity (even in alteration or failure) as a point to be moved towards, and, even more importantly, affirming the ability of the imagination to concretise itself. It thus becomes a point of narrative posteriority, guaranteeing the movement towards itself. And so, for example, the recounting of Hillela's life is constantly interspersed with apparently extra-textual references from future 'factual' works. These serve as points of posterior reference upon her history, establishing it as history even as it passes through the present of the novel's creation.

Hillela essentially exists then for the novel *beyond* the action recounted; this future tense of its protagonist is hinted at often through the novel. At times this is done obliquely, as in the joking moment when Joe says to Hillela:

Now that's the correct way with the verb! Future tense! You and Carole used to drive us crazy by using it in the context of something achieved ... (142)

At other times it is expressed more overtly, as in the words of the 'dear old one' after Whaila's assassination:

White people who settled in other countries have no past, so you're not surrounded, like me ... but you tried to live – there's something von Kleist wrote – 'in a time that hasn't yet come'! Ridiculous, crazy, but I like it. (269-70)

Hillela is created to be 'historical' in another sense too; we are told: 'No history of her really can be personal history then; its ends were all apparently outside herself' (261). Her significance is meant to lie, if not in her typicality (in the Lukácsian sense) at least in her ultimate representativeness of a certain progressive force. This sounds like a positive strategy in terms of the representations of history we have evaluated thus far in this book, but Margaret Lenta (1988) has effectively spelt out what seems to be Gordimer's failure in this regard: trapped in a realist mode she is reluctant to discard, her protagonist cannot take on the allegorical weight necessary to establish her as a guide into an unknown future. Hillela, no less than the culminating ceremony celebrating South Africa's metamorphosis, suffers from an 'impoverishment' in this regard, an impoverishment Jameson identifies as occurring 'when the literary work attempts to use ... utopian material directly, as content, in secular fashion ...' This is due, says Jameson, 'to the reduction of the multiple levels of the utopian idea to the single, relatively abstract field of social planning' (1971:145-46). Certainly the resistance provided by *A Sport of Nature* to the present is the weaker for the literal level of its social content. Too overtly a realised conception of the future lacks the ability to evoke a convincing sense of judging the present because its historical terms are limited in their very (formal) concreteness.

The trouble, then, with Gordimer's futurist strategy in *A Sport of Nature*, lies, to use Paul Q. Hirst's distinction between Hegel's dialectic and conventional philosophies of history, in its too strict a use of the teleological – a use which blocks the dialectical, or open-ended, potential of the form. This is a distinction that it will be salutary for us to bring into our account of the utopian use of teleology as it stands thus far. Hegel's dialectic, says Hirst, explains a *process* but not its end ... it is, to use Althusser's phrase, 'a process without a subject'... It differs from teleological realizations of a given end (Comte, Spencer, etc.) in this rigorous openness, or all but the *form* of its process to knowledge. (1985:89)

On this view, the concretising of the future, no matter how positively, always risks realising the fictional and historical failure we referred to in the first section of this chapter; instead of affirming the present, it all too easily becomes an attempt, as Jameson puts it, to 'outsmart' it. The sense of an ending, whether it be teleological in the utopian sense we sketched in 'Utopia (One)' or more openly dialectical, is most useful when it stresses process, not closure, strategic ends, not final ones. It is precisely the unconvincing representation of a social world in the inadvertently hollow ceremony that concludes *A Sport of Nature* – it is too brief, too thin and almost perfunctory in its utopianism to carry the weight the novel asks of it – that makes it less of a success as a 'future history' than the more personal, more tentative, but ultimately more effective conclusion to *July's People*. No matter that the actual ceremony Gordimer predicted also rang a little hollow at times when it did come into being; perhaps it did this because amidst all the jubilation, people realised this end of so much history was, in Visser's terms, the annunciation of another, in which the players would now have to play a very different part. The present progressive tense in which we leave the protagonist of *A Sport of Nature* – 'Hillela is watching a flag slowly climb ...' (396) – expresses rather too much a sense of a simple continuous history for the forces she has come to represent – especially as far as its implications for the future beyond the future called up here are concerned. It is to a fuller sense of the materiality of tense as a vehicle for the future that we must next shift.

DESIRE

... what strikes the random observer of the history of philosophy is the lack of attention given the future as such, as though there were something essentially frivolous in a consideration of that which does not yet exist, when so much exists already. In that the philosophers resemble M. Terentius Varro, 'most learned of all the Romans', who 'is supposed to have forgotten the future tense in the first version of his Latin grammar'.

– Bloch, *Das Prinzip Hoffnung*, (quoted in Jameson 1971:125)

It would certainly be taking things too far to suggest that, of the Germanic characteristics retained in the English language, the reduction of the numerous tense and aspect forms of Indo-European verbs (preserved and added to in Latin, despite Varro's lapse) could be related to the anomalous position of works concerned with the future in our general cultural text. English, solidly equipped with past and present tenses, may have no future tense, but non-tense systems within the language convey temporal meanings; future time is easily evoked by use of modal expressions, usually reinforced or clarified by adverbs. In any event, a concern with units of expression as complex as narrative tends to keep us in the past tense, regardless of deictics; narration, after all, usually represents all experience linguistically as past experience, if only as a reflex of the rupture between the moment of narration and the material narrated.

Yet a hint of suspicion remains regarding the slightly awkward conjuncture of tense and the future, prompting us at least to consider the ontological uncertainty surrounding the status of the future. Perhaps this may be traced back to the trope regarding tense of the narrative attitude, but what we should recognise is that, just as narrative tense is not a sufficient indicator of the temporal situation being treated, so grammatical mood in narrative does not necessarily reflect the actual manner of the statement made. The utopian mode, to illustrate with an example central to our concerns in this chapter, is that of the implied subjunctive; despite its surface grammatical tense (past) and mood (indicative), the utopian form is ruled by the future tense and the subjunctive mood. We are involved here then with, to appropriate a prevalent contemporary term, the grammar of desire.

I use this formulation partly to pick up on its origin in the Lacanian opposition of the 'discourse of the real' and 'the discourse of desire', where history and wish-fulfilment represent the standard historical text and the 'future history' respectively, but I do not wish to push this too far. I mainly wish to shift the formally grammatical into the social space opened up by Lacan – and, with now-standard necessary disclaimers regarding ideology, the Althussarian reading of Lacan – where language becomes an image of the unconscious as the effect of social relations rather than a private realm 'within', and grammar becomes significant in terms of discourse.

The grammar of desire involves a definite rhetorical shift from the past tense and indicative mood associated with history writing. As such, it suggests a deliberate strategy of running against realist expectations of reference. Yet the one case does not necessarily follow upon the other, as Raymond Williams makes clear in his distinction between the categories of science fiction and utopian fiction. 'It is tempting,' he writes,

> to extend both categories until they are loosely identical, and it is true that the presentation of otherness appears to link them, as modes of desire or warning in which the crucial emphasis is attained by the elements of discontinuity from ordinary 'realism'. But this element of discontinuity is itself fundamentally variable. Indeed what has most to be looked at, in properly utopian or dystopian fiction, is that form of continuity, of implied connection, which the form is intended to embody. (1979:54)

A similar observation is found in Dominic Baker-Smith's essay, 'The Escape from the Cave: Thomas More and the Vision of Utopia':

> At the centre of all utopian writing is a concern with the mediating process between ideal forms and the inadequate provisions of experience ... Whether it is utopia or dystopia that we are considering, the separation from fantasy is absolute: both imply a reference back to the world of concrete acts and familiar experience which fantasy excludes. The central feature of utopian writing is the effort to reconcile ideal possibilities with the recalcitrance of the known. Even in the case of dystopian writing it is that emphasis on the obstinate features of a known world which suggests desirable alternatives ... (Baker-Smith and Barfoot 1987:8)

It is from this perspective that the utopian mode makes available to us on positive terms the very logical grounds that A.C. Danto, in his *Analytical Philosophy of History*, uses for his ultimate rejection of any place for the future in history. 'Philosophies of history attempt to capture the future without realizing that if we knew the future, we could control the present, and so falsify statements about the future, and so such discoveries would be useless', writes Danto (1965:284). Far from being useless, this is precisely the logic behind the use of the utopian mode – and the *formally* identical dystopian mode. It is not so much predictive as pre-emptive. Whether inspirational or admonitory, utopias are explicitly interventionist. Thus we move from the overt indicative of the utopian text, by way of an implicit subjunctive, to a new, or at least different, form of the indicative. Utopian projections declare their reference to the present just as historical meaning attaches itself in important ways to events to come beyond the present. Desire, in the sense of a process set in motion by the temporal differences represented here, writes the future into the past, the present into the future.

These are the formal terms which indicate the integration of the future in the historical, but desire is more than simply a formal element. As we saw Baker-Smith insist, utopian and dystopian forms 'both imply a reference back to the world of concrete acts and familiar experience' and it is finally on these terms that we must analyse fictions which make the future their subject. Apartheid was formally as utopian a vision as anything proposed by its opponents, so it is on the grounds of their social content that we must judge the texts that we have termed 'future histories'; it is precisely their commitment to such a content that makes them *histories*. The conviction they carry then can be measured, no less than we measured past and present historical fiction, by their ability to render the terms, if not the exact material conditions, of a fully realised society to reflect upon their own time. Upon this depends the success of their resistance to the crippling effects of the social system they oppose. It is for this reason that we may ultimately call their projection into the future historical; it is for this reason we may treat these texts of the future as legitimate uses of history; it is for this reason that we must examine these novels closely in terms of their historiographical strategies.

COETZEE: MINIMALISM

'One notes how explanation is involved with prophecy', writes Phyllis Lewsen with the conventional historian's standard disapproval of such a thing (1970:357). Her observation is especially true of explanation in any nomological sense; Paul Q. Hirst stresses, for example, the merely illustrative nature of the historical examples given in *Capital*, and takes Marx's 'Preface to the First German Edition' seriously when it states:

> It is a question of these laws themselves, of these tendencies working with iron necessity towards inevitable results. The country which is more developed industrially only shows, to the less developed, the image of its own future. (Quoted in Hirst 1985:68)

The identification of laws, then, moves us quickly from an historical to a predictive emphasis. '*Capital,*' Hirst insists, 'is not a history, but that is because Marx claimed to be writing capitalism's *future*' (68; Hirst's emphasis). Hirst fights for this point only to make clear 'that both Marx's conception of capitalism and of the method by which it should be studied are untenable' (68), as (along with his co-author, Hindess) his rejection of teleological causality in *Pre-Capitalist Modes of Production* would lead us to expect. It is with an equal awareness of such tropes of explanation that Coetzee approaches his portrayal of the future. The venerable structure of the dialectic itself, if it cannot finally be refused, must, it seems, be resisted in the extreme minimalism of Coetzee's style.

Stephen Watson has written of the 'failed dialectic' in Coetzee's work (1986:370), but Stephen Clingman has countered this with his illuminating claim that 'it is more accurate to talk of a more principled "negative" dialectic in which Coetzee's work stands as the ostensible second term'. Reading *Life and Times of Michael K* (1985 [1883]) against Braudel's concept of the *longue durée*, Clingman sees in Michael K's refusal to create a 'rival line' of any kind Coetzee's recognition of the ways in which resistance risks 'duplicating in alternative form the dominant terms of power' (1990b:49). David Attwell reads a more paradoxical resistance into a similar formal apprehension; in answer to those critics who accuse Coetzee of idealist strategies, he finds 'in Coetzee's refusal to "complete" the historical trajectory of decolonization' evidence 'of the very palpability of historical forces' (1990b:116). There is a sense in which these approaches complement each other, especially if read in relation to Foucault's challenge to the totalising effects of all linear, progressive history. 'Continuous history' (as we have had occasion to note before in more detail in this study), be it Marxist, liberal, positivist, even empiricist, attempts to control or domesticate the past in the form of knowing it; 'future history' in any continuous form would, of course, perform the same operation upon the future. It is for this reason that the true figure of the future – we are taken just far enough into the future to characterise Michael K as such – must constantly recede before attempts to know it. The future itself must be taken by allegorical extension as a figure here, of course: a figure of the play of meaning, irreducible and knowable only as difference. Thus Michael becomes known only as 'a great escape artist, one of the great escapees' (228). His drawing inexorably away from the pursuing medical officer/narrator is a prime illustration of Jameson's 'History is what hurts, it is what refuses desire ...' (1981:102).

Life in the camps is threatening to Michael specifically in terms of meaning:

Am I at last learning about life here in a camp? It seemed to him that
scene after scene of life was playing itself out before him and that the
scenes all cohered. He had a presentiment of a single meaning upon
which they were converging or threatening to converge ... (122)

It is difficult, however, to free Michael of the one important sense in which he
becomes meaningful to the medical officer (the doctor diagnosing the symptom):

'Your stay in the camp was merely an allegory, if you know that word.
It was an allegory – speaking at the highest level – of how scandalously,
how outrageously a meaning can take up residence in a system without
becoming a term in it.' (228)

Michael himself must raise his right hand to this (see p. 229), and, in answer to
the invitation Coetzee's work so often makes (critics on Coetzee consistently
demonstrate the invitation in their response) we relate this to its extra/intertextual
echoes; in this case they are myriad, but let us select one from Roland Barthes
that will also serve to bring us back to our theme:

Pigeonholed: I am pigeonholed, assigned to an (intellectual) site, to
residence in a caste (if not in a class). Against which there is only one
internal doctrine: that of atopia (of a drifting habitation). Atopia is
superior to utopia (utopia is reactive, tactical, literary, it proceeds from
meaning and governs it). (1974:49)

We recognise Michael K as atopian, but the very fact that we are able to indicate
that means that *Life and Times of Michael K* is not. It inhabits meaning, or
meaning inhabits it, to at least this degree, and in its being 'reactive, tactical' and
definitely (if predominantly in its reactive and tactical form) '"literary"', it is also
utopian. We located the deep grammatical mood of the utopia in the subjunctive,
and the last eight pages of Part II of *Life and Times of Michael K* (the conclusion
of the medical officer's narration) are, quite crucially, entirely in the subjunctive.
Governed by 'would' and infiltrated by 'should', the whole passage enacts its
own grammar, the grammar of (frustrated) desire. It recounts, of course, the desire
for knowledge, for humble (no matter how humble, still threatening) mastery

through meaning: "'I was the only one who saw that you were more than you seemed to be,' I would have proceeded', says the medical officer of 'Michaels' (the cutting irony of the misnomer resonates through his certainty). Further, later:

> 'This is not my imagination,' I would say to myself. 'This sense of a gathering meaningfulness

(we remember what threatens Michael in the camp; here is the logic of his escape)

> is not something like a ray that I project to bathe this or that bed, or a robe in which I wrap this or that patient according to whim. Michaels [sic] means something, and the meaning he has is not private to me. If it were,

he continues, launching into the subjunctive in its hypothetical form within the subjunctive in its dominant form of desire,

> if the origin of this meaning were no more than a lack in myself, a lack, say, of something to believe in, since we all know how difficult it is to satisfy a hunger for a belief with the vision of *times to come* that the war, to say nothing of the camps, presents us with [my emphasis],

moving away from the past as originary, staying within the utopian to counter the dystopian,

> if it were a mere craving for meaning

no meaning of course is ever this innocent, or incidental, hence Michael's insistent retreat before all this

> that sent me to Michaels and his story

('history'),

> if Michaels himself were no more than what he seems to be (what you seem to be),

the parenthesis returning us to reference, reminding the narrator and the reader of the overall subjunctive mood in which all this is couched

> a skin-and-bones man with a crumpled lip (pardon me, I name only the obvious), then I would

(a subjunctive conclusion within the subjunctive)

> have every justification for retiring to the toilets behind the jockey's changing-rooms and locking myself into the last cubicle and putting a bullet through my head.' (226)

The medical officer's desire is not legitimated or negated; it remains unconsummated ('"Am I right?" I would shout. "Have I understood you?"' [229]) in all respects except that noted above ('you are a great escape artist'; Michael's escape confirms this much about him). Part III of the novel follows this and moves back into the authority of the third person or free indirect discourse, emphasising Michael's escape from the medical officer's extended hypothesis, his return to himself ('the truth, the truth about me. I am a gardener' [247-48]), but the novel itself concludes in the utopian mood. The minimalist vision of Michael's capacity for survival under even the most limited circumstances is imagined (by Michael) in the subjunctive, the utopian future: 'And if ... he, Michael K, would ...' (250). Surely here Coetzee's prose takes on the strength George Steiner notes of the future tense:

> Future tenses are an example of the more general framework of non- and counter-factuality. They are part of the capacity of language for the fictional and illustrate absolutely central powers of the human word to go beyond and against 'that which is the case'. (*After Babel*, 61, quoted in Waugh 1984:121-22)

Few authors have avoided the present as a setting for their works as militantly and systematically as Coetzee, as we have noted already. Generally it has been the past which has served as his point of oblique reference to the present (in the second part of *Dusklands*, *In the Heart of the Country*, and *Foe* – even the atemporal and unlocalised *Waiting for the Barbarians* carries overtones of a preponderantly past sense), but in *Life and Times of Michael K* his use of the future approximates an impulse common to, in crucially different ways, all the texts dealt with thus far in this chapter. This impulse is concerned to define the terms upon which the present becomes 'meaningful' with reference to a future, no matter how minimal and hypothetical that future may be. The concluding vision of *Life and Times of Michael K* is couched, I have claimed, in what I have chosen to call a utopian tense; even in a story set in the future, it remains in the future. Yet as a social vision it holds convincingly before us the fundamental elements of survival: it is communal (in the most basic sense, it concerns Michael and an old man), creative (the old man is imagined from evidence), and ultimately (in the face of adversity) materially sustaining:

> And if the old man climbed out of the cart and stretched himself (things were gathering pace now) and looked at where the pump had been that the soldiers had blown up so that nothing should be left standing, and complained, saying 'What are we going to do about water?', he, Michael K, would produce a teaspoon from his pocket, a teaspoon and a long roll of string. He would clear the rubble from the mouth of the shaft, he would bend the handle of the teaspoon in a loop and tie the string to it, he would lower it down the shaft deep into the earth, and when he brought it up there would be water in the bowl of the spoon; and in that way, he would say, one can live. (250)

In his survival upon his own terms Michael K becomes a figure of – as befits Coetzee's aesthetic – the minimal requirements of resistance and in this he judges the surfeit all too often considered necessary for sustaining a meaningful existence. As a point of ultimate difference he stands against the domesticating power of the present, yet he is not outside history; to the extent that he inhabits the future he does so in a utopian sense, playing back upon the present the basic conditions of meaning that allow past, present, and future to (meaningfully) exist. What has come to pass since the publication of *Life and Times of Michael K* in no way cancels this future vision from 1983; if anything, Michael K still teaches us to look beyond the futures imagined for us so that we may interrogate them with the full weight of a history informed with an ever-reflexive utopianism.

UTOPIA (TWO)

A word on preaching about how the world should be. For that, philosophy always arrives too late. As the thought of the world, it only makes its appearance after the actuality has finished its process of development and is over. What the conception teaches, history also shows to be necessary. Only in the maturation of actuality does the ideal appear to confront the real. Then the ideal reconstructs this world for itself in the form of an intellectual realm comprehending it in its substance. When philosophy paints its grey in grey then the form of life has grown old, and this grey in grey is not capable of rejuvenating it, merely of understanding it. The owl of Minerva only begins its flight when the twilight falls.
    – Hegel, Preface, *The Philosophy of Law*
    (quoted in Jameson 1971:364)

For Hegel, as Jameson comments, 'one ... has to posit an end to history in order for historical thought to take place', and Hegel's controversial doctrine that it ends in the present is not unrelated to the problem in hand. Indeed, R.G. Collingwood finds Hegel's position the only defensible one, even if he chooses to reject the specific philosophical and political significance Hegel attached to it:

> History must end with the present, because nothing else has happened. But this does not mean glorifying the present or thinking that future progress is impossible. It only means recognizing the present as a fact and realizing that we do not know what future progress will be. As Hegel put it, the future is an object not of knowledge but of hopes and fears; and hopes and fears are not history. (1983:3)

'Hopes and fears' may not be history, but is it in fact possible to divorce them from history? Agnes Heller, in her *A Theory of History*, demonstrates how not. While she does reject the philosopher of history's claim to be able to make true statements about future history, she nevertheless allows such statements a legitimate role. They may not be true simply because they are neither true nor untrue; they are rather 'value-commitments'.

> The image of future history is meant as a promise or a warning ...
> Whilst depicting the future, the philosopher of history intends to induce

others to commit themselves to the same values; to the same lifestyle and activities as contained in his or her philosophy. The philosopher wants the addressee to create the future designed in the philosopher's imagination. (1982:239)

Thus Heller can quote Herder: 'a philosophy of history, too, is needed for the education of mankind' (223), and entitle her penultimate chapter, 'The Need for Utopia'.

Paul Ricoeur has probably come closest to spelling out the philosophical basis for the way in which the utopian may function towards such an end. The fullest account of Ricoeur's position on this issue is set out in his *Lectures on Ideology and Utopia* (1986), which is based on a series of lectures given at the University of Chicago in 1975. Briefly, Ricoeur's concern is to break with the bind of the ideology/science distinction as proposed by Althusser and others, especially with the sense it conveys of distortion versus the 'real'. Drawing upon his concept of the symbolic nature of all action (established in *The Rule of Metaphor*), which he equates with all perspectives being ideological, Ricoeur then seeks a concept of ideology which is thoroughly pervasive and yet not necessarily pejorative. He achieves this by recourse to the idea of the utopian. Ricoeur identifies three levels upon which ideology works. The first two accord with more conventional concepts of ideology: distortion (in the sense that all perspectives are of a symbolic order, and thus noncongruent with the 'real'), and legitimation (ideology fills the gap between the claims of the rulers and the beliefs of the ruled). Ideology at its third and deepest level, however, also plays an integrative social role. 'All social action is already socially mediated, and it is ideology that plays this mediating role in the social realm. Ideology is integrative at this stage; it preserves social identity' (Taylor, Introduction, Ricoeur 1986:xix). Given the ideological nature of all perspectives, how then can one validly challenge a particular ideological position?

It is at this point that Ricoeur introduces the ideology/utopia relationship to escape any false appeals to a non-ideological 'scientific' perspective. Utopia, like ideology, is not necessarily a pejorative term. Like ideology, it too operates on three levels: at its weakest, it is a mode of fantasy and escape. But it also functions by challenging present authority (questioning the legitimation of power) and, at its best, exploring the possible (putting in question what presently exists).

In fact,

> what we must assume is that the judgment on ideology is always the judgment from a utopia. This is my conviction: the only way to get out of the circularity in which ideologies engulf us is to assume a utopia, declare it, and judge an ideology on this basis. Because the absolute onlooker is impossible, then it is someone within the process itself who takes the responsibility for judgment ... It is to the extent finally that the correlation ideology-utopia replaces the impossible correlation ideology-science that a certain solution to the problem of judgment may be found, a solution ... itself congruent with the claim that no point of view exists outside the game. If there can be no transparent onlooker, then a practical concept is what must be assumed. (172-73)

This position is developed out of Ricoeur's belief in the need for both a negative and a positive hermeneutics. Fredric Jameson draws upon this distinction in Ricoeur's work when, in his 'Conclusion' to *The Political Unconscious* he attempts to move Marxism criticism away from its concentration on the former – 'to unmask and to demonstrate the ways in which a cultural artifact fulfils a specific ideological mission' (291) – in order to include the latter: 'its simultaneously utopian power' of 'symbolic affirmation' (291).

The novels I have concentrated upon up to this point have each tried, in their own way and with greater and lesser degrees of success, to use the future as a strategy for a hermeneutic which includes both positive and negative forms. In this the best of them realise their complicity with a particular 'ideology', but try to find a point of resistance within this from which to generate a genuine critique, rather than a simplistic criticism, of the 'history' produced by that ideology. The utopian mode, as set out by Ricoeur above, is central to such projects, and I hope to emphasise its importance by concluding this study of 'future histories' with an analysis of two texts which present the future stripped of this kind of utopian resistance.

The first of these works is contemporary to the period that has been our main focus, and the second is the classic form of the negative hermeneutic ghosting through all the efforts to generate something of a positive hermeneutic out of the South African historical future.

HOPE: KENOSIS

I take the term 'kenosis' from Terry Eagleton. In defining some forms of deconstruction as mere power-games, he states that 'It is just that now, in a religious twist to the old ideology, victory is achieved by kenosis or self-emptying: the winner is the one who has managed to get rid of all his cards and sit with empty hands' (1983:147).

The last two works we shall consider each in their own way drain the future of its meaning-giving capacity altogether. Chronologically Hope's novel was published just after the other works we have looked at from the early to mid-1980s, and so it fits naturally after them in our order of analysis; its sense of the future, however, is of a very different order and represents something of a break with what I have called the utopian thrust of the 'future histories' we have studied. *Kruger's Alp* (1985 [1984]) develops the full implications of a tradition of thought about the future in South Africa that goes back some way chronologically. We will conclude this chapter by tracing into the past, via Keppel-Jones's *When Smuts Goes*, this conception of the future which lies behind not just Hope's novel, but also, as something to be challenged, the other texts we have dealt with so far.

Christopher Hope's *Kruger's Alp* spins out of the South African political scandals *circa* 1970 a dreamscape which, while not specifically located in the future, has important implications for history and the future – specifically, it represents a history with no future, at least in any voluntarist sense.

In 'The Great South African Novel' (1983), J.M. Coetzee lists as chief among the features making the appearance of such a phenomenon unlikely the lack of a shared national consciousness, one that can cut across or underlie differences of language, race, and class. Hope's first novel, ironically entitled *A Separate Development* (1983 [1981]), employs a protagonist meant to embody within himself the divisions resulting from apartheid. Hope attempts to make out of Harry a representative unity of the commonly experienced separateness of South African society: he is white with a dark skin and crinkly hair, male with overlarge breasts, and so on. His life history, too, carries him through a variety of 'typical' experiences from across the spectrum of South Africa's structural divisions.

In *Kruger's Alp*, Hope reverses the terms of his national equation. Here a host of characters socially differentiated in a number of typically South African ways are, one is first led to expect, united in their different relations to a common nationalism. Their differences depend upon their places within a national struggle, but these differences are revealed as being increasingly illusory as that nationality is systematically emptied of significance. The future, or a lack of one, has a key place in this. What we will see in *Kruger's Alp* is the logic of utopianism turned against itself, or at least demonstrated by its absence. This has important effects for the kind of social vision we have seen the 'future histories' considered up to now striving towards.

The guidance of the presiding tutelary figure in *Kruger's Alp*, Father Lynch, depends upon a binary set of defining interests. He has, on the one hand,

> alarming gifts for prophecy; he prophesied often, with tremendous conviction, of the future which lay ahead for his boys; prophecies truly imaginative, but magnificently inaccurate (5),

the narrator tells us, but this internal (he enters his own dream at points) narrator proves to be a fallible one, and chiefly with respect to Father Lynch's unlikely prophecies which all too often prove (ironically, of course) extremely accurate. This accuracy turns out to depend upon Father Lynch's other defining interest, his

> strange addiction to South African history, or at least

and this proves crucial

> to one of its distant and probably mythical sub-themes, the question of the missing Kruger millions ... (5)

Father Lynch's combination of prophecy and history enables him to guide the protagonist, Theodore Blanchaille, through the illusion of history as a moral, political, or philosophical process and reveal its material base. History, like Father Lynch's interest in South African history, has at its centre a heart of gold: 'Gold it was and gold it always has been, the dream, the rumour, the hope and despair of the conquerors and of the conquerors before them ...', says Lynch (71), a sentiment which proves to be allegorical only to the degree that it represents the essentially determining nature of material interest. This is not, as it may at first glance appear, to be confused with a theory of historical materialism. The whole panorama with which we are presented is not an ideologically-mediated superstructure; we are talking knee-jerk determinism and the resulting absurdity of agency in any serious sense. Each of the characters is imprisoned to the degree that he fails to understand the necessity of his or her actions. This is perhaps most clearly demonstrated in the tour Blanchaille is given of the prison cells which hold prisoners representing a variety (ostensibly) of South African political positions. Based to a greater or lesser degree on actual people (Zandrotti relates to Breytenbach, Horatio Vilakaze to Mandela, and so on), each is revealed to be dependent upon his imprisonment for his significance. Similarly, Blanchaille's attempts to escape the South African system simply reveal its implication in an infinite regression of international meta-systems – all ultimately of economic interdependence.

Thus, when it comes to the individual experience of each of the characters portrayed, we have constant references to what Blanchaille calls at one point 'the first rule in African politics': 'what begins as tragedy turns into farce at a blink' (228-29) – a sentiment of one of the characters that turns out to be limited only in that he sees it as a specifically African rule: it turns out to be a universal one, as the conclusion of the novel is at pains to make clear. The most persistently idealistic character, Looksmart Dladla (and he is a political idealist), battered into idiocy during the course of the novel, remains persistent in his idealism to the end, only to be arrested as an illegal immigrant at the gates of the utopia in the Swiss Alps. The narrative terminates with the observation:

> And as I saw him turned away from the gates of Uncle Paul's great white location in the sky, expelled from the sacred Alp, I realised that it's a long way down at the best of times and that the pit may wait at the end of the American rainbow, or open beneath the feet in some seeming Swiss paradise just as surely as it does in the city of destruction where I was born. (279)

There is a special sense in which such a vision is in fact, for Hope, a South African one, however. Hope is a writer who has left South Africa but writes mainly of it. Like others in this position, he is keenly aware of the divided opinions regarding the political relevance of leaving (this is not, after all, the exile of a Serote). Usually evaluations of this point turn on the level of effective commitment it represents. Another tack, the one taken by *Kruger's Alp*, is to undercut the relevance of the choice. This is achieved by presenting history in what Hayden White, in *Metahistory*, calls the Satiric mode – a mode generated 'by the apprehension of the ultimate inadequacy of consciousness to live in the world happily or comprehend it fully' (1973:10). What emerges is an ironic debunking of the validity of political choice or moral responsibility. When, for example, the representatives of a government so long seen as setting new standards of injustice and repression are revealed to be merely a band of cheap, vicious criminals (only in it for the profit), the status of opposition to that government is equally reduced by inverse implication, as Zandrotti's story is designed to illustrate. Blanchaille, in his new illumination, tells Kipsel:

> Zandrotti was broken, he'd lived his whole life in the belief that the Regime was genuinely, thoroughly, consistently and impressively, let's face it, evil. He grew up in that belief, he'd suffered for it, he'd gone to jail for it, he'd lived in exile for it. It was, when you think about it, a very high expectation. He had a worthwhile enemy. You can imagine what it did to him when Ferreira told him he was dealing with a bunch of crooks. He hadn't been a hero. He'd been a fool. (233)

When, too, that government's chicanery implicates international politics, the deconstruction of a meaningful political universe should be complete. *Kruger's Alp* does not achieve a convincing sense of universal absurdity, however; the universal comes about a little too obviously and easily as a necessary corollary to the meaninglessness of political partisanship in South Africa.

Another level built into the narrative mode of the novel exhibits its distrust of finding any firm base in even an allegorical appeal to the South African political situation. Coherence is ultimately guaranteed by the work's being intertextually patterned upon *The Pilgrim's Progress*. It is at this level we return to the importance of the future in *Kruger's Alp*, for the progress of Bunyan's pilgrim is affirmed, against all satiric attack, by the fact that it is meaningful, made so by its ultimately attainable end. Historical progress in *Kruger's Alp* is inevitably satirised, chiefly in terms of the falsity of its goals: all the scenarios for the South African future presented end in destruction (46), and Blanchaille's 'progress' results only in the insight: '… going forward. No illusion is more precious' (257).

One might read such an insight as a healthy corrective to the evolutionary historicism ingrained in the South African as much as any other version of liberalism, but the trouble is Hope simply debunks the content of a progressive idea of history, rather than deconstructing its form. He can only empty its form, and then play with its shell, not, as we have seen in at least some of the novels considered above, experiment with new forms. A teleology without an end, or the possibility of an end, is rendered absurd, not alternatively meaningful. Hope then, in *Kruger's Alp*, remains within the terms he is trying to challenge, illustrating that they are dead, to switch metaphors, but only by playing with their bones. The idea of future alternatives, or even, as we have seen in Coetzee, the idea of seriously resisting the idea of future alternatives, is tellingly absent.

Thus Hope's novel illustrates in an important sense the end, in South Africa, of what Raymond Williams identifies elsewhere as 'the path travelled ... by bourgeois cultural theory':

> from the universal liberation, in bourgeois terms, through the phase
> in which the minority first educates and then regenerates the majority,
> to the last sour period in which what is now called 'minority culture'
> has to find its reservation, its hiding place, beyond both the system
> and the fight against the system. (1979:61)

Taken as a figure for the history of liberalism, this account can easily and accurately be translated into South African circumstances. As Williams reads his observation into the 'now dominant mode of dystopia', it becomes even more revealing as to the nature of the failure lurking behind *Kruger's Alp*. He distinguishes within the utopian mode two potential readings: one in which 'its defining subjunctive tense is part of a grammar which includes a true indicative and a true future', and another in which 'it has seized every paradigm and become exclusive, in assent and dissent alike'. The latter opens itself to a particularly insidious 'collusion',

> in that the State warned against, satirized – the repressions of
> autonomy, the cancellation of variations and alternatives – is built
> into the fictional form which is nominally its opponent, converting
> all oppositions into agencies of the repression, imposing, within its
> excluding totality, the inevitability and the hopelessness which it
> assumes as a result. (62)

It is difficult to avoid the play of 'Hope' against the type of strategic 'hopelessness' described here, for *Kruger's Alp* performs much the operation given in this extract.

The terms of the novel's exclusion become altogether too complete, even, perhaps especially, in relation to the South African cultural phenomenon that is the real target of its satire: hope.

KEPPEL-JONES:
THE BREAKDOWN OF NARRATIVE

The ghost Christopher Hope tries unsuccessfully to exorcise in *Kruger's Alp* is one that has haunted a particular element of the tradition of liberal thought as brought to South Africa: this is its belief in the nature of history as developmental, hierarchical, and, in the formal sense at least, progressive. Historicism of this sort is central to crucial points in the liberal agenda: its gradualism, evolutionism, rationalism, even its universalism, depend upon such an ideological formation. The intractability of social reality in South Africa just prior to and certainly in the decades immediately after the National Party's accession to power prompted a degree of despair in this regard, at least in some liberal quarters. The despair was limited, however, to the course of the historical progression; it did not extend to its informing historicist assumptions. If the historical form of progression was not providing any achieved content of progress, this could only be accounted for by asking, in the words of the title of an article by Arthur Keppel-Jones in the liberal journal *Race Relations*, 'Where did we take the wrong turning?' (1938). Retroactive explanation in this case confirms the very mode of thought that should be in question; proactive explanation follows the same form into the future.

If, as we saw claimed by Robert Bundy above, 'the future is a prologue to all history', this is nowhere more strikingly evident than in the work of Arthur Keppel-Jones. An historian, his first major publication was quite literally a 'future history'. *When Smuts Goes: A History of South Africa from 1952 to 2010* (claiming to have been first published in 2015) was published in 1947. Its publishing history is evidence of its popular reception; so well received was it that when Keppel-Jones published his more conventional *South Africa: A Short History* two years later, one review was headed 'Before Smuts Went' (Saunders 1988:126). In 1953 one 'Jan Toekoms' published a tentative counter-history entitled *'When Malan Goes': A Progressive Programme for South Africa*, which concludes with a brief positive 'Peep Into the Future' (a dramatised interchange illustrating an ideal relationship between a black lawyer about to form his own firm and the senior partner of the firm he is leaving) and an alternative description of nature taking over in the wake of the total destruction unleashed by a failure to settle South Africa's 'squabbles' ('If we go on as we are, squabbling over the shadows instead of the substance of life, we shall have no posterity to record our follies or admire our ruthlessness. Life will disappear ...' [140]). As late as 1991, Keppel-Jones's influence was felt in another literal history of the future, *South Africa 1994-2004: A Popular History* (1991) by 'Tom Barnard' (a pseudonym adopted by historian Deon Geldenhuys). In its interventionist intentions this work is strongly reminiscent of *When Smuts Goes*, but its reliance upon a simple gradual reversal of oppressor/oppressed roles under a majority government make its strategic pessimism less engaging than it could have been.

When Smuts Goes is important to us not because it initiated obvious follow-ons such as these to its concern with the future, but because it is the not entirely effaced original text of the palimpsest upon which the 'future histories' we have considered are written. If *Kruger's Alp* illustrates this in the way it intensifies fears raised in *When Smuts Goes*, the more utopian texts we have considered also register its influence: it defines the nature of the problem that the utopian form as we have used it is concerned to counter.

In some respects Keppel-Jones's 'future history' is similar in form to the novels with which we have been concerned. Bearing in mind the comments above on the pre-emptive character of the utopian/dystopian mode, *When Smuts Goes* is classically interventionist; 'the book was written', as Saunders notes, 'to prevent what he [Keppel-Jones] predicted coming about' (1986:50). Keppel-Jones shows himself to be conscious of this point in his introduction:

> Some people have tried to perform this service [of waking a dreaming white South African public] by a frank consideration of the future of the gold industry; others have done it in terms of soil erosion. This book attempts it by working out the next half-century of South African history as it is likely to be shaped by the political forces which at present dominate the scene. (1947:7-8)

Na die Geliefde Land echoes this impulse in its method of historical reversal, *July's People* and *To Every Birth its Blood* in their apocalyptic vein; *Life and Times of Michael K* attempts to construct the minimum conditions upon which this is possible, while *A Sport of Nature* most clearly approximates the 'working out' of historical forces. More important, however, is the way in which the texts with which we have been concerned implicitly react to the attitude *When Smuts Goes* expresses to the potentials latent in a South African future.

Immediately following on the quotation above from his introduction, Keppel-Jones continues: 'Everyone must hope that it will not work out that way. If there were no grounds for such hope it would have been a waste of time to write this book.' Yet the work is again classical in its expression of the pessimistic obverse that is so quick to appear from behind liberalism's often-noted optimism. 'The great and fundamental assumption' is 'that the National Party will come into power' (9). The plot that follows includes their arbitrary authoritarian rule and their imposition of a racially-exclusive Afrikaner Republic. This results in widespread black uprising, which is met by an even more extreme white government coming to power. It suppresses opposition with bloody force, upon which the United Nations intervenes in the form of an armed invasion. Power is handed over to a moderate black government which is promptly overthrown amidst assassination and violence. The country then suffers a 'return to barbarism' (the title of the final chapter), complete with a plague.

Even this thumbnail sketch should make it plain that the work enacts all the major facets of the South African liberal's nightmare. This is not to suggest that other ideologies do not fear the potential for things going massively wrong in South Africa's future, but the specific fears expressed here are those related to a liberal interpretation of the country's history. In stating this I am aware that I must avoid making a monolith out of the complex phenomenon that is liberalism in South Africa, but the element I wish to focus upon is central enough to allow of some generalisation. Evolution as the preferred mode of change (and the historicism informing this) confronting a social reality as intractable as it was in South Africa generated the sort of negative vision *When Smuts Goes* represents. That this was not the only response may quickly be established by looking at the work of Alan Paton, for example, which rejects the sort of apocalyptic imagery drawn on by Keppel-Jones, but Keppel-Jones's vision was widespread enough to make it representative of one major liberal response to South African history and its future. Of especial interest to us will be the way this vision is formally enacted.

De Kiewiet called *When Smuts Goes* 'a study in historical extrapolation' (Saunders 1988:125), and Keppel-Jones is careful to qualify his calculation based on the known terms of the series in terms of its possible variables. He identifies as assumptions factors he has not built in, such as remarkable changes in international relations (World War III for example), major scientific or military developments, and the fate of 'South-West Africa' (then before the United Nations). The computation results in a fair degree of accuracy: 'the growth in executive tyranny, the destruction of the rule of law, the coming of the Republic, increased isolation' all, as Saunders notes (1986:50), came about. Inaccuracies such as an overemphasis on the role of anti-Semitism, and the inability to envisage the thoroughness of apartheid policy on Group Areas and resettlement, the period of a dramatic rise in the price of gold that would for a while resist the story of economic depression he tells, the shift in the international power balance (especially in relation to Britain and the United Nations), the dynamics of internal resistance, and the changed perspective the events following the turnabout of 2 February 1990 gave to all this are less important than the significance of the structure embodying the working out of historical laws.

Keppel-Jones is, understandably (given his extrapolative method), concerned to stress the causal logic of his 'future history'. 'The desolation left by the plague' which effectively ends South African history is, he emphasises, 'no more than the ultimate result of causes that, as we have seen, were operating before. This latest affliction merely accelerated a decline of which it was not the primary cause' (228). He wonders too, of those who have survived the history he has recounted, 'how many ... are able to see the events of those sixty years as a logical series, every change the necessary consequence of those that preceded it?' (229).

Extrapolation, forwards or backwards, is of course dependent on such logic, but its explanatory power rests finally more in the narrative role it plays. Hayden White, in attempting to summarise (and conclude) the lengthy and often messy interchange on explanation (nomological versus narrative) carried out in the journal *History and Theory* between the late 1960s and his own contribution of 1984, expands the concept of narrative into an all-inclusive category, certainly, indeed primarily, capable of containing 'explanation' in its more narrow nomological sense. Narrative is in itself, he would claim, a form of meta-explanation, but narrative explanation in this sense is qualitatively different from the overt 'explanations' a given narrative may have embedded in it as commentary, description, or nomological aside. In narrative these, no less than the 'events, agents, and agencies', are 'transformed', 'encoded' as 'story-elements' in recognisable 'story-types'. Comprehension in narrative consists of recognising the specific story type, because 'it is the choice of the story-type and its imposition upon the events which endow them with meaning. The effect of such emplotment', he goes on to say, may be regarded as an 'explanation' if one chooses so to view it, but in this case it would have to be recognized that the generalizations that serve the function of universals in any version of a nomological-deductive argument are the topoi of literary 'plots', rather than the causal laws of science. (1984:20-21)

The ahistorical typology which an approach such as White's leaves itself open to (and which ultimately bedevils his whole concept of 'tropics of discourse') must be avoided, and we can do this by situating our general points about narrative and *When Smuts Goes* within the story of decline well mapped by Paul Rich in his article referred to above, 'Apartheid and the decline of the civilization idea'. Keppel-Jones's pamphlet *What is Destroying Civilization in South Africa?* is invoked in this essay (Rich 1984a:365), essentially for its pessimistic depiction of the concept of a nonracial 'civilisation' liberalism was increasingly forced to fall back upon as the only positive possibility in the South African scenario. Keppel-Jones's despair in this regard is most evident in his decision to leave South Africa, a decision typical of a certain strand of liberalism in the period his writing represents – historians in particular seemed subject to this, with all the early leading liberal historians emigrating (see Saunders 1987, esp. 146) – and one that was to be all too typically repeated: Christopher Hope, as we have seen, tries to write (and live) himself out of just such a narrative, and with similar, if differently deployed, generic tools. Hope's dream mode and Keppel-Jones's future mode equally distance their narratives from the realistic, allowing for the latitude of satire. In Keppel-Jones the satiric points towards the emptying function it will ultimately play in Hope; history, still conceived teleologically, becomes meaningless in the frustration of its ends.

The story of the future of South Africa ends for Keppel-Jones most compellingly not in the content he affords it, but in the stasis of its concluding form: in the final chapter, 'The Return to Barbarism', Keppel-Jones surrenders narrative in favour of description and explanation:

No good purpose would be served by making of this chapter a narrative of the complex political history of South Africa since 1989. Of more value to the reader would be a description of the changing condition of the country and an attempt to account for that condition. (1947:209)

Description and explanation are no longer, even in White's inclusive sense, aspects of narrative; they are indicative of a narrative collapse, an inability to write the future further into the narrative form. Narrative progress is disabled, and static events are only open to a symptomatic reading. The work concludes with the remarks of one John Dudd (naming throughout the work is this obviously allegorical), a typical South African 'of European descent', which are mediated to us through the consciousness of 'Dr. Matterhorn of the Swiss Red Cross'. Dudd ends with a question, one which ends the work too: 'Nothing has been spared us. What have we done to deserve this? Why have we had to suffer this? Why?' (230). The 'history' related in *When Smuts Goes* renders such questioning rhetorical. Stripped of any utopian direction, *When Smuts Goes* becomes more than an intervention concerned to define the conditions upon which a future is possible; it becomes overwhelmed with its own pessimism and breaks down as narrative. Along with narrative structure goes social structure: South Africa as a community collapses before its problems and the future is emptied of any positive historical resistance to the present. The judgement it presents is a purely negative one which, one ultimately fears despite its stated objective, carries not so much the strength of a dystopian vision as the attempt at a genuine prediction. Here we meet a very different future with no future to the one represented in *July's People*. In Gordimer's novel the future is open if not otherwise definable; in Keppel-Jones's history of the future the future as a meaning-giving force finally disappears altogether.

The heights of a Swiss utopia will later preside again, as we have seen, over the conclusion of another South African story of the future, rendering the situation just as hopeless. But if *Kruger's Alp* represents the fullness of the failure inherent in Keppel-Jones's approach to the future, if history there finds no future and is thus emptied of meaning, we have also considered forms which more radically question the nature and role of pessimism concerning South Africa's future. Coetzee does not leave us breathless in the footsteps of his earnest medical doctor, vainly trying to diagnose the significance of a figure drawing ahead of us into the future; he allows the utopian tense of his questioning to carry over to a conclusion based upon the minimum conditions upon which the future will be meaningfully possible. The contrast between this not-quite private moment of realisation and the massed audience overflowing the celebration of a utopia coming to a not-quite convincing finale in *A Sport of Nature* could not be more marked, but the spirit of willing the future into being belongs to a related impulse – just as the running Maureen and Michael are parallel figures hastening to meet the unknown future from their position just inside the future. And if the future represents a large degree of chaos – and in some cases complete collapse – for certain South African narrative forms, then we have also considered in *To Every Birth its Blood* a narrative which precisely finds its structure in the future and through this gives communal shape to its broken past. The best South African 'future histories' then, while they may suffer the limits of some degree of failure, still manage to find their significance in a bodying forth of the utopian form that has been our ultimate concern in this chapter. In this they join the many other works considered in this book which make of history – each in their own particular way – something novel enough to be a form of resistance.

PART FOUR

■

CONCLUSION

9

RESISTING A NATIONAL LITERARY HISTORY

———■———

... only those who think that the past was
different from the present are enabled to imagine
that the future may be so too.
— John Barrell (1980:88)

This book represents the sort of project which, despite itself, will be pulled into one of the categories it has most sought to confront; whatever else it is read as, *Novel Histories* will be categorised as a contribution – however rated – to a specific form of history: 'South African literary history'. Given my theme, it will be prudent for me to conclude with an attempt to hold this process at bay for as long as possible. This I will do by ending with some comments directed towards the common current preoccupation with 'Re-thinking South African Literary History'.

This was the theme of a colloquium held by the University of Durban-Westville's Centre for the Study of Southern African Literature and Languages in May 1995. The invitation to this event included the announcement of the Centre's particular interest in 'producing a comprehensive South African national literary history'. It will be obvious in the current cultural climate that such a project is not the inevitable consequence of such a theme. 'Re-thinking' a national literary history in any serious sense today must involve examining the assumptions behind 'producing' such a thing at all; the 'theorising' of such an enterprise should not be limited to serving as the groundwork for its practicality (as the Centre's invitation suggested) – it must begin by interrogating its desirability (that is, its tactical value) in the first place.

It is hardly necessary to observe that it is the word 'comprehensive' in the statement of the Centre's aims that highlights the fraught status of each of the terms that follow in its formulation. The generous inclusiveness undoubtedly intended can be read all too easily as claustrophobic appropriation. 'Nation', 'literature', and 'history' are each signifiers central to the acts of totalisation that the culture of 'posts' has specifically set itself against. Perhaps more tellingly, local conditions associated with the national, literary, and historical are especially marked by plurality, fracture, contingency, and contestation. Attempts to reconstruct the traditional terms of both cognitive and material mapping in these areas, then, risk – indeed, almost invite – the old charges of imposition and invasion.

Even the care with which the Centre for the Study of Southern African Literature and Languages's journal, *Alternation*, redefines the reference points of its national literary historical project does not save it from awkward rhetorical shifts that illustrate the potential contradictions of its programme: the lurch from the language of 'a systematic knowledge of the literary history and languages of the region' (Wade 1994:1) to that of 'post-absolutist radical democratic practice, affirming indeterminacy and difference' (4) is difficult to accommodate within one discursive practice. Being asked, too, as those of us invited to the colloquium were, to collaborate on a document which in form expresses the essence of Enlightenment practice ('a comprehensive encyclopaedia of South African literature') was a peculiarly 'modern' request within what otherwise announced itself as a 'broadly "post-modernist"' (6) context of inquiry.

Clearly, however, the colloquium's aims went beyond the essentialisms that recent critical activities have spent so much effort in removing from notions of the national, the literary, and the historical; there was no need there to rehearse the arguments for the contingent constructedness of these terms, their varying specificities, or their investments in particular relations of power. The question remains, however, whether a vigilant reflexivity is enough to allow us to re-engage in a project still defined within these terms. Exposing their institutional investments from a 'rigorously interdisciplinary' (Wade 1994:2) perspective is certainly a good place to start, but what will be, in Barthes's vocabulary, the 'new object' and 'new language' (1977:155) of this interdisciplinarity? The old object and language of national literary histories has been as conservative as it has precisely because in them the national, the literary, and the historical are so radically implicated in each other. We have had occasion, in the body of this book, to consider why this is so. I have followed Benedict Anderson in tracing the connections between 'the birth of the imagined community of the nation' and the novel form (one of the 'technical means for "representing" the kind of imagined community that is the nation' (1983:30); more particularly, I have followed Georg Lukács in looking at the chronological relation between modern concepts of the nation and the sub-genre of the historical novel.

This is just the most obvious of the ways in which nationality, literature, and history intersect – not only in a crudely deterministic sense, but also in so far as cultural forms are vital in the creation of the grounds for the possibility of certain political, economic, and historical manifestations, even as they are products of them.

The intersection of nations, literatures, and histories is emphasised even further when we become aware that the institutionalisation of a literature is not only an internal aspect of the invention of a nation and its history; this may be illustrated by the fact that the study of 'English Literature' began at the margins of empire (India), where the self-definition so necessary to the creation of an Other suitably placed in relation to that sense of Self was most urgently needed. This example would seem to suggest that literatures, like nations and histories, begin at their limits, not their centres, and are defined relationally, not essentially – although the point of contact with the something other that gives the necessary sense of shape and proportion to a defined area is, in this case, all too often a point of non-relation. The generally exclusivist programme of most national literary histories gives them a history of, at best, a begrudged accommodation between themselves, which is why the more recent phenomenon of comparative literary history is so dismissive of national literary histories.

Mario J. Valdés, in his introduction to the volume *Comparative Literary History as Discourse*, writes of the 'artificial barriers of nationalism', claiming that 'literature has no national orders'; as language communities seem to form the main basis for his idea of nationalism, the ease of modern participation in more than one language and the widespread availability of translation make nationalism, like language, 'a permeable membrane' (1992:4). Valdés still speaks, however, of 'the developmental sociocultural specificities of a literature', and praises comparative literary history for recognising that 'categories and concepts are intellectual abstractions used heuristically and cannot be drawn from one literature to describe the articulations of another' (7). It is hard to imagine how the subtleties of current thought on nationalism could be divorced from the way in which the concept of specific literatures is used here, but the difficulties associated with *comparative* literary history – as opposed to national literary history – are, in any event, intensified when, as in the South African case, the differences of specific literatures – often presented as national – are internalised within one nation state.

So the shift from 'comprehensive' to 'comparative' still leaves us at something of a loss. Helize van Vuuren is concerned by the fact that 'a comparative literary history of the totality of South African literature is clearly an ideal which is far from being realised' (1994:18). This comes from her conclusion to an overview of 'Recent changes in South African literary historiography' which, like other overviews, makes it plain that the various South African literary histories have invariably been exclusivist and constructed around one or another of the features usually identified as forming the bases of different nationalisms. Early surveys of South African literature depended upon a combination of *geography* and *race*, with their attendant linguistic associations. Later conservative studies made *language* the prime organising principle which, in a separatist state, had deep material class and race implications. Radical critiques of such methods moved *history* in as a master narrative against which the various literary developments – suitably loosened from generic 'literary' limitations in order to more accurately allow for the registering of the historical – could be read. History, however, like the comparativist appeals of the more sociologically inclined 'one society/one literature' literary historians, has provided no firmer purchase for an inclusive literary history, for two reasons: history, no less than society, has remained fractured and plural in South Africa, and it is, in any event, no less 'real' than (that is, it is as much a construct as) the nationalisms we are much more ready to identify as a product of our earnest imaginings.

Anderson's point (invoked in Chapter One) that the constructedness of nationalism does not make nations 'false' communities ('all communities', he reminds us, 'are imagined communities' [1983:15]) makes the call for acknowledging the *rhetorical* organising principles possibly the most important break away from the traditional bases for identifying national literary histories. The linguistic, historical, and continental links for the southern African archipelago of literature that Stephen Gray proposed in his *Southern African Literature: An Introduction* gives way in his later work to a *thematic* basis: 'our system is not divided, but it is *about* division. That is our common heritage, and comparisons may begin with confidence only from that common point' (1979:21). The move away from the essentialisms fundamental to conservative national projects – race, language, history

– is vital and vitalising in the understanding of national literary histories, but not without its dangers. Michael Chapman gives a *narrative* structure to his attempt 'to delineate a *single literature* from this country' (his emphasis), 'a narrative of conflict and disunity that in different ways has involved the entire population' (1993:36). Yet Leon de Kock, who praises Gray's thematic focus for translations between diverse cultural representations (1993:48), takes great exception to what he sees as Chapman's reduction of South Africa's many literatures and literary histories to one 'central South African story' (43). 'Instead,' writes de Kock, 'we will continue to have many stories, and they should be told differently' (53).

Debates of this nature are valuable in that they emphasise the degree to which the task of constructing a literary history for South Africa is a particularly – and importantly – imaginative act; the 'South African nation', as we saw in Sol Plaatje's work, is one that more overtly than most must be constructed outside the usual definitions of the nation state. At the heart of the problems – and advantages – surrounding the creation of this nation is the fact that here the narrativised nature of ethnos is so overt, and the differences that must be held – dynamically – together are so obvious.

All well and good, but the challenge for what I have called 'rhetorical' national description goes further than this; the question central to its definition is whether it is able to represent difference as a meaning constantly deferred, always produced by its difference from other meanings, volatile, unstable, disturbing as much to its own narratives as to any others that are appropriative of the discontinuities, unevennesses, resistances, that are the chief features of the experience of material histories.

I wonder, then, if we should bewail the fact 'that well into the last decade of the twentieth century an inclusive literary history has yet to be published' (Wade 1994:1)? In my Introduction I considered the case of the revisionist South African historians of the 1970s and 1980s, whose inability to produce a single narrative for itself did not prevent the production and maintenance of generalised and often unspoken assumptions which have begun to form the base for a new and dominating orthodoxy. One wonders if 'progressive' South African literary history's strengths thus far have not depended upon similar strategies to those that characterised the early moments of historical revisionism – a sort of academic guerrilla warfare – and whether, as it now approaches the orthodox itself, it too will be in danger of losing its reflexivity and suffocating under the dominance of its own unchallenged assumptions.

This danger is emphasised by the present context in which the battles fought with reactionary academic discourses are rapidly becoming something of a rearguard action; when our invitation to participate in the Centre for the Study of Southern African Literature and Languages's colloquium invited us to 'break with hegemonic critical practices', I for one was unsure if this referred to 'New Critical' or 'Post-modern' ones. In one sense, it hardly matters which, for, if the 'historical' must be abandoned on the grounds that the past as a point of reference is only a construct of the present, the point of *Novel Histories* is to ask how, equally, the literary, or for that matter, the national, can exist with enough purchase to resist being governed by whatever mode or modes are dominant in the present. I have thus tried to argue for a critical practice that will allow the objects of its study to adequately resist the appropriations of totalising concepts like nation, literature, and history, yet, at the same time, recognise the ways in which these concepts construct those objects of study.

Out of this has come a desire to find a balance between the rejection of and search for 'national literary histories', but literary history *per se* has not been my most basic prompt in this. I am made most aware of what is at stake in these debates at the pedagogical level of teaching one fracture of South Africa's literary history, 'literature in English', to a rapidly changing student constituency. Here the tension between 'literature' (with its infrastructures of nation and history) and its lived moment in its completion in consumption is acted out theoretically and experientially.

A practical admission of difference in pedagogic relations must, it seems to me, include seeing the very limits of the 'disadvantaged' or 'underprepared' status of many of the students now able to enter tertiary institutions in South Africa more positively than we have tended to do. They must be seen in relation to the literary history we wish to construct and promote as one of the forms of 'difference' it created and was previously unable to relate to as part of its own blindness. Differences of this sort protect the further marginalisation of cultures (and I do not mean only 'traditional' ones) which we continuously erode in our ignorance of them; they reveal too the degree to which we, as the purveyors of one historically dominant literature or another, or, indeed, a comparative assessment of them all, are the 'disadvantaged' and 'underprepared' ones when it comes to lacking the skills – as far as other languages and cultural positions generally are concerned – necessary for carrying out our vocation. Resistance can be structural rather than simply voluntarist, but none the less effective and necessary for this.

What resistances of this sort should inspire in us is the way in which the position of the teacher and critic – and the point of this conclusion is to extend this to the historian of literature – must be open to the interrogation of his or her subject as it is created in the audience he is addressing, and must include, in our context, 'disruptions' of the sort all too common in our teaching of particular literatures to those 'disadvantaged' by the histories of those literatures.

This will result in a sense of a community created out of difference which may also be read directly into current attempts to transform the signifier 'South Africa' from a term of deeply contested geographical reference to a national one that is able to encompass fractures of region, religion, ethnicity, gender, class, and culture. 'History' (and 'literary history' partakes fully in this) is constantly and urgently mobilised by the different factions created in such a project, and if the material of that history is not to be merely subsumed into an all too often bloody and vicious present-mindedness, we must find terms upon which the objects of study within these 'totalisations' can challenge the present and force the different positions within the present to examine the specificities of their positionality. To do this, artefacts from the past (a common area of contestation for all of us), no less than from the other forms of difference out of which the politics of the present are formed, must be accorded a force of their own and treated as valid in their historicity, and not simply as things entirely open to the manipulation of the present.

Literary history, then, no less than the works of 'historical fiction' we have looked at, becomes a new and powerful historicising form when it so operates upon its material – not necessarily bound to a particular temporal location, as I have argued, but open to the past, present, and future – as to make of its historical material a moment of resistance that leads to an intervention with its own moment of production or consumption. In this way, the history that a work or a literary history enacts is no mere reflex of that work's or that history's own history, but acts upon its construction within that history in the very act of its construction.

It is common now to concede that a 'national literary history' is not an invisible medium within which works find their relations across the material divisions of a nation as divided as the one in which we operate. Fair enough, but even a national literary history understood as contingent construct should be careful of the insidious ways in which, almost by definition, it will be inclined to become an agent in the present's imperialisation of the past or other areas of difference –

languages, media, forms – within the present. National literary historical structures and the activities they demand in their specific deployment become visible in relation to the resistance a particular text presents to those structures and activities. A work's 'meaning' (always slipping out of any, even its 'own' or its 'moment of production's', attributions of this) must be historicised sufficiently to challenge the activity of a particular literary history to know it. At some point the resistance a work presents to our attempts to appropriate it results in our admission of failure, and out of that failure is born the moment of 'knowing' that constructs around itself a particular literary history; but for the history (here non-'continuous') of literary histories to remain open, 'meaning' must be recognised as a term within a constant temporary yet necessary failure. These are the terms – sought in different ways throughout this work – of what I would call *Novel Histories*.

Nowhere, today, is this act of defamiliarisation able to take place as strongly as it does where this fundamental experience of reading occurs at the borders between literatures; the crossings, the translations (literal and otherwise) that force us to acknowledge the resistance of a text, are a model for reading in general, and the construction of literary histories in particular.

A national literary history, formed as it is by the literatures it forms, must be able to identify the creative collapse of 'meaning' implied by these observations as its contingent foundation, while always looking forward to the regeneration that will mark the end of its period or place and the beginning of others. The moment in which the work begins to blur, to slip out of the field of vision that delineates its mode in the present, is the moment when the appropriative placing within one literary history gives way to the resistance, re-thinking, re-working of another. When asked to focus on the question of a national literary history, we must remember that peripheral vision, not hindsight, makes the best history.

BIBLIOGRAPHY

■

PRIMARY SOURCES

Abrahams, Peter. 1948. *The Path of Thunder*. New York: Harper.

———1950. *Wild Conquest*. New York: Harper.

———1953. *Return to Goli*. London: Faber and Faber.

———1954. *Tell Freedom*. London: Faber and Faber.

'Adamastor' [Oliver Walker]. 1950. *White Man Boss: Footsteps to the South African Volk Republic*. London: Gollancz.

Bosman, Herman Charles. 1977. *Willemsdorp*. Cape Town, Pretoria: Human and Rousseau.

Christie, Agatha. 1962 (1924). *The Man in the Brown Suit*. London: Pan.

Coetzee, J.M. 1974. *Dusklands*. Johannesburg: Ravan Press.

———1985 (1983) *Life and Times of Michael K*. Harmondsworth: Penguin.

Doyle, Sir Arthur Conan. 1928. *Sherlock Holmes: The Complete Short Stories*. London: John Murray.

Drummond, June. 1971. *Farewell Party*. London: Gollancz.

Ebersohn, Wessel. 1979. *A Lonely Place to Die*. London: Gollancz.

———1980. *The Centurion*. Johannesburg: Ravan Press.

———1981. *Divide the Night*. London: Gollancz.

———1984 (1980) *Store Up the Anger*. Harmondsworth: Penguin

———1987. *Klara's Visitors*. London: Gollancz.

———1990. *Closed Circle*. London: Gollancz.

Fugard, Athol. 1981 (1974). *Boesman and Lena and Other Plays*. Cape Town: Oxford University Press.

Fugard, Athol, Kani, John and Ntshona, Winston. 1974. *Statements: Three Plays*. London, Oxford, Cape Town: Oxford University Press.

Gordimer, Nadine. 1982 (1981). *July's People*. Harmondsworth: Penguin.

———1988 (1987). *A Sport of Nature*. Harmondsworth: Penguin.

Hope, Christopher. 1983 (1981). *A Separate Development*. London: Granada.

——1985 (1984). *Kruger's Alp*. London: Sphere (Abacus).

'Jan Toekoms'. 1953. *'When Malan Goes': A Progressive Programme for South Africa*. Johannesburg: Central News Agency.

Keppel-Jones, Arthur. 1947. *When Smuts Goes: A History of South Africa from 1952 to 2010*. Cape Town: The African Bookman; London: Gollancz.

Manqupu, Mbokotwane. 1989 (1955). Love Comes Deadly. In Michael Chapman (ed.), *The Drum Decade: Stories from the 1950s*. Pietermaritzburg: University of Natal Press.

McClure, James. 1983 (1971). *The Steam Pig*. Harmondsworth: Penguin.

Millin, Sarah Gertrude. 1926. *The South Africans*. London: Constable.

——1941. *The Night is Long*. London: Faber and Faber.

——1950 (1949). *King of the Bastards*. Melbourne, London, Toronto: Heinemann.

——1952. *The Burning Man*. Melbourne, London, Toronto: Heinemann.

——1980 (1924). *God's Stepchildren*. Johannesburg: Ad. Donker.

Mogale, Arthur [Arthur Maimane]. 1953. Crime for Sale. *Drum* 3, No. 2 (February).

——1953. You Can't Buy Me! *Drum* 3, No. 12 (December).

——1989 (1953). Crime for Sale. In Michael Chapman (ed.), *The Drum Decade: Stories from the 1950s*. Pietermaritzburg: University of Natal Press.

Plaatje, Solomon T. 1975 (1930) *Mhudi*. Johannesburg: Quagga Press.

Rooke, Daphne. 1953. *Ratoons*. London: Gollancz.

——1957. *Wizards' Country*. London: Gollancz.

——1961. *A Lover for Estelle*. London: Gollancz.

——1965. *Diamond Joe*. London: Gollancz.

——1968 (1960). Fikizolo. In A. Lennox-Short and R. E. Lighton (eds), *Stories South African*. Johannesburg: Perskor, pp.46-59.

——1974. *Margaretha de la Porte*. London: Gollancz.

——1987 (1951). *Mittee*. Diep River: Chameleon Press. Introduction by Ian Glenn.

——1989 (1946). *A Grove of Fever Trees*. Diep River: Chameleon Press. Introduction by the author. First published as *The Sea Hath Bounds*.

——Undated. Yesterday's Child. Cape Town, University of Cape Town Libraries, BC 995 A3.

Schoeman, Karel. 1972. *Na die Geliefde Land*. Cape Town and Pretoria: Human and Rousseau.

——1979 (1978). *Promised Land*. Trans. Marion V. Friedmann. London: Futura. (First published in English in 1978, Johannesburg: Julian Friedman)

Serote, Mongane. 1981. *To Every Birth its Blood*. Johannesburg: Ravan Press.

Sharpe, Tom. 1983 (1971). *Riotous Assembly*. London: Pan in association with Secker and Warburg.

Smith, Wilbur. 1976 (1964). *When the Lion Feeds*. London: Pan in association with Heinemann.

Walker, Oliver. 1949. *Kaffirs Are Lively: Being Some Backstage Impressions of the South African Democracy*. London: Gollancz.

———1949. *Proud Zulu*. London: Werner Laurie.

———1949. *Wanton City: An Escapade*. London: Werner Laurie.

———[As 'Adamastor']. 1950. *White Man Boss: Footsteps to the South African Volk Republic*. London: Victor Gollancz.

———1951. *Shapeless Flame*. London: Werner Laurie.

———1953. *Sailor Malan: A Biography*. London: Cassell.

———1957. The Baas Comes Home. *Africa South* 1, No. 2 (January-March), pp.107-14.

———1961. *Zulu Royal Feather*. London: Hutchinson.

———1964. *Kaffirs Are Livelier*. London: Frederick Muller.

———1967. *The Hippo Poacher*. London: Cassell, 1967.

SECONDARY SOURCES

Documents in the Killie Campbell Museum are referenced as KCM with file numbers.

Adey, David, Beeton, Ridley, Chapman, Michael and Pereira, Ernest. 1986. *Companion to South African English Literature*. Johannesburg: Ad. Donker.

Anderson, Benedict. 1983. *Imagined Communities: Reflections on the Origin and Spread of Nationalism*. London: Verso.

Attwell, David. 1990a. Political supervision: The case of the 1990 Wits History Workshop. *Pretexts* 2(1):78-85.

———1990b. The Problem of History in the Fiction of J.M. Coetzee. In Trump (ed.) 1990a:94-133.

Baker, Ernest A. 1968 (1914). *A Guide to Historical Fiction*. New York: Argosy Antiquarian.

Baker-Smith, Dominic and Barfoot, C.C. (eds). 1987. *Between Dream and Nature: Essays on Utopia and Dystopia*. Amsterdam: Redopi.

Ballard, Charles. 1985. *John Dunn: The White Chief of Zululand*. Johannesburg: Ad. Donker.

Barboure, Doriane. 1984. Mongane Serote: Humanist and Revolutionary. In Daymond *et al*. 1984:171-81.

Barnett, Ursula A. 1983. *A Vision of Order: A Study of Black South African Literature in English (1914-1980)*. London: Sinclair Browne; Amherst: University of Massachusetts Press.

Barrell, John. 1980. *The Dark Side of the Landscape: The Rural Poor in English Painting 1730-1840*. Cambridge University Press.

Barthes, Roland. 1970. Historical Discourse. In Lane (ed.), *Structuralism: A Reader*. London: Jonathan Cape, pp.145-55.

———1974. *Roland Barthes*. Trans. Richard Howard. New York: Hill and Wang, 1974.

———1977. From Work to Text. In Heath, S. (ed.), *Image-Music-Text*. London: Fontana Cape.

Belsey, Catherine. 1980. *Critical Practice*. New Accents. London and New York: Methuen.

Berthoud, Jacques. 1989. Writing under apartheid. *Current Writing* 1(1):77-87.

Binyon, T.J. 1989. *Murder Will Out: The Detective in Fiction*. Oxford: Oxford University Press.

Birkby, Carel. 1948. *The Pagel Story*. Cape Town: Howard O. Timmins for Hodder and Stoughton.

Bonner, Philip, Hofmeyr, Isabel, James, Deborah and Lodge, Tom (eds). 1989. *Holding Their Ground: Class, Locality and Culture in 19th and 20th Century South Africa*. Johannesburg: Witwatersrand University Press and Ravan Press.

Boonzaier, Emile and Sharp, John (eds). 1988. *South African Keywords: The Uses and Abuses of Political Concepts*. Cape Town and Johannesburg: David Philip.

Bozzoli, Belinda (ed.). 1983. *Town and Countryside in the Transvaal: Capitalist Penetration and Popular Response*. Johannesburg: Ravan.

———1987. *Class, Community and Conflict: South African Perspectives*. Johannesburg: Ravan.

Bozzoli, Belinda and Delius, Peter (guest eds). 1990a. *Radical History Review: History from South Africa* 46/47.

———1990b. Editors' Introduction: Radical history and South African society. *Radical History Review: History from South Africa*. 46/47:13-46.

Braudel, Fernand. 1980. *On History*. Trans. Sarah Matthews. London: Weidenfeld and Nicolson.

Brontë, Emily. 1967 (1847). *Wuthering Heights*. Introduction by Elizabeth Jennings. London and Sydney: Pan.

Brookes, E.H. and Webb, C. de B. 1965. *A History of Natal*. Pietermaritzburg: University of Natal Press.

Brown, Audrey. 1995. Survival of an African Identity. *Weekly Mail and Guardian* 24-30 March.

Bryant, A.T. 1949. *The Zulu People as They Were Before the White Man Came*. Pietermaritzburg: Shuter and Shooter.

Bulpin, T.V. 1986 (1985). *The Reader's Digest Illustrated Guide To Southern Africa*. 4 edn. Cape Town: Reader's Digest.

Bundy, Robert (ed.). 1976. *Images of the Future: The Twenty-First Century and Beyond*. Buffalo: Prometheus Books.

Butler, Jeffrey, Elphick, Richard and Welsh, David (eds). 1987. *Democratic Liberalism in South Africa: Its History and Prospect*. Middletown, Conn.: Wesleyan University Press; Cape Town and Johannesburg: David Philip.

Callinicos, Luli. 1987. *Working Life 1886-1940*. Vol. 2 of *A People's History of South Africa*. Johannesburg: Ravan.

Carr, E.H. 1987 (1961). *What is History?* 2 edn. Harmondsworth: Penguin.

Chapman, Michael. (ed.). 1982. *Soweto Poetry*. Johannesburg: McGraw-Hill.

———(ed.) 1989a. *The Drum Decade: Stories from the 1950s*. Pietermaritzburg: University of Natal Press.

———1989b. More Than Telling a Story: Drum and its Significance in Black South African

Writing. In Chapman (ed.) 1989a:183-232.

——1990. How do mimic men, and women, become New South Africans? *Current Writing* 2(1):187-91.

——1993. Red People and School People from Ntsikana to Mandela: The significance of 'Xhosa Literature' in a general history of South African literature. *English Academy Review* 10:36-44.

Chase, Richard. 1960 (1957). *The American Novel and its Tradition.* Garden City N.Y.: Doubleday.

Christie, Sarah, Hutchings, Geoffrey and Maclennan, Don. 1980. *Perspectives on South African Fiction.* Johannesburg: Ad. Donker.

Clingman, Stephen. 1986. *The Novels of Nadine Gordimer: History from the Inside.* London: Allen and Unwin.

——1988. Beyond the Limit: The Social Relations of Madness in Southern African Fiction. Unpublished paper delivered at an African Studies Seminar, University of the Witwatersrand, Oct.

——1990a. Literature and history in South Africa. In Bozzoli and Delius (eds) 1990a.

——1990. Revolution and Reality: South African Fiction in the 1980s. In Trump (ed.) 1990:41-60.

Cobbing, Julian. 1988a. Jettisoning the Mfecane (with Perestroika). Unpublished paper delivered at the University of the Witwatersrand African Studies seminar, Sept.

——1988b. A Tainted Well: The Objectives, Historical Fantasies, and Working Methods of James Stuart, with Counter Argument (Review Article). *Journal of Natal and Zulu History* 11: 115-54.

——with Wright, John. 1988c. The Mfecane: Beginning the Inquest. Unpublished paper delivered at the University of the Witwatersrand African Studies Seminar, Sept.

Coetzee, J.M. 1980. Blood, flaw, taint, degeneration: The case of Sarah Gertrude Millin. *English Studies in Africa* 23(1):41-58; repr. in *White Writing: On the Culture of Letters in South Africa.* New Haven and London: Yale University Press, 1988, pp.136-62.

——1983. The great South African novel. *Leadership S.A.* 2(4):74-79.

——1988. The novel today. *Upstream* 6(1):2-5.

Collingwood, R.G. 1983 (1946). *The Idea of History.* Oxford University Press.

Cornevin, Marianne. 1980. *Apartheid: Power and Historical Falsification.* Paris: UNESCO.

Coupland, R.F. 1948. *Zulu Battle Piece: Isandhlwana.* London: Collins.

Couzens, Tim. 1971. The dark side of the world: Sol Plaatje's *Mhudi. English Studies in Africa* 14(20):187-203.

——1973. Sol Plaatje's *Mhudi. Journal of Commonwealth Literature* 8(1):1-19.

——1975. Introduction. In Sol. T. Plaatje, *Mhudi.* Johannesburg: Quagga Press.

Coward, Rosalind and Ellis, John. 1977. *Language and Materialism: Developments in Semiology and the Theory of the Subject.* London: Routledge and Kegan Paul.

Culler, Jonathan. 1983. *On Deconstruction: Theory and Criticism after Structuralism.* London, Melbourne and Henley: Routledge and Kegan Paul.

Danto, Arthur C. 1965. *Analytical Philosophy of History*. Cambridge University Press.

Davenport, T.R.H. 1987. *South Africa: A Modern History*. 3 edn. Johannesburg: Macmillan.

Daymond, M.J., Jacobs, J.U. and Lenta, M. 1984. *Momentum: On Recent South African Writing*. Pietermaritzburg: University of Natal Press.

Dean, Elizabeth, Hartman, Paul and Katzen, May. 1983. *History in Black and White: An Analysis of South African School History Textbooks*. Paris: UNESCO.

Degenaar, Johan. 1987. Nationalism, Liberalism, and Pluralism. In Butler *et al.* (eds) 1987: 236-49.

———1988. Understanding Little Red Riding Hood. In I. Cilliers (ed.), *Towards Understanding Children's Literature for Southern Africa*. Cape Town: Maskew Miller Longman, pp.14-29.

De Kock, Leon. 1993. The central South African story, or many stories? A response to 'Red People and School People from Ntsikana to Mandela'. *English Academy Review* 10:45-55.

Delius, Anthony. 1951. Study in black and white. *Standpunte* 5(3):1-16.

Derrida, Jacques. 1978. *Writing and Difference*. Trans. Alan Bass. London and Henley: Routledge and Kegan Paul.

———1985. Racism's Last Word. Catalogue to exhibition, *Art contre/against Apartheid*. Published in *Critical Enquiry* 12.

Donatich, John. 1988. Borders of the Imagination. Review of Bell Gale Chevinny and Gari Laguardia (eds), *Reinventing the Americas: Comparative Studies of Literature of the United States and Spanish America* (Cambridge University Press 1986). *American Book Review* 9(6):14 & 21.

Dovey, Theresa. 1988. *The Novels of J.M. Coetzee: Lacanian Allegories*. Johannesburg: Ad. Donker.

Duminy, Andrew and Ballard, Charles (eds). 1981. *The Anglo-Zulu War: New Perspectives*. Pietermaritzburg: University of Natal Press.

Duminy, Andrew and Guest, Bill (eds). 1989. *Natal and Zululand from Earliest Times to 1910: A New History*. Pietermaritzburg: University of Natal Press and Shuter and Shooter.

Dunn, John. 1886. *John Dunn, Cetywayo and the Three Generals*. Ed. D.C.F. Moodie. Pietermaritzburg: Natal Printing and Publishing Co.

During, Simon. 1990. Postmodernism or Post-colonialism Today. In Andrew Milner, Philip Thompson and Chris Worth (eds), *Postmodern Conditions*. New York, Oxford, Munich: Berg.

———1991. Waiting for the Post: Some Relations between Modernity, Colonization, and Writing. In Ian Adam and Helen Tiffin (eds), *Past the Last Post: Thinking Post-Colonialism and Post-Modernism*. New York, London, Toronto, Sydney, Tokyo, Singapore: Harvester Wheatsheaf.

Eagleton, Terry. 1983. *Literary Theory: An Introduction*. Oxford: Basil Blackwell.

Ensor, Robert. 1990. The Novels of Peter Abrahams and the Rise of Nationalism in Africa. Ph.D. thesis, University of Amsterdam.

Essa, Saira and Pillai, Charles. n.d. *Steve Biko: The Inquest. A Documentary Based on the Inquest Hearing into the Death in Detention of Steven Bantu Biko*. Durban: Art Printers; first performed 1985.

February, V.A. 1981. *Mind Your Colour: The Coloured Stereotype in South African Literature*. London and Boston: Kegan Paul.

Flather, Horace. 1977. *The Way of an Editor*. Cape Town, Johannesburg, London: Purnell.

Fleishman, Avrom. 1971. *The English Historical Novel: Walter Scott to Virginia Woolf*. Baltimore and London: Johns Hopkins University Press.

Forster, Margaret. 1980. Secrets of a Glittering Prize. *Sunday Times* (London), 26 Oct.

Foucault, Michel. 1972 (1969). *The Archeology of Knowledge*. Trans. A.M. Sheridan-Smith. London: Tavistock.

————1979 (1975). *Discipline and Punish: The Birth of the Prison*. Trans. Alan Sheridan. London: Penguin (Peregrine).

Fukuyama, Francis. 1989. The end of history? *National Interest* 16.

————1992. *The End of History and the Last Man*. London: Hamish Hamilton.

Fuze, Magema M. 1982 (1979). *The Black People and Whence They Came: A Zulu View*. Trans. H.C. Lugg, ed. A.T. Cope. Pietermaritzburg, Durban: University of Natal Press, Killie Campbell Africana Library.

Gallie, W.B. 1964. *Philosophy and the Historical Understanding*. London: Chatto and Windus.

Gardiner, Patrick (ed.). 1959. *Theories of History*. Glencoe: Free Press.

Gikandi, Simon. 1992. The Politics and Poetics of National Formation: Recent African Writing. In Rutherford (ed.) 1992.

Glenn, Ian. 1987. Introduction. In Daphne Rooke, *Mittee*. Diep River: Chameleon Press.

————1989. Interview with Daphne Rooke. Unpublished.

Goldblatt, David and Gordimer, Nadine. 1973. *On the Mines*. Cape Town: Struik.

————1989. Interview with Daphne Rooke. Unpublished.

Gray, Stephen. 1979. *Southern African Literature: An Introduction*. Cape Town: David Philip; London: Rex Collins.

————1989. Some problems of writing historiography in Southern Africa. *Literator* 10(2):16-24.

————1990. The long eye of history: Four autobiographical texts by Peter Abrahams. *Pretexts* 2(2):99-115.

Green, Michael. 1991. Interview with Wessel Ebersohn. Unpublished.

————1992. Interview with Daphne Rooke. Unpublished.

Guy, Jeff. 1979. *The Destruction of the Zulu Kingdom: The Civil War in Zululand, 1879-1884*. London: Longman.

————1983. *The Heretic: A Study of the Life of John William Colenso 1814-1883*. Johannesburg and Pietermaritzburg: Ravan and University of Natal Press.

Hawthorne, Nathaniel. 1851. *The House of the Seven Gables: A Romance*. Boston: Ticknor, Reed, and Fields.

Head, Bessie. 1984. The Search for Historical Continuity and Roots. In Daymond *et al.* 1984.

Heller, Agnes. 1982. *A Theory of History*. London: Routledge and Kegan Paul.

Hirst, Paul Q. 1985. *Marxism and Historical Writing*. London, Boston, Melbourne and Henley: Routledge and Kegan Paul.

Hobsbawm, E.J. 1971. Class Consciousness in History. In Mészáros (ed.) 1971.

———1990. *Nations and Nationalisms since 1780: Programme, Myth, Reality*. Cambridge, New York, Port Chester, Melbourne, Sydney: Cambridge University Press.

Hofmeyr, Isabel. 1987. Building a Nation from Words: Afrikaans Language, Literature and Ethnic Identity, 1902-1924. In Marks and Trapido (eds) 1987, pp.95-123.

———1990. History Workshop positions: Introduction. *Pretexts* 2(2):61-71.

———1993. *'We spend our years as a tale that is told': Oral Historical Narrative in a South African Chiefdom*. Social History of Africa: Series editors Allen Isaacman and Jean Hay. Johannesburg: Witwatersrand University Press; Portsmouth NH: Heinemann; London: James Currey.

Jameson, Fredric. 1971. *Marxism and Form: Twentieth-Century Dialectical Theories of Literature*. Princeton University Press.

———1981. *The Political Unconscious: Narrative as a Socially Symbolic Act*. London: Methuen.

———1988a. *The Ideologies of Theory: Essays 1971-1986*. Vol. 2: *The Syntax of History*. London: Routledge.

———1988b. Marxism and Historicism. In *The Ideologies of Theory: Essays 1971-1986*, pp.148-77.

———1991. *Postmodernism, or, The Cultural Logic of Late Capitalism*. London, New York: Verso.

JanMohamed, Abdul R. 1985. The economy of Manichean allegory: The function of racial difference in colonialist literature. *Critical Inquiry* 12:59-87.

Jennings, Elizabeth. 1967. Introduction. In Brontë, 1967 (1847).

Karis, Thomas and Carter, Gwendolen (eds). 1972-1977. *From Protest to Challenge: A Documentary History of African Politics in South Africa, 1882-1964*. 4 vols. Vol.2 (1973), *Hope and Challenge, 1935-1952*. Stanford: Hoover Institution Press.

Keppel-Jones, Arthur. 1938. Where did we take the wrong turning? *Race Relations 5*.

———1975 (1949). *South Africa: A Short History*. 5 edn. London: Hutchinson University Library.

Kierson, S. 1958. English and Afrikaans Novels on South African History. Cape Town, University of Cape Town School of Librarianship. Mimeograph.

Knight, Stephen. 1980. *Form and Ideology in Crime Fiction*. Bloomington: Indiana University Press.

Leavis, F.R. 1962 (1948). *The Great Tradition: George Eliot, Henry James, Joseph Conrad*. Harmondsworth: Penguin.

Legassick, Martin. 1972. The dynamics of modernization in South Africa. *Journal of African History*, 13(1):145-50.

———1973. *Class and Nationalism in South African Protest: The South African Communist Party and the 'Native Republic', 1928-34.* Syracuse, USA: Eastern African Studies Programme.

———1980. The Frontier Tradition in South African Historiography. In Marks and Atmore 1980:44-79.

Lenta, Margaret. 1988. Fictions of the future. *English Acadamy Review* 5:133-45.

Lerumo, A. 1971. *Fifty Fighting Years: The South African Communist Party, 1921-1971.* London: Inkululeko Publications.

Lewsen, Phyllis. 1970. The language of the historian. *English Studies in Africa* 13(2):337-58.

Lodge, Tom. 1983. *Black Politics in South Africa since 1945.* London and New York: Longman.

Lugg, H. C. 1948. *Historic Natal and Zululand.* Pietermaritzburg: Shuter and Shooter.

Lukács, Georg. 1981 (1937). *The Historical Novel.* Trans. Hannah and Stanley Mitchell. Harmondsworth: Penguin.

Lyotard, Jean-François. 1984 (1979). *The Postmodern Condition: A Report on Knowledge.* Trans. Geoff Bennington and Brian Masumi. Minneapolis: University of Minnesota Press.

MacCabe, Colin. 1989 (1974). Realism and the Cinema: Notes on some Brechtian Theses. In Philip Rice and Patricia Waugh (eds), *Modern Literary Theory: A Reader.* London, New York, Melbourne, Auckland: Edward Arnold, pp.134-42.

Macherey, Pierre. 1978 (1966). *A Theory of Literary Production.* Trans. Geoffrey Wall. London, Henley and Boston: Routledge and Kegan Paul.

MacKeurtan, (H.) G. 1930. *The Cradle Days of Natal, 1497-1845.* London and New York: Longmans, Green.

Mailer, Norman. 1971 (1968). *The Armies of the Night.* Harmondsworth: Penguin.

Marks, Shula. 1970. African and Afrikaner history. *Journal of African History* 11(3):435-47.

———1986. *The Ambiguities of Dependence in South Africa: Class, Nationalism, and the State in Twentieth-Century Natal.* Johannesburg: Ravan Press.

Marks, Shula and Atmore, Anthony (eds). 1980. *Economy and Society in Pre-Industrial South Africa.* London: Longman.

Marks, Shula and Rathbone, Richard (eds). 1982. *Industrialization and Social Change in South Africa.* London: Longman.

Marks, Shula and Trapido, Stanley (eds). 1987. *The Politics of Race, Class and Nationalism in Twentieth Century South Africa.* London and New York, Longman.

Marwick, Arthur. 1983 (1970). *The Nature of History.* 2 edn. London and Basingstoke: Macmillan.

'Matsix' [Matsemela Manaka]. 1981. The Babalaz people. *Staffrider* 4(3):32-34.

Maughan-Brown, David. 1990. Raising Goose-Pimples: Wilbur Smith and the Politics of Rage. In Trump (ed.) 1990a:134-60.

McClintock, Anne and Nixon, Rob. 1986. No names apart: The separation of words and history in Derrida's '*Le dernier mot du racisme*'. *Critical Enquiry* 13:140-54.

Mészáros, István (ed.). 1971. *Aspects of History and Class Consciousness*. London: Routledge and Kegan Paul.

Modisane, William 'Bloke'. 1986 (1963). *Blame Me on History*. Craighall (Johannesburg): Ad. Donker.

Morgan, Janet. 1984. *Agatha Christie: A Biography*. London: Collins.

Morris, Donald R. 1966 (1965). *The Washing of the Spears: A History of the Rise of the Zulu Nation under Shaka and its Fall in the Zulu War of 1879*. London: Jonathan Cape.

Mphahlele, Ezekial. 1962. *The African Image*. London: Faber and Faber.

Mutloatse, Mothobi (ed.). 1981. *Reconstruction: 90 Years of Black Historical Literature*. Johannesburg: Ravan Press.

Nairn, Tom. 1977. *The Break-up of Britain: Crises and Neo-Nationalism*. London: NLB.

New Nation/New History. 1989. Vol. 1. Johannesburg: New Nation and the History Workshop.

Nkosi, Lewis. 1981. *Tasks and Masks*. Harlow: Longman.

Ogungbesan, Kolawole. 1979. *The Writing of Peter Abrahams*. London, Sydney, Auckland, Toronto: Hodder and Stoughton.

Parker, Kenneth (ed.). 1978. *The South African Novel in English*. London: MacMillan.

Parrinder, Patrick (ed.). 1979. *Science Fiction: A Critical Guide*. London and New York: Longman.

Pippin, Robert B. 1991. *Modernism as a Philosophical Problem: On the Dissatisfactions of European High Culture*. Cambridge Mass. and Oxford: Basil Blackwell.

Porter, Dennis. 1981. *The Pursuit of Crime: Art and Ideology in Detective Fiction*. New Haven and London: Yale University Press.

Posel, Ros. 1993. An Evaluation of the Witchcraft Suppression Act No. 3 of 1957. Working paper presented at the University of Natal Workshop on Natal and Zululand since the 1890s. Pietermaritzburg, Oct.

Poster, Mark. 1984. *Foucault, Marxism and History: Mode of Production versus Mode of Information*. Cambridge and Oxford: Polity Press and Basil Blackwell.

Rabkin, David. 1978. Race and Fiction: *God's Stepchildren* and *Turbott Wolfe*. In Parker (ed.) 1978, pp.77-94.

Rabkin, Lily. 1952. The works of Daphne Rooke. *Forum* 1(1):36-37.

Ramsey, Sally. 1980. Keeping Control. *The Times Literary Supplement* 19 Sept.

Renan, Ernest. 1990. What is a Nation? In Homi K. Bhaba (ed.), *Nation and Narration*. London and New York, Routledge.

Rich, Paul. 1982. Tradition and revolt in South African fiction: The novels of Andre Brink, Nadine Gordimer and J.M. Coetzee. *Journal of Southern African Studies* 9(1):54-73.

———1984a. Apartheid and the decline of the civilization idea: An essay on Nadine Gordimer's *July's People* and J.M. Coetzee's *Waiting for the Barbarians*. *Research in African Literatures* 15(3):365-93.

———1984b. Romance and the Development of the South African Novel. In White and Couzens (eds) 1984:120-37.

————1984c. *White Power and the Liberal Conscience: Racial Segregation and South African Liberalism 1921-60*. Manchester University Press.

Ricoeur, Paul. 1986. *Lectures on Ideology and Utopia*, ed. H. Taylor. New York: Columbia University Press.

Robertson, Janet. 1971. *Liberalism in South Africa, 1948-1963*. Oxford: Clarendon Press.

Ross, Andrew. 1986. *John Philip (1775-1851): Missions, Race and Politics in South Africa*. Aberdeen: University Press.

Rowse, A.L. 1978. *The Annotated Shakespeare*. 3 vols. New York: Clarkson N. Potter.

Rubin, Martin. 1977. *Sarah Gertrude Millin: A South African Life*. Johannesburg: Ad. Donker.

Rutherford, Anna. 1992. *From Commonwealth to Post-Colonial*. Australia, Denmark, United Kingdom: Dangaroo Press.

Sachs, Bernard. 1965. *Personalities and Places*. Second Series. Johannesburg: The Dial Press.

Said, Edward K. 1992. Figures, Configurations, Transfigurations. In Rutherford (ed.) 1992: 3-17.

Sampson, Anthony. 1983 (1956). *Drum: An African Adventure – and Afterwards*. London, Sydney, Auckland, Toronto: Hodder and Stoughton.

Samuel, Raphael (ed.). 1981. *People's History and Socialist Theory*. London: Routledge and Kegan Paul.

Saunders, Christopher 1986. *When Smuts Goes* revisited. *Die Suid-Afrikaan* Winter:48-50.

————1987. Liberal Historiography before 1945. In Butler *et al.* (eds) 1987.

————1988. *The Making of the South African Past: Major Historians on Race and Class*. Cape Town and Johannesburg: David Philip.

————(Consultant Editor). 1992. *Reader's Digest Illustrated History of South Africa: The Real Story*. Expanded 2 edn. Cape Town, London, New York, Sydney, Montreal: Reader's Digest.

Schoeman, A.E. 1938. *Coenraad de Buys: The First Transvaler*. Pretoria: J.H. de Bussy.

Simmons, James C. 1973. *The Novelist as Historian: Essays on the Victorian Historical Novel*. The Hague: Mouton.

Simpson, David. 1988. Literary criticism and the return to 'History'. *Critical Enquiry* 14(4):721-47.

Smith, Anthony. 1986. *The Ethnic Origins of Nations*. Oxford: Basil Blackwell.

Smith, H. Lindsay. 1946. *Behind the Press in South Africa*. Cape Town: Stewart.

Smith, Ken. 1988. *The Changing Past: Trends in South African Historical Writing*. Johannesburg: Southern.

Smith, Rowland. 1984. Masters and servants: Nadine Gordimer's *July's People* and the themes of her fiction. *Salmagundi* 62, Winter:93-107.

Sole, Kelwyn. 1989. 'But then, where is home?': Time, Disorder and Social Collectives in Serote's *To Every Birth its Blood*. Unpublished paper presented at the Africa Seminar of the Centre for African Studies, University of Cape Town, 27 Sept.

————1990. Real toads in imaginary gardens: A response to David Attwell. *Pretexts* 2(1):86-93.

————1991.'This time set again': The temporal and political conceptions of Serote's *To Every Birth its Blood*. *English in Africa* 18(1):51.

Stadler, Alf. 1987. *The Political Economy of Modern South Africa*. Cape Town and Johannesburg: David Philip; London: Croom Helm.

Stewart, R.F. 1980. ... *And Always a Detective: Chapters on the History of Detective Fiction*. Newton Abbot, London, North Pomfret: David and Charles.

Symons, Julian. 1972. *Bloody Murder: From the Detective Story to the Crime Novel: A History*. London: Faber and Faber.

Thompson, E.P. 1978. *The Poverty of Theory and Other Essays*. London: Merlin.

Thornycroft, Peta. 1980. Acclaimed SA Novel is 'Not Literature' say Local Experts. *Sunday Express* (Johannesburg) 23 Nov.

Traversi, Derek. 1958. The Brontë Sisters and *Wuthering Heights*. In Boris Ford (ed.), *The Pelican Guide to English Literature: From Dickens to Hardy*. Vol. 6. Harmondsworth: Penguin, pp.256-73.

Trump, Martin (ed.). 1990a. *Rendering Things Visible: Essays on South African Literary Culture*. Johannesburg: Ravan Press.

————1990b. Serote's *To Every Birth its Blood* and Debates within Southern Africa's Literature of Liberation. Unpublished paper delivered at the University of the Witwatersrand History Workshop, 6-10 Feb.

Valdés, Mario J. 1992. Why Comparative Literary History? In Mario J. Valdés, Daniel Javitch and Owen A. Aldridge (eds), *Comparative Literary History as Discourse: In Honour of Anna Balakian*. Bern, Berlin, Frankurt a.M., New York, Paris, Vienna: Peter Lang.

Van Niekerk, Ada Joyce. 1956. South African Writer who Stormed America. *Milady* Feb.:28-29.

Van Onselen, Charles. 1982. *Studies in the Social and Economic History of the Witwatersrand 1886-1914: New Babylon*. London: Longman.

Van Vuuren, Helize. 1994. Recent changes in South African literary historiography: Theory and practice. *Alternation* 1(1):8-20.

Vaughan, Michael. 1982. Literature and politics: Currents in South African writing in the seventies. *Journal of Southern African Studies* 9(1):118-38.

Visser, Nicholas. 1987. Fictional projects and the irruptions of history: Mongane Serote's *To Every Birth its Blood*. *English Academy Review* 4, Jan.:67-76.

————1990a. Beyond the Interregnum: A Note on the Ending of *July's People*. In Trump (ed.) 1990a, pp.61-67.

————1990b. Towards a political culture. *Pretexts* 2(1):69-77.

Wade, Jean-Philippe. 1994. Introduction. *Alternation* 1(1):1-7.

Wade, Michael. 1972. *Peter Abrahams*. London: Evans.

————1974. Myth, truth and the South African reality in the fiction of Sarah Gertrude Millin. *Journal of Southern African Studies* 1:91-108.

Walsh, Peter. 1987 (1970). *The Rise of African Nationalism in South Africa*. Johannesburg: Donker.

Watson, Colin. 1971. *Snobbery with Violence: Crime Stories and their Audience*. London: Eyre and Spottiswoode.

Watson, Stephen. 1986. Colonialism and the novels of J.M. Coetzee. *Research in African Literatures* 17(3):370-90.

Watt, Ian. 1974 (1957). *The Rise of the Novel: Studies in Defoe, Richardson and Fielding*. Harmondsworth: Penguin.

Waugh, Patricia. 1984. *Metafiction: The Theory and Practice of Self-Conscious Fiction*. London and New York: Methuen.

Webb, Colin. 1981. The Origins of the Angle-Zulu War: Problems of Interpretation. In Duminy and Ballard (eds) 1981, pp.1-12.

White, Hayden. 1973. *Metahistory: The Historical Imagination in Nineteenth-Century Europe*. Baltimore and London: Johns Hopkins University Press.

———1982. The Politics of Historical Interpretation: Discipline and De-sublimation. *Critical Inquiry* 9(1):113-37. Reprinted in White 1987:58-82.

———1984. The Question of Narrative in Contemporary Historical Theory. *History and Theory* 23(1):1-33. Reprinted in White 1987, pp.26-57.

———1986 (1978). *Tropics of Discourse: Essays in Cultural Criticism*. Baltimore and London: Johns Hopkins University Press.

———1987. *The Content of the Form: Narrative Discourse and Historical Representation*. Baltimore and London: Johns Hopkins University Press.

White, Landeg and Couzens, Tim (eds). 1984. *Literature and Society in South Africa*. Pinelands (Cape Town): Maskew Miller Longman.

Willan, Brian. 1984. *Sol Plaatje: South African Nationalist 1876-1932*. London: Heinemann.

Williams, Raymond. 1979. Utopia and Science Fiction. In Parrinder (ed.) 1979:52-66.

———1983 (1976). *Keywords: A Vocabulary of Culture and Society*. London: Fontana (Flamingo).

Woollacott, Martin. 1995. Moral Engine in a Fragile State. *Mail and Guardian* 10-16 Nov., p.27.

Young, Robert. 1990. *White Mythologies: Writing History and the West*. London and New York: Routledge.

INDEX

■